FOR CHRIST AND COUNTRY

A BIOGRAPHY OF BRIGADIER GENERAL GUSTAVUS LOOMIS

FOR CHRIST AND COUNTRY

A Biography of Brigadier General Gustavus Loomis

Printed in the United States of America

ISBN: 978-1-935507-47-5

Cover Design & Page Layout by David Siglin of A&E Media

AMBASSADOR INTERNATIONAL
Emerald House
427 Wade Hampton Blvd.
Greenville, SC 29609, USA
www.ambassador-international.com

AMBASSADOR BOOKS
The Mount
2 Woodstock Link
Belfast, BT6 8DD, Northern Ireland, UK
www.ambassador-international.com

The colophon is a trademark of Ambassador

FOR CHRIST AND COUNTRY

A Biography of Brigadier General Gustavus Loomis

Kenneth E. Lawson

Ambassador International

Greenville, South Carolina & Belfast, Northern Ireland

www.ambassador-international.com

As a Vermonter whose great great grandfather fought in the Civil War I can't commend Kenneth Lawson enough for writing this book about the life of Gustavus Loomis. A Vermonter and a man of God, Loomis is one of the many unsung heroes of the war. Thanks to Lawson's dedication to detail he has preserved the story of not only a great Vermonter, but also a great American.

—HONORABLE SCOTT WHEELER
Vermont House of Representatives
Publisher of *Vermont's Northland Journal*

Colonel Lawson has rescued the memory of his fellow Vermonter and given us a detailed portrait of a unique soldier. Most of us have never heard of General Loomis, but none of us----after reading this narrative of his life----is likely to forget him. A worthy read, it combines military history with the personal story of a man who balanced well his obligations to God, to family, and to country; and performed them with joy.

In this telling we learn of wars with Britain, with Mexico, with American Indian tribes, and with fellow Americans in the War Between the States. We learn of the seeming naturalness of the General's concern for the spiritual well-being of his men and his concern for blacks and their education, much ahead of his times. In its reading we find pleasure and profit. Having received both, I recommend it.

—DR. EDWARD M. PANOSIAN
Professor of Church History (ret'd.), Bob Jones University

AUTHOR AND HISTORIAN Chaplain (Colonel) Ken Lawson has accomplished a feat with this thrilling story of a forgotten American hero, Brigadier General Gustavus Loomis. Lawson digs through a scant historical record in a compelling effort. The historian's task here is daunting. General Loomis did not write a book or keep a journal. Relying on obituaries, tangential journal references, census records, newspaper articles and various published and unpublished documents, aided by a little speculation, Lawson recreates the epic story of a man who lived and died for his savior Jesus Christ, and for his nation in its formative years.

From Vermont during the Second Great Awakening with the preaching of Rev. Asa Burton, through West Point, the War of 1812, numerous Indian Wars, the Mexican War, and ending in the Civil War, Gustavus Loomis served more than fifty-five years in uniform. He was a solid military professional, a good husband, father and grandfather, as well as a consistent Bible reader and teacher. Inspired by the Gospel command to love one's neighbor, Gustavus Loomis was an early foe of slavery, a hero in combat yet a compassionate man who showed mercy to the downtrodden, especially Native Americans, former foes on the battlefield, displaced from their tribal homelands to reservations in the West. I enjoyed this book. As a fellow West Pointer, and Christian soldier, this book is an inspiring and fascinating look at a forgotten age in American history. Highly recommended!

—CHAPLAIN (BRIGADIER GENERAL) EUGENE R. WOOLRIDGE
US Army Reserve, Assistant Chief of Chaplains, Mobilization and Readiness

CHAPLAIN (COLONEL) KENNETH Lawson has done a masterful job intertwining the biography of brevet Brigadier General Gustavus Loomis with the times in which he lived. Loomis stands out as a Christian officer for all seasons, with service that spanned most of the nineteenth century. Loomis functions not only as a role model for leadership from the War of 1812 through the end of the Civil War, but also as a prism through which one may see many historical events in a new light. I am pleased to recommend this scholarly but entertaining book to anyone interested in American military or religious history.

—DR. JOHN W. BRINSFIELD
Army Chaplain Corps Historian
Adjunct Professor, Wesley Theological Seminary

Table of Contents

INTRODUCTION:

GUSTAVUS LOOMIS (1789-1872) HAS BEEN overlooked by history. His life was a gradual rise in authority and influence. Historians are hindered in discovering Loomis, in that he never kept a journal and his limited correspondence is all within a military context, short paragraphs summarizing significant events. Before now, no biography was written about this very religious career military officer. Actually, only one journal article has ever been written about Gustavus Loomis, a nine page article published by the Oklahoma Historical Society in 1940.[1]

Loomis was born into a religious home in rural Thetford, Vermont. In his youth he participated in revivals historians call the Second Great Awakening. He was educated in a one-room schoolhouse but was able to secure an appointment to the United States Military Academy at West Point, graduating in 1811. Through his fifty-six years of military service, Gustavus Loomis fought the British in Canada; served throughout the United States and its western territories; fought Indians in places as far away as Florida, Wisconsin and Texas; served in Mexico in the Mexican American War; and ended his career in uniform as a seventy-eight year old brevet Brigadier General serving with the Union Army in the Civil War. Loomis was a prisoner of war; a respected staff officer; a careful administrator; and was fearless in combat. He suppressed a mutiny at sea and was respected nationally for his military and

---

1 Carolyn T. Foreman, "Gustavus Loomis: Commandant of Fort Gibson and Fort Towson," *Chronicles of Oklahoma*, vol. 18, no. 3 (September, 1940), pp. 219-228.

civil dealings with Indians. Loomis was fair and compassionate while always manly and self-controlled. Above all his attributes he was known as a devout and sincere Christian, a Calvinist who encouraged revivals. His men loved him.

There was nothing impressive about the physical appearance of Gustavus Loomis. He was of average height and slim. What little of his correspondence that exists shows that he was educated, reasonable, and he made sound decisions. Loomis had a lifelong aversion to alcohol and profanity. His tent in the field and his home in the garrison were places of hymn singing and prayer meetings. In his military activities against Indians and against the Confederate States of America, Loomis was seen as compassionate, fair and honest. In his over five decades of military service he had no fiscal or moral indiscretions.

Loomis' military career covered fifty-six of his eighty-two years of life. Counting his time at West Point, Gustavus Loomis wore the military uniform of his country for an amazing fifty-nine years. He froze in the snows of Minnesota and he perspired in the deserts of Mexico. He marched in the swamps of Florida, protected settlers along the Oregon Trail, and he skirmished with the Comanche in Texas. In his last military assignment he served in the Civil War as commandant of a prisoner of war camp and as commander of a fort in New York Harbor. His was a rich and rewarding military career.

Brevet Brigadier General Gustavus Loomis was a devoted family man. Only his relationship with God came before his relationship with his family. God and family were always above his career, a fact that brought him some criticism from fellow officers. The army was the only job Loomis ever held. For almost six decades he served his Lord Jesus Christ and his country. While some officers questioned his religious zeal, no one questioned his devotion to his family or his capability as a military officer.

There are numerous detailed studies of the U.S. Army in the nineteenth century. Nevertheless, Gustavus Loomis is frequently overlooked in most of these texts. For example, in the excellent book, *Frontiersmen in Blue: The United States Army and the Indian, 1848-1865*, Loomis is not mentioned, even though he was a senior Lieutenant Colonel and then a Colonel dealing with Indians in the American west and southwest at that time.[2] There are a couple of passing references to Gustavus Loomis in *An American Profession of Arms: The Army Officer Corps, 1784-1861*, but they are random references that say nothing about Loomis' overall military career.[3] The religious life of soldiers in the Civil War has received quite a bit of literary attention. During this war Colonel and later brevet Brigadier General Gustavus Loomis was conducting prayer meetings and encouraging revivals at his location at Fort Columbus, New York Harbor, but these religious activities have been overlooked by historians. An exception to the overlooking of Loomis in military history relates to his activities in the Florida Seminole Wars. In the Second Seminole War Loomis had a major role in the battle of Okeechobee and in other operations. In the Third Seminole War, Gustavus Loomis was the senior military officer in Florida. In both of these cases history has briefly recorded Loomis' successes.[4]

While Loomis' name has been mostly lost to history, the men who served under him greatly admired him for his tactically sound decisions; his reasonable but firm standards for discipline; and for his courage in the face of the enemy. Others who served

---

2 Robert M. Utley, *Frontiersmen in Blue: The United States Army and the Indian, 1848-1865*, (University of Nebraska Press, 1967).

3 William B. Skelton, *An American Profession of Arms: The Army Officer Corps, 1784-1861*, (University of Kansas Press, 19920, pp. 322, 351-352.

4 For mention of Loomis in the Second Seminole War, see John K. Mahon, *History of the Second Seminole War, 1835-1842*, (University of Florida Press, 1985), pp. 253, 306. Loomis' leadership in the Third Seminole War is found in Joe Knetch, *Florida's Seminole Wars, 1817-1858*, (Charleston, SC: Arcadia Press, 2003), pp. 153, 156.

with Loomis did not like his repudiation of slavery and his insistence in teaching blacks and Indians how to read the Bible. A select few saw Loomis as a religious nut, an eccentric. Others saw him as a fair and devout Christian.

At his death in 1872, brevet Brigadier General Gustavus Loomis was called, "One of the oldest and most faithful servants of the country in the United States Army."[5] He was remembered at his death for his "firmness of purpose and a resolute and untiring perseverance," and that he was a valiant soldier of the cross and of his country.[6] This biographical study of Gustavus Loomis focuses on a career military man who lived through innumerable cultural, political and technological changes in the nineteenth century United States. Yet his devotion to his God, his family, and his country remained unchangeable.

Photograph of the exterior of the Fort Columbus Chapel, Governor's Island, New York Harbor. Although this image is from 1905, the building looks much the same as it did when constructed in 1846. Notice the military and civilian clothing on the parishioners and the military sentry near the door. Here Gustavus Loomis worshipped from 1861 to 1867. Public domain image.

---

5 *The New York Times*, March 10, 1872.
6 *Third Annual Reunion of the Association of the Graduates of the U.S. Military Academy at West Point, N.Y., June 14, 1872,* (New York: Crocker and Company, 1872), pp. 46-47.

CHAPTER ONE

THE EARLY YEARS

AN EIGHT YEAR OLD BOY sat in the Congregational Church in Thetford, Vermont, named Gustavus Loomis. The year was 1797. The spring weather was refreshing after a long Vermont winter. The small village of Thetford, founded in 1761, was a stable community of farmers and merchants in touch with the outside world mostly through the adjacent Connecticut River. The Congregational Church was the center of the community, the focal point of life in Thetford. A religious revival was sweeping through Thetford and surrounding communities. Reverend Asa Burton (1752-1836) was the most influential man in Thetford, though he was not always the most liked. Gustavus Loomis was baptized as an infant by Rev. Burton in November 1789. All of his young life, Loomis attended religious services and was dedicated to the gospel message preached by Pastor Burton. Gustavus Loomis and his whole family attended church regularly, they walking a few minutes from their home across the town common to the meeting house. Nobody sitting in that small Thetford Congregational Church in 1797 could have imagined that there would be a future war hero in their midst. Nobody could have predicted that young Gustavus Loomis was destined to become a brevet Brigadier General in the United States Army, a veteran of wars against the British, against numerous Indian tribes, against Mexicans, and against his own countrymen in a horrific Civil War.

Thetford, Vermont was initially settled by proprietors, investors and adventurers from Connecticut. In 1761, Governor Benning Wentworth of New Hampshire sold the land he probably named after the Viscount of Thetford to a group of Connecticut investors. For some time it was said that Thetford was named for the English town of Thetford, one-time capital of the kings and bishops of East Anglia. Recently, however, it has become accepted that Thetford was probably named for one of Governor Benning Wentworth's British relatives, Augustus Henry Fitzroy, Duke of Grafton, Earl of Arlington and Euston, Viscount of Thetford and Baron of Sudbury. Governor Wentworth used all of Fitzroy's titles in naming towns in Vermont and New Hampshire.[7] Governor Wentworth granted charters for sixty towns in 1761, one of these being Thetford, Vermont.

The first settlers of Thetford, mostly from Hebron, Connecticut, migrated north throughout the 1760s. First settling along the Connecticut River and gradually moving inland, these pioneers were avid fishermen and farmers. An industrious group, they soon developed saw mills for lumber and grist mills for refining wheat. The land was eventually cleared, new settlers from New England and New York arrived, babies were born, and the town gradually prospered. One of those Connecticut families that moved north to Thetford, Vermont was the Beriah Loomis family.

The Loomis family of Connecticut has a distinct history. The first Loomis descendant to come to America was Joseph Loomis (m.1614 to Mary White), who arrived in Boston in 1638 and settled in Windsor, Connecticut in 1639. Originally from Braintree, England, Joseph Loomis was a fervent supporter of the Protestant Reformation, a puritan typical of those devout settlers of New England in the seventeenth century. Because of religious persecution in Braintree, Joseph Loomis immigrated to the New World as a middle aged man with his wife and children. Over the

7 "Virtual Vermont Internet Magazine," www.virtualvermont.com/towns/thetford. Charles Latham, *A Short History of Thetford, Vermont 1761-1870*, (Lebanon, NH : 1999), p. 4.

next twenty years, several dozen Loomis descendants followed the example of Joseph Loomis and migrated to Connecticut. From these original Loomis descendants arose numerous persons of distinction in the ministry, in foreign missions, in various civil positions, in education, in science and in the military.[8]

As part of this long line of Loomis descendants in Connecticut, Beriah Loomis notes our attention. As one of the upper middle class Loomis' in Connecticut, Beriah Loomis (1753-1819) arrived in Thetford, Vermont around 1780. He appears as a land owner in Thetford in 1781.[9] Like almost all the Loomis family in Connecticut, he was proud of his Protestant and puritan heritage. He was born in Bolton, Connecticut and was married in 1774 in Tolland, Connecticut. Beriah and his wife Mary (Benton) Loomis (1757-1820) eventually had eleven children, the ninth who was Gustavus. The lure from Connecticut to Thetford was strong and abundant land cheaply obtained. Beriah quickly rose to prominence in Thetford, he being elected by his peers as a Selectman for Thetford in 1785. As one of the first if not the first settler to build a home in the Thetford Hill community, Beriah Loomis eventually built four homes along the common, two which are still standing and in good condition today.

Beriah Loomis served as a private in the Connecticut Militia during the Revolutionary War. As with all able bodied men in Colonial New England, Loomis was a member of the militia. His brief active duty service was for seventeen days, in April and May of 1775. His service was in response to the "Lexington Alarm," a call for New England militia to support Massachusetts after the British raids against Lexington and Concord. Beriah Loomis was one of about four thousand Connecticut militiamen

8 *The Loomis Family in America*, (Hartford, CT: 1905), pp. 9, 11, 18, 21-24, 29-30, 32.
9 Charles Latham, *A Short History of Thetford*, p. 22.

who marched to Boston for duty.[10] Some of the units returned home before reaching Boston, as they learned their service was not needed. Beriah Loomis had a brief but positive experience as a soldier, an experience that inevitably had some influence upon his son Gustavus and the pursuing of an education for Gustavus at the United States Military Academy at West Point, New York.

When the Revolutionary War veteran Beriah Loomis arrived in Thetford with his wife Mary around 1780, they were already the parents of three sons. In November, 1780 their first daughter was born in Thetford. Seven more children were born to Beriah and Mary while they lived in Thetford. Only two of the children did not live to an older age, as Edna (1782-1817) and Horatio (1784-1802) died relatively young. Their ninth child, Gustavus, lived much longer than all his siblings, he seeing all ten of his brothers and sisters predecease him before he died at age eighty-two and a half years in 1872.[11]

Like most of his Loomis ancestors, Beriah Loomis was a man of deep personal faith in Jesus Christ. Loomis fully accepted the doctrines of the Protestant Reformation and happily endorsed the Westminster Confession of Faith. The household of Beriah Loomis was devout and principled, with family catechism and prayer common events. Upon his arrival in Thetford, he discovered that the Thetford church met in a crude log meeting house in the eastern part of town near the Connecticut River. Loomis offered to finance the construction of a new meeting house for Thetford. He proposed

10 *Connecticut Military Record 1775-1848: Record of Service of Connecticut Men in the War of the Revolution...*, (Hartford, CT: 1889), p. 23.
11 Elias Loomis, *The Descendants of Joseph Loomis,* (New Haven, CT: 1875), p. 152.

building the church structure on Thetford Hill, on the condition that he design a common in front of the meeting house and he purchase building lots around the proposed common. In 1787, two years before Gustavus Loomis was born, Thetford had the beginnings of a new meeting house on the south side of the common. This structure is considered the oldest meeting house in the State of Vermont to be in continuous operation. In 1830 the building was moved from the south side of the common to its present location on the north side of the common.[12]

Throughout the early 1790s the final construction details on the Thetford meeting house were completed. Beriah Loomis and his growing family lived a few minutes walk from the meeting house and had the only home on Thetford Hill at that time. Loomis had the duty in the 1790s to keep the key and sweep the building twice a month in summer and once a month in winter for an annual salary of twenty shillings.[13] It is not difficult to imaging the awe in the boy Gustavus Loomis, as he  and his father cleaned and maintained the building he could see from his window, a meeting house where the word of God was preached and the authority of holy scripture was proclaimed. We can only imagine the religious talks father and son had in the quiet shadows of that empty building with its commanding pulpit and wooden pews. The lessons learned through the ministry of the Thetford Congregational Church were a vital part of Gustavus Loomis for all of his almost eighty-three years of life.

---

12 Janine Weins, "The Church Built on Thetford Hill," www.acornhillfarmweather.com. Accessed November 2, 2009.

13 Charles Latham, *A Short History of Thetford*, p.18.

The early settlers of Thetford seem to have been more reli-
gious-minded than other Vermonters.[14] The childhood of Gustavus Loomis in Thetford was secure. His father Beriah had various
positions in local and later Vermont state government. For example, Beriah Loomis represented Thetford to the state assembly
from 1782 to 1790; he was Councilor from 1801 until 1814; he
was the Assistant Judge of Orange County, Vermont from 1797 to
1818; he was a member of the Constitutional Convention in
1791.[15] From 1807 to 1808 Beriah Loomis served on the Gover-

nor's Council.[16] This meant that Gustavus
and his ten siblings were reasonably well off
for Vermonters at that time. Two of the four
homes Beriah Loomis built in Thetford are
still standing. They are nice, comfortable
homes but are certainly not mansions or
overly extravagant. It is safe to say that
Gustavus Loomis grew up in a home where
there was always food on the table, but at a
table where his father Beriah was often away
on government business. The main occupa-
tion of the men in Thetford was farming, with some employed on
the Connecticut River as fishermen, as boat operators, or as ice-
men in the long Vermont winters. The Thetford census for 1800
had a total population of 1,478 people; the 1810 census had 1,785
people.[17] Overall, the residents of Thetford were an industrious
and God-fearing people.

While the original settlers of Thetford struggled financially

14 Charles Latham, *A Short History of Thetford*, p.6.

15 LaFayette Wilber, *Early History of Vermont*, (Jerico, VT: Roscoe Printers, 1902), vol.
   III, p. 354.

16 *Records of the Governor and Council of the State of Vermont*, vol. V, (Montpelier,
   VT: 1877), p. 184.

17 Charles Latham, *A Short History of Thetford*, p.23.

through the Revolutionary War years, the world into which Gustavus Loomis was born in Thetford in 1789 was rural but stable. Each family grew most of its own food. At least one cow was in every barn with the horses. Residents wore homespun clothing. The men hunted, fished and farmed in the abundant Vermont countryside. Religiously, the people of Thetford in 1779 were called "ignorant about the doctrines and precepts of the gospel," they being mostly irreligious although not antagonistic towards Christianity.[18] This all changed with the arrival in 1779 of Reverend Asa Burton, who would minister in Thetford for over fifty-five years.

A most influential person upon the life of Gustavus Loomis was his first minister, Rev. Asa Burton of the Thetford Congregational Church. When Beriah Loomis settled in Thetford around 1780, Rev. Burton had just recently arrived. Burton ministered in Thetford for ten years when Gustavus Loomis was born in 1789. Reverend Asa Burton was Gustavus Loomis' minister from his birth until Loomis departed Thetford for the U.S. Military Academy at West Point in 1808. Pastor Burton baptized the infant Gustavus Loomis. The handwritten records of the Thetford Congregational Church state, "Gustavus ye Son of Beriah Loomis baptized November 1789."[19]

Reverend Asa Burton (1752-1836) was a fascinating and influential man. He was born in Stonington, Connecticut but moved to Norwich, Vermont as an infant, part of the huge migration of puritans from Connecticut moving north for cheap and productive land. Raised on a farm, he entered the nearby Dartmouth College, a decidedly evangelical Protestant institution, graduating in 1777. After graduation he remained at the college

---

18 Asa Burton, *The Life of Asa Burton, Minister in Thetford, Vermont, 1779-1836,* (Thetford Historical Society, 1998), p. 29.

19 *The Records of the Church of Christ, Thetford, Vermont, 1773-1832,* (Thetford Historical Society), p. 163.

to prepare for the ministry, occasionally preaching at rural New England meeting houses as an itinerant minister. He was ordained January 19, 1779, as pastor of the fledgling Congregational church at Thetford, Vermont, where he remained for approximately fifty-five years. Rev. Burton was an avid supporter of the revivalist spirit of his day, known today as the Second Great Awakening.[20]

The Second Great Awakening created the evangelical climate which compelled Asa Burton to minister in rural Thetford. From around 1800 to the Civil War, this sporadic religious awakening manifested itself in various locations throughout the United States. Rural Vermont was no exception. The Second Great Awakening was characterized by prolonged religious meetings within existing churches; outdoor revival meetings with large crowds; new churches being started; existing churches dividing over theological issues; and a general increase in religious sensibilities within various towns.[21] Asa Burton was the human instrument of spiritual awakening in his growing parish in Thetford. One of his parishioners who fully accepted the awakening and developed a lifelong zeal for evangelical Christianity was the youth Gustavus Loomis.

Theologically, Asa Burton was an adherent of what was later called the New England Theology. This theological perspective believed that the Calvinistic piety of New England had grown stale and indifferent. While maintaining an insistence on the Calvinist doctrine of predestination, the New England Theology asserted passionately that sinners surrender themselves to the grace of God through the blood of Christ for conversion and personal holiness. While still maintaining the Calvinist doctrine of depravity, Asa Burton and other early New England Theology

---

20 Sydney E. Alstrom, *A Religious History of the American People*, (New Haven: Yale University Press, 1972), pp. 403-428.

21 Mark A. Noll, Editor, *Eerdman's Handbook to Christianity in America*, (Grand Rapids: Eerdman's Publishers, 1983), pp.172-187.

proponents asserted that all people had an obligation to repent and believe in Jesus Christ for personal regeneration. The older Calvinists regulated church membership by those who within the state-sponsored church participated in baptism and communion. The New England Theology based church membership on a personal testimony of conversion.[22]

Asa Burton preached a masculine Christianity, bold and blunt yet with scriptural support and practical application. Upon his arrival in Thetford in 1779, Burton admonished his congregation for their poor parenting, their indifference to religion, their amusements of dancing and card playing, their use of alcohol, and their general ignorance of experiential Christianity. Rev. Burton began to teach the Bible to his parish both on Sundays and in small groups during the week. He focused on the youth while insisting on compliance from the parents. Asa Burton stated, "I was much opposed in this town." He continued, "It was my practice to preach against every evil practice prevalent, and, if any found fault, to preach more plainly and pointedly. This convinced them I was not intimidated by any opposition, and that opposition did not avail anything." Burton continued, "This operated as a restraint upon them... There were also frequent instances of hopeful conversions, and the church was yearly increased in numbers."[23]

Gustavus Loomis was a disciple of Asa Burton. Rev. Burton mentored the young Loomis into the essentials of Protestant theology with a revivalistic application. Loomis was present when his minister had special youth meetings to discuss theology and the Christian life with the young people in Thetford. Gustavus Loomis was converted under his pastor's ministry. He was thoroughly supportive of the spiritual awakening preached by Rev.

22 Douglas A. Sweeney and Allen C. Guelzo, *The New England Theology*, (Grand Rapids: Baker Books, 2006), pp. 14-17. This book has a chapter on Asa Burton, pp. 179-186.
23 Asa Burton, *The Life of Asa Burton*, p. 29.

Burton. In 1804, Burton received the degree of Doctor of Divinity from the evangelical Middlebury College. Dr. Burton was noted as a theological teacher and author, training about sixty young men for the ministry. He was twice asked to preach Election Sermons and served as a Chaplain to the Vermont General Assembly on several occasions. Burton had numerous local ministerial responsibilities outside his parish, such as serving as President of the Orange County Bible Society and serving as President of a local religious tract society. His congregation gave him a colleague in 1825, and after 1831 Dr. Burton retired altogether from his labors. He died on May 1, 1836 in Thetford.

Although not so much in New England, within the Second Great Awakening there were religious fanatics and emotional zealots.[24] The awakening in Thetford was calm and balanced. Beginning in 1797 a strong and enduring awakening covered Asa Burton's ministry in Thetford. Gustavus Loomis, who was eight years old at that time, was completely absorbed into the revival within his church. This spirit of awakening lasted beyond the time Loomis left Thetford for West Point in 1808. The entire formative years of Gustavus Loomis were spent amidst an increased religious awareness, with hundreds of his fellow Thetford residents experiencing conversion from outward religion to inner faith in Jesus Christ. Rev. Burton wrote of these converts as individuals who were "under strong impressions;" as those who were "seriously impressed;" and as ones who "gave evidence of a change of heart." The Thetford revival developed slowly, peaked for about four years, and gradually leveled off. However, Asa Burton recorded the after affects of the awakening lasting until 1817, as every month individuals came forward on Communion Sunday to give evidence of conversion with a request for church membership.[25]

24 Sydney E. Alstrom, *A Religious History of the American People*, pp. 433-435.
25 Asa Burton, *The Life of Asa Burton*, pp. 49-50.

Evangelical Christianity was not the only lifelong conviction Gustavus Loomis received as a youth in Thetford. A second life-long enduring principle Loomis received as a youth in Thetford was his aversion to slavery.

It is not difficult to understand Gustavus Loomis' position towards blacks and towards the institution of slavery. Essentially, Loomis despised slavery and he loathed the fact that some men claimed to be inherently superior to others based on race. To Loomis, who believed that all people were made in the image of God and therefore all are equally valuable, slavery was reprehensible. The fact that slave owners did not allow blacks to read meant to Loomis that slave masters were preventing human beings from reading the Bible and accepting Jesus Christ as Lord and Savior. In his later years, Loomis was stationed as an Army officer in southern slave states. He saw the evil of slavery firsthand and was repulsed. While serving in southern slave states, Loomis held reading classes for blacks and he developed Sunday Schools for blacks, both illegal activities in slave states. Needless to say, his fellow Army officers from southern states were furious at Loomis for such activities. But Loomis answered to a higher authority than the man-made rules of southern slave owners, and he persisted in his educating and evangelizing of blacks.

As a child in Thetford, Gustavus Loomis had limited but significant exposure to blacks. Reverend Asa Burton was friends with a mulatto minister named Rev. Lemuel Haynes. In 1785, Lemuel Haynes (1753-1833) made his first preaching tour through Vermont and then served as a pastor in the same church in Rutland, Vermont for thirty years. Originally from Connecticut, Rev. Haynes in 1804 was the Field Secretary for the Connecticut Missionary Society, and after moving to Vermont he was appointed to the same position with the Vermont Missionary Society in 1809.[26] In this position, Haynes worked closely with Asa Burton. Physically, Haynes looked like a black man. As a Field Secretary, one of Haynes' responsibilities was to go out to Vermont churches and promote the Missionary Society. We can only imagine what went through the mind of Gustavus Loomis as he sat in the Thetford Congregational Church as a boy and heard appeals from Rev. Lemuel Haynes related to missions and evangelism. Asa Burton and Lemuel Haynes preached the same revivalist message and promoted the same gospel with identical missionary zeal. To Gustavus Loomis, the message was essential, not the color of the skin of the messenger.

There were blacks living in Thetford while Gustavus Loomis was a youth. The 1791 census, taken when Gustavus was three years old, reveals that in a town of less than nine hundred residents there were three black households in Thetford with a total of thirteen people. In addition, one white resident is listed as having a black person in their household. Of these total fourteen blacks in Thetford in 1791 we know the most about Mr. George Knox. Mr. Knox was a servant to General George Washington in the Revolutionary War. After the war, Washington urged Knox to go north away from southern slavery. Arriving in Thetford around 1783, George Knox and his wife had four children and were active members of the community. Perhaps as a child, Gustavus Loomis played with these young black girls and boys. George Knox died in 1825 and is buried in Thetford.[27] Blacks worshipped with whites in the Thetford Congregational Church, with two pews reserved for the blacks in the gallery. Blacks were baptized in the meeting house and received communion from Rev. Asa Burton alongside the white congregants.

26 Wilber H. Siebert, *Vermont's Anti-Slavery and Underground Railroad Record*, (Columbus, OH: 1937), pp. 6-10.
27 Charles Latham, *A Short History of Thetford*, pp. 23-24.

A black youth in Thetford that departed before the 1791 census was Mr. Prince Saunders (c.1780-1839). The Saunders were from Lebanon, Connecticut. Cuff Saunders served with his master throughout the Revolutionary War and was granted his freedom for faithful service. Cuff Saunders married a servant of Charles Hinckley of Lebanon named Phyllis. Their son Prince Saunders was born shortly thereafter. The son was baptized in 1784 either in Lebanon, Connecticut or in Thetford, Vermont. At age four, Prince Saunders' father died. His mother moved back into the Charles Hinckley home in Lebanon. Charles invested in land in Thetford and around 1784 Charles' son George moved to Thetford and took the black child Prince Saunders with him. George Hinckley married and settled into a law practice in Thetford and had children of his own, with the black boy Prince Saunders always considered an equal part of the family. Although Prince Saunders was several years older than Gustavus Loomis, they were both children at the same time in Thetford. With Hinckley's sponsorship, Prince Saunders was able to attend Dartmouth College. Saunders then taught at a school for black children in Connecticut and later at the African School in Boston.

Mr. Prince Saunders' later life reads like a novel. He started numerous schools for blacks in Boston; he became a leader in the black colonization movement to Africa; and he travelled to England and met with the famous abolitionists William Wilberforce and Thomas Clarkson. While in England he was recommended to serve in the first black republic in the New World, Haiti. King Henri Christophe of Haiti enthusiastically received Saunders and allowed him to develop educational and medical programs in Haiti. Saunders saw Haiti as a paradise for black slaves in the United States and facilitated blacks to immigrate to Haiti. After some back and forth movements, Saunders settled in Haiti in

1820 and died in Port-au-Prince in 1839.[28] How the intellectual and cultural successes of Prince Saunders affected his fellow citizens in Thetford is unclear. But it is certain, as one author stated, "The career of this negro, Prince Saunders was another example known to Vermonters in the time of the anti-slavery agitation of a negro who achieved distinction."[29]

The world of Gustavus Loomis in Thetford was passionately against slavery. One author spoke of Vermont as "a state which took slavery as a moral evil."[30] Within Thetford there developed a station in the Underground Railroad, which assisted runaway black slaves to freedom into Canada.[31] Some of the Vermont distinctions in the anti-slavery movement are as follows:

1777 - Vermont's Constitution was the first to outlaw adult slavery

1786 – Vermont Legislature fines all those who sell or remove negroes

1791 – With a prohibition on slavery, Vermont becomes the 14th state

1805 – Vermont US Senators create a bill prohibiting the importation of slaves to the US (the bill failed)

1819 - The First State Colonization Society founded in Vermont

1820 – Vermont becomes a key location for the Underground Railroad

1820 – The Vermont Legislature adopts a resolution opposing Missouri as a slave state because slavery was in-

28 For a summary of Saunders career, see Frank Bayard, "Prince Saunders," in *Dictionary of American Negro Biography*, (New York: W.W. Norton & Company, 1983), pp. 541-542, and Arthur D. White, "Prince Saunders: An Instance of Social Mobility among Antebellum New England Blacks, *Journal of Negro History* 55, (1975), pp. 526-535.

29 Wilber H. Siebert, *Vermont's Anti-Slavery and Underground Railroad Record*, p. 12.
30 Charles Latham, *A Short History of Thetford*, p. 43.
31 Wilber H. Siebert, *Vermont's Anti-Slavery and Underground Railroad Record*, p. 97.

compatible with a free government. Thereafter Vermont resisted the admission of every slave state and Territory into the Union.

Within the town boundaries of Thetford, Gustavus Loomis enjoyed his youth. Typical of the educational systems of that day, Loomis attended school only in the winter months. His education in Thetford was in a one room schoolhouse located on the common near the meeting house. When Asa Burton arrived in Thetford in 1779 there was no schoolhouse. As the town grew the population was divided into various districts, each district eventually having its own schoolhouse.

Since Gustavus Loomis and his family lived on Thetford Hill by the common, they resided in District 10. The District 10 schoolhouse began holding classes in 1782, seven years before Gustavus was born. There was a summer school for girls, taught by a woman, and a winter school for boys, taught by a man. The schoolhouse was endorsed by Rev. Asa Burton and funded by Beriah Loomis. Black and white children were educated together. In the winter the boys were expected to bring their own firewood for the schoolhouse woodstove. Starting in 1801, the number of "scholars" was reported every few years, a scholar being a child in school between the ages of four and eighteen.[32]

In 1801, a few years before Gustavus Loomis was old enough for school, there were seventy-two scholars in the District 10 school. The next year there was an attendance record is 1806, when Loomis was definitely in the District 10 school, he being one of the seventy-four students. Using the seventy-four students in 1806 as an example, we can divide that number evenly between the summer school for girls and the winter school for boys,

32 Charles Latham, *A Short History of Thetford,* p. 25. See also "School District 10 Records," Thetford Historical Society.

meaning that Gustavus Loomis was in the one room District 10 schoolhouse in 1806 with approximately thirty-five or so male classmates, ages four through eighteen. Gustavus was definitely educated sitting alongside black male students. There is no question that this fact influenced Gustavus in later years in his insistence in teaching blacks to read and write.

We know virtually nothing about the teenage years of Gustavus Loomis in Thetford. We know that by 1800, when Loomis was eleven years old and in school in the wintertime, the town had 1,478 residents. Thetford was the third largest town in rural Orange County, Vermont. In 1810, when Gustavus was twenty-one years old and a student at West Point, the population of Thetford increased to 1,785 people, a significant increase for a small New England town in the early nineteenth century.

Typically, a school age child in early Thetford history ended his or her formal education at or before their eighteenth birthday. We do not know at what point Gustavus Loomis completed his education at the District 10 schoolhouse in Thetford. We do know that because Beriah Loomis was reasonably wealthy although not rich, his son Gustavus did not have to work to contribute to the survival of the family. We also know that Gustavus was the ninth born of eleven children. Therefore an inheritance as the firstborn son was out of the question, since Gustavus had four older brothers and four older sisters.

In the early 1800s, what did a healthy, devout young man in rural Vermont from a large family with no anticipated inheritance do with his life? Beriah Loomis was a firm advocate of education, evidenced by his purchase of the materials to build the District 10 schoolhouse in Thetford. As Gustavus approached the customary age eighteen deadline for his education, his career choices were limited. He could work for his father as some type of low level civil clerk. He could farm or fish for a living, skills he acquired in Thetford. As a devout and active Christian young man he certainly could study for the ministry. All of these options were legitimate and worthwhile. But Gustavus Loomis chose another career path, he deciding on a military career that began in 1808 and ended fifty-nine years later in 1867.

The District 10 schoolhouse, Thetford, Vermont. This photograph was taken many years after Gustavus Loomis was a student, but the size of the building and the general design of the structure were unchanged. Image provided by the Thetford Historical Society.

CHAPTER TWO

THE WEST POINT YEARS, 1808-1811

GUSTAVUS LOOMIS BECAME A CADET at the United States Military Academy, West Point, on June 15, 1808. We may never know exactly why Loomis chose an education at West Point. But we can know of the instrumental factors that influenced his decision.

First, Gustavus Loomis came from a long line of men who performed military service. Beginning with the first Loomis' who settled in Connecticut in the 1640s, men of the Loomis genealogy served in the military. Gustavus Loomis' father, Beriah, served in the Connecticut militia and had a brief active duty experience related to British raids at Lexington and Concord, Massachusetts in 1775. Beriah's brother Nathaniel Loomis III was a militia captain and their father Nathan Loomis, Jr. was a sergeant in the militia. The senior Nathaniel Loomis, the great-grandfather of Gustavus Loomis, was an ensign in the Connecticut militia in the 1660s. Prior to that, Sergeant Daniel Loomis and Ensign Nathaniel Loomis, distant relatives of Gustavus Loomis, served in the Connecticut militia in the 1640s.[33] It is not clear what emphasis should be placed on this military genealogy, since most young men in early nineteenth century New England could claim a similar family history of militia service.

Another factor that influenced Gustavus to attend the U.S. Military Academy was the leadership of his father, Beriah Loomis.

33 "Hickok Family Genealogy," www.hickokfamilygenealogy.com/hickok/b163. htm#P9848. Accessed August 1, 2009.

The influence of Beriah Loomis was local, statewide, and national. Locally, Beriah was a Thetford Representative from 1782-1790. More regionally, he served as an Assistant Judge for the Orange County Court from 1797-1818. On a national level, Beriah Loomis was a Vermont member of the United States Constitutional Convention of 1791. Significantly, in the 1807-1808 timeframe in which Gustavus Loomis was seeking an appointment to the U.S. Military Academy, his father Beriah served on the Governor's Council of Vermont. In this capacity, Beriah Loomis served as an advisor to Vermont Governor Israel Smith, Loomis making frequent trips to work with the Governor in Montpelier.[34] It is not hard to imagine Beriah Loomis speaking to Governor Smith about a recommendation for his son Gustavus to attend the U.S. Military Academy. Such a prestigious recommendation would almost assure the acceptance of Gustavus into the Academy.

As far as the acceptance into the U.S. Military Academy, the influence of Rev. Asa Burton should be considered. Reverend Burton was well known throughout New England and New York. Burton was a published author who travelled widely as an itinerant preacher. Gustavus Loomis was a dedicated member of Burton's parish and was an outspoken advocate of Burton's revivalist preaching. It is unclear if Asa Burton had a direct influence on Loomis' acceptance into the Academy. But an endorsement from a clergyman, a valuable commodity in that day, would have meant a lot in the potential appointment of Loomis as a cadet at West Point.

A consideration for any potential cadet at a military academy is the emotional, spiritual and physical condition of the individual. Life as a military cadet was not for the faint of mind or heart. Rigorous academic studies, combined with military tactics and physical exercise, made for long and exhausting days.

---

34 *Records of the Governor and Council of the State of Vermont,* (Montpelier: 1877), vol. V, p. 184.

As a young man, Gustavus Loomis was emotionally and spiritually mature. Physically, he was an outdoors person, enjoying hunting, fishing, hiking and horseback riding. Not every young man was capable of surviving life as a military cadet, but Loomis had all of the emotional, mental, spiritual and physical qualifications to be successful.

Gustavus Loomis traveled several days by boat with the current from Thetford down the Connecticut River through Massachusetts to the ocean port of Lyme, Connecticut. From Lyme he took a boat west along the Connecticut coastline into New York Harbor. In New York City Loomis again changed boats and sailed about fifty miles north along the Hudson River to West Point.

The U.S. Military Academy that greeted Gustavus Loomis in June of 1808 was a fledgling school, underfunded and with limited supplies and facilities. The school was founded in 1802 amidst the controversy whether or not it was appropriate for a democratic nation to have a military academy to train professional soldiers. Many favored the colonial militia system of citizen soldiers, fearful of a standing Army with elite officers professionally trained in the art and science of war.[35] Located on high ground overlooking the bending Hudson River fifty miles north of New York City, the U.S. Military Academy was in 1808 understaffed and over extended. It was a transitional time in which there were few standards for admission, curriculum or length of study. Some of these early graduates studied for a year or two while others studied several years before graduating. There was no age requirement for a cadet, as some were young teens while other cadets were men in their late thirties. The Academy was located within the well-defended military fort designed during the Revolutionary War to prevent British shipping along the Hudson River.

---

35 Allan R. Millett and Peter Maslowski, *For the Common Defense: A Military History of the United States of America*, (New York: The Free Press, 1994), p. 135.

The military garrison at West Point was first developed and occupied in 1778 and played a strategic role in the Revolutionary War. Congress formally authorized the establishment and funding of the U.S. Military Academy on March 16, 1802, though artillery and engineering students had been undergoing training at the garrison since 1794. Few records survive that describe the day-to-day life of cadets in the early West Point years. The impending War of 1812 caused Congress to authorize a more formal system of education at the academy, and increased the size of the Corps of Cadets.

Although scant records exist from the years that Gustavus Loomis was a cadet at the Academy, there is abundant evidence as to why the Academy was founded. During the American Revolution there were few experienced military officers. The Colonial Army was very dependent upon European military officers for its senior leadership. These European "soldiers of fortune," as Cullem called them, were employed with "high rank and extravagant pay."[36] Both French and Prussian officers filled the senior ranks of the Colonial Army, a fact that deeply irritated Benjamin Franklin and many other colonial leaders. It became obvious to the founding fathers that a national school for the education of military officers was essential for the United States to survive. While some lamented the idea of a federally funded military school, political

A portrait of Colonel Jonathan Williams, Superintendant of the U.S. Military Academy at West Point, c. 1810. Public domain image.

36 George W. Cullum, *Biographical Register of the Officers and Graduates of the United States Military Academy, at West Point, New York,* (New York: 1868), pp. v-vi.

momentum led to the founding of the United States Military Academy at West Point in 1802.

From its beginning the Academy was intended to train cadets for future General Officer level commands. The intent was not merely to teach tactics, as any capable man could learn lower level military tactics in a few months. Rather, the glaring need in the U.S. Army was leaders who could think and plan on the operational and strategic level, looking beyond the battlefield to long term issues related to engineering, sustainment of large numbers of troops, maneuvering huge numbers of men, and developing coordinated and sustained aggressive techniques for artillery, infantry and cavalry. Warfare in the nineteenth century was rapidly modernizing, resulting in the urgent need for senior officers who were trained in science and in history as well as martial arts. Warfare was seen as arising from set rules and principles which a senior commander must master to effectively lead soldiers.

West Point has always sought to blend knowledge with experience. The goal, according to Cullum, was to produce "practical generals and learned scholars." Students were taught skills to "conceive of great projects and devise extraordinary means for their accomplishment." The principles of training senior military commanders was to make them tactically proficient and strategically orientated, thinking and planning as well-read scholars familiar with history and science and especially engineering. The outcome was to out think and out maneuver a potential enemy, utilizing a minimum of resources while exhausting the resources of the enemy. Graduates were expected, when they became senior officers, "to know how to organize and form the character of an army, as well as to lead it when formed."[37]

---

37 George W. Cullum, *Biographical Register,* pp. vi-viii.

The one room school house education of Gustavus Loomis in Thetford was put to the test at the U.S. Military Academy. At West Point, Loomis had classes in Tactics, specifically Artillery, Infantry and Cavalry Tactics. There were numerous classes in Engineering, Mathematics, Drawing, Ordinance and Gunnery. The curriculum also included courses in Chemistry, Geography, History, Ethics, French, and what was then called Natural and Experimental Philosophy, what we would call Physics today. While Loomis took classes in all of these fields, in his student years there were only three structured academic departments, namely the Department of Mathematics (begun in 1802); the Department of Drawing (begun in 1803); and the Department of French (begun in 1803).[38] Class instructors were a combination of military officers and civilian professors who lectured on a rotating basis. The Superintendant of the U.S. Military at West Point during the Loomis years was Lieutenant Colonel and later Colonel Jonathan Williams.

The first Superintendant at West Point was Jonathan Williams (1751-1815). Williams was born in Boston, Massachusetts into an affluent merchant family. He was a grand-nephew of the U.S. diplomat Benjamin Franklin, and assisted Franklin in Europe from 1770 to 1785 with various business and political affairs. In 1801, President John Adams appointed Williams a Major in the Corps of Artillerists and Engineers, a controversial move since Williams had no prior military experience. That same year he was designated to be the first Superintendant of the U.S. Military Academy and was given additional engineering duties in and around New York City. When the Academy officially opened in 1803, Superintendant Williams was the presiding officer. In addition to his academic and military duties at West Point, from 1807-1812 Colonel Wil-

---

38 George W. Cullum, *Biographical Register,* pp. 42-56.

liams designed and supervised the construction of Castle Williams and Castle Clinton in New York Harbor.[39] A year after Gustavus Loomis graduated, in 1812, Colonel Williams resigned his position at West Point over a dispute with the Secretary of War, Henry Eustis. He then moved to Philadelphia and was involved in coastal construction and fortification projects as a civilian. He was elected to the U.S. Congress from Philadelphia but died before he could assume that position.

The early years of the Military Academy at West Point under Colonel Williams were a transitional time of slow and often painful growth. The Williams appointment as Superintendant was a good selection.[40] Yet Williams was hindered in directing this fledgling school by the uncertain legal status of the Academy; by budget constraints; by an uncertain curriculum; and by unclear supervision by the Secretary of War and by President Jefferson. Williams himself was pulled in two directions, as an academic administrator and as an Army Engineer coordinating numerous construction projects around New York City. Cadets had no provisions for their uniforms; had difficulties obtaining books in English; and were constricted by uncertain academic requirements.[41] Yet the final products of those early years, the first graduates of the Academy, were an outstanding group of men who greatly contributed to the military and civil development of the United States.

In the early nineteenth century, all colleges in the United States had some type of religious foundation. The oldest colleges in America had a religious disposition towards conservative Protestantism. In the early nineteenth century, as the Second Great

---

39 Robert McDonald, *Thomas Jefferson's Military Academy,* (University of Virginia Press, 2004), pp. 157-159.

40 Stephen E. Ambrose, *Duty, Honor, Country: A History of West Point,* (The Johns Hopkins Press, 1999), pp. 21-22.

41 Robert McDonald, *Thomas Jefferson's Military Academy ,*pp. 135-137.

Awakening captured the attention of many, evangelical colleges began to arise throughout the country. The first college in America to not be founded on a religious foundation was the U.S. Military Academy at West Point. This does not mean that the students, faculty and staff were anti-religion or were unbelievers. It does mean that the Academy was founded as a military college on a military facility with an army officer as Superintendant. The initial academic focus of West Point was army tactics and operations, military history, and specifically engineering. The non-religious basis of the Academy created many critics. George W. Cullum addressed these accusations of irreligion directly. Cullum stated:

> A GRAVE CHARGE has been made against West Point, that it is immoral and irreligious…Now suppose this was actually true, is it not equally true of every college in the land? Is it not a high compliment to West Point to expect its young men to be perfect [mature, complete] when it is not expected of any college in the country. I undertake to say, without fear of contradiction, that there is more restraint and less temptation to dissipation at West Point than there is at Harvard, Yale or Princeton. What restraint is there at Harvard or Yale to prevent dissipation or immorality among young men to any extent? Would it be difficult to find Harvard students in gross dissipation? Would it be difficult to find Yale students where the laws of the college forbid them to go? On the other hand, it is barely possible for the cadets at West Point to escape at night and engage in some immorality. This is possible, but it is not common and it is not easy. The whole establishment and grounds belong to the government; the discipline is strict and most rigidly enforced, and the outward temptations small. The public services of religion are properly

attended to, and there is a cadet's prayer meeting once a week for those who are religiously inclined."[42]

The first chaplain was assigned to West Point in 1813, two years after Gustavus Loomis graduated. For the first ten years of the Academy's existence, the religious needs of the students were attended to by local civilian clergy. The cadets were allowed to attend a civilian church on Sundays and to attend a prayer meeting during the week. The prayer meetings were held at West Point, directed by cadets for cadets and other soldiers and civilians who desired to attend. The prayer meetings were a combination of singing, testimonies, prayer and scripture reading. No sermon was preached, although occasionally a cadet would read a sermon previously preached and published. It is certain that Gustavus Loomis attended civilian church services on Sundays and that he participated in the weekly West Point prayer meetings as a cadet. Whether or not Loomis read published sermons by his pastor in Thetford, Rev. Beriah Loomis, we can not be sure. But we do know that simultaneous to Loomis's cadet years at the Academy there were numerous revivals and awakenings throughout the Hudson River Valley all around West Point. Both small farming communities and more urban areas experienced spiritual renewal movements common to the Second Great Awakening. In speaking of the awakenings in the vicinity of West Point, one eyewitness recorded, "The work was powerful and rapid, and all ages from twelve to sixty years old, were gathered from the broad way that leads to hell and brought to Christ and his church, but yet little noise or confusion has been heard, through the whole transaction."[43]

---

42 George W. Cullum, *Biographical Register*, pp. 7-8.
43 Joshua Bradley, *Accounts of Religious Revivals*, (Albany, NY: G.J. Loomis and Co., 1819), p. 166.

Gustavus Loomis attended the U.S. Military Academy from 1808 through 1811. In 1809 there were six graduates. Because of various administrative issues, there were no graduates of the class of 1810. In Loomis' third and final year at West Point he was one of eighteen graduates of the class of 1811. These eighteen young men were residents of Pennsylvania, New Jersey, Connecticut, Maine, New York, Vermont, Maryland, Massachusetts, District of Columbia, New Hampshire, and Virginia. The majority of these eighteen cadets were students for three years, as was Gustavus Loomis. A few of the students graduated after two years, while one cadet was a student for six years and other was a cadet for five years. Of the eighteen graduates of the class of 1811, five of these men died in the War of 1812, four from combat and one from disease. Two more died while in the Army of unspecified causes, in 1817 and in 1832. In addition, one was wounded in 1814 and discharged from the army in 1815. Three would serve as prisoners of war, including Gustavus Loomis. Four others were disbanded from the army in 1815, at the conclusion of the War of 1812. Another was discharged in 1814. Others resigned in 1816, 1819 and in 1824. Two cadets resigned their obligation to the military upon their graduation in 1811.[44] Astonishingly, Gustavus Loomis would serve in uniform until 1867.

Only two of the eighteen graduates of the West Point class of 1811 had extended careers in the military. One of these successful long-term military members was John J. Albert (1785-1863). Cadet Albert graduated last in his class of eighteen cadets. He resigned his commission upon graduation and studied law in Maryland. He served as a private in the Maryland militia and saw combat in the War of 1812. In 1814 John Albert was reappointed in the U.S. Army as a brevet major in the Topographical Engineers. From 1814

---

44 George W. Cullum, *Biographical Register*, pp. 114-122.

through 1829 Albert conducted topographical research along the north Atlantic coastline, as well as along various inland canals in Ohio and Kentucky. In 1829 he was placed in charge of the Topographical Bureau in Washington, D.C., a position he held until retirement in 1861.[45] In 1838 he achieved the rank of Colonel in the U.S. Army and was given command of the Corps of Topographical Engineers, another position he held until his retirement. Virtually every map used by both sides in the U.S. Civil War was produced under Albert's supervision. Colonel John J. Albert was retired from active military service on September 9, 1861 with a medical disability resulting from long and faithful service. He died in Washington, D.C. in 1863, at age seventy-eight.[46]

Another cadet from the West Point class of 1811 who had an extended and successful military career was Gustavus Loomis. Of the eighteen graduates of his class, Loomis ranked at number ten. Loomis lived to be almost eighty-three years old, outliving all his classmates. His years of military service, including his time as a cadet at West Point, totaled fifty-nine years, far exceeding all his classmates. Gustavus Loomis fought against the British in Canada and in the United States; he fought against Indians from Texas to Wisconsin to Florida; he fought in Mexico in 1848 during the Mexican War; and in his mid-seventies he served his country as a Union officer with the rank of brevet Brigadier General in the Civil War.

Gustavus Loomis was the only member of the West Point class of 1811 to become a General Officer. Throughout his almost six decades of military service, Loomis was always known as a clear thinker, a fearless combatant, a friend of common soldiers, an advocate for the oppressed, an able administrator, and a devoted Christian.

45 *The American Almanac and Repository of Useful Knowledge for the Year 1860*, (Boston: Crosby, Nichols and Company, 1860), p. 102.
46 George W. Cullum, *Biographical Register*, pp. 121-122.

CHAPTER THREE

THE FIRST TOUR OF DUTY AT FT. COLUMBUS, 1811-1813

WHEN GUSTAVUS LOOMIS GRADUATED FROM the U.S. Military Academy in 1811, his immediate plans were already certain. Second Lieutenant Loomis was ordered to report for duty as an artillerist at Fort Columbus, New York City. New York City in 1811 was, like most of America, experiencing restlessness, an urgency for growth and expansion and cultural advancement. The fledgling United States was eager to develop and prosper. This was a time of inventions and ingenuity and a period where bold entrepreneurs made fortunes in shipping and commerce. Numerous citizens along the east coast moved west, bought land, built a home, sold the home for profit and moved west again. The desire to experience material abundance drove men and woman to invent, design, innovate and imagine.[47] The United States became a trading partner with much of the world, as new ideas, inventions, clothing, customs and material goods flooded eastern cities. There were a percentage of people at the time who were dishonest rascals, taking advantage of the vulnerable. But most of America in 1811 was prosperous and forward looking with unlimited potential.

Politically, the United States in the early nineteenth century had experienced excellent executive leadership by a series of exceptionally talented and intelligent Presidents. After the Presidency

---

47 Larry Schweikart and Michael Allen, A *Patriot's History of the United States*, (New York: Sentinel Press, 2004), p.187.

of George Washington (1789-1797) was the Presidency of John Adams (1797-1801); Thomas Jefferson (1801-1809); and James Monroe (1809-1817). These talented men solidified the political foundation of the country while asserting military prowess overseas in the Quasi-War with France (1798-1800) and in the conflict with the Barbary Pirates (1801-1805). Militarily, tension still existed between the United States and Great Britain. Treaties signed between the United States and Great Britain after the Revolutionary War was not always honored by both sides. In particular, the U.S. Congress and governors of western states were furious at England for its meddling into Indian affairs and its alleged supplying of arms to Indians to hinder American expansion into the western territories. This and other factors would lead to the War of 1812 between England and the United States.[48] But in 1811 in New York City, all was right with the world for Gustavus Loomis.

The Gustavus Loomis who graduated from West Point in 1811 was a different man that the naïve rural Vermonter from Thetford who first stepped on the Academy campus in 1808. Unlike most in Thetford, Loomis was now a college educated man who had travelled throughout New England and New York. One can only imaging the stir in tiny Thetford when Gustavus returned home as a graduate of West Point or the celebrations when he came home on military leave in his uniform.

Loomis was a graduate of a military academy when there was no war. America was at peace with the world in 1811. As a newly commissioned Second Lieutenant, Loomis reported to Colonel Jonathan Williams, Commander of Fort Columbus, New York City, in March of 1811. Colonel Williams was the Superintendant at West Point and therefore already knew Loomis. Perhaps Loomis was familiar with Fort Columbus, as we can imagine

---

48 Allan R. Miller and Peter Maslowski, *For the Common Defense: A Military History of the United States of America*, (New York: The Free Press, 1994), pp. 104-106.

Colonel Williams taking his West Point cadets for a visit to Fort Columbus to discuss engineering fortifications and artillery tactics. For Loomis this was a good first assignment, as the fort was brand new, he already had a relationship with the Commander, and he was reasonably close to home in Thetford, Vermont.

The Fort Columbus that greeted Gustavus Loomis in March, 1811 was a recently built fort on the site of the previous Fort Jay. Located on Governor's Island in New York Harbor, Fort Columbus was fully capable of defending New York City from any maritime attacks. The fort consisted of an enclosed pentagonal structure with four bastions holding one hundred guns. On three of its sides it was constructed the same as the old Fort Jay with the addition of fourteen feet on each side. On the fourth (north) side there was a V-shaped ravelin with further artillery pieces. Fort Columbus had eighteen pound and twenty-four pound canons as well as French mortars. Some of the artillery pieces were mobile, not in fixed firing locations. The parapet had fifty-two embrasures (firing positions). The walls of the fort were about forty feet high, twelve feet thick at the base and seven feet thick at the summit. The two stone magazines held at least two hundred barrels of gunpowder, an enormous amount. Within the well was an inexhaustible supply of fresh water, easily supplying the men and any ships needing refreshment. It was a fort capable of supporting one thousand men.[49]

Life for Second Lieutenant Gustavus Loomis at Fort Columbus was predictable and routine. The unmarried twenty-two year old Loomis lived in one of the single officer's barracks either on the east side or the west side of the fort. In 1811, Loomis was under the direct Command of Colonel Jonathan Williams, Commander of Fort Columbus. The overall Commander for all

49 Edmund B. Smith, *Governor's Island: Its History under Three Flags, 1637-1913*, (New York: 1913), pp. 55-56, 72.

troops in the New York City vicinity was Colonel Henry Burbeck (1754–1848). Colonel Burbeck was considered the "grand
old man" of the U.S. Artillery, he being the senior Colonel in the
Army in 1813. A Bostonian, Henry Burbeck served throughout
the entire Revolutionary War. He then became the Commander
at the U.S. Military Academy at West Point (1787–1790) and then
continued his career in the artillery. He retired in 1815 at the
conclusion of the War of 1812.[50]

Colonel Burbeck practiced strict discipline upon his soldiers
in the New York City area. For example, guards on patrol were
required to report "All's Well" every fifteen minutes throughout
the night. All people were forbidden to sit on the perimeter parapet, denied the enjoyment of the spectacular views. The use of
liquor was strictly rationed. Prisoners confined to the guardhouse
were given limited privileges. The "smoking of pipes or segars"
was strictly forbidden. Soldiers involved in fighting each other
were denied certain amenities. The use of passes for the men to
visit New York City was strictly monitored. None except non-
commissioned officers could enter the gunpowder magazine and
all had to take their shoes off before entering. The firing of salutes
by the artillery throughout the day had to be done with exact
precision. Strict formality was observed in the numerous court
martial cases of desertion, absence with out leave, rowdiness and
disobedience of orders, although the sentences were often lenient
due to the fact that the nation was not at war. The strict use of the
sign and countersign was at all times observed entering Fort Columbus. In one case, a Private caught stealing and convicted of his
theft was humiliated by being drummed up and down the parade
field for one week with the band playing the Rogues' March and
with his uniform on upside down and the word "Thief" attached

50 David S. Heidler, Editor. "Burbeck, Henry," *Encyclopedia of the War of 1812,* (Naval
    Institute Press, 2004), pp. 69-70.

to his chest. Some convicted offenders were placed in solitary confinement on Fort Columbus in the "Black Hole." Occasionally a soldier convicted of a serious crime was executed.[51]

Second Lieutenant Gustavus Loomis appeared for duty at Fort Columbus in his brand new lieutenant's uniform for the artillery. Historically, uniform standards were lax, as the impoverished U.S. Congress found it impossible to uniformly and properly dress and supply an entire army. The standard army uniform was not even decided until 1779 and was poorly implemented. By 1792 Infantry and Artillery officers wore saber swords. As a junior officer serving at the Company level, Loomis' sword was two and a half feet long, while more senior officers wore swords that were three feet long. The artillery officer's uniform Loomis wore had a dark blue shoulder strap

A sketch of Fort Columbus, New York, looking from the northwest bastion across the North River to New York City, 1816. Public domain image.

trimmed in red, red being the color of the Artillery. The coat was dark blue and knee length. The vest was white with red trim. The boots of an artillery officer were different from other officers, as were the color and style of buttons on the jacket.[52] No longer wearing a cadet uniform at West Point, Loomis at his first assignment wore an impeccably groomed uniform and fully looked the part of a junior Artillery officer.

---

51 Edmund B. Smith, *Governor's Island: Its History under Three Flags,* pp. 59-65.
52 Oscar F. Long, "Changes in the Uniform of the Army, 1774-1895" *US Army Quartermaster Foundation, Fort Lee, Virginia,* www.qmfound.com/changes_in_the_army_uniform_1895. Accessed September 7, 2009.

Fort Columbus had the advantage of beautiful sea breezes that kept the air fresh, minimized mosquitoes and helped prevent disease. This same advantage was a disadvantage in the winter, as frozen winds off the ocean penetrated through New York Harbor to freeze Fort Columbus. Year round the fort was illuminated with whale oil. In the winter, rooms were heated by open fireplaces or stoves. Mostly wood and some bituminous coal were used for heating. The fort was connected to the mainland through a horse powered ferry system. After 1812 more and more steam powered boats connected Fort Columbus to the rest of New York City, but steam power was slow in developing. As far as weapons, there was no change in U.S. small arms since the Revolutionary War. The same flint lock muskets were used. The pistols were identical.[53] The location of the fort was beautiful but living conditions were humble, even primitive. Common soldiers slept in open bay stone barracks while officers shared smaller rooms. Toilet and hygiene facilities were crude. Privacy was virtually non-existent.

A primary point of interest for Second Lieutenant Gustavus Loomis at Fort Columbus was the availability of religious services. Loomis' years at the secular West Point did nothing to diminish his religious zeal. There was no chapel at Fort Columbus but there was a chaplain. A New York militia chaplain named John X. Clark mustered in on April 13, 1812 as chaplain to the 10th Brigade of Militia. He was stationed in and around New York City.[54] It is impossible to determine any details of Chaplain Clark and Second Lieutenant Loomis' religious conversations or their participating together in religious services. Reverend Peter VanPelt performed religious services at Fort Columbus before he was commissioned as a U.S. Army chaplain on April 2, 1813. Chaplain VanPelt coordinated all

---

53 R.S. Guernsey, *New York City and Vicinity during the War of 1812,* (New York: Charles L. Woodward, 1889), vol. I, pp. 194-195.
54 R.S. Guernsey, *New York City and Vicinity,* p. 432.

religious activities in the Army's Third Military District, located in New York City. VanPelt served throughout the War of 1812 and was honorably discharged in June, 1815.[55]

As the first official regular Army chaplain for Gustavus Loomis, Chaplain Peter VanPelt (1778-1861) deserves further examination. VanPelt was a native New Yorker raised in the Dutch Reformed Church. As a boy he lived through the difficulties all New Yorkers faced in the early years of the American Revolution. Sometime around 1800, while a young minister in New York, VanPelt met the aged and respected Methodist itinerant minister Francis Asbury (1745-1816). As a well travelled revivalist minister, Asbury was the patriarch of Methodism in America. Asbury travelled tens of thousands of miles throughout all of the American Colonies and later the United States. Over the decades Francis Asbury visited Staten Island in New York City nineteen times, preaching at least forty times.[56] Even before Peter VanPelt was born, Asbury preached in and around New York City. The young minister Rev. VanPelt met the elderly Asbury and immediately asked the aged preacher to minister at his church, the Reformed Church of Staten Island.

Francis Asbury was a key component in the Second Great Awakening in America. Asbury was a relentless organizer, a tireless traveler, and an enthusiastic but not eccentric preacher. Asbury also showed remarkable compassion to both the rural and the urban poor. The influence of Asbury on Peter VanPelt was significant. For example, shortly after meeting Asbury, VanPelt began a ministry to quarantined immigrants on Staten Island. Fearful of various plagues, immigrant ships were unloaded and fumigated while thousands of people were detailed in temporary medical

---

55 Herman A. Norton, *Struggling for Recognition: The United States Army Chaplaincy, 1791-1865*, (Washington, DC: Office of the Army Chief of Chaplains, 1977), pp. 15, 17.

56 Gladys Kimmerer, Editor, *A Story of faith: A History of Faith United Methodist Church, Staten Island, New York*, (copyright 1976 by Faith United Methodist Church), p. 2.

facilities for examinations. Beginning in 1798, VanPelt, who was twenty years old, developed a ministry of compassion and evangelism to the immigrants that was directly linked to the influence of Francis Asbury.[57] In 1802, Rev. VanPelt established a church affiliated school called "a seminary of learning," which provided English bible classes to immigrants and others. In 1812, through his ministry at the Dutch Reformed Church on Staten Island, VanPelt started one of the first Sunday Schools in America.[58]

As Fort Columbus completed its construction around 1810, numerous soldiers were ordered to man the fort. The influx of soldiers far away from home and in a strange place was not lost on the evangelistically minded Rev. Peter VanPelt. First he began volunteering as a civilian chaplain to the troops. Then he developed a preaching and pastoral ministry to local militia units. As one source stated,

> The role of chaplains in the American armed forces was as yet undeveloped. Ordained personnel willing to take upon themselves such responsibilities were rare, but local ministers often held services for troops stationed in the neighborhood. Sometimes a commission as militia chaplain was awarded to a prominent clergyman because of his popularity with the soldiers, as was the case of Peter VanPelt, whose Independence Day sermon in 1812 led to his appointment as a chaplain to a local regiment.[59]

The ministry of Chaplain Peter VanPelt was appreciated by the Commander of Fort Columbus, Colonel Jonathan Williams, and by the senior Army officer in the region, Colonel Henry

---

57 Gladys Kimmerer, Editor, *A Story of Faith,* p. 3.
58 Margaret Lundrigan, *Staten Island,* (Arcadia Publishing, 1999), p. 42.
59 William Gribben, *The Churches Militant: The War of 1812 and American Religion,* (New Haven: Yale University Press, 1973), p. 75.

Burbeck. In late 1812, Williams and Burbeck passed their commendation and recommendation of VanPelt to Washington. This resulted in VanPelt's commissioning as a U.S. Army chaplain on April 2, 1813. Chaplain VanPelt served primarily at the U.S. Army Third Military District Headquarters in New York City throughout the entire War of 1812. Second Lieutenant Gustavus Loomis arrived at Fort Columbus in March, 1811. This is when Loomis met Chaplain VanPelt. They were theologically similar, both coming from Reformed or Calvinist traditions. They both supported revivals. And both Loomis and VanPelt encouraged bible studies, evangelistic meetings and extended church activities outside routine Sunday services.

After the War of 1812, VanPelt returned to the civilian ministry and served in the New York City area at the Staten Island Reformed Church in Tompkinsville. He guided the church through a period of growth resulting in a building program for a new meeting house in 1818. Rev. VanPelt served this congregation until around 1823.[60] He then served as pastor at the Dutch Reformed Church on Staten Island in the town of Port Richmond. In this capacity VanPelt in 1836 ministered to the dying Aaron Burr, the former Vice President of the United States. For months Burr was confined to bed

A painting of Reverend Peter VanPelt, c. 1810.
Source: www.artnet.com.

---

60 "Brighton Heights Reformed Church Demolished," www.preserve.org/stgeorge/bhrc.

in Port Richmond. VanPelt frequently visited the dying Aaron Burr, knowing that Burr was not a believer in Jesus Christ. As VanPelt pressed Burr on his need to trust in the merits of Jesus Christ for salvation, Burr was evasive. Upon Burr's death, Rev. VanPelt held a small memorial service in the home where he died and then accompanied the body to Princeton, New Jersey where VanPelt participated in the burial ceremonies.[61] Details about the later years of Peter VanPelt are scant. We know that in 1852, at age seventy-four, he performed a wedding ceremony which was announced in the *New York Times*.[62] As an older minister in the 1850s he served as Chaplain to the Veteran's Corps of the War of 1812. VanPelt died in 1861 and was buried in New York City.

As a brand new Second Lieutenant on his first military assignment, Gustavus Loomis was centrally located within a force structure consisting of enlisted soldiers, non-commissioned officers, and commissioned officers. As a commissioned officer his rank was above the enlisted soldiers and the non-commissioned officers, though most of these men had more military experience than Loomis. As far as the commissioned officers, Loomis was at the very bottom. His West Point education may have given Loomis prestige or it may have served as a point of envy or even ridicule from less educated senior officers.

Upon Loomis' arrival at Fort Columbus in 1811 there were approximately eight hundred Army soldiers in the New York City area. Second Lieutenant Loomis was assigned to a company level position, the lowest position for an officer. He was not a company commander, as this position was reserved for senior First Lieutenants or Captains. Before the War of 1812 a company had

---

61 Charles B. Todd, *The True Aaron Burr: A Biographical Sketch*, (Bibliolife: 2009), p. 63.
 Samuel H. Wandell, *Aaron Burr*, (Kessinger Publishers, 2003), vol. II, pp. 333-335.
62 The wedding date was August 12 and the announcement was in the *New York Times*,
 August 26, 1852.

forty or fifty men. After the war began a company was increased to one hundred men.[63] As a low level artillery officer, Loomis was responsible for inspecting the guns; training artillery crews; and drilling the troops in general soldier skills. His additional responsibilities included night duty as the officer on call; inventorying of supplies; inspections of the guards; and whatever else was assigned to him by his company commander. As the United States was at peace with the world, Loomis and his fellow soldiers trained, rehearsed, and lived the highly disciplined and monotonous life of a military unit in garrison.

There were numerous factors that led up to the War of 1812. Unspoken was the lingering antagonism by Great Britain against the United States after the Revolutionary War. More tangible factors were the outrage of U.S. coastal cities against British seizure of American merchant ships and the impressments of U.S. citizens into the British Navy. The British claimed that they were justified in seizing American ships that traded with England's enemy, France. And the British claimed that their boarding of American ships and their impressments of American seamen was nothing more than a collection of deserters from the British Navy. Many Americans saw these acts of the British Navy as moral outrages against a sovereign nation and demanded a stern political or military response. The location of the most anti-British clamor was from the most western U.S. states and the Northwest Territories. Here Americans claimed, with good reason, that the British were in violation of treaties implemented after the Revolutionary War, that the British were supplying Indians with English weapons and inciting the Indians against the vulnerable westward expanding American population.[64]

Great Britain, already in an expensive and protracted conflict with Napoleonic France, did not want a war with the

---

63 R.S. Guernsey, *New York City and Vicinity*, pp. 116, 119, 193.

64 John K. Mahon, *The War of 1812*, (Gainesville: University of Florida Press, 1972), pp. 3-7.

United States. President James Madison's use of political and economic pressures against Great Britain almost avoided the war. The revival of the Non-Intercourse Act against Britain, prohibiting all U.S. trade with England and its colonies, coincided with a poor grain harvest in England and with a growing need of American provisions to supply the British troops fighting the French. As a result, on June 16, 1812, the British Foreign Minister announced an adjustment of policy related to American shipping. Had there been an Atlantic cable, war might have been averted. President Madison sent a message to Congress on June 1 listing all the complaints against England and asking for a congressional declaration of war. Dividing along sectional lines the House voted for war on June 4, but the Senate approved it on June 18 and then by only six votes.[65] The New England states were adamantly opposed to war, while the western states firmly supported the war.

The news of the declaration of war reached New York City the morning of June 20, 1812. All of the New York City newspapers were opposed to the war, while the citizenry was divided. The United States' declaration of War against Great Britain was made on the eighteenth, the news taking two days to reach New York. Brigadier General Joseph Bloomfield, who was then in command of all army forces in the New York City area, wrote an official memorandum to his soldiers as follows:

GENERAL ORDERS.

General Bloomfield announces to the troops that war is declared by the United States against Great Britain.

By order,

R.H. McPherson, Adjutant General[66]

---

65 "History of the War of 1812," www.militarysocietyofthewarof1812.com.

66 R.S. Guernsey, *New York City and Vicinity*, p.1.

Life for Second Lieutenant Gustavus Loomis and his fellow soldiers immediately became more intense and focused. Only the most senior officers had war experience, against the British in the Revolutionary War. A few lower level officers and sergeants were veterans of Indian campaigns, but the majority of military personnel in New York City were like Loomis, inexperienced in war. At the time of the declaration of war, the most significant ships in the U.S. Navy were in New York Harbor or outside the harbor at Sandy Hook on the New Jersey shore. The day after the war declaration, the senior naval officer, Commodore John Rodgers, received orders to gather all naval vessels under his command and to get out of the potential British blockade of New York Harbor. Loomis and his fellow army officers watched with serious contemplation as Commodore Rodgers sailed out of the harbor on his ship, the *President*, accompanied by the *Essex* and the *Hornet*.

One need not wonder about the moral or religious position of Gustavus Loomis related to war. Loomis came from a long line of men who proudly served in the Connecticut militia. His father briefly served in the American Revolution. The fact that Gustavus attended and graduated from the U.S. Military Academy at West Point is evidence that he had no moral or theological objections to war. As Loomis examined his bible he read of numerous examples of men of faith engaged in war. Whether Abraham or Moses from the Old Testament, or the Roman Centurion Cornelius in the New Testament, there were various examples from scripture to support Loomis' conviction that there are appropriate times for a man of faith to go to war. Loomis was of the mindset that the Creator God maintains providential control over this world. There are times under the providence of God, so goes the theory, that war is not only necessary but an absolute duty. There may be times of war to secure peace and prosperity. Other times

of war may be necessary to correct a wrong to protect the innocent.[67] A few days after the declaration of War, a public meeting
in New York City passed numerous resolutions in support of the
war. One of the resolutions specifically stated:

RESOLVED,

> *That in placing our reliance in the Most High, and soliciting
> his benediction on our just cause, we pledge to our government,
> in support of our beloved country, our lives, our fortunes, our
> sacred honor.*[68]

At the commencement of the War of 1812, Gustavus Loomis
was a twenty-three year old Second Lieutenant on his first active
duty assignment. Fort Columbus maintained a strategic position in
the defense of New York City. At the commencement of the war,
Loomis was one of about one thousand soldiers stationed in and
around Fort Columbus and New York Harbor. Fort Columbus was
a busy place, with thousands of New York and New Jersey militiamen being trained and supplied at the fort. The declaration of war
by President James Madison authorized privateering, meaning that
many New York Harbor civilian ships were refitted and commissioned as a paramilitary naval force raiding British vessels, returning
with their spoils under the safe guns of Fort Columbus.

On January 22, 1813, several British war vessels appeared off
the New Jersey coast near Sandy Hook, in the vicinity of Fort
Columbus but well out of firing range. On April 10th a civil-
ian American schooner was boarded by the British off of Sandy
Hook, causing local outrage. On May 29, several boats from the
British squadron located between New York and New Jersey at-

---

67 Loraine Boettner, *The Christian Attitude Toward War,* (Phillipsburg, NJ: Presbyterian
    and Reformed Publishing, 1985), pp. 18-39.
68 R.S. Guernsey, *New York City and Vicinity*, p. 13.

tempted a covert night raid in Sandy Hook. The militia discovered the raiding party and skirmished with the British, driving them back to their ships. A British attack directly upon New York City was unlikely and in fact never occurred throughout the war. The stone fortress of Fort Columbus and smaller fortifications throughout the harbor discouraged a naval assault of New York City. British vessels under sail power would have difficulty navigating in the harbor. Local mariners formed a naval militia called "Sea Fencibles," composed of men who were local sailors and boatmen that knew the shoals, the flow of the tides, the sandbars, and the dynamics of the turbulent and wind swept harbor. They formed a gun boat fleet of about one thousand sailors on orders for one year at a time. They were placed under the leadership of a naval officer and they greatly discouraged any small boat British operations. And with over five thousand militia and a thousand regular army soldiers in and around the harbor, a British attack or invasion of New York City would be suicidal.[69]

As an artillery officer at Fort Columbus, Second Lieutenant Gustavus Loomis worked with various types of weaponry. Specifically, the ammunition used by the canons at Fort Columbus was designed to destroy ships at sea. The guns fired iron balls, hot shot, bar shot, canister and grape shot, double-headed shot, star shot and langrel shot. This ammunition could be used to destroy sails and rigging; to penetrate wooden vessels; or to cause maximum damage to a crew on deck.[70]

At the beginning of the War of 1812, the British Navy did not make an aggressive attempt to blockade New York Harbor. England was at war with France and the British needed American goods. Only later, when the Napoleonic war with France ended did the British tighten the blockade. Meanwhile in September

69 R.S. Guernsey, *New York City and Vicinity*, pp. 168, 173-174.
70 R.S. Guernsey, *New York City and Vicinity*, p. 78.

and October, 1813, the British conducted brief raids in Long Island Sound, burning some small vessels. On November 3rd a British naval vessel chased and grounded an America schooner at Long Branch, New Jersey near Sandy Hook. The ship was bound from New Orleans to New York laden with sugar and lead. The grounded schooner was boarded by the British who then found themselves in a skirmish with local militia. Several British were killed and one American was killed and a few more were wounded, with the schooner retaken by the Americans.[71]

Numerous small scale skirmishes occurred in the vicinity of New York Harbor and Long Island Sound, but the guns of Fort Columbus, inside the harbor, did not directly engage the enemy. While the British harassment of the Americans around New York City was bothersome, it was not the main theater of war. By the summer of 1813, upstate New York, along the Canadian border, was the center of combat operations in the northeastern United States. It eventually became obvious that New York City was not going to receive a direct attack from a major British force. Therefore, numerous troops assigned to the defense of New York Harbor were reassigned to combat operations in other areas. Gustavus Loomis was one of those soldiers ordered to depart Fort Columbus for reassignment to the New York-Canadian border for direct combat operations against the British in Canada.

71 R.S. Guernsey, *New York City and Vicinity*, p. 332.

Chapter Four

Combat Operations on the New York/ Canadian Border

As the War of 1812 continued into the winter of 1812-1813, Gustavus Loomis and his almost one thousand soldiers at Fort Columbus were missing the main military activities of the war. The British would be insane to attack heavily fortified New York City, and they never attempted to do so. By the beginning of the War of 1812, the strength of Fort Columbus was augmented by that of a second major fortification on Governors Island, Castle Williams, and by a third defense work, South or Half-Moon Battery. Castle Williams, a circular, casemated masonry work, was located on a rocky promontory on the northwest side of the island. Its ability to mount approximately 100 guns and its solid

A sketch of the Castle Williams on the northwest side of Governors Island, next to Fort Columbus overlooking New York Harbor, 1823. Public domain image.

construction allowed the Castle to effectively command the North River and the harbor to the southwest toward the Narrows. South

Battery, a smaller masonry work with thirteen guns, was mounted to protect the entrance to Buttermilk Channel east of Governors Island. The strength of the fortifications on Governors Island and elsewhere in the harbor effectively protected the city and the harbor from attack.[72]

Upon his graduation from the U.S. Military Academy in West Point in March, 1811, Gustavus Loomis was commissioned as a Second Lieutenant in the Corps of Artillerists. The U.S. Army at that time was tiny with only a few dozen artillery officers and a few hundred artillerymen. Because of the war, in 1812 two regiments of artillery were added to the army, each having twenty companies, for a total of about two thousand artillery soldiers.[73] While at Fort Columbus, Loomis was transferred from the Corps of Artillerists to the new First Artillery Regiment, in March 1812. His superior officers were obviously satisfied with Loomis' military service, as he was promoted from Second to First Lieutenant on May 5, 1813.[74]

The first year of the War of 1812 was successful for the American Navy but disastrous for the U.S. Army. At the outbreak of the war the northwestern U.S. was protected from British Canada by a series of small and undermanned forts. The actual strength of the U.S. Army in June, 1812 was almost twelve thousand total regular army soldiers. In contrast, the British in Canada totaled about one thousand six hundred regular army troops mostly along the United States border. Numerically the U.S. had almost ten times the force of the British, and an easy and quick victory was predicted. Such predictions were sorely mistaken.[75]

72 Barbara A. Yocum, *Fort Jay Historic Structure Report,* (National Park Service, 2005), p. 53.

73 William L. Haskin, "The First Regiment of Artillery," (U.S. Army Military History Institute), p. 301.

74 Correspondence from Richard Baker, U.S. Army Military History Institute, September 16, 2009.

75 Pierre Berton, *The Invasion of Canada, 1812-1813,* (Anchor Canada Books, 2001), p. 25.

The United States strategy for the war was simple: attack the British in Canada in simultaneous operations and expel the British from all of North America. At the same time the U.S. Navy would attack British naval vessels while privateers harassed British shipping. British reinforcements would be slow in coming due to a prolonged war in Europe against France.

The American army pursued a three-pronged coordinated strategy, in direct contradiction to the long held truism than an army must almost never divide its forces. The first blows of the war were struck by invading Americans in the Detroit area, resulting in leadership failures and the surrender of the American forces. A second invasion of Canada was directed between Lake Erie and Lake Ontario. The Americans fared better here than in the Detroit area, but again, leadership failures and rivalries between regular army and militia general officers created chaos and ultimately defeat for the Americans. The third invasion route was through Lake Champlain on the New York-Vermont border, northwards into Canada with the intention of attacking Montreal. This large American force was mismanaged, hesitant and uncoordinated. After many delays the Americans assembled at Plattsburg, New York on Lake Champlain, but most of the invading force never made it past the Canadian border before the militia disbanded and the regular army went into winter quarters.

As 1813 arrived, the American strategy was to recapture Detroit from the British and to attack the British along Lake Ontario. A winter campaign in early 1813 along the western shore of Lake Erie resulted in the defeat of the Americans and the massacre of the wounded by British allies, the Indians. A better planned and executed strategy called the Ontario Campaign was entrusted to General Henry Dearborn, who was ordered to move his army from Plattsburg, New York on Lake Champlain to Sacket's Harbor, Lake Ontario. There Commodore Isaac

Chauncey was assembling an invasion fleet. Dearborn planned to move across the lake to capture Kingston and destroy the British flotilla there, then proceed to York (now Toronto), the capital of Upper Canada, to capture military stores. Finally he was to co-operate with a combined regular army and militia force from Buffalo in a coordinated attempt to seize the forts on the Canadian side of the Niagara River.[76]

Having learned painful lessons in 1812, this American strategy was sound. The intention was to give the U.S. control of the lake and, by cutting the British lines of communications, frustrate enemy plans for operations in the west. After the fall of Kingston, the operations against York and the Niagara forts would be simple mopping-up exercises. A last minute decision changed the first objective from Kingston to York. About one thousand seven hundred men were embarked and sailed up Lake Ontario without incident, arriving off York before dawn on April 27. The landing, four miles west of the town, was almost unopposed. The British garrison of about six hundred men, occupying a fortification about halfway between the town and the landing, was overwhelmed after sharp resistance. Accidently, a powder magazine exploded killing or disabling many Americans and a number of British soldiers. Remnants of the British garrison fled toward Kingston, one hundred and fifty miles to the east. The losses were heavy on both sides—almost twenty percent of Dearborn's forces had been killed or wounded. Then the U.S. troops apparently got out of hand. They looted and burned the public buildings in York and destroyed the provincial records. After holding the town for about a week, they re-crossed Lake Ontario to Niagara to attack the British forts on the Canadian side of the Niagara River.[77]

76 "The Military Society of the War of 1812," www.militarysocietyofthewarof1812.com/history, p. 11. Accessed September 5, 2009.
77 "The Military Society of the War of 1812," pp. 11-12.

The failure of a quick American victory in 1812, and the re-commencement of military campaigns in 1813, meant that the U.S. needed more officers and soldiers than first expected. It is at this point that First Lieutenant Gustavus Loomis would see his first active combat assignment, in the Niagara theater of operations.

For Loomis and his fellow soldiers at Fort Columbus in New York Harbor, life was routine and uneventful. It was obvious that the major military operations were not in the vicinity of New York City but were to the north and west along the Great Lakes. For this reason, the numbers of regular army soldiers at Fort Columbus was reduced and replaced by militia, freeing up regular army troops for campaigns to the northwest. In the fall of 1812 the first troops departed Long Island, New York for the Niagara frontier. In February, 1813 a large number of soldiers departed Fort Columbus and the New York City area for duty in the Niagara region between Lake Erie and Lake Ontario.[78] One of the soldiers who headed north from New York City up the Hudson River to the assembly area in Albany was Gustavus Loomis.

As a First Lieutenant in the First Artillery Regiment, Loomis travelled from Albany to northwest New York. West of the Niagara River he joined the large American force which previously departed York in victory and was preparing for operations around Niagara. General Henry Dearborn was intent on invading the Canadian side of the Niagara River, a British stronghold centered at Fort George.

Fort George was first constructed in 1796. At that time the British complied with the terms of the 1783 Treaty of Paris, which granted the nearby Fort Niagara to the United States. To protect their interests in Upper Canada, the British set work immediately to construct Fort George across the Niagara River, in plain

78 R.S. Guernsey, *New York City and Vicinity in the War of 1812*, (New York: Charles L. Woodward, 1889), vol. I, pp. 118, 141, 167.

view of the United States and Fort Niagara. By 1802, Fort George had been completed and became headquarters for the British army, local militia and the Indian Department. The imposing new fort stood guard over transportation on the Niagara River and protected vital warehouses and wharf facilities. It was a substantial installation, boasting six earthen and log bastions linked by a wooden palisade and surrounded by a dry ditch. Inside the walls, the Royal Engineers constructed a guardhouse, log blockhouses, a hospital, kitchens, workshops, barracks, officers' quarters, and a stone powder magazine. Some of this fortification remains today while much has been carefully reconstructed.

At the beginning of the War of 1812, Fort George served as the headquarters for the Centre Division of the British Army. These forces included British regulars, local militia, Indian warriors, and a corps of freed slaves. Fort George was destroyed by American artillery fire and captured during the Battle of Fort George, May 25-27, 1813. The U.S. forces then used the fort as a base to invade the rest of Upper Canada, but were unsuccessful.

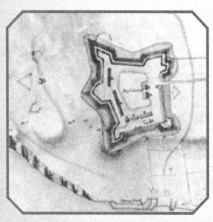

After a seven month occupation, the fort was retaken in December and remained in British hands for the remainder of the war.[79]

The British forces on the Niagara front were commanded by Brigadier General John Vincent. He had a total of just over two thousand regulars and a few hundred militia spread out hundreds

A pencil sketch of Fort George in 1816.
Source: www.pc.gc.ca/eng/lhn-nhs/on/fortgeorge/edu/edua.

---

79 "Fort George History," www.niagaraghosts.com/HFort, p. 1. Accessed August 22, 2009.

of miles. Under his direct command at Fort George were one thousand men from the 8th and 9th Regiments of Foot, the Royal Newfoundland Regiment and the Glengarry Light Infantry Fencibles, supported by three hundred Canadian militia. Tactically, General Vincent was in a weak position, as Fort George itself was reasonably strong but vulnerable to siege and to being cut off from reinforcements. The Americans chose a maritime assault from Lake Ontario with support from across the Niagara River. The attack on Fort George was a well coordinated naval and army assault led by Army Lieutenant Colonel Winfield Scott and Navy Commodore Oliver Hazard Perry.

The attack on Fort George would require detailed quartermaster support. On May 14, 1813 Lieutenant Gustavus Loomis wrote to the Secretary of War John Armstrong that he would accept the position of Assistant Deputy Quartermaster in preparation for the attack. Further, Loomis stated that the supplies he purchased had been bonded by his contacts in Vermont for sureties.[80]

The American attack began at sunrise on May 25th with a naval bombardment of Fort George. The wooden buildings inside the fort were soon on fire, although the outer stone fortifications were not so badly affected. British commander General Vincent sent out patrols to try and anticipate the location of the American ground attack. U.S. General Henry Dearborn was ill, so Lieutenant Colonel Winfield Scott, his Adjutant General, took command of the landing. Those landings began early on May 27, two miles west of Fort George. Winfield Scott's men were supported by heavy fire from the American naval squadron on the lake under the command of Commodore Perry. The British forces were split into three brigades, each searching for the location of the ground

---

80 Adjutant General's Office, "Old Files." Quoted in Carolyn T. Foreman, "Gustavus Loomis: Commandant of Fort Gibson and Fort Towson," *Chronicles of Oklahoma*, vol. 18, no. 3. (September, 1940), p. 219.

attack. Once the attack was identified the other brigades would reinforce. The Americans were met by British Light Infantry and a sharp engagement resulted. The British and Indian forces on the lakeshore were forced to retreat, and when Vincent's reinforcements from the Eighth Regiment arrived they found it difficult to launch a counterattack. The majority of the British fifty-two dead and three hundred wounded or missing were suffered during this phase of the fighting.[81]

After failing to prevent the American landings, General Vincent pulled back to a new position inland, out of the range of the naval guns, where he prepared to resist an American attack. Another firefight occurred and the Americans continued to advance. However, after half an hour he discovered that the Americans were attempting to turn his right flank by the Niagara River, and that he was outnumbered by at least four to one. By the third hour of the battle, General Vincent suffered almost four hundred casualties. British Dragoons continued to harass the advancing American army. Vincent decided to abandon his defensive line along the Niagara River. The guns of Fort George were spiked and Vincent withdrew south, moving parallel to the river until he reached the hills south of Queenston. There he met up with other British forces and retreated west, taking up a new position at Burlington Heights, at the western end of Lake Ontario. At a cost of forty dead and one hundred and twenty wounded the Americans had finally established a foothold west of the Niagara. As one author stated, "In proportion to the numbers engaged, the contest resulted in severe British casualties. The Battle of Fort George was serious and decisive, for it left the American Army in possession of the entire Niagara region."[82]

---

81 "Fort George History," www.niagaraghosts.com/HFort, pp. 1-2. "The Capture of Fort George – May 1813," www.war1812.tripod.com/ftgeo., pp. 1-2. Accessed August 29, 2009.

82 Gilbert Collins, *Guidebook to the Historic Sites of the War of 1812*, Toronto: Dundurn Press, 2006), p. 83.

First Lieutenant Gustavus Loomis fought with the First Artillery Regiment in the Battle of Fort George. The artillery was a supporting force for the main maritime invasion. While the main attack under Lieutenant Colonel Winfield Scott approached Fort George from the west, Loomis and the artillery located themselves on the high ground between Butler's Farm and the contemporary Niagara Historical Museum. Loomis and his artillerymen fired direct fire upon the British forces engaging the American landing, and then subsequently fired upon the retreating British. Artillerists also fired directly upon Fort George. The heated shot used in the bombardment of Fort George was a very dangerous and delicate operation for the gunners of the American artillery. Cannon balls were put into a small furnace near the guns until they became literally red hot. Then the ammunition handlers carried the ammunition in a special carriage to the gun. The cartridge of gunpowder was rammed in and then a well soaked wad of cloth was inserted. Then the steaming hot cannon ball was rammed in with another well soaked wad of cloth inserted in the cannon. Then the gun was

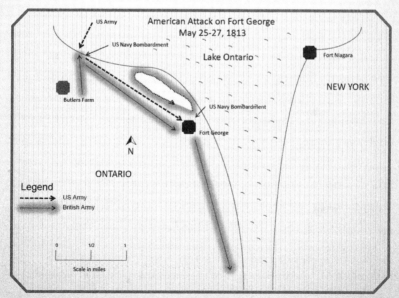

American Attack on Fort George
May 25-27, 1813

US Army

US Navy Bombardment

Lake Ontario

Fort Niagara

NEW YORK

Butlers Farm

US Navy Bombardment

Fort George

N

ONTARIO

Legend

- - - → US Army
———→ British Army

0   1/2   1

Scale in miles

quickly fired before the red hot ball burned through the wet cloth and destroyed the gun and killed the gun crew.[83] Heated shot fired in this way against the wooded buildings and barricades of Fort George has a devastating effect.

During the battle Loomis and his artillerymen moved their artillery cannons in support of the advancing American troops. The battle lasted a few hours before the British began retreating.[84] After the battle at Fort George, Gustavus Loomis as an artillery officer provided limited support to American operations in various skirmishes with the British near the Niagara River. Since artillery requires set targets, its use in fluid and sporadic skirmishes was severely limited.

During the summer and fall of 1813, Loomis and his fellow officers were concerned with the rebuilding and repairs on Fort George, as the British destroyed most of the fort before retreating. It was here that Loomis' engineering skills learned at the U.S. Military Academy were especially helpful. American units in the Niagara region used the fort for resupply and rearming and continued to confront the British throughout northwestern New York and into Canada. The nearby town of Newark (now called Niagara-on-the-Lake) was occupied by American troops throughout most of 1813. In December, U.S. Brigadier General George McClure senselessly ordered Newark to be burned to the ground. The townspeople were given thirty minutes in the dead of winter to evacuate. After this cruel incident the war in the Niagara Theater entered a much more brutal phase, where acts of cruelty and vicious retaliation were commonplace. That same month the U.S. Army realized it was unproductive to retain a large force in the vicinity of Fort George. They then destroyed

---

83 "The Capture of Fort George – May 1813," p. 2.

84 Ernest Cruikshank, *The Battle of Fort George,* (Niagara-on-the-Lake Historical Society, 1990), pp. 46-51.

the buildings they had repaired six months earlier and abandoned the fort, also burning the town of Niagara. The British repossessed Fort George without firing a shot and held the fort until the end of the war.

As the Americans left the ruins of Fort George in Ontario, some crossed the Niagara River to spend the winter within Fort Niagara in New York, while others proceeded east by boat to Sackets Harbor in order to join a proposed U.S. Army campaign against Montreal. Lieutenant Gustavus Loomis was with the soldiers who headed to Fort Niagara for winter quarters. This was a fateful decision.

Fort Niagara was strategically located on the eastern side of the Niagara River, where the river joins Lake Ontario. The French had a fort at this spot as early as the 1680s. The English captured the fort from the French in 1759. During the American Revolution, the British used the fort as a staging area for many Tory and Indian raids against the Colonists in Pennsylvania and New York. The Fort Niagara that Gustavus Loomis entered in December, 1813 was essentially the French fort from decades earlier, with many improvements.[85] The Americans anticipated quiet winter quarters at Fort Niagara but they were mistaken. The British were furious at the senseless burning of the town of Newark which caused great hardship to innocent British and Canadian citizens, many of whom were friends or family members of the British soldiers.

Determined to avenge the hardships upon the citizens of Newark, a plan was presented to Lieutenant General William Drummond to capture Fort Niagara and humiliate the Americans. The U.S. Army in Fort Niagara was a small force, already divided by those who departed for Sackets Harbor for the proposed attack upon Montreal. The British with great difficulty hauled

85 Gilbert Collins, *Guidebook to the Historic Sites of the War of 1812*, p. 91.

boats from fifty miles away and secretly gathered a large force. British soldiers involved in the attack were from the 100th and the 41st Regiments, the Royal Artillery, and some Canadian militia, for a combined force of about five hundred and fifty men. On the evening of December 18, 1813, this force marched south about three miles in the opposite direction of Fort Niagara. They then crossed the Niagara River and proceeded north in darkness for a surprise attack. To insure quiet, each British soldier was ordered to unload his musket and to clip on his bayonet. The troops were instructed to advance in silence and to attack only with their bayonets, insuring the element of surprise.

Under the cover of darkness, the Americans were completely surprised. The northward advancing British bayoneted some pickets and spared the lives of others who revealed the passwords. The British advanced close to the fort and successfully used the challenge and password, then captured the sentry. The gate was opened and the British poured into the fort. Some used scaling ladders but most simply ran into Fort Niagara with their bayonets fixed, fighting the Americans in hand-to-hand combat. After a short but furious skirmish, the overwhelmed Americans surrendered. The British had five soldiers wounded and six killed, while capturing almost four hundred and fifty U.S. troops, tons of supplies and various munitions. Fort Niagara in New York State remained in British hands until the end of the war.

At the December 19, 1813 capture of Ft. Niagara, First Lieutenant Gustavus Loomis and hundreds of his fellow American soldiers became prisoners of war. Or was he? There appears to be conflicting information on this subject. On one hand, the official U.S. Military Academy biographical summary of Loomis states, "taken prisoner at the surprise of Fort Niagara, NY Dec.

19, 1813."[86] However, official correspondence from New York Governor D.D. Tompkins implies that Loomis and a few other soldiers may have escaped capture at Fort Niagara.

LETTER FROM GOVERNOR D. D. TOMPKINS AT ALBANY, TO THE SECRETARY OF WAR

December 24, 1813

"Sir--Upon my arrival in this place today I was met by an express bringing dispatches of which I send you a copy. The express further informs that on his arrival at Batavia he learned from Major Allen (the contractor's agent at Niagara) and from Lt. Loomis, who, with three or four others had made their escape, that Fort Niagara had been taken by the British. The garrison was surprised. Captain Leonard (1st Regiment of Artillery) had the command, but it is rumored he was not in the fort at the time but with his family some miles off. What became of the rest of the garrison those that escaped do not know."[87]

Whether Gustavus Loomis was an escaped prisoner of war, or he evaded capture as the fort was taken, we may never know. We do know that Fort Niagara was captured by the British around sunup on December 19, 1813. As Jere Brubaker, Curator at Old Fort Niagara stated, "For a courier from Batavia to be in Albany on the 24th, he would have to depart Batavia no later than the morning of the 20th. To have met the courier in Batavia, therefore, Loomis would have had to be in Batavia by the morning of the 20th as well. Since a journey from Fort Niagara to Batavia in 1813 would have taken at least one very full day, and that day had

86 George W. Cullum, *Biographical Register of the Officers and Graduates of the U.S. Military Academy, at West Point, N.Y.*, (New York: 1868), p. 118.

87 Ernest Cruikshank, *The Documentary History of the Campaigns upon the Niagara Frontier in 1812-1814*, (Welland, Ontario: 1908), vol. IX, p. 42

to have been the 19th, there remains no time for Loomis to spend as a prisoner."[88] This is an extremely tight timeline to follow. Loomis may have been within the fort as the British attacked on the 19th, fought the British and then avoided capture. Loomis may have been captured and been a prisoner of war very briefly before escaping and furiously riding on horseback to Batavia. Or Loomis may have been outside the fort and was not technically a prisoner of war. Although the timeline is very tight, there is no reason to doubt the integrity of the U.S. Military academy biographical summary of Loomis, that he was taken as a prisoner of war (however briefly) at Fort Niagara on December 19, 1813.

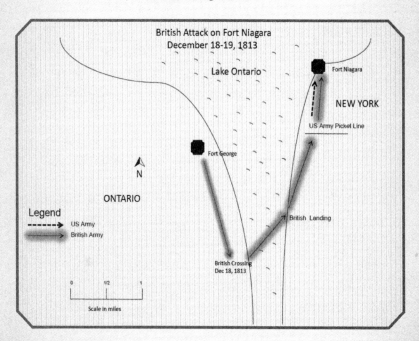

In early 1814, with Fort Niagara captured from the Americans, the British and their Indian allies marched south on the

88 Correspondence from Jerome Brubaker, October 5, 2009.

New York side of the Niagara River, destroying farms and villages as far as Niagara Falls. American army and militia troops fought numerous skirmishes against the British, who continued to use Fort Niagara as a base of operations. The British firmly held this section of American territory, a factor in the pending peace negotiations. Meanwhile, across the Niagara River in Ontario, the British built Fort Mississauga from the ruins of Fort George and from a destroyed lighthouse. This small fort was strategically better located that Fort George, as Fort Mississauga was closer to Lake Ontario. This fort remained controlled by the British throughout the war, and visitors today can tour the historic grounds.

In May of 1814, Lieutenant Loomis was on a short furlough in Vermont. This may be related to acquiring food and supplies in his quartermaster capacity. On May 21st Loomis wrote from Montpelier, Vermont to General George Izard, commander of the Northern Army on Lake Champlain. Loomis stated he desired permission to go to British controlled Fort Niagara to look after cash vouchers which he feared had been lost at the taking of the post.[89] We do not know what became of this request.

On May 12, 1814 Lieutenant Gustavus Loomis was transferred from the First Artillery Regiment to the Corps Artillery. The Corps Artillery was a merger of three Artillery Regiments under one unified command. The prolonged War of 1812 forced U.S. Artillerists to expand and reorganize their artillery firepower.

As a First Lieutenant in the Corps Artillery, Gustavus Loomis' steps are difficult to trace. We do know that elements of the Corps Artillery fought at the Battle of Chippeway in Ontario (July 5, 1814); the Battle of Niagara Falls in Ontario (July 25, 1814); and at the Battle of Plattsburg, New York (September 11, 1814). But there is no mention in Loomis' West Point bio-

89 Carolyn T. Foreman, "Gustavus Loomis," p. 219.

graphical summary of him participating in any of these battles. There is a notation in the *Biographical Register* of Loomis on April 19, 1813 being given the additional duty of "Assistant Deputy Quartermaster General." Loomis' name may be absent from the roster of these battles not only from his additional duties as a Quartermaster. On April 26, Loomis was given the additional duties of an Acting Adjutant. On October 10, Loomis was appointed the Garrison Adjutant at Fort Niagara. We cannot be certain, but this may explain why Lieutenant Loomis was not listed as a veteran of various battles fought by the Corps Artillery. He was instead in a rear operations capacity, insuring that the wounded received medical care and those more forward units were supplied with critical food, ammunition, weapons, horses, wagons and other necessary supplies.[90]

In 1814, the United States was in a desperate military and economic situation. The British, having defeated the French monarch Napoleon, began to transfer large numbers of ships and combat veterans to America. The British planned to attack the United States in three main areas: in New York along Lake Champlain and the Hudson River in order to sever New England from the union; at New Orleans to block the Mississippi; and in Chesapeake Bay as a diversionary maneuver. The British goal was to obtain major territorial concessions in a peace treaty, particularly around the Great Lakes Region. The United States was bankrupt by the fall of 1814. In New England, opponents of the war were discussing separation from the federal government. The Hartford Convention that met in Connecticut in December 1814 and January 1815 stopped short of such an extreme step but suggested a number of constitutional amendments to restrict federal power. The country was still much divided over the war.

---

90 George W. Cullum, *Biographical Register*, p. 118.

The British appeared near success in the late summer of 1814. American resistance to the diversionary attack in Chesapeake Bay was weak. The British, after winning the Battle of Bladensburg, Maryland on August 24, marched into Washington, D.C., and burned most of the public buildings. President James Madison and his wife had to flee into the countryside. The British then turned to attack Baltimore but met stiffer resistance and were forced to retire after the American defense of Fort McHenry, which inspired Francis Scott Key to write the words of the "Star-Spangled Banner."

In the north, Americans and British continued their fighting along the Niagara Frontier. To the northeast, almost ten thousand British veterans advanced into the United States from Montreal. Only a weak American army stood between them and New York City, but on Sept. 11, 1814, American navy Captain Thomas Macdonough won the maritime Battle of Lake Champlain (Plattsburg Bay), destroying the British fleet carrying their massive army. Fearing the possibility of a severed line of communications, the British army retreated back into Canada to reevaluate and receive further instructions. The northern U.S. border was now secure. A military stalemate began. Meanwhile, diplomats were at work. In December, 1814 the Treaty of Ghent was signed, which basically restored relations between the two countries to *status quo ante bellum*. In January, 1815, after the peace treaty was signed, General Andrew Jackson led a huge U.S. victory over the invading British at the battle of New Orleans. The war of 1812 was over.

In the War of 1812, First Lieutenant Gustavus Loomis served in the Niagara Region for approximately two years or longer. During this period he fought in two major battles, a victory at Fort George in Ontario and a defeat at Fort Niagara in New York. Due to his additional duties as a Quartermaster and an Adjutant, much of his time was filled with support and administrative responsibilities within the First Artillery Regiment and later the Corps Artillery. During these two years in the Niagara region, the religiously minded Loomis had minimal military chaplain support. The U.S. Army chaplain for the region, Chaplain Peter VanPelt, maintained an office in New York City. It is unknown if Chaplain VanPelt visited troops on the Niagara frontier. If he did so it was inconsistent. However, Gustavus Loomis did have access to a significant clergyman in the Niagara region, Rev. Robert Addison.

During the War of 1812, the only prominent clergyman in the Niagara region was Rev. Robert Addison (1754-1829). A graduate of Trinity College, Cambridge, Addison came to the Ontario side of the Niagara River in 1791, dedicating his life to ministry in this region. Settling in Newark, Addison founded Saint Mark's Anglican Church and used his pulpit as a base for ministry throughout the region. Early in the War of 1812, Rev. Addison was captured by the Americans and paroled as a prisoner of war to his own home. In 1813, as Gustavus Loomis and the Americans captured Fort George and burned Newark, Rev. Addison was again the victim of American aggression and again a prisoner of war. Saint Mark's Anglican Church was the only established church in the entire region. One wonders what Loomis thought, as a devout Christian, of the burning of the church building and the imprisonment of a clergyman by the Americans.[91]

The stone structure of Saint Mark's Anglican Church was located between Newark and Fort George. Rev. Addison was the only ordained clergyman in the region. He served as a chaplain to the soldiers at Fort George, receiving a British military

---

91 "Rev. Robert Addison," www.2ministries-online.org/tbfuller/addison. Accessed October 4, 2009. "History of Saint Mark's Anglican Church," www.stmarks1792.com/page/historyofsaintmarks. Accessed October 6, 2009.

pension after the war. During the war the church building was used by both the British and the Americans as a hospital and supply depot. The Americans dug foxholes in the church cemetery, the indentations of these holes still visible today. While a prisoner of the Americans, Rev. Addison provided chaplain services to his American captors. Whether or not the devout Lieutenant Loomis attended these religious services is unknown, but likely. In late December, 1813, after the Americans abandoned Fort George and burned Newark, the British replaced the Saint Mark's Church roof and again utilized Robert Addison as a chaplain to troops at the derelict Fort George and nearby Fort Mississauga. After having ministered to his civilian congregation for nearly forty years, Robert Addison died in 1829, in his seventy-fifth year.[92]

It is interesting to consider the state of mind of Gustavus Loomis as a combat veteran of the war of 1812. Physically, Loomis was fit, spry and athletic. His technical abilities in military matters were excellent, evident by the many additional responsibilities given him by senior officers. Religiously, he remained firm in his evangelical Protestant faith. Based on his behavior in subsequent military assignments, Loomis kept himself spiritually refreshed by personal Bible study, by attending religious meetings whenever possible, by sharing his faith with others, and by maintaining a small library of Christian literature.

A year after the end of the war, Lieutenant Loomis was still seeking financial compensation from the federal government related to his quartermaster activities. Apparently Loomis used his own money, or used his personal promise of surety, to purchase army supplies. In March, 1816 the U.S. Senate considered

92 "Saint Mark's began our Diocese, and Continues a Fine Ministry," *Niagara Anglican*, September, 2008, p.1. Robert Addison," *Dictionary of Canadian Biography Online*, www.biographi.ca/009004-119.01-e.php?&id_n-br=2727, pp. 1-3. Accessed October 8, 2009.

a bill called, "An Act for the Relief of Gustavus Loomis." The bill passed and Loomis was compensated.[93]

At the end of the War of 1812, Gustavus Loomis departed the Niagara Region and returned to Fort Columbus in New York City. The inner drive, the life passion of Loomis, remained his faith. The piety of Gustavus Loomis was a small part of a national religious movement that, while dormant during the war, rekindled itself after the end of the war. Many Americans remained a fervently evangelical and spiritually minded people. For example, during this period the American Board of Commissioners for Foreign Missions was formed (1810), the first organized group in the United States to sponsor foreign Christian missions. In 1816 the American Bible Society was formed in New York City. In 1817 the American Sunday School Union was organized in Philadelphia. While evangelical leaders such as Timothy Dwight (d.1817) and Francis Asbury (d.1816) were passing away, new fervent preachers took upon themselves the ministry of revivalism and awakenings. Men such as Peter Cartwright (1785-1872), Charles G. Finney (1792-1875), Lyman Beecher (1775-1863) and Asahel Nettleton (1783-1844) spread the gospel message of repentance from sin and acceptance of Jesus Christ as personal savior. In this Second Great Awakening, a movement which swept America, U.S. Army First Lieutenant Gustavus Loomis was a firm supporter.

---

93 "Journal of the United States of America, 1789-1873," *Senate Journal*, Friday, March 15, 1816.

CHAPTER FIVE

QUARTERMASTER DUTIES, U.S. COASTAL SURVEY, MARRIAGE

THE UNITED STATES AT THE end of the War of 1812 was
a nation on the rise. Twice the fledgling nation had defeated Great
Britain in war. By 1816 the Barbary Pirates were defeated and the
prestige of the infant United States was developing. The U.S. had no
enemies. Washington received an increasing amount of foreign diplomats, eager to develop economic treaties with the upstart nation.
As the nation expanded west and south, Indian relations became an
ongoing problem. Indeed, for soldiers like the twenty-six year old
Lieutenant Gustavus Loomis, the next several decades would be
spent mostly fighting Indians or coordinating Indian affairs.

American religion in 1815 continued its course developed
before the war. Churches, sects and individuals still argued about
doctrine and liturgies and cults. Theological battles filled religious newspapers, as Calvinists and Arminians debated free will
and human depravity. While the War of 1812 did nothing to heal
religious divisions, the war did stimulate a feeling of national-
ism and patriotism. A type of cultural pride developed among
most people, a sense of individual identity as a nation. America, it
seemed to most, was now at the threshold of greatness. Endless
possibilities existed for the nation. Evangelical religion burned in
many people's hearts. Others lamented the war and the loss of life
and property, questioning the wisdom of the war and the will of

God for the future of America.[94] Meanwhile deists debated evangelicals; Unitarians clashed with Baptists; Presbyterians began infighting over doctrine; and Mormonism brought a new religious movement into America.

In the first decades of the nineteenth century, serious voices to abolish slavery were heard in America. Temperance movements appeared throughout the country. America began to display cultural, political and economic divisions. Pluralism developed rapidly from economic prosperity, from immigration, from industrialization, and from westward expansion. The United States around 1815 was rapidly departing from its homogenous origins and was quickly becoming a diverse and expanding nation. In less than three generations since the founding of the United States, the nation had increased its territory over five times. Americans began to dream of a gigantic nation from the Atlantic to the Pacific, a land ruled by democratic freedom and benevolence. The other side of the story was far less idealistic. Only white men could truly experience the blessings of an expanding America. White women could not vote. Indians continued to lose their land as they retreated westward. And chattel slavery of Negros made a mockery of the claims that America was a land of freedom and opportunity for all.[95]

During the last months of the War of 1812, it is difficult to follow Lieutenant Gustavus Loomis. At one point he was briefly part of the Northern Army at Plattsburg, New York. In June, 1814 he was home in Thetford, Vermont. And in May, 1815 he was in Montpelier, Vermont. This may have been related to his duties to acquire food and supplies for the army. There were briefly some questions about Loomis' financial dealings, as he

---

94 William Gribbin, *The Churches Militant: The War of 1812 and American Religion*, (New Haven: Yale University Press, 1973), pp. 129-132.

95 Daniel W. Howe, *What Hath God Wrought: The Transformation of America, 1815-1848*, (Oxford University Press, 2007), p. xiii.

apparently paid for supplies with his own money. But these questions amounted to nothing.[96]

At the conclusion of the War of 1812, Gustavus Loomis returned to his assignment in New York City, at Fort Columbus. The New York City that greeted Loomis after the war was fully consumed in the movement to transform America. During the war, the city defended itself while suffering the hardships of the British naval blockade. The city after the war displayed all the economic and technological changes in the culture, both positive and negative. New York thrived after the war, eventually acquiring the nickname, "The Empire State." New York City quickly became a receiving point for travelers, businessmen, adventurers, criminals, immigrants, and opportunity seekers. Often called a "city of contrasts," New York had an expanding downtown crowded with people and buildings. Busy with trade, commerce and businesses, elegant buildings were built next to structures made of scraps. Some streets were cobblestone while most were dirt. There was mud and horse manure everywhere, as portions of the city stank from poor sanitation. Beggars walked the same streets as the very wealthy. Prostitution, bankruptcy, disease, an increasing number of orphans, and unscrupulous businessmen were common. Simultaneously, many churches experienced revival movements and saw hundreds converted. These evangelical churches sought to minister to both the spiritual and physical needs of their bustling city.[97]

In the spring of 1815, Lieutenant Gustavus Loomis was back at Fort Columbus on Governor's Island. Much had changed in

96 Carolyn T. Foreman, "Gustavus Loomis: Commandant of Fort Gibson and Fort Towson," *Chronicles of Oklahoma,* vol. 18, no. 3, (September, 1940), p. 219.

97 "History of New York City," www.inetours.com/New_York/Pages/NYC_History. "New York City and the Developing Republic," www.nyhistory.org/seneca/nyc. Accessed November 2, 2009.

the defense of New York Harbor since Loomis departed over two years earlier. The New York and New Jersey militias greatly expanded defensive structures and built new blockhouses and numerous small forts. Dozens of new artillery positions and ammunition bunkers were constructed along the many rivers and islands in New York Harbor.[98] At the end of the war the militia returned home. Hundreds of valuable artillery cannons, tons of munitions, and huge amounts of military equipment had to be accounted for. Someone with skills as a quartermaster had to be assigned to inventory, catalogue, recycle or dispose of U.S. Army weapons, munitions and supplies. Lieutenant Gustavus Loomis was assigned this task.

While on the Niagara frontier, Lieutenant Loomis was assigned the additional duty of "Assistant Deputy Quartermaster" on April 19, 1813. He served in this capacity for approximately two years. His superior officers were impressed with his honesty and his attention to detail. While Quartermasters are always under the temptation to steal from the government, no such allegations were ever placed against Loomis. In fact, his skills as a Quartermaster were so well respected that upon his arrival back to Fort Columbus in the spring of 1815, he was placed on full-time ordinance duty.[99] Ordinance duty was not sensational or necessarily fulfilling work, but Loomis did his job well. He served in this capacity from 1815 to 1817. His primary responsibilities during this time were to evaluate the serviceability of the artillery; catalogue and dispose of outdated military supplies; relocate artillery canons to other military forts; coordinate with New York City officials for financial compensation; disassemble dozens of military fortifi-

98 R.S. Guernsey, *New York City and Vicinity During the War of 1812 – Being a Military, Civil and Financial Local History of that Period,* (New York: 1895), vol. II, pp. 389-400.

99 George W. Cullum, *Biographical Register of the Officers and Graduates of the U.S. Military Academy, at West Point, N.Y.,* (New York: 1868), p.118.

cations in and around New York City; provide property account-ability; validate graves registration for those militiamen who died while on duty in the New York City area; and evaluate financial claims from the New York and New Jersey militias.

While serving as a Quartermaster on ordinance duty at Fort Columbus, Gustavus Loomis did more than his military duties. On June 20, 1817, Loomis married Miss Julia Ann Mix. The always religiously minded Lieutenant Loomis clearly understood the biblical command to not be "unequally yoked to an unbeliever" (II Corinthians 6:14). The faith of Gustavus, implanted in his heart in Thetford, Vermont as a boy, would never allow him to marry a woman who did not share his evangelical zeal. By all accounts, his marriage to Julia was happy. Julia Ann Mix (1797-1849) was eight years younger than Gustavus when they married. They were married in rural Washington, New York.[100] This town is located about one hundred and fifty miles north of New York City, about twenty miles northeast of Poughkeepsie, between the Hudson River and the Massachusetts border. We can only speculate as to why the young couple were married in such a remote location where neither one had any family. Gustavus was stationed in this area briefly before he deployed to the Niagara Theater in 1813. In all likelihood the couple eloped and spent their honeymoon in the beautiful mountains along the Hudson River in upstate New York. Upon their return from their honeymoon, at age twenty, Julia Loomis became an army wife at Fort Columbus, New York City.

We cannot be certain how Gustavus and Julia met. We know she was born on June 23, 1797, the tenth of ten children born to Jonathan and Nancy (Sears) Mix. Jonathan Mix was a descendent of Puritans who settled in southern Connecticut in the 1640s.

---

100 William P. Blake, *A Brief Account of the Life and Patriotic Services of Jonathan Mix of New Haven, being an Autobiographical Memoir,* (New Haven: 1886), p. 96.

Born in 1753, he grew up "in the midst of plenty and contentment and under good religious influences." Jonathan Mix was a Revolutionary War veteran with both the Colonial Army and the Colonial Navy, seeing action in both services. Towards the end of the Revolutionary War, Jonathan Mix was a prisoner of war and was in poor health. The war ruined his fortune and he had to begin again to build his economic standing in New Haven. Mix had limited success as an inventor. He designed and patented novel equipments for artillery and was praised for his invention of steel axel springs for carriages, an invention that slowly achieved universal use.[101]

Julia was born and raised in New Haven, Connecticut in a middle-class home of stable but not wealthy financial means. Her father Jonathan was involved in maritime activities, evidenced by two of his ten children being born overseas, one in South America and the other on the island of Guadeloupe in the West Indies. Julia's mother died in 1799, when Julia was two years old. Her father soon remarried. The name of Mix was very popular in southern Connecticut, with dozens of families with that name living in New Haven, Wallingford, Norwich and other places.

For business reasons, Jonathan Mix in 1808 moved his large family to New York City. Julia was age twelve at the time. Apparently Jonathan thought he could best sell his inventions in New York City. It is here that the Jonathan Mix family may have first met Lieutenant Gustavus Loomis. Shortly before the War of 1812, Jonathan Mix invented and patented improvements in cartridge boxes for cannons, and invented a type of smokeless fuse and improved sighting techniques for artillery. In this capacity he worked closely with senior U.S. Navy commanders, Commodore Stephen Decatur and Captain David Porter. On November 14, 1814, Jonathan Mix accepted a commission as an officer in the Sea Fencibles, serv-

---

101 William P. Blake, *A Brief Account...*, p. xi.

ing for six months in New York Harbor with this lightweight mobile maritime artillery force. Perhaps Lieutenant Loomis and the Jonathan Mix family met at this time, it is impossible to tell.[102]

Lieutenant Gustavus Loomis and Miss Julia Ann Mix may have met in a different way. We do know that Gustavus had various Loomis relatives in southern Connecticut, in proximity to the numerous Mix families in the same area. Perhaps Gustavus and Julia met while Gustavus was stationed at Fort Columbus after the War of 1812, while he was visiting his relatives in southern Connecticut. Perhaps the couple was intentionally fixed-up by plotting relatives on both sides. Maybe they met at one of the large revival meetings frequently held in New Haven, as that city was a hotbed for the Second Great Awakening. While we can not be sure how the couple met, we know that they had a successful marriage of thirty-

An undated early sketch of Fort Columbus on Governor's Island, New York City. Beginning in 1817, Lieutenant Gustavus Loomis and his wife Julia and infant daughter Eliza lived within the walls of the garrison on the center of the island. Source:www.govisland.com/Images/historic_maps/GI_map_-1855%20(Bachmann).

one years. Julia and Gustavus had three children, Eliza (b.1818 at Fort Columbus, New York); William (b.1819 at New Haven, Connecticut); and Gustavus (b.1821 at Baton Rouge, Louisiana). Only their first-born child, Eliza, lived past infancy.[103] Julia traveled with her husband and their daughter to his various military assignments and fully supported his military career. Religiously,

102 William P. Blake, *A Brief Account…*, pp. 59-62.
103 William Blake, *A Brief Account…*, pp. 96-97.

the couple was as one, both evangelical in their faith and both firmly devoted to God and to their country.

In 1817, the living accommodations at Fort Columbus for the newly married Gustavus and Julia Loomis were humble. The couple lived in officer's quarters, a section of which were divided up for married officers.[104] Called "Officer's Pavilions," these small stone rooms adjacent to the parade field made for simple living accommodations, a big step down from what Julia was used to as a girl in New Haven. All day long Mrs. Loomis heard bugles sounding, troops marching and guns firing in artillery practice. As an officer's wife, Julia Loomis was esteemed and almost revered by the soldiers. Strict protocol separated enlisted soldiers from officers, and an officer's wife was considered a treasured and respected commodity in a military installation. The lack of privacy for a woman in any U.S. Army fort in the 1800s was stifling. Yet Mrs. Loomis appears to have taken it all in stride, adjusting well to her role as an army officer's wife. Gustavus was able to eat his meals at home. He and his wife enjoyed walks along the island and enjoyed picnics on the spacious grassy fields outside the fort walls. In May, 1818, a daughter was born to Gustavus and Julia Loomis named Eliza, born at Fort Columbus.

Stationed on Governor's Island in the harbor of New York City, the Loomis family had direct access to the most thriving city in America. As there was no war at the time, Gustavus and Julia and later baby Eliza could visit New York City as they wished. Ferry boats connected Governor's Island and Fort Columbus to various parts of the city. The economy was booming and prosperity was everywhere evident. In November, 1816 a public meeting was held to discuss the radical idea of forming a savings bank in New York City. The city prospered even in the winter, as huge

---

104 Barbara A. Yocum, *Fort Jay: Historic Structure Report*, (Lowell, MA: National Park Service, 2005), p.51.

shipments of ice carved out of the Hudson River were sold to markets in South America, Asia, and southern U.S. states.

By 1817, thousands of Irish Roman Catholic immigrants had arrived in the city. An underclass of the impoverished formed a dark shadow against the prosperity of the city. Soup kitchens and orphanages were created to address the needs of the urban poor. Meanwhile the city developed sewer systems, fresh water supplies, hospitals, schools and elegant homes for the very rich. Theaters, balls, plays and other gaieties were readily available. Churches, both Protestant and the newer Roman Catholic churches, ministered to the growing population. In 1818 the first savings bank in the city opened. In April, 1818 the New York State Library was founded. In June, U.S. President James Madison visited the city. On February 23, 1819, General Andrew Jackson, fresh from his victories in Florida against the Seminoles, visited New York City with a hero's reception. One wonders if Lieutenant Gustavus Loomis met Andrew Jackson at this time. If they did not speak, it is likely that Loomis was part of a formal military reception or parade, where Loomis would have at least seen the famous General and future President of the United States. Loomis had no way of knowing that as he departed New York City in 1820, he would be following in the footsteps of Andrew Jackson as a soldier in northern Florida dealing with the Seminoles.

After the War of 1812, Lieutenant Gustavus Loomis served at Fort Columbus, Governor's Island in New York City, on ordinance duty from 1815-1817. He then served in the same location on garrison duty from 1817-1819. On April 7, 1819, Loomis was promoted to the rank of Captain the Corps of Artillery,[105] making him one of only twenty-five or so captains in the entire U.S. Army Corps of Artillery. However, since the nation was not at war,

---

105 *Niles Weekly Register, September, 1819 to March, 1820*, (Baltimore, 1821), p. 6.

meaningful duties for artillery officers were at a premium. There simply was not enough work for the Corps of Artillery and its officers in peacetime. This being true, Captain Gustavus Loomis, while remaining assigned to Fort Columbus, was detailed from 1819-1820 to the United States Coastal Survey.

The Office of Coast Survey was first established by President Thomas Jefferson in 1807 as the Survey of the Coast. Not until after the War of 1812 did Mr. Ferdinand Rudolph Hassler (1770-1843) return from Europe to the United States with the proper navigation and mathematical instruments. From the Coast Survey flowed much of the structure and the manner of conducting modern federally funded science projects. As one source stated of Mr. Hassler,

> Introducing the best European practice in surveying, Hassler forged a union of applied and theoretical science through a precise measurement of lines and angles and a rigorous search for errors. He was solicitous about training his "assistants" (their formal designation) so that there would be a uniform practice in mapmaking, and he initiated studies in such affiliated subjects as tides, currents, and magnetism.[106]

The Coastal Survey instituted regular and systematic observations of the tides and the Gulf Stream, and investigated magnetic forces and directions. During the nineteenth century, the Coastal Survey was loosely organized with no competition in federally funded scientific research. Graduates of West Point filled the ranks of the Coastal Survey. Various Coastal Survey superintendents developed expertise in fields as diverse as astronomy, cartography, meteorology, geodesy, geology, geophysics, hydrography, navigation, oceanography, exploration, pilotage, tides and topography.

---

106 Thomas G. Manning, *U.S. Coastal Survey vs. Hydrographic Office: A Nineteenth Century Rivalry in Science and Politics,* (University of Alabama Press, 1988), p. 1.

Rudolph Hassler's plans were to employ triangulation to establish his mapping system. Work began in the vicinity of New York City in 1816. The first base line was measured and verified in 1817. The army and navy were placed at the forefront of the Survey which generated a lull in activity. The Coastal Survey was without a Superintendent during the fourteen years from 1818 to 1832 when the army was the primary authority. Mr. Hassler eventually brought together mathematicians, cartographers, geodesists, metrologists, hydrographers, topographers, sailors, soldiers, laborers, and administrators, and molded them into a coherent organization with the goal of surveying the coast of the United States.[107] Captain Gustavus Loomis, as an artillery officer, was very interested in the best shoreline locations in which to build a coastal fortification system for the United States.

As a U.S. Military Academy graduate, Gustavus Loomis had the engineering, mathematical and cartography skills to greatly assist the U.S. Coastal Survey. The expanding nation needed accurate maritime charts for shipping, commerce and national defense. Loomis served in the capacity from 1819-1820. It is not difficult to imaging Captain Loomis and his wife Julia and infant daughter Eliza cruising with the U.S. Coastal Survey in fair weather along the New York, New Jersey and Connecticut coastlines. Since exact measurements could only be taken in fair weather and calm seas, Loomis spent part of his time editing Coastal Survey maps at Fort Columbus and part of his time on the water often with his family in mapmaking and cartographic activities.

In early 1819, Julia Loomis was pregnant with her second child. Gustavus Loomis and his wife were enjoying a happy time in their lives. They were newly married with a healthy baby daughter. He was recently promoted to Captain in the U.S. Army,

107 "The Coast and Geodetic Survey – The Beginning," www.history.noaa.gov/legacy/ coastsurvey. Accessed November 6, 2009.

almost guaranteeing him a long career as an army officer. His work with the Coastal Survey was fulfilling and also allowed him maximum time with his young family. While at Fort Columbus they lived in officer's quarters. While at sea in fair weather they lived in small but private quarters on board a vessel leased by the Coastal Survey. Loomis' piety was everywhere evident. He did not drink alcohol or use profanity. He was not a brawler. Whenever possible he sang hymns and read the Bible with his family. In his job with the Coastal Survey he showed technical engineering and cartographic skills. His high moral standards may have seemed odd to some of the sailors and laborers he served with in the Coastal Survey, but his competence as a military officer could not be reproached.

In the fall of 1819 the first tragedy struck the Loomis family. Gustavus and Julia Loomis had a baby boy born October 11, 1819 in New Haven, Connecticut. Why the baby was born in New Haven is uncertain. Medical doctors in New York City near Julia's home at Fort Columbus were as capable as any doctors in New Haven. We do know that Julia had many Mix family members in New Haven. Perhaps she had a difficult pregnancy and needed her family's support. Perhaps as the birth date came close, she and her daughter Eliza were staying with relatives while Gustavus was on a coastal cruise with the U.S. Coastal Survey. For whatever reason the child was born in New Haven, the baby was not well. The sickly child was named William Beriah Loomis. This was a grievous trial to his parents who prayed for the child and dedicated the baby to the Lord. The infant lived for about nine months and died on July 30, 1820.[108]

From sometime in late 1819 into early 1820, Captain Loomis was placed on Recruiting Duty in the New York City area.[109]

108 William Blake, *A Brief Account...*, p. 97
109 George W. Cullum, *Biographical Register*, p. 118.

Loomis must have had an office in New York City, commuting to his office back and forth every day by ferry boat to his home on Fort Columbus. It is likely that Loomis did not like recruiting duty. Any army must reproduce itself, even in peace, as newer soldiers are required to fill in the bottom of the ranks as others leave the military or advance in their careers. With thousands of unemployed immigrants swarming into New York City, recruiting new soldiers for the army must have been relatively simple. Loomis was assigned to recruit troops to accompany him to his next assignment in Florida. No doubt Captain Loomis was eager to get out of commanding a recruiting officer's desk and was excited to again take the field in a more tactical and operational tour of duty. His next assignment was on garrison duty at Fort Gadsden, in Spanish Territory in the Florida panhandle.

CHAPTER SIX

MILITARY DUTIES IN FLORIDA AND IN LOUISIANA

IN THE EARLY SUMMER OF 1820, Captain Gustavus Loomis and his wife Julia, their two year old daughter Eliza and their infant son William departed New York Harbor for Florida. Neither Gustavus nor Julia had been to Florida. Gustavus, as a rural Vermonter, had never been outside New England and New York, except when he crossed the Niagara River during the War of 1812 and served a few miles within Ontario, Canada. The several weeks travel from New York to Fort Gadsden, with numerous stops along the way, was a severe trial for the Loomis family. Actually, this time period was a low point in the life of Gustavus Loomis, only comparable to the deep sadness he experienced at the death of his wife Julia and as he later saw his country divide into bloody Civil War.

Two traumatic experiences faced Loomis on the southern sailing trip to Florida. First, his infant son William died. The child had been sickly all along and Julia had experienced a difficult pregnancy. Tradition at the time stated that the salty sea air was healthy. Gustavus and Julia had high hopes that the southern cruise on the vessel *Robert* would invigorate their sickly son. This was not to be. On July 30, 1820, the child died. With no chaplain on board the *Robert*, it fell to Captain Loomis to conduct a brief memorial service for his deceased son William. Although always devout and committed to Jesus Christ as his savior, this memorial service must have been very difficult for the grieving Gustavus Loomis. His only son had died as an infant, less than one year old. The child's body was committed to the deep, with an emphasis on the future resurrection at the return of Jesus Christ from the Bible verse, "The sea gave up the dead who were in it, and death and hades delivered up the dead who were in them. And they were judged, each one according to his works" (Revelation 20:13).[110]

The second event on the southern cruise to Florida that made this trip especially stressful and challenging for U.S. Army Captain Gustavus Loomis was the mutiny of the soldiers on board the *Robert*. Shortly after departing New York City on the chartered civilian vessel *Robert*, Loomis discovered a plot to take over the ship. The vessel was full of new recruits. Something caused the new recruits to change their mind about military service. Life on the *Robert* was confining and unsanitary. The food was bad, the men were dirty, and fear of Yellow Fever in Florida possessed the men. Many of the recruits recanted their oath of enlistment and wanted to go home. It was getting hot and humid as they went farther south. A mutiny erupted.

Captain Loomis was the senior army officer on board the *Robert*. When the ship arrived for supplies in Havana, Cuba, Loomis wrote a letter to Secretary of War John C. Calhoun. In this letter dated August 19, 1820, Loomis reported that he discovered a plot among the army recruits on the ship shortly after leaving New York Harbor. The plot was to take possession of the ship, kill Captain Loomis and Mrs. Loomis, and kill Lieutenant Chester F. Tracy. Then the mutinous recruits planned to kill the civilian captain of the vessel and his crew. Then the army non-commissioned officers who watched over the recruits would be killed if they did not join the mutiny. Loomis reported that he had twenty-one of the mutineers arrested on the ship and placed in irons. In his letter

---

110 George W. Cullum, *Biographical Register of the Officers and Graduates of the U.S. Military Academy, at West Point, N.Y.*, (New York: 1868), p. 118.

to Secretary of War Calhoun, Captain Loomis complimented the cool, prompt and energetic conduct of Lieutenant Tracy and the non-commissioned officers. The U.S. Consul in Havana, Francis C. Black, promptly ordered aid and assistance for Loomis' men.[111]

On September 22, 1820, Loomis wrote a second letter to Secretary of War Calhoun. This letter was written from Apalachicola Bay, Florida, a few miles from the inland Fort Gadsden. Captain Loomis presented the Secretary of War a bill for $413.00 to be paid to the U.S. Consul in Havana, a bill to pay for the provisioning of Loomis' troops as they entered Florida. Loomis also stated that the Spanish Governor on Cuba treated him friendly and offered his assistance. This was an unusual move, as Captain Loomis was taking a military force to occupy Fort Gadsden in Spanish Territory. Loomis wrote that he arrived at the Apalachicola River on September 11, ready to move inland to Fort Gadsden, but the senior army officer in the area, Major Alexander C.W. Fanning, ordered him to encamp at the bay due to Yellow Fever in the Fort Gadsden area.[112]

In the early fall of 1820, Captain Loomis sailed up the Apalachicola River a few miles to Fort Gadsden. The location of Fort Gadsden had a recent and volatile history.[113] During the final year of the War of 1812, the British decided to attempt a "Southern strategy" that would include attacks from the Gulf Coast against New Orleans, Mobile and Georgia. The plan called for the enlistment of Creek and Seminole warriors, along with free blacks and liberated slaves. To help accomplish this goal, a fort was established at Prospect Bluff on the Apalachicola River. Constructed during the summer of 1814,

111 W. Edwin Hemphill, Editor. *The Papers of John C. Calhoun, Volume V, 1820-1821,* (University of South Carolina Press, 1971), pp. 333-334.

112 W. Edwin Hemphill, Editor. *The Papers of John C. Calhoun, ...*p. 359.

113 Much of the following narrative is taken from "British Post on the Apalachicola," "Attack on the Negro Fort," and "Fort Gadsden in the First Seminole War," at www.exploresouthernhistory.com/fortgadsden. Accessed October 15, 2009.

the works consisted of an octagonal central magazine surrounded by palisades and moats and an earthen battery overlooking the river. Indian warriors came here to receive arms, ammunition and other supplies, while the British used the fort as a base for a large force of auxiliary Royal Marines. This British Post on the Apalachicola became a major supply point and training installation which quickly attracted the attention of U.S. military leaders.

The British left the fort on the Apalachicola after the end of the War of 1812, in May of 1815. When the British departed they placed the fort and its massive store of artillery, ammunition and weaponry in the hands of Native American and Negro allies. The British flag continued to fly over the fort, which quickly became a beacon for escaped slaves from all along the Southern frontier. Outraged American officials began calling the post the "Negro Fort" in their official correspondence, and it was not long before they began to develop plans to deal with the former British Post on the Apalachicola River. A political difficulty was that the Negro Fort was in Spanish Territory.

The well-defended former British fort offered a natural refuge for blacks fleeing slavery. The senior U.S. Army Commander, Major General Edmund P. Gaines, was authorized to move against the fort. The attack was lead by Colonel Duncan Clinch. On the morning of July 27, 1816, U.S. river gunboats moved within range of the fort and opened fire. Cannon fire was returned from the fort and a brief but intense battle followed. After firing four shots to test the range, the sailors loaded their guns with "hot shot," cannonballs heated until they were red hot. This shot sailed over the wall of the fort and into the magazine. The entire "Negro Fort" was instantly blown to pieces.

The death toll at the Negro Fort was horrendous. Of the three hundred and twenty men, women and children in the fort when the attack began, two hundred and seventy were killed and many others were horribly wounded. The few survivors of the explosion were carried upstream to Fort Scott in Alabama by Colonel Clinch and notices posted so the slave owners could come and claim them. The artillery and other supplies were seized by the Americans over the objections of Spanish officers who arrived in Apalachicola Bay a short time later.[114]

The site of the Negro Fort was abandoned for about two years after the fateful 1816 explosion. In the fall of 1817 the First Seminole War began. By the spring of 1818, Major General Andrew Jackson arrived in the Florida panhandle with an army of regulars, militiamen and more than one thousand Creek warriors. Authorized to invade Spanish Florida, Jackson crossed the international boundary between the U.S. and Spanish Territory in March of 1818 and moved his army down the east bank of the Apalachicola River.

Impressed with the location of the original Negro Fort, General Jackson ordered the construction of a new post at the same site to serve as a supply depot for his army. The task of designing the new fort was given to Lieutenant James Gadsden, a U.S. Army Engineer. The young officer's efforts impressed Jackson and he named the new outpost Fort Gadsden in his honor. Lieutenant Gadsden used the old British Battery as the foundation of his new fort, adding a rectangular bastioned work to its rear. The walls were made of earth and topped with a heavy log stockade. Strongly built for a frontier fort, remnants of Fort Gadsden can still be seen today. The earthworks have survived remarkably well for more than 190 years. Standing within Fort Gadsden, a visitor can see the indented ground, all that remains today of the pulverized Negro Fort. The later Fort Gad-

114 Joe Knetsch, *Florida's Seminole Wars, 1817-1858,* (Charleston, SC: Arcadia Books, 2003), pp. 19-22.

sden earthworks are worn but clearly visible, outlining this medium sized fort on the Apalachicola River.

Jackson's army marched east along the coast from Fort Gadsden in late March of 1818, pushing to attack any Indians that confronted them. They mostly found abandoned villages in the Tallahassee vicinity and on the Suwannee River. Many of these villages had scalps from white people hanging prominently on poles in the center of the villages.[115] He also captured the Spanish fort at St. Marks, Florida. Jackson returned to Fort Gadsden believing the First Seminole War was over, having cleared the Florida panhandle of all Indians.[116] Instead he learned that warriors were being sheltered and supplied to the west by the Spanish and British in Pensacola. Taking an army of more than one thousand men and two pieces of artillery, he left Fort Gadsden on an overland march that led to the surrender and capture of Pensacola later that spring.[117]

The historical marker for Ft. Gadsden, Florida. During the First Seminole War this site was the location for operations under General Andrew Jackson against the Seminoles.
Photo by Ken Lawson.

Despite the fact that it was located in Spanish territory, Fort Gadsden was held by U.S. troops before Florida was turned over to the United States in 1821. It was at this location of the former

115 Joe Knetsch, *Florida's Seminole Wars*, p. 31.

116 John Missall and Mary Lou Missall, *The Seminole Wars: America's Longest Indian Conflict*, (University Press of Florida, 2004), pp. 42-43.

117 Joe Knetsch, *Florida's Seminole Wars*, p. 36.

British fort and the former Negro Fort that Captain Gustavus Loomis and his wife and daughter arrived, in Spanish Territory, in September, 1820. The Fort Gadsden that welcomed them was quite different from their former residence at Fort Columbus in New York Harbor. The weather in Florida was sickly for almost half the year, as high temperatures, Yellow Fever and high humidity made life uncomfortable. Mosquitoes and other insects, along with snakes, panthers, alligators and other creatures, made life outside the fort an adventure. Here the Loomis' home was made of wood and not stone. All the floors were pressed dirt, meaning that dust or mud was a constant problem. Fort Gadsden was only a fraction of the size of Fort Columbus. While the Loomis family could wander around Governor's Island outside the walls of Fort Columbus, no such wandering was allowed at Fort Gadsden. At Fort Gadsden there were no ferries to take the Loomis's into New York City for social engagements. Outside the walls of their new home were swamps and Indians.

The missions of Fort Gadsden were several. The fort was situated to provide a forward deployed U.S. military presence in an area recently contested by Great Britain and Spain; to facilitate friendly relations with the numerous Indians in the area; and to insure that the Apalachicola River remained open to American citizens traveling and settling in the southeastern United States.

It was at Fort Gadsden that Captain Gustavus Loomis had his first contact with American Indians. When General Andrew Jackson left the Florida panhandle in the spring of 1818, it was assumed that the Indian problems in northern Florida were over. This was a mistake. Confrontations and bloodshed between small groups of whites and Indians were common around Fort Gadsden. There were continuous border skirmishes, as white Georgians came south into Florida to steal Indian cattle and capture runaway slaves. The Indians retaliated by raiding white settlements both in northern Florida and in Georgia. In addition, there was always the threat that large numbers of Seminole warriors would return west across the Suwannee River and reclaim their homelands in northern Florida.

In 1820, Major General Andrew Jackson departed the army to accept a position as the first Governor of Florida. Also serving at the same time was the Spanish Governor of Florida, Jose Callava. The two rival governors squabbled over various issues, but it was clear that the United States was in Florida permanently and the Spanish had to go.[118] Meanwhile, isolated from the political intrigues of the time, Captain Gustavus Loomis assumed his duties at Fort Gadsden.

The author at the Fort Gadsden site, Bristol, Florida. Notice the bulwarks on the left of the photograph. These mounds of dirt were the base for the timber palisades surrounding the fort.
Photo by Ken Lawson.

Garrison life at Fort Gadsden, Florida was similar to garrison life at most other army installations. Loomis drilled the troops. He maintained sentries to watch maritime traffic on the Apalachicola River. He patrolled the region both with Infantry on foot and with small boats along the many rivers and marshy areas nearby. Captain Loomis also negotiated with Indians related to their claims against the U.S. Government. Loomis was responsible to feed and clothe

118 Joe Knetsch, *Florida's Seminole Wars*, p. 43.

and protect over one hundred soldiers at Fort Gadsden, with a few dozen civilians as well. While always watchful of the infiltration of the Spanish and their Indian allies, Loomis was deeply moved by the plight of runaway slaves. Loomis detested slavery. Since his days as a boy in Thetford, Vermont, Gustavus was taught that slavery was a moral evil and contrary to the will of God. Now Loomis was in a position as a representative of the federal government to assist in the enforcement of the slave laws from southern states.

Captain Loomis was exposed to the horrors of southern slavery at Fort Gadsden. Here he saw furious white Georgians and other southerners spend inordinate amounts of time and money to search for their runaway slaves. To Loomis, all people were made in the image of God and all people are therefore equal in the sight of the Lord. In the tropical swamps around Fort Gadsden traveled runaway slaves, seeking to join other runaways with the goal of immigrating into Indian culture and society.[119] Along the Apalachicola River, slaves in makeshift boats travelled south at night into the safety of Spanish Florida and freedom. This certainly presented a moral dilemma for Captain Loomis. Personally, he despised slavery. As a professional army officer he was under orders to assist in the enforcement of southern states' laws, as slaveholders descended into Florida in search of their slave property. Did Loomis choose his obligation to follow his faith in God over his sworn oath as an army officer, and hide runaway slaves? If he did so he would simply be acting out what he learned as a boy in Thetford, as his hometown by the 1820s was soon to become a stop on the developing Underground Railroad.[120] There is no documentation one way or the other as to how Captain Loomis

---

119 For more information, see Kenneth W. Porter, *The Black Seminoles: History of a Freedom-Seeking People,* (University of Florida Press, 1996).

120 Wilber H. Siebert, *Vermont's Anti-Slavery and Underground Railroad Record,* (Columbus, OH: 1937), pp. 67, 97.

dealt with the runaway slave issue in Florida. We do know, however, two decades later, as he served at Fort Gibson in Oklahoma Indian Territory, that Loomis protected runaway Negro slaves from their white masters and taught the Negros how to read and write and understand the Bible.[121]

The U.S. Congress in 1820 passed a bill greatly reducing the size of the army. At that time there were still many of the founding fathers of the nation still alive. Their dislike of a large standing army influenced the next generations. Secretary of War John C. Calhoun sought to buffet the full effects of a hasty military downsizing, with little success. Congress slashed the size of the army to about six thousand total soldiers by eliminating regiments and reducing the number of officers.[122] The reorganization of the army directly affected Captain Gustavus Loomis at Fort Gadsden. Loomis was an artillery officer, but in the reorganization of the army he was transferred to the infantry. The notation of this change of his branch in the records at West Point simply states, "Captain, 1st Infantry, in Reorganization of the Army, June 1, 1821."[123]

Captain Loomis did not like his branch changed, from artillery to infantry. The implementation of the 1820 military downsizing from Congress took effect in June, 1821. On June 11, 1821, Captain Loomis wrote to Secretary of War Calhoun from Fort Gadsden. Loomis stated that the change in his branch from artillery to infantry was mortifying for him, in that he had waited eight years to serve as a Captain in the artillery, only to be transferred to the infantry. Loomis' note to Secretary Calhoun is also insightful in that it states that Mrs. Loomis was in "delicate health"

---

121 Jeff Guinn, *Our Land Before We Die: The Proud Story of the Seminole Negro*, (New York: Tarcher Publications, 2005), p. 112.

122 Allan R. Millett and Peter Maslowski, *For the Common Defense: A Military History of the United States,* (New York: The Free Press, 1994), pp. 127-128.

123 George W. Cullum, *Biographical Register...*, p. 118.

and that he also was not feeling well. Captain Loomis wrote, "I shall leave this post as soon as practicable and report at Baton Rouge if I can not obtain [a] leave of absence to carry Mrs. Loomis to the north."[124]

Loomis served at Fort Gadsden, Spanish Territory for one year. Why was he transferred so quickly? There was no doubt that his brief time at Fort Gadsden was exceedingly difficult both personally and professionally. On the way to Fort Gadsden his infant son died and was buried at sea. He then fought a mutiny on board the southern sailing vessel *Robert*, as the new army recruits destined to Florida rebelled and created an insurrection. Then Captain and Mrs. Loomis and their two year old daughter Eliza came to Fort Gadsden and saw the primitive living conditions and experienced the sickly weather. Indians were everywhere, disease was prevalent,

Poster in French advertising the auction of a group of slaves at Baton Rouge, Louisiana, March 1823. Source: www.bridgemanartonde-mand.com. Accessed September 6, 2009.

and the international political situation in northern Florida was tenuous at best. Captain Loomis must have thought this was no place for his wife and baby daughter. Added to this uneasiness was the fact that Loomis was disgruntled with the army transferring him from the artillery to the infantry. One further consideration should be mentioned. In early 1821 it was learned that

124 This letter from Loomis is in the Adjutant General's Office, "Old Files," quoted in Carolyn T. Foreman, "Gustavus Loomis, Commandant of Fort Gibson and Fort Towson," *Chronicles of Oklahoma*, vol. 18, no. 3, pp. 219-220.

Mrs. Loomis was again pregnant. For all of these reasons, Captain Loomis was happy to get out of rural tropical Florida to be transferred to the southern city of Baton Rouge, Louisiana.

In Loomis's West Point biographical summary it simply states, "In garrison at Baton Rouge, LA 1821-1825."[125] Captain Loomis and his pregnant wife and two year old daughter travelled by boat from Fort Gadsden to Baton Rouge. Gustavus Loomis had never seen a city like this. Baton Rouge was a prosperous southern city built upon slavery. Although not as large as New York City, Baton Rouge was a growing maritime city located on the Mississippi River. The city was trilingual – French, English and Spanish. Evidences of slavery were everywhere present. The city wreaked of alcohol, prostitution, and gambling. City streets were covered in mud with dilapidated wooden buildings along the riverfront. Charlatans, pioneers, mariners and businessmen crowded the city streets. Ferry boats came up the Mississippi River from New Orleans loaded with chained Negros for auction in Baton Rouge. The city also supported a wealthy upper class, mostly businessmen who worked in cooperation with plantation owners outside the city.

Baton Rouge, Louisiana in the 1820s was a city only recently under U.S. control. The city, founded in 1699, passed from France to Britain in 1763, from Britain to Spain in 1779, and from Spain to an independent American force in 1810. The city was officially annexed with western Florida to the U.S. in December, 1810. Captain and Mrs. Loomis were introduced to Baton Rouge as a very European city, perhaps the most European and eclectic city in the United States at that time. Spanish, British and French foods were readily available. Wealthy women's fashions were more European than American. European newspapers in three different languages were for sale. Baton Rouge owed its location to its site

---

125 George W. Cullum, *Biographical Register...*, p. 118.

upon the Istrouma Bluff, the first bluff upriver from the Mississippi delta, which protected the city's residents from flooding and was a natural location for a military fortification. Incorporated in 1817, Baton Rouge became Louisiana's state capital in 1849.[126]

During the war of 1812, Baton Rouge was unharmed. In the early nineteenth century the city grew steadily as the result of steamboat trade and Mississippi River transportation. The first steamboats arrived in 1812. Ten years later, while the Loomis' lived in Baton Rouge, eighty-three steamboats, one hundred and seventy-four barges, and four hundred and forty-one flatboats docked at local wharfs.[127] In 1816, Congress established a U.S. Army post and arsenal at Baton Rouge. Construction of the five-sided Pentagon Barracks began in 1819. Captain and Mrs. Loomis lived within the fort, called Pentagon or Pentagonal Barracks, for four years, 1821-1825. The fort was designed by James Gadsden, the same army engineer that designed and built the Loomis' former home station at Fort Gadsden, Florida.

A major expansion of the Pentagonal Barracks was made in 1819-1823, when new barracks were built and a large Arsenal Depot was established to serve the southern United States. The four, two-story brick buildings were completed in 1825 after six years of planning. Captain James Gadsden prepared the schematics for the barracks and coordinated the construction. Originally, there were five buildings, Gadsden having intended for a group of buildings arranged in a pentagon-shaped configuration to be erected for the housing of enlisted soldiers.[128] Soon to be called

---

126 Walter Prichard, *History of Baton Rouge and its People,* (States Historical Publication Company, 1932). Sylvia F. Rodrique, *History of Baton Rouge: An Illustrated History,* (Historical Publications Network, 2006).

127 Ralph Draughon, Jr. *Down by the River: A History of the Baton Rouge Riverfront,* (U.S. Army Corps of Engineers, 1998), p. 8.

128 "Pentagon Barracks," www.nps.gov/history/Nr/travel/louisiana/pen. Accessed September 15, 2009.

the Baton Rouge Arsenal and Ordnance Depot, the Army Quartermaster Department built warehouses and a commissary. Army engineers constructed enlisted and officer housing, bulwarks, artillery firing positions, and a parade field. What made the Baton Rouge Arsenal and Ordnance Depot unique was that in addition to being a military installation, it was also a Federal Arsenal of military supplies for the entire southwestern United States.

A photograph of a portion of the renovated Baton Rouge Arsenal and Ordnance Depot. The buildings were under construction and some were completed while the Loomis' were stationed here, 1821-1825. Source:www.house.legis.state.la.us/pubinfo/virtual%20tour/pentagon_barracks

The Baton Rouge Arsenal and Ordnance Depot was a good assignment for Captain Gustavus Loomis. Here he and his family were comfortable and safe. Although the ongoing construction might have been a noisy irritation to the Loomis', the fort was brand new and had modern sanitation, fresh water, and no Yellow Fever. Although the summers were intensely hot and humid like at Fort Gadsden, the elevation of the fort allowed for steady breezes. The facility was clean and agreeable for the Loomis family. In Baton Rouge Mrs. Loomis could get medical care as she was pregnant. Gustavus was able to spend maximum time with his wife and daughter, as his position in a military fort in a large city did not require him to do much traveling.

Shortly after arriving at the Pentagonal Barracks, Julia Loomis gave birth to a baby boy. The child was named Gustavus Loomis, Jr. The baby was born on October 8, 1821. It had been a little over a year since Gustavus and Julia buried their nine month old son at sea on their way to Fort Gadsden, Florida. This child, like their previous child, was not a strong baby. Perhaps Julia had a touch of Yellow Fever which weakened the child. Whatever the cause of the child's ill health, he lived only two weeks. Baby Gustavus Loomis, Jr. died on October 23, 1821.[129] Their first child, Eliza, was three years old at this time. Two sons born two years apart had both died. The heartache for the Loomis family was intense. Gustavus and Julia grieved for their loss but still trusted in the wisdom and compassion of a benevolent God. There was no chaplain assigned to the Baton Rouge Arsenal and Ordnance Depot. The Loomis continued to attend religious services in Baton Rouge. The couple, though wounded, experienced no long term crisis of faith.

When Gustavus and Julia Loomis walked the streets of Baton Rogue with their little daughter Eliza, they fully understood that they were a long way from home in New England. The rural Vermonter Gustavus and his Connecticut wife from New Haven, both with puritan values, were appalled by the moral depravity of Baton Rouge.

Life within the walls of the Baton Rouge Arsenal and Ordnance Depot was structured, orderly and disciplined. The facility was impeccably neat and sanitary. But life on the streets of Baton Rouge was often hectic, indecent and vulgar. It was in many areas a filthy city. An ill-bred underclass made large sections of the city unsafe. A small upper class portrayed the dignity, decorum and affluence expected of the very rich. Middle class merchants bought and sold various goods and slaves from the ever present riverboats. Gustavus studied French at the U.S. Military Academy and he would have had ample opportunities to practice his

---

129 William P. Blake, *A Brief Account of the Life and Patriotic Services of Jonathan Mix*, (New Haven: 1886), p. 97.

French language skills. Perhaps Julia picked up some French from her father's mercantile interests in the Caribbean. But the most enduring memory from their four years in Baton Rouge was their exposure to the reprehensible business of chattel slavery. The city sold thousands of slaves to support the gigantic plantations in Louisiana. Such plantations could have hundreds of slaves living in shacks and working for affluent white masters. Slave markets with their auctions of human beings were a sight familiar and disturbingly unforgettable to Gustavus and Julia Loomis.[130]

The Baton Rouge Arsenal and Ordnance Depot was of particular military importance due to its location on the southern Mississippi River. From this garrison the entire southern access to the inland United States was protected. Expanding settlers into the Northwestern Territories could be supplied from the Mississippi River and its tributaries. Such a forward deployed garrison assisted with the settlement and development of the entire southwestern United States. There were civilian immigrants to feed and shelter as they headed west; there were military quartermaster duties to perform for soldiers heading for duty on the great prairies; there were an incessant amount of riverboats to resupply, boats leased to the U.S. Government for quartermaster duties; and there was the routine administration, training and drilling expected on garrison duty.

Captain Gustavus Loomis served at the Baton Rouge Arsenal and Ordnance Depot from 1821-1825. Relieved to be out of rural sickly and tropical Florida, Gustavus and Julia enjoyed military life within the walls of the garrison. We do not know what church they attended in Baton Rouge, but we do know that there were few Protestant evangelically-minded churches in the

---

130 For a contrast between very wealthy whites and Negro slaves on a Baton Rouge plantation, see Lois E. Bannon, *Magnolia Mound: A Louisiana River Plantation,* (New York: Penguin Books, 1984).

city in the 1820s. Methodist, Baptist or perhaps Presbyterian missionaries came and went through the city. When no itinerant missionary was available, the Loomis family created their own simple home church, inviting others to attend. Military duties at the garrison were routine but fulfilling. Although the Loomis' had fond memories of living in the brand new, clean and safe military fort in Baton Rouge, their memories of these years was scarred by the death of their son Gustavus, Jr. and by their relentless exposure to the enslavement of Negros. In 1825, Captain Gustavus Loomis received orders to report for duty in Alabama to work with the Creek Indians.

CHAPTER SEVEN

CREEK INDIANS, FLORIDA, NEW ORLEANS

IN 1825, CAPTAIN GUSTAVUS LOOMIS received orders assigning him to military duty working within the Creek Nation. The location of his activities was north of the Florida panhandle in the states of Alabama and Georgia. As an infantry officer his skills were needed to insure the implementation of treaties between the Creek Indians and the U.S. Government. From his brief time at Fort Gadsden in northern Florida, Loomis knew the terrain and had exposure to the Creek peoples. He was a natural selection for this duty.

The name Creek, from the shortening of "Ocheese Creek" Indians, was given by the English colonists to the tribes living along the Ocmulgee River in central Georgia. The Creek Indians belong to the Muskhogean linguistic stock. They are composed of several separate tribes that occupied Georgia and Alabama in the American Colonial period. Originally these peoples came from lands as far east as the Carolinas and as far west as the Mississippi River. It is believed that the Creek culture began as a way to guard against other larger conquering Indian tribes of the region. Their confederacy was in constant flux, its numbers and land possessions ever-changing as small bands joined and withdrew from the alliance. But later the Cherokee and then the American colonists forced them southwestward to Alabama and Georgia. The Creek were sedentary, living year round in thatched huts. They farmed and domesticated livestock.[131] They built sophisticated ceremonial centers to which they travelled for religious or civil occasions. The Creeks were an intelligent people who adjusted well to their environment and who learned much from contact with Europeans and American colonists.

The U.S military first came to blows with the Creeks in 1813. What became known as the Creek War of 1813-1814 was actually a civil war between the Creek peoples. The larger of the two, the Upper Creeks, also called Red Sticks, settled in the heart of Alabama along the Coosa, Alabama and Tallapoosa Rivers. The smaller group, the Lower Creeks, was more open to interaction with Americans, having settled along both sides of the Chattahoochee River which runs along the Georgia-Alabama border. In February 1813 a band of Red Sticks killed a white family along the Ohio River. Instead of handing the criminals over to U.S. authorities, the older chiefs decided to execute the war party themselves. To the Red Sticks this was seen as accommodation of the white man over the Indian, and the Creek civil war began.

The first clash between Red Stick Creeks and the U.S. Army was at the Battle of Burnt Corn, July 21, 1813. American troops from Fort Mims stopped a group of Red Sticks heading north from Pensacola, the Indians recently armed and supplied by the Spanish. The Creeks fled into the swamps and the Americans looted what they had found and took the Creek horses. The Creeks then noticed that the Americans were getting carried away with their looting and had dropped their guard. The Creeks stealthy launched a surprise attack which scattered the Americans. The Red Sticks considered this confrontation to be a declaration of war by the American settlers. Since the American

---

131 John Tebbel and Keith Jennison, *The American Indian Wars*, (London: Phoenix Press, 2001), p.163.

militia had attacked from Fort Mims, the Red Sticks directed their next offensive at that fort.

On August 30, 1813, the Upper Creeks or Red Sticks attacked Fort Mims, north of Mobile, Alabama. Fort Mims was poorly defended by militia troops and was overcrowded with Lower Creeks and mixed race Creeks friendly to the Americans. The Fort Mims Massacre began at noontime while no American scouts were out. About five hundred men, women and children were killed or murdered in this afternoon fight. Much of the fighting was Upper Creeks against Lower Creeks. The Upper or Red Stick Creeks took about two hundred and fifty scalps but kept alive dozens of Negros to use as their own slaves.[132]

The slaughter at Fort Mims spread panic throughout the southeast United States. Since the U.S. Army was busy fighting the War of 1812 against the British, state militias from Tennessee, Georgia, Mississippi and some others raised large numbers of citizen soldiers to fight the Creeks. Colonel Andrew Jackson of the Tennessee militia rose to prominence. He led various state militias in a series of small battles against the Red Stick Creeks with various results. On February 6, 1814, the 39th U.S. Infantry, a disciplined regular army unit, reported for duty under Andrew Jackson.

For the next several weeks Jackson trained his combined force of militia, Lower Creeks and regular army soldiers. On March 27, 1814, the combined American force soundly defeated the Red Stick Creeks at the Battle of Horseshoe Bend, located in central Alabama. This five hour battle, complete with an artillery barrage and a bayonet charge by Jackson's troops, resulted in the deaths of five hundred and fifty enemy warriors killed in combat and another two hundred and fifty killed while retreating. Red Stick Chief Menawa was severely wounded but survived and led only

---

132 Gregory A. Waselkov, *A Conquering Spirit: Fort Mims and the Redstick War of 1813-1814*, (University of Alabama Press, 2009).

about two hundred of the original one thousand Creek warriors into safety among the Seminole Indians in Spanish Florida.

The Red Stick Creeks were broken. Andrew Jackson, no friend of any Indians, sought to make the best treaty deal for the United States with the Creeks. It was not a high priority for Jackson to compensate the Lower Creeks who supported him.[133] On August 9, 1814, Andrew Jackson forced the defeated Creeks to sign the Treaty of Fort Jackson, also called the Treaty of Horseshoe Bend. Despite the protests of the Lower Creek chiefs who had fought with Jackson, the Creek people signed away twenty three million acres of their homeland to the U.S. government, land that is now part of the states of Alabama and Georgia. Jackson saw the Creek War as an Indian civil war so that both sides owed compensation to the United States for money spent and American lives lost. Some Creeks accepted the terms and vowed to live in peace. Others rejected the treaty and fled to Florida and joined with their cousins the Seminoles, which would lead to forty more years of intermittent Indian warfare against the U.S. in Florida.[134]

The August 9, 1814 treaty began a series of treaties with the Creek Indians. In was for the signing and enforcement of these treaties with the Creeks that Captain Gustavus Loomis was sent to the Creek Nation. After the First Seminole War of 1817–1818 (discussed in the previous chapter), the Creeks and the U.S. again signed a treaty on January 8, 1821. This treaty with the Creeks at Indian Springs, Georgia, ceded additional Creek lands to the U.S. Government. Two more treaties were signed in 1825 and 1826.

---

133 For an elaboration on this theme, see Sean M. O'Brien, *In Bitterness and in Tears: Andrew Jackson's Destruction of the Creeks and Seminoles,* (Guilford, CT: The Lyons Press, 2005).

134 Carl Waldman, *Atlas of the North American Indian,* (New York: Checkmark Books, 2000), p. 143.

Captain Gustavus Loomis was present to support the signing and enforcement of these 1825 and 1826 treaties.

The 1825 treaty was called the Treaty of Indian Springs. On February 12, 1825, a Creek chief with a white father and a Creek mother named William McIntosh signed a treaty with other chiefs as representatives of the Creek nation. McIntosh signed away almost all the remaining Creek land in Georgia. The Creeks were therefore required to migrate across the Mississippi River where compensation acre-for-acre would be granted. Also, a huge government annuity was granted the Creek nation by the U.S. Government.

The Creek spokesman at the signing of the 1825 Treaty of Indian Springs was William McIntosh (1778-1825). Raised as Creek, he never knew his white Tory father. Since the Creeks were a matriarchal society, it mattered little to the Creeks that McIntosh had a white father. In the 1813-1814 Creek War McIntosh fought along Andrew Jackson as a leader of the allied Lower Creeks. In the 1817-1818 First Seminole War McIntosh again fought along-side Andrew Jackson.[135] Despite the fact that the Upper or Red Stick Creeks vowed to kill anyone who signed a treaty with the U.S., McIntosh and eight other Creek chiefs signed the February, 12, 1825 Treaty of Indian Springs.

McIntosh was a flamboyant individual and a skilled military tactician. He was a slave owner, a successful farmer and supported U.S. Indian Agents in bringing American civilization to the Creeks. He also personally benefited from enormous financial compensation given to him by the U.S. Government for signing the Indian Springs Treaty. One wonders what Captain Gustavus Loomis thought of the eccentric William McIntosh. Loomis and his infantry soldiers were on security duty for the signing of the 1825 treaty. Loomis and McIntosh met and may have spoken but were

---

135 David S. Heidler and Jeanne T. Heidler, *Old Hickory's War: Andrew Jackson and the Quest for Empire,* (Louisiana State University Press, 2003), pp. 15, 27, 140-143.

not friends. It was part of the U.S. Army's responsibilities to provide safety to all individuals involved in the treaty signings. In this
the Army failed. On April 30, 1825, the Creek Red Stick leader
Menawa led a war party against William McIntosh for signing the
peace treaty. His house was set on fire and as he attempted to escape he was killed by his fellow Creeks.

In addition to the 1825 Treaty of Indian Springs, Captain
Gustavus Loomis was also on duty within the Creek Nation for
the negotiations related to the 1826 treaty called the Treaty of
Washington. This treaty was an adjustment to the 1825 Treaty of

Indian Springs and essentially voided
it. After the murder of William McIntosh in April, 1825, the Creeks and the
U.S. Indian Agents continued to argue,
debate and negotiate. The stress level
was very high. This was a tense time for
Captain Loomis and his soldiers, as the
Creeks already expressed their willing-
ness to kill if they continued to be dis-
respected and their demands for compensation were not met. Negotiations
dragged on for months, as the majority
of Creeks wholly rejected the February 12, 1825 Treaty of Indian Springs.

Painting of William McIn-
tosh, by Charles B. King,
early 1820s.
Public domain image.

Captain Loomis and his troops were busy keeping Creeks from
killing Creeks, were providing physical security for provisions
donated by the U.S. Government, were maintaining guard and
patrol duties, and served as a show of force to the Indians. The
Treaty of Washington, signed on January 24, 1826 by Secretary
of War James Barbour in Washington, had many Creeks present
at the signing. This new treaty allowed Creeks to keep three

million acres in Alabama, provided a huge financial incentive, and guaranteed a perpetual annuity to the Creeks guaranteed by the U.S. Government.

During his time within the Creek Nation it is impossible in detail to trace Captain Gustavus Loomis' activities. We do know he was mobile, at various locations within Creek lands. We do know he was at Indian Springs, Georgia, located between Atlanta and Macon, for the signing of Indian Springs Treaty in 1825. Whether or not he spent time at Fort Deposit, in northern Alabama on the Tennessee River, or at Fort Strother in central Alabama, we do not know. Captain Loomis must have been stationed at Fort Mitchell along the Chattahoochee River, for a few reasons. First, Fort Mitchell was a key location for Creek and American negotiations. Second, the fort was renovated in 1825, meaning that it was the best location for him to reside within the Creek Nation. Also, Loomis with his engineering background from West Point and experience as an artilleryman was a key person to consult with about construction plans and artillery lanes of fire for Fort Mitchell.

Captain Loomis served for almost two years within the Creek Nation. His West Point biographical summary simply states, "in Creek Nation, 1825-26."[136] An article about Gustavus Loomis states he served "two years in the Creek Nation in Alabama."[137] Whatever Loomis thought of his duty with the Creeks is not recorded. We do know, however, that in mid-1826 he received orders to report for duty at Cantonment Clinch, near Pensacola, Florida.

After the conclusion of the First Seminole War in 1818, the Indians were slow to move onto reservation lands in central Florida.

---

136 George W. Cullum, *Biographical Register of the Officers and Graduates of the U.S. Military Academy, at West Point, NY,* (New York: 1868), p. 118.

137 Carolyn T. Foreman, "Gustavus Loomis: Commandant Fort Gibson and Fort Towson," *Chronicles of Oklahoma,* Vol. 18, September, 1940, pp. 219-220.

The Treaty of Moultrie Creek was an agreement signed in 1823 between the United States and numerous chiefs of the Seminole Indians. The intent was to settle the Seminoles on a reservation in the central part of Florida, away from the coasts and the influence of Spanish traders. The treaty was negotiated in September 1823 at Moultrie Creek, south of St. Augustine. About four hundred and twenty-five Seminoles attended the meeting.

In obedience to the terms of the treaty, the Seminoles placed themselves under the protection of the United States and gave up all claims to lands in Florida in exchange for a reservation of about four million acres. A show of U.S. military force was needed to encourage the Seminoles to migrate to the reservation and to help minimize local raids. A series of incidents in the mid-1820s over land and cattle raised the tension between Indians and white settlers. The local militia was on duty and off duty depending on the crisis at hand. Although the Seminoles did not know it, the U.S. policy was to concentrate the Seminoles on a reservation so that they may later be easily moved west of the Mississippi.[138]

Under the 1823 Treaty of Moultrie Creek, the U.S. Government was obligated to safeguard the Seminoles as long as they remained peaceful and law-abiding. The federal government was supposed to distribute farming tools and livestock, seeds, financial compensation for their relocation, and provide rations for the year, until the Seminoles could plant and harvest new crops. The U.S. government also pledged to pay the tribe an annuity for twenty years and provide economic and civil incentives. In turn, the Seminoles had to allow roads to be built across their reservation and had to return any runaway slaves to United States jurisdiction. The Moultrie Creek treaty was difficult to enforce,

---

138 John K. Mahon, *History of the Second Seminole War*, 1835-1842, (University of Florida Press, 1895), p. 56. John Missall and Mary Lou Missall, *The Seminole Wars: America's Longest Indian Conflict,* (University Press of Florida, 2004), pp. 69-72

as the U.S. Government supplies were slow in coming; as the rations supplied were distasteful; as financial compensation was soon traded away for alcohol; and as crops did not grow as well in central Florida as in the homelands of the Seminoles. Further, the Seminoles were very attached to runaway Negro slaves and welcomed them into their clans, meaning that they were slow to return them to the whites or refused to do so.[139]

In mid-1826, Captain Gustavus Loomis was sent to Florida to encourage the last remnants of Seminoles in north Florida to migrate south to the reservation. He was also responsible to insure that the Seminoles stayed on their reservation, that U.S. Government supplies were properly delivered and distributed, and that skirmishes between whites and Indians were eliminated. Of particular irritation to Loomis were the unscrupulous whites who sought to take advantage of the Seminoles through corrupt business deals and overpriced alcohol sales. As Captain Loomis and his soldiers in the First Infantry Regiment arrived in Florida to enforce the Moultrie Creek Treaty, they were assigned to Cantonment Clinch, near Pensacola.

Located three miles north of Pensacola, Cantonment Clinch was in existence from 1823-1834. It was built along the Escambia River near the Alabama border as an outpost to encourage Creeks and Seminoles in the Florida panhandle to migrate to reservation lands in central Florida. The U.S. also wanted a fort near Pensacola to discourage any activities by the Spanish or English in the area. Fort building in Florida was not based on a consistent policy but on expediency. They were built to respond to immediate and local needs. Some forts were more permanent, especially those along the coast. Others were temporary supply depots or hastily constructed fighting positions. Hundreds of forts were built in Florida in the

139 John K. Mahon, *History of the Second Seminole War*, pp. 60-61.

mid–1800s, most of which are long forgotten. Cantonment Clinch was one of the hundreds of Florida forts that served a specific purpose for a set period of time, and was disbanded.[140]

At Cantonment Clinch, Captain Loomis was ever mindful of Creeks and Seminoles desiring to leave Florida and return to their traditional homelands in Alabama. This could not be allowed. In addition to his duties enforcing the Treaty of Moultrie Creek, Gustavus Loomis was active in a variety of military missions throughout northern Florida. The U.S. Army in Florida was involved in numerous engineering projects. Roads needed to be built. Swamps needed to be drained. Supply depots needed to be assembled. And forts needed to be built. Soldiers with engineering training, like that which Captain Loomis received at the U.S. Military Academy, were invaluable in opening inland waterways by dredging operations so that the army could use steam boats in inland Florida.[141] One project that Loomis worked on was the congressionally mandated road to be built and maintained between Saint Augustine on the Florida Atlantic coast, to Pensacola on the Florida Gulf of Mexico coast. Loomis and his troops at Cantonment Clinch participated heartily in this engineering project.

There was not much fighting for the U.S. Army to do in Florida in the 1820s. True, there were occasional opportunities for the army to display its power to intimidate deviant whites and Seminoles. But for most of the time the army was focused on engineering projects to open up central Florida to white settlers. In the 1820s, soldiers were more familiar with the axe and the shovel than the musket. Soldiers herded animals, chopped wood, planted crops and of course built forts, supply depots and roads. Many soldiers from throughout the United States enjoyed

---

140 Ernest F. Dibble, "Giveaway Forts: Territorial Forts and the Settlement of Florida," *Florida Historical Quarterly*, vol. 78, Fall, 1999), pp. 210, 219-222.
141 Ernest F. Dibble, "Giveaway Forts...", pp. 223-224.

Florida, and at the end of their military enlistment settled in the area. As the army moved so did the camp followers, always eager to make easy money off of lonely soldiers or wayward Seminoles. Former soldiers and militiamen started businesses near the army camps and in proximity to the Seminole Reservation, intending to make fast money off of the vulnerable.

While serving at Cantonment Clinch, Captain Loomis had access to nearby Pensacola. Pensacola was a historic city settled by the Spanish in 1559. This strategically located multicultural city had many rulers, namely the First Spanish Period (1559-1719); the French Period (1719-1722); the Second Spanish Period (1722-1763); the British Period (1763-1781); the Third Spanish Period (1781-1819); the First United States Period (1819-1861); the Confederate States Period (1861-1865); and the Second United States period (1865-Present). The Pensacola that Captain Gustavus Loomis and his family enjoyed in the mid-1820s was a city only recently acquired from Spain. In 1825 the U.S. Congress approved a site for the Pensacola Naval Yard and appropriated six thousand dollars for a lighthouse. Pensacola did not grow as large as other Gulf of Mexico ports such as New Orleans, as there was no inland waterway connecting Pensacola to river ports within the Unites States. Pensacola was primarily a strategic military location with a deep port and a sheltered harbor.

Much of the United States in the early nineteenth century was consumed with Protestant evangelical awakenings and revivals. The city of Pensacola in the 1820s was directly affected by this movement. Only since 1821, when Florida became an official United States territory, was religious freedom for Protestants allowed. The first evangelical Christians to arrive in Pensacola in 1821 were Methodists and Presbyterians, the Methodists having the greatest initial influence through the missionary Rev. Alexander Talley of the Mississippi Conference. Initially the Methodists held church in the Pensacola courthouse and in a theater, with their first church services conducted in their own new building in June, 1828.[142] The Presbyterians also arrived in Pensacola in 1821, but had a much slower start than the Methodists, with only two Presbyterians in Pensacola in 1827.

There is no doubt that the majority of soldiers who served with Gustavus Loomis in the 1820s in Florida had significant exposure to a turbulent and sectarian Christianity. The religious culture of the south was open to diverse religious trends and rivalries, from Mormonism to Millennialism and even to Spiritism. In this turbulent period, the most dominant religious force was still the conservative Christian revivalism of men like Captain Loomis. Nevertheless there was a growing secularism. In the developing states, a jingoism or patriotic chauvinism was epidemic.[143] While evangelical type religion was the most visible and vocal trend of this period, there remained a significant number of Americans, both rural and urban, who made no profession of the historic Christian faith and were instead secular, nationalistic, irreverent, atheistic, or perhaps simply inattentive to the religious controversies of the period.

While stationed at Cantonment Clinch near Pensacola, Captain Loomis and his wife Julia and daughter Eliza attended church services at the Methodist Episcopal Church in Pensacola. This church dates back to 1821, when a mission was established by the Mississippi Conference and the Rev. Alexander Talley was appointed as missionary to Mobile, Pensacola and adjoining areas. The mission began by holding meetings in the courthouse and the old theater

---

142 "History of the First United Methodist Church of Pensacola," www.pensacola-firstchurch.com.

143 Sidney E. Ahlstrom, *A Religious History of the American People*, (Yale University Press, 1972), pp.474-476.

of Pensacola. In 1827 a lot was purchased on the northeast corner of Intendencia and Tarragona Streets and a church structure was built. The first services were held in the new building on June 2, 1828. Rev. Alexander Talley (c.1790-1835) was first recommended to the ministry through the South Carolina Conference in 1809. He was ordained a deacon in 1811 and elected an elder in 1814. Talley was a circuit riding, evangelistic preacher who sought to build churches and to save souls. He had medical training which assisted his church ministry. There is no doubt that Gustavus Loomis fully supported his ministry. In speaking of Alexander Talley, "While he was not as elegant and eloquent as some others in the pulpit, yet he was a popular and successful preacher. His pulpit was commanding and impressive... He was a man of

An early representation of the first building of the Methodist Episcopal Church, Pensacola, Florida. The building was completed in 1828 and served the church until a new building was constructed in 1881. Source: *First United Methodist Church History,* www.pensacolafirstchurch.com.

strong Christian character, and of more than ordinary mental ability... he was a steady devotee of the cause he espoused."[144]

In December, 1827, Rev. Alexander Talley was reassigned to the Choctaw Mission in Mississippi, replaced by Rev. Charles Hardy. In 1825 we know that there were thirty-seven white members and forty-seven black members of the Methodist Episcopal Church in Pensacola.[145] Two of the white members were Gustavus and Julia Loomis. In 1827 there were between twenty-five

144 Anson West, *A History of Methodism in Alabama,* (Nashville, TN: 1893), pp. 250-251.
145 Anson West, *A History of Methodism in Alabama, p. 254.*

and forty Sunday school scholars, three of whom were Gustavus Loomis, Julia Loomis and eight years old Eliza Loomis. Captain Loomis' commanding officer at Cantonment Clinch, Colonel Duncan Clinch, was also an active member of the Methodist Episcopal Church in Pensacola.

Colonel Duncan Clinch (1787-1849) was a native of North Carolina and a career Army officer, commissioned as a First Lieutenant in July of 1808. He had undistinguished service in the War of 1812, was rapidly promoted through the officer ranks, and achieved some notoriety in July of 1816 in a successful military action against the Negro and Seminole stronghold in Florida called the Negro Fort. Later he became in 1819 a colonel of the 8th Infantry. In this capacity he became in January, 1827 the senior army commander in all Florida. He had direct command over his own 8th Infantry Regiment as well as a battalion of the 1st Infantry Regiment. Captain Gustavus Loomis was in the 1st Infantry and was under the orders of Colonel Clinch. As senior officer, Duncan Clinch was known as a fair and compassionate man, one who spoke well to common soldiers and was steady under pressure. As a child of the south he supported slavery, and was known as a man of "deep religious convictions."[146] Colonel Duncan Clinch lived at Cantonment Clinch near the Loomis family. They attended the same church in Pensacola and considered each other brethren in the faith. Years later, an enlisted soldier in the Second Seminole War mentioned, "I only remember one man that made even a profession of Christianity and that was our commander, Gen. D.L. Clinch."[147] No doubt it was a pleasure for Captain Gustavus Loomis to serve under a dedicated Christian commander.

The Loomis family at Cantonment Clinch had a good life.

---

146 John K. Mahon, *History of the Second Seminole War*, p. 66.

147 John Bemrose, *Reminiscences of the Second Seminole War*, (1856[?]: Reprinted by University of Florida Press, 1966), p. 54.

Gustavus was able to be home most evenings, Julia was content as a military wife and mother, and Eliza was advancing well in school, taught at home by her mother. As the head of his home, Captain Loomis led the family in daily prayers and devotional readings. The entire family experienced good health. Spiritually, they were happy with the revivalist preaching at the Methodist Episcopal Church in Pensacola. The Seminoles and Creeks in northern Florida had mostly moved onto reservation lands in central Florida. The Indian threat in the Florida panhandle was almost nonexistent. This meant that changes were coming for the stationing of soldiers in Florida. Under orders from Brevet Major General Winfield Scott, in late 1827 four companies of regular army soldiers were pulled away from Colonel Duncan Clinch at Cantonment Clinch and sent to New Orleans.[148] One of those soldiers was Captain Gustavus Loomis.

New Orleans in 1827 was a booming city. Located where the Mississippi River empties into the Gulf of Mexico, the city had a distinct European culture. Its location was beautified and stabilized out of the surrounding swamps. The city quickly became a haven for travelers along the Mississippi River, an island of civilization in an ocean of wilderness.[149] In the early 1800s, France owned New Orleans, but the city's annexation to the United States was inevitable. After the Louisiana Purchase from France in 1803, thousands of settlers, pioneers and adventurers came to New Orleans as the gateway to the Mississippi River and the massive newly acquired lands from France. In 1803 the U.S. Army Corps of Engineers began work on the never-ending task of containing and controlling the outlet of the Mississippi into the Gulf of Mexico. The expanding U.S. used the Mississippi River as a

---

148 John K. Mahon, *History of the Second Seminole War*, pp. 66-67.
149 Donald McNabb and Louis E. Madere, Jr., "A History of New Orleans," www. Madere.com/history, p. 6.

water highway moving people and goods thousands of miles in safety. It was the work of army engineers that allowed riverboats and later steamboats safe access in and out of New Orleans.

By around 1810 the U.S. Congress was being urged by representatives from the western states and territories to explore, dredge and map the Mississippi River and its tributaries. River traffic was rapidly expanding in pace with westward expansion. Farmers in the Ohio Valley shipped their produce all the way to New Orleans and safe maritime passage was essential. In 1819 Congress authorized an engineering survey of the Mississippi and its tributaries for the purpose of improving river navigation. By 1821 the Mississippi River was mapped from Saint Louis to New Orleans. In 1824 federal funding poured into various Mississippi River projects, as President James Monroe signed the first law committing the federal government to improve transportation on the Mississippi River.[150] It was within this surge of interest and activity that Captain Gustavus Loomis was transferred from Cantonment Clinch in Florida to New Orleans.

The 1810 Census revealed New Orleans to have a population of ten thousand, making it the fifth largest city in the U.S. behind New York, Philadelphia, Boston, and Baltimore. By 1830 New Orleans was America's third largest city, behind New York and Baltimore. The rapidly expanding city of New Orleans needed major assistance in developing its strategic location for westward expansion. Soldiers with engineering training like Captain Gustavus Loomis were quickly utilized in figuring out how to improve navigation and flood control. The engineering goal was to develop and maintain safe river channels for commerce and migration. This was a dangerous waterway with fast currents, hidden shoals, numerous snags (toppled trees), wrecked ships and tons of

---

150 Albert E. Cowdrey, "Land's End: A History of the New Orleans District, U.S. Army Corps of Engineers," (Office of the District Engineer, 1977), pp. 4-6.

garbage that floated downstream. The Army Corps of Engineers was directed to make the waterways in and around New Orleans safe, a task that continues to this day.

Captain Loomis worked on engineer projects in New Orleans from 1827-28. His mathematic and cartographic skills were utilized and tested in the areas of flood control, hydraulics, soils erosion, the building of levees, and maritime navigation. This work with the engineers was somewhat similar duty to that which he performed several years earlier with the U.S. Coastal Survey in and around New York City. There is no doubt that an outdoorsman with a keen analytical mind like Loomis enjoyed this engineering work around the waters surrounding New Orleans.

The raucous and expanding city of New Orleans with its annual Mardi Gras revelry did not appeal to the New England puritan roots of the Loomis family. The largely Roman Catholic city with its mix of European and frontier culture was certainly an interesting place to live. Like all cities in America at that time, there were commerce districts that were safe and other neighborhoods where hoodlums dwelt. The waterfront culture attracted crooks, prostitutes, gamblers and other adventurers. In 1824 New Orleans began to develop its lasting reputation as a party town, as Quadroons (one-quarter Negro blood) and Octoons (one-eight Negro blood) began to celebrate in earnest. Reports abounded that private parties with alcohol were being held, with "masking and intimate goings-on" said to be taking place.[151] Dancing and sexual promiscuity were routine. The wealthy lived along side the destitute. New Orleans was dominated by the large Saint Louis Cathedral, constructed in 1794 in a prominent location by the gardens on Jackson Square. The Loomis' were living in New Orleans when the well-beloved priest of Saint Louis, Father Pere

---

151 "New Orleans & Mardi Gras History Timeline," www.mardigrasdigest.com/html/ mardi_gras_history_timeline. Accessed November 4, 2009.

Antoine, was laid to rest on January 22, 1829 after the largest funeral service in the city up to that time. For more than forty years this remarkable Capuchin priest labored in New Orleans.[152] Overall, New Orleans was a comfortable place for the Loomis family to live, though the cultural norms of the city did not appeal to the Loomis' tastes.

In 1828 Captain Loomis was transferred from engineering duties to recruiting service in New Orleans. He served in this new capacity from 1828 to 1830. This was the kind of military move that made Mrs. Loomis very happy. She did not have to move her household, disrupt her daughter's home education, or settle into another church. In 1830, Eliza was becoming a young lady of twelve years old. The job of military recruiting that Captain Loomis commenced was similar to his recruiting duty in New York City in the early 1820s. New Orleans, like New York, was a city overwhelmed with immigrants, settlers and adventurers. Many were unemployed or disenfranchised. While Loomis must have enjoyed recruiting young men into the army, such administrative duties can become routine and monotonous. Loomis' mundane life of an army recruiting officer was interrupted by the joyful news that he was promoted to the rank of brevet Major on April 7, 1829 for faithful service ten years in one grade.[153]

Captain and later brevet Major Gustavus Loomis and his family attended church in New Orleans at the First Presbyterian Church. The church organized in 1818 and first met in 1819 as the second protestant church to be founded in New Orleans. The first minister, Rev. Sylvester Larned, began services in 1818 but died in 1820 of Yellow Fever at only twenty-four years old.

152 "History of Saint Louis Cathedral," www.stlouiscathedral.org/early_history. Accessed November 7, 2009.

153 George W. Cullum, *Biographical Register,* p. 118. A brevet rank meant the soldier had the rank and prestige but not more pay. It typically preceded an official promotion.

Pastor Larned (1796–1820) was well educated through Middle-bury College and Princeton Seminary. As an evangelical Calvin-ist, Rev. Larned was a firm supporter of revivals and the Sec-ond Great Awakening. He laid a strong doctrinal foundation for the church.[154] After his death in 1820, the next minister was Rev. Theodore Clapp. The unorthodox theology of Theodore Clapp (1792–1866) split the congregation into Unitarians verses Cal-vinists. Rev. Clapp attended Calvinistic and revivalist schools, namely Yale and Andover. As early as 1824, Pastor Clapp shared with the First Presbyterian Church his reservations about tradi-tional Protestant Reformation doctrines. The Mississippi Presby-tery convicted Clapp of heresy and expelled him. The majority of the church went with their pastor across the street to form a church which became Unitarian and Universalist.[155] Meanwhile the First Presbyterian Church retained its name and its building but was small in membership. The new pastor who ministered to the Loomis family was Rev. Joel Parker.

The First Presbyterian Church that welcomed Rev. Joel Parker (1799–1873) was in desperate need of leadership. Parker studied at Hamilton College and Auburn Theological Seminary and in 1826 was ordained pastor of the Presbyterian Church in Rochester, New York. He first came to New Orleans in 1829 or 1830 to preach at the First Presbyterian Church and was called to be pastor shortly thereafter. A native Vermonter, Rev. Parker and Major Loomis had much in common. Both supported reviv-als and the Second Great Awakening. Both were intellectually bright and conversant on a wide range of theological issues. Both were Vermonters. And both rejected Unitarianism. After serving

---

154 *Biographical Sketch and Obituary of Rev. Sylvester Larned,* (1822), pp. 1–5.

155 "Theodore Clapp," *Dictionary of the Unitarian and Universalist Association,* http:// www25.uua.org- /uuhs/duub /articles/theodoreclapp, pp. 1–2. Accessed November 2, 2009.

in New Orleans, Rev. Joel Parker returned to New York where he served as a pastor and as President of Union Theological Seminary. Later he pastored in Philadelphia and Newark. Princeton Seminary granted him the degree of Doctor of Divinity in 1839. Dr. Parker was a frequent contributor to the religious press and was a guest lecturer at Princeton Seminary, sharing research and writing projects with the Princeton seminary faculty. A summary of Pastor Joel Parker's preaching is as follows:

> His sermons are marked by strong and deep excitement; yet the excitement is calm, subdued, never rising into passion, never seeming to throw the mind of the speaker from his balance. This sort of excitement, this earnest breathing through every argument, and every expression, yet never growing tempestuous, is the most favorable to the triumph of excellence.[156]

The Gustavus Loomis family enjoyed their tour of duty in New Orleans. In his military career, brevet Major Loomis was progressing. He now was undoubtedly a career military officer, devoting his life to his God, his family and his country. Upon leaving New Orleans in 1830, Gustavus Loomis completed almost twenty years of military service. As far as we know, Loomis had not fired a weapon against an enemy since 1813, but that would all change at his next assignment, as he reported to Fort Crawford, Michigan Territory, in the present state of Wisconsin.

---

156 "Universalism," *The Quarterly Christian Speculator*, (vol. V, 1833), p. 267.

CHAPTER EIGHT

FORT CRAWFORD AND THE BLACK HAWK WAR, 1830-1833

IT WAS A LONG RIVERBOAT ride against the current which took brevet Major Gustavus Loomis and his family north from New Orleans to Ft. Crawford in Michigan Territory. The Loomis' had never visited this part of the United States before. No doubt the refreshing change of climate made Gustavus and Julia Loomis homesick for New England. Their relaxing riverboat voyage north allowed them to see various traders, merchants, mariners and settlers on makeshift vessels plying their way along the Mississippi River. Stops along the way in such bustling cities as Memphis and Saint Louis allowed the Loomis family to see an expanding and progressing America. The newly promoted brevet Major Gustavus Loomis had nothing but positive thoughts about his new assignment at Fort Crawford.

Fort Crawford was constructed in 1816 as a wooden fort as a forward deployed presence for the U.S. Army. The town of Prairie du Chien, on the upper Mississippi River in what was later called Wisconsin, was the location for Fort Crawford. Because of annual flooding, the army abandoned the unhealthy fort in 1826. Indian troubles caused the army to relocate a few troops at the derelict fort. Major General Edmund Gaines inspected Fort Crawford in 1827 and reported that the fort was so moldy and decayed that it was unhealthy for the troops.[157] In 1829 new land at a better location was selected to rebuild Fort Crawford under the direction of the new commander, Lieutenant Colonel Zachary Taylor. The War Department insisted on a stone fort which could better withstand the annual flooding of the Mississippi River. When the Loomis family arrived at Fort Crawford in 1830 they were welcomed to a new fort under construction in an increasingly volatile part of America.

Brevet Major Loomis joined an army force at Fort Crawford of ten officers and one hundred and seventy-three men, all of the 1st Infantry Regiment. Indian troubles were raging. In 1804, William Henry Harrison as a government agent negotiated a treaty with the Sauk and Fox Nations. This gave the white man all the lands these Indians possessed east of the Mississippi River. For all this land the Indians received financial compensation and promises that they could still use the land until the white settlers arrived. One of the Sauk Indians that was infuriated by this treaty was Black Hawk.[158]

An experienced shaman, leader and warrior of the Sauk Indians was Black Hawk (1767-1838). He was not a hereditary chief of the tribe but was nevertheless influential. He was born in Saukenuk, the historic and holy village of the Sauk people. Black Hawk came to prominence as a forty-five year old warrior fighting with the British against the Americans in the War of 1812. He had always hated the idea of ceding land to the whites, especially when the ceded land included the sacred Saukenuk. Black Hawk saw the 1804 treaty with the whites as invalid, in that a full tribal council had not been called and that those who did represent the

---

157 Bruce E. Mahon, *Old Fort Crawford and the Frontier*, (State Historical Society of Iowa: 2000), p. 120.

158 Black Hawk dictated his biography in 1833 to John B. Patterson. See *Black Hawk: An Autobiography,* (1833: reprinted in 1955 by the University of Illinois Press).

tribes at the treaty signing had no authority to speak for the Sauk and Fox peoples. During the War of 1812 Black Hawk was granted the rank of brevet Brigadier General by the British. After the war Black Hawk signed a peace treaty with the Americans which reaffirmed the treaty of 1804, of which Black Hawk later protested his ignorance.

As a result of the 1804 treaty and the expanding white settlements, various tribes such as the Chippewas, Winnebagoes, Kickapoos, Sioux, Potawatomies, Sauks, and Foxes began slowly migrating west. It was not until 1828 that the remaining Sauk and Fox Indians moved west of the Mississippi River, including Black Hawk. Between 1828 and 1830, Black Hawk could not adjust to life west of the Mississippi River. He could not accept the fact that his people were driven off their historic farming and hunting lands. Most important, Black Hawk refused to accept the fact that the sacred village of Saukenuk, his birthplace and the

A painting of Black Hawk, c.1835.
Public domain image.

place of the graves of his ancestors, was no longer controlled by his people. Beginning in 1830, around the time that brevet Major Gustavus Loomis and his family arrived at Fort Crawford, Black Hawk began his military activities against the United States.[159]

Life at Fort Crawford for brevet Major Loomis and his wife and daughter was somewhat predictable. Garrison life within the walls of the fort began at dawn with trumpeters playing reveille. Roll call was taken, the facilities were cleaned and the horses

---

159 Kerry A. Trask, *Black Hawk: The Battle for the Heart of America,* (New York: Henry Holt & Company, 2006), pp. 101-107.

were attended. After breakfast at 0900 the tasks of the day were begun. The officer of the day made sure that all the troops were working and that all went smoothly. Tasks accomplished consisted of gardening, chopping wood, patrols, stone quarrying, guard duty, and construction of the fort. At 1500 hours another role call was performed and then dinner. More work was then completed and drills and ceremony were performed before the dress parade every day at sunset.[160]

For entertainment the officers occasionally held formal balls and invited residents, especially ladies, from Prairie du Chien to at-

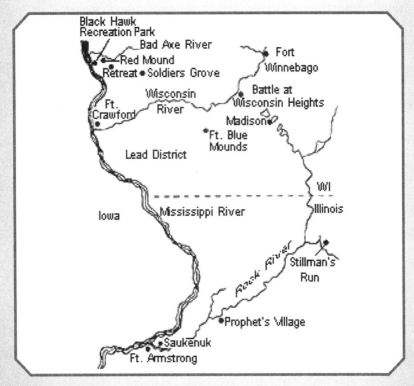

Battles and other key sites of the Black Hawk War.
Source: http://blackhawkwar.webs.com/battlesblackhawkwar.

---

160 Bruce E. Mahon, *Old Fort Crawford and the Frontier,* pp. 241-250.

tend. Fort Crawford had a library but at this time there was no chapel and no chaplain. The physician at the fort, Dr. William Beaumont, often taught school for the children, sharing this responsibility with officers who had graduated from West Point and with the mothers. During the winter, families were resigned to winter quarters within the fort, but the rest of the year there was a social network of soldier's wives between Fort Crawford, Fort Snelling and Fort Winnebago. For recreation, soldiers hunted and fished. Brevet Major Gustavus Loomis held a Bible study at the fort. Soldiers found innocent ways to amuse themselves. The abuse of alcohol was strictly forbidden. Visiting Prairie du Chien offered some distractions to the mundane garrison life at Fort Crawford.

While stationed at Fort Crawford the Loomis family worshiped at the First Congregational Church of Prairie du Chien. The basis of the church was a small Sunday School which began meeting in 1824, as there was no Protestant church in town. The Loomis family arrived in 1830 and quickly added three to this fledgling group. In March, 1831 the first minister arrived, Rev. Oratus Kent. He stayed as pastor of the Congregational Church in Prairie du Chien from March to November, 1831. The small group then reverted to various men reading sermons and leading prayer meetings, one of which was

An undated image of Rev. David Lowry. Source: www.cumberland.org/hfcpc/minister/LowryDavid.

Gustavus Loomis. Then in 1832 a school teacher came for six months and preached to the group on Sundays; his name is lost to history. Finally in the fall of 1832 Rev. David Lowry arrived to serve as the Congregational Church pastor from 1832-1840.[161]

---

161 *Historical Sketch of the First Congregational Church, Prairie du Chien*, Wisconsin, (Prairie du Chien: 1891), pp. 1-3.

Pastor David Lowry (1796-1877) was a poor Kentuckian who was converted in a revival at age eighteen. He soon became a candidate for the ministry and was quickly licensed and then ordained. His early ministries were associated with the Cumberland Presbyterians in Kentucky and Indiana. He preached an evangelical Calvinism that was less rigid than that of Princeton Seminary and other orthodox bastions of the faith. His early years of ministry were spent as a revival preacher at camp meetings. While debating Unitarians his defense of the divinity of Jesus Christ was compelling.[162] Around 1830 Lowry was editor of a religious magazine that promoted evangelicalism and the Second Great Awakening in Nashville, Tennessee. While in Nashville he became acquainted with General Andrew Jackson, who encouraged Rev. Lowry to accept a position as an Indian Agent near Prairie du Chien. At this new location he started a mission school for Indians, served as an Indian Agent for the U.S. Government, and pastored the First Congregational Church in Prairie du Chien. For approximately two years David Lowry was the pastor for the Gustavus Loomis family. Of Rev. Lowry it was written;

> MR. LOWRY WAS in many respects a remarkable man. His ability was as marked as his kindness, both, winning for him the warmest friendship and the truest respect of the whole community. His activity and zeal were undaunted... He was an able man, a good man, and the best Indian Agent I ever knew."[163]

In 1830, the U.S. Army was well aware of the tensions with the Indians in the Illinois and Michigan areas. Skirmishes between Indian tribes, or between Indians and whites, were com-

---

162 J.I.D. Hinds, "Memorial Sermon for Rev. David Lowry, D.D.," *The Cumberland Presbyterian*, April 12, 1877, p. 2.
163 *Historical Sketch of the First Congregational Church, Prairie du Chien*, pp. 3-4.

mon. Fort Crawford at Prairie du Chien would play a significant part in these Indian activities. The north quarter of the new fort was completed in the summer of 1830, along with a powder magazine in the southwest corner. All of these structures were made of stone blocks. Meanwhile the Sauk and Fox Indians were crossing and recrossing the Mississippi River. In early 1831 they refused to leave the vicinity of Rock Island for their new promised home in Iowa. In June of 1831, brevet Major Gustavus Loomis and a number of regular army soldiers under the command of General Edmund Gaines pursued the Indians under Black Hawk and forced them to return west of the Mississippi. Because of furloughs and deployments, in July, 1831 Gustavus Loomis was assigned as Commander of Fort Crawford. In this garrison he commanded eleven officers and two hundred and twenty-five men. Loomis remained the Commander at Fort Crawford until turning over command to Colonel Zachary Taylor at the conclusion of the Black Hawk War in August, 1832.[164]

As the Commander of Fort Crawford, brevet Major Loomis oversaw the details of the stone construction of the fort. The construction was interrupted by a cholera outbreak and the constant need to deploy soldiers in support of Indian operations. He was also responsible for the protection, supply and shelter for both the soldiers and their families, and to protect the flow of pioneers who stopped at the fort.

Angered by the loss of the resting place of his ancestors and his birthplace at Saukenuk, in 1830 Black Hawk began a number of military excursions across the Mississippi River, in violation of treaties. Perhaps these were probing missions to test white man's resistance. Each time Black Hawk led the Sauk and Fox warriors back across the Mississippi River without bloodshed. In

---

164 Bruce E. Mahon, *Old Fort Crawford and the Frontier*, p. 135-136.

April, 1832, Black Hawk planned what he must have known was a futile mission. He intended to cross the Mississippi River, join up with other Indian tribes, be resupplied by the British, and then attack the United States. Leading about one thousand warriors and others he entered Illinois and was confronted by the Illinois militia. This lead to the Battle of Stillman's Run on May 14, 1832, where two hundred and seventy-five Illinois militia under Major Isaiah Stillman briefly fought but then fled in a panic from a larger number of Sauk warriors. During the engagement twelve militiamen were killed while making a stand on a small hill. The engagement was the first battle of the 1832 Black Hawk War.

As white women were kidnapped and other families plundered or killed, there developed an attitude that the Indians around northern Illinois and Michigan Territory had to be exterminated. Indian raids grew bolder and more intense, with virtual impunity. On June 9 a raiding party crossed the Mississippi River and began to ransack farms south of Galina, Illinois. On June 14, six white men were farming when attacked. The four killed were scalped and mutilated. On June 16 the militia under Henry Dodge attacked a Sauk and Fox war party by the Pecatonica River and won a small but decisive hand-to-hand skirmish inappropriately called the Battle of Pecatonica. On June 24 Black Hawk and a large war party attacked a small fort along the Apple River where less than twenty-five militiamen held off a much larger Indian force. The next day Black Hawk led his warriors in successful skirmishes against both militia and civilian farmers. Upper Illinois and the lower Michigan Territory was a war zone.[165]

Terrified white settlers, pioneers and farmers flooded into Fort Crawford, under the command of brevet Major Gustavus Loomis. Both local civilians and national newspapers became very critical

---

165 Kerry A. Trask, *Black Hawk: The Battle for the Heart of America*, pp.218-232.

of the U.S. Army in this region. Many were dissatisfied with the leadership of Brigadier General Henry Atkinson, the senior commander. Henry Atkinson (1782-1842) was a North Carolinian who entered the army in 1808 at age twenty-six as a captain in the 3rd Infantry. He saw considerable combat in the War of 1812. In 1813 he was appointed Inspector General for the army and quickly rose through the ranks. In 1814 he became a Colonel in the 45th Infantry. After the War of 1812 Atkinson led two exploratory missions for the army along the Yellowstone River, in 1819 and 1825. His experience working with Indians was extensive. In the Black Hawk War he was a middle-aged officer who had developed a reputation for being careful, calculated and well-organized. Not a person of external bravado, Atkins was reliable and respected by the Indians as a fair and honest man. Often criticized for his hesitancy, General Atkins did ultimately lead the army to a resounding victory in the Black Hawk War.[166]

While brevet Major Gustavus Loomis was fairly autonomous within the walls of his command at Fort Crawford, any significant activities he planned outside the fort had to be approved by General Henry Atkinson. As the senior commander, General Atkinson coordinated army activities over a huge rural geographic area, from Jefferson Barracks at St. Louis in the south, to Fort Snelling in the northern Michigan Territory wilderness. Numerous reports came to Atkins about the Sauk and Fox Indians making war against white settlements. The army and local Indian agents were agreed that the Indians had to be pushed back across the Mississippi River. General Atkins did not quickly go to meet Black Hawk and his warriors in battle. Instead he coordinated his chain of command, consolidated his forces, resupplied his forts, conferred with local Indian agents, and met face to face with his senior commanders.

166 For a detailed study of Henry Atkinson, see Roger L. Nichols, *General Henry Atkinson: A Western Military Career,* (University of Oklahoma Press, 1965).

On April 16, 1832, Brigadier General Henry Atkinson disembarked from the steamer *Enterprise* and met with brevet Major Gustavus Loomis at Fort Crawford. Atkins inspected the troops and discussed with Loomis how to respond to Black Hawk and how to avoid an Indian war between the Sauk and Foxes against the Winnebagos and the Sioux. They discussed protecting white settlers and mining interests in the area. A few days later Atkins ordered Loomis to provide him three companies of soldiers for immediate deployment.[167] Here Loomis was in the thick of the Black Hawk War. Civilians fled to Fort Craw-

ford for protection. The wounded were cared for at the Fort Crawford hospital. Loomis strategized with the senior commander, Brigadier General Atkins. Loomis was responsible for training and equipping troops who came to his fort before deploying. Soldiers, civilians and militiamen who were killed were buried at the Fort Crawford cemetery. And troops assigned to brevet Major Loomis at Fort Crawford were deployed into direct combat with the Sauk and Fox Indians under Black Hawk.

An undated sketch of Brigadier Genera Henry Atkins. Source: www.patriotfiles. com/gallery/showphoto. php?photo=15175.

As General Atkins slowly and methodically prepared for a major campaign against the Sauk and Fox Indians under Black Hawk, the Indians disappeared into the thick swamps of what would later be southern Wisconsin. Black Hawk intended to put distance between his forces and the U.S. troops by heading north into the wilderness, then turning west and evading the Americans until he could lead his people across the Mississippi to safety. At

---

167 Kerry A. Trask, *Black Hawk: The Battle for the Heart of America,* pp. 155-156.

times Black Hawk appeared indecisive and desperate; at other times his strategies were successful. Overall, Black Hawk's plan was a poor one, with the only long-term goal being to return where they had started from months earlier. Through June and July of 1832, the Sauk and Fox Indians under Black Hawk successfully evaded the Americans, while food supplies and stamina were running low. On July 21 Black Hawk was trapped against the Wisconsin River by about seven hundred pursuing militiamen. The Indian warriors fought the militia while their women, children and elderly crossed the river to temporary safety, later joined by the warriors who survived. The fight lasted about one hour and ended with a bayonet charge from the militia which sent the Indians scattering. Casualties at this Battle of Wisconsin Heights were at least forty Indians dead and many more wounded; U.S. casualties were one dead and eight wounded.[168]

Specifically, brevet Major Loomis at Fort Crawford chartered the steamboat *Warrior,* armed the vessel with canon and about twenty men, and sent the vessel north to recruit assistance from the Sioux. Meanwhile some of the fleeing Sauk and Fox Indians reached the Mississippi, only to see the heavily armed *Warrior* waiting for them. With the *Warrior* armed and anchored just fifty yards from shore, the Sauks and Foxes abandoned their efforts to cross the river. Under a white flag, Black Hawk waded out into the river and tried, once again, to surrender. As at Stillman's Run and Wisconsin Heights, the soldiers could not understand him. After ten or fifteen minutes of failed communications, the soldiers on the *Warrior* saw an increasing amount of Indians

---

168 For a full treatment of this battle see Crawford B. Thayer, *The Battle of Wisconsin Heights: An Eyewitness Account of the Battle of Wisconsin Heights of 1832*, (published by the author, 1833 [reprinted 1983]). For a short summary see Robert O. Dodsworth, *The Battle of Wisconsin Heights of 1832*, (Wisconsin Department of Natural Resources, 1996).

gathering at the shore. The Americans opened fire on the Sauks and Foxes. A number of the warriors around Black Hawk died instantly; the rest found cover and returned fire. After a two hour fight the *Warrior's* fuel supply was nearly exhausted and it headed off downriver. The battle with the *Warrior* left nearly two dozen Sauk and Fox warriors dead. It also convinced Black Hawk that safety lay to the north among the Winnebago or Ojibwa villages, rather than to the west across the Mississippi. He pleaded with his people, but few were willing to follow him, as the Indians were intent on returning west to their ancestral lands. Late on August 1, Black Hawk, White Cloud, and thirty or forty others (mostly members of their families) left the main band and headed north. A few more Sauks and Foxes crossed the river before darkness made it too dangerous. Most of the Indians remained on the eastern bank, fatigued and starving.[169]

After the Battle of Wisconsin Heights, hundreds of Sauk and Fox men, women and children made crude rafts and attempted to float down the Wisconsin River away from the Americans. This was a disaster. Many of the Indians drowned while brevet Major Loomis deployed a large flatboat with a canon and twenty-five soldiers to anchor in the middle of the river. On July 29, the lieutenant in charge reported that several canoes full of Indians tried to sneak past them at night and many were killed by army canon and small arms fire.[170] Meanwhile Winnebago and Menominee mercenaries in support of the U.S. hunted through the woods for Sauk and Fox refugees and took many scalps. The U.S. Army was determined to avenge the hundreds of deaths of innocent white settlers, farmers and pioneers, men, women and children, by delivering a decisive and crippling blow to Black Hawk and his Sauk and Fox warriors. Gustavus Loomis then dispatched a

---

169 James Lewis, *The Black Hawk War of 1832,* (Illinois Humanities Council, 2000).
170 Kerry A. Trask, *Black Hawk: The Battle for the Heart of America*, p. 280.

lieutenant to go upriver to the Winnebago and Sioux villages to enlist their support in fencing in Black Hawk and his followers, support which was eagerly granted by the rival tribes. Trapped and surrounded by adversarial Indians, the Mississippi River and the advancing U.S. Army, Black Hawk abandoned his people and fled into the wilderness.[171] All of these activities set up the final battle of the Black Hawk War, the Battle of Bad Axe. Brevet Major Loomis wrote about this as follows:

> LAST EVENING THE steamboat Warrior returned from up the river. Lieut. Kingsbury, who commanded the guard, reports that about 40 miles up the Mississippi River they saw the Sacs and Foxes to a very large number—he presumes their whole force of effective men—on the bank of the river. They hoisted a white flag—but would not send a canoe aboard the steamboat. He told them if they did not do so, he would fire upon them, and did so. He supposes there were five at least of the killed. They were seen to fall by some of the gentlemen on board the steamboat. They appeared much alarmed by the 6 pounder. Lt. K. saw some but not many horses. The boat was obliged to come down for wood.—Lt. K. had gone to the Sioux at Prairie Auxiles to notify them that the Sacs and Foxes were expected to cross into their country—to say to them that they had again been defeated and closely pursued by the army—that we did not want them to fight, but to stop their crossing until the army could come up with them.—150 Sioux started down the river almost immediately and passed the steamboat while she was scraping her boilers a little above Wabashaw's Prairie. They must have heard

171 Kerry A. Trask, *Black Hawk,* pp. 281–282.

the firing of the six pounder, and a half Winnebago was sent by Lt. Kingsbury, to Wabashaw to let him know the Sacs and Foxes had arrived upon the Mississippi. I [Loomis] expect General Atkinson and his combined army, 1600 men strong, will be upon the Mississippi to-day. The steamboat Warrior was sent back with an additional guard, and two Mackinac boats to interrupt their crossing—support the Sioux and communicate with General Atkinson.[172]

Gustavus Loomis made a significant contribution to the Battle of Bad Axe and to the end of the Black Hawk War. Brigadier General Atkinson led the regular army and militia forces in a relentless pursuit westward, trapping Black Hawk and his people against the Mississippi River. Black Hawk expected canoes to be waiting for him at the river but he was disappointed.[173] On August 1, Black Hawk's band of perhaps five hundred starving men, women, and children reached the eastern bank of the Mississippi, a few miles downriver from the Bad Axe River. The leaders called a council meeting in which Black Hawk and the Winnebago prophet White Cloud suggested breaking into small groups, turning north, and hiding out in the Winnebago villages. Others suggested fleeing into the swamps to the north and east. But most of the Sauks and Foxes wanted to build rafts or canoes and cross the river as quickly as possible. There was a crisis in leadership, as Black Hawk could not control or lead his followers. Around this time, brevet Major Gustavus Loomis, who was still being paid as

---

172 Extracts from an August 2, 1832 letter from Gustavus Loomis appeared in the *Sangamo Journal*. See the Northern Illinois University Digitization Projects, http://lincoln.lib.niu.edu/cgibin/philologic/getobject-.pl?c.3952:5:17.lincoln. Accessed September 14, 2009.

173 Allan W. Eckert, *The Twilight of an Empire: A Narrative*, (Ashland, KY: Jesse Stuart Foundation, 2004).

a Captain, wrote a letter to his commanding officer, Brigadier General Henry Atkins.

CAPTAIN GUSTAVUS LOOMIS TO GENERAL HENRY ATKINSON

Fort Crawford, M[ichigan]. T[erritory]... July 31. 9 ock.

The Winnebagos have just bro't in 7 to 9 more prisoners, squaws & children, among them a part Menominie Squaw who says that the whole of the Women and Children are coming down the Ouisconsin. That she cannot count the Canoes -- That they thought they would come and give themselves up to their relations the Menominies -- That there were but 7 men with her party. She does not think there were many men coming down, they had gone with the main Band. She has not seen that band since the battle [on July 21], says they lost in killed 68 men.

I have requested Genl. [and Indian agent Joseph] Street to tell the Winnebagos to go out with flags and endeavor to persuade them all to come in and surrender themselves. I have great hopes that they will do so. I think the possession of the Women and Children will give you a great hold upon the band of B. Hawk. Genl. Street was also of the opinion that we had better take them prisoners. I deem it very important that you should know that Black Hawk is relieved from his women and children -- for he will be able to fly the more rapidly. I could not get any body to go on Express yesterday and now am obliged to pay an exorbitant price for they think that there is great risk of life.

The S.B. [steam boat] Warrior now up the Miss: is to go as far as Wa-ba-shaw and get the Sioux to watch the Shores of the river that the men (Hos. [Hostile] Indians) do not cross with impunity -- the boat has a 6 Pr. [six pound cannon] on

board, Lt. [Reuben] Holmes is also on board and has provi-
sions with him. Wi-ni-shec has not come in with his band. I
fear he is too friendly with the S. & Foxes.   Genl. Street
wishes me to say he is too busy to write. I tried but couldn't
not get a man to go to Galena nor hire a Canoe. I wished
to inform Col. [James M.] Strode and get him to send some
Mounted men to guard the Ouisoncin &c. and prevent their
passing around the ferry by land.

My whole Guard & 6 Pr. are now at the Ferry: I found
that the Musketry of the Guard at the Ferry stopped nearly all
from passing and rendered the 6 Pr. useless below. The Win-
nebago Chief Caramonie has gone out with a part of his band,
2 Frenchmen & a Sac Squaw goes along to assure the fugitives
of security and good treatment as prisoners, until the pleasure
of the President is known.

I have the honor to be very Respectfully, Yr. mo. Servt. G:
Loomis Cap. 1t. Infy. Commg. [Captain, 1ˢᵗ Infantry, Com-
manding]

At 2:00 a.m. on August 2, 1832 the Battle of Bad Axe resumed.
Black Hawk was gone. Bugles roused Brigadier General Henry
Atkinson's men, who dressed, gathered their equipment, collected
their horses, broke camp, and set out before sunrise. Within a
few miles militia scouts under Henry Dodge met the Sauk rear
guard. The warriors tried to slow the army's advance, retreating
and leading the Americans away from the main camp. This tac-
tic succeeded until a militia regiment stumbled across the main
trail and led Atkinson's army toward the Sauk and Fox camp. The
warriors continued to fight, hoping to allow time for more of
the women and children to cross the Mississippi River. Just as
Atkinson's troops pushed them back toward the river, the refueled

steamboat *Warrior* returned and began firing its cannon into them from behind. U.S. army soldiers and Illinois militia fought the Sauk and Fox warriors for eight hours. The battle became a rout. Soldiers shot at any Indian that moved. Other Indians drowned. The steamship *Warrior*, ordered by brevet Major Loomis to attack the Indians, was especially deadly; its canon blasts indiscriminately killing men, women and children. Those who were able to escape across the Mississippi River were hunted down by Sioux warriors, who collected many Sauk and Fox scalps. Prisoners captured by the Americans were brought to Fort Crawford, where they were placed under the supervision of Gustavus Loomis.[174]

At the conclusion of the Black Hawk War, Fort Crawford and its Commander, brevet Major Gustavus Loomis, are frequently mentioned in official army correspondence. General Atkinson set up a temporary headquarters on the east bank of the Mississippi near the Bad Axe battle site. A simple aid station was created with the wounded then sent to Fort Crawford. Soon thereafter General Atkins moved his command post from the field south to Fort Crawford. At the Battle of Bad Axe there were many acts of cruelty upon the Sauk and Fox peoples. Some called the battle a massacre.[175] That all ended at Fort Crawford, where Gustavus Loomis insisted that the Indians be fed, clothed, respected and protected. Loomis was gratified that the starving and disheveled Indians were received and treated with humanity, stating that the U.S. was not at war with women and children.[176]

About one week after the Battle of Bad Axe, brevet Major Loomis was very busy with administrative issues with the local Indian agents and with caring for the needs of hundreds of Indian

174 Kerry A. Trask, *Black Hawk: The Battle for the Heart of America*, pp. 281-290.

175 John A. Wakefield, *Wakefield's History of the Black Hawk War*, (Jacksonville, Ill: 1834), chapters 7-8.

176 Kerry A. Trask, *Black Hawk: The Battle for the Heart of America*, pp. 292.

refugees from various tribes that sought shelter from the raging Indian skirmishes. Keeping peace around Fort Crawford between rival Indian tribes was a difficult task but was performed well by the soldiers. Loomis also spent time visiting the wounded, sharing his faith with those who had faced death and had survived. One of his administrative tasks was to report to his superior officer. Loomis wrote to General Atkinson as follows:

COMMANDER, FORT CRAWFORD

Fort Crawford, / M.T. [Michigan Territory] August 8, 1832.

Sir/ With regard to the measures pursued by me and the operations of the Troops under my command, commencing on the 25th. July 1832, intended to cooperate with the Army in the field under your command to prevent the escape of the hostile Indians, either across the Mississippi or in their descent of the Ouisconsin.

I have the honor to report.—that soon after the receipt of Genl: Dodge's letter 22d. July, a copy of which is enclosed marked 1. Some Winnebago's came down the Mississippi, up which they had gone but a few days before, avowedly to be out of the Way of war, and encamped below this Fort in the Prairie. This circumstance increased my suspicions of their honesty. I requested Genl: Street their Agent to order them above the Fort, which he did. They obeyed an encamped on the Slough about ./3 of a mile above the Fort that evening. I then ordered the A.A. Qr. Mr. [assistant quartermaster] to furnish a light Canoe well manned to send up the Mississippi River to order down the Winnebagos encamped above last their Canoes should facilitate the crossing of the hostile Indians should they arrive on the shores of said River. I requested Genl. Street to send an Interpreter & his Sub-agent which he readily complied with.

That afternoon accompanied by Capt. Estes I examined the Ouisconsin River at the Ferry as to the practicability of a piece of Artillery preventing the enemy's descent of it. On my return I found the Steam Boat Enterprise at the landing with the two Comps of the 4th. Regt of the Infty, from Baton Rouge under the command of Lt. Torrence of said Regiment. I immediately decided to charter the S. Boat and send her up the Mississippi to support those previously sent in the light Canoe and to endeavor to show a force ready to compel obedience.

On the 27th. July I ordered Lt. Torrence to ascend the Mississippi as far as Prairie Le Cross and order down the Winnebago Chief Win-o-sheck and his band. He was again accompanied by the Sub. Ind. Agent and an Interpreter furnished by the Genl. Street. The report of this Trip is marked 3.

On the return of the S. Boat to the Prarie on the evening of the 28th., understanding that the S. Boat Warrior would be at Prairie on the 29th. or 30th., I discharged that Enterprise.

The Detachment of the 4th. under Lt. Ritner, stationed at the mouth of the Ouisconsin with a 6 Pr. in a Flat boat and one Mackinac — Killed some of the enemy in his attempt to pass his command on Saturday night the 28th. July. Lt. Ritner's report is marked 4. The Ferry Guard, the same night fired upon some Canoes passing & in the morning killed one Indian on the Island in front of the Ferry house. These circumstances convinced me that the enemy was, so far as he could, disencumbering himself of his ineffective men and his Women and children — and pointed out his ultimate object to regain the West bank of the Mississippi. On the 30th. the Steam Boat Warrior arrived with Provisions. I ordered the Qr. Mr. to charter her and directed Lt. Kingsbury to take command of the detachment sent on board and also a Six Pr., which put on board and to proceed up the Mississippi. If the Winnebago Chief Win-o-shec had not started to come down from Black River, to hasten him and to proceed as

far as to Wa-ba-shaw's Village and notify the Sioux that the Sacs
and Foxes were flying before the Americans and were expected
to cross the Mississippi into their Country which we hoped to
prevent. Lt. Kingsbury in descending the Missi. had an action
with the hostile Sacs & Foxes who were on the bank of the Missi.
endeavoring to construct rafts to facilitate their crossing. For want
of Wood the S. Boat was obliged to come to Prairie Du chien. I
increased the Guard on board the S. Boat and sent her back under command of the same officer. On the 4th. August Lt. Kingsbury sent me his letter marked 5.1 still required a report which
he has sent me this day and is marked 6.I cannot but speak with
high approbation of the Officers and men under my command.
The support which I have received from those of the 1st Infty left
here in Garrison when the Detachmt. of three Companies from
this Post were cali'd into the field, merits my thanks.I would
also bring to the notice of the General the detachment of the 4th.
Regt who arrived from B. Rouge in 15 days, burning with ardor
to find the enemy and who promptly and cheerfully performed
the duties assigned them. In the operations detailed above I received prompt support from Genl: Street, in all that relates to the
Indian Department.

   I have the honor to be Respectfully your obt. Servt. G: Loomis
Capt. 1ft. Infy Commg. Bridgr Genl. H. Atkinson Commanding, N. W. Army

While the August 1-2, 1832 Battle of Bad Axe was going on,
Black Hawk, "in an act of undisguised self-interest,"[177] abandoned
his followers and travelled northeast through Winnebago country
and made camp in the thick forests of what was later called Wisconsin. Eventually the Winnebagos found Black Hawk and his

---

177 Kerry A. Trask, *Black Hawk: The Battle for the Heart of America*, p. 294.

few dozen companions and persuaded the defeated warrior to give himself up to the Indian Agent, Joseph Street. For over three weeks the whites wondered what happened to Black Hawk. On August 27, Black Hawk and his cohorts entered Prairie du Chien and surrendered at Fort Crawford. This was the first time brevet Major Gustavus Loomis saw the elderly and emaciated war chief. Colonel Zachary Taylor returned from the field and was now in his rightful place as Commander at Fort Crawford, Gustavus Loomis holding that position only in Colonel Taylor's absence.

While staying at a Winnebago village before his surrender, Black Hawk had a special vestment prepared. His surrender was planned by him to be a dignified event. Black Hawk then spoke to the whites, including Gustavus Loomis, as if the Indians were always noble and virtuous. Black Hawk spoke of his bravery in battle and the virtue of his people. No doubt the white refugees who had family members murdered and scalped; or the soldiers who understood that Black Hawk abandoned his people at the battle of Bad Axe; thought that the aged warrior was a fool, an idiot, a beast or a coward. In remembering his surrender, Black Hawk stated,

> DURING MY STAY at the [Winnebago] village, the squaws made me a white dress of deer skin. I then started, with several Winnebagos, and went to their agent [James Street], at Prairie du Chien, and gave myself up… I was then given up by the agent to the commanding officer [Colonel Zachary Taylor] at Fort Crawford… We remained there a short time, and then started to Jefferson Barracks [Saint Louis] in a steam boat, under the charge of a young war chief who treated us with much kindness.[178]

---

178 *Black Hawk: An Autobiography,* Donald Johnson, editor, (1833: Reprinted by the University of Illinois Press, 1955), pp. 139-140. The "young war chief" was Lieutenant Jefferson Davis.

While the capture of Black Hawk established the end of the Black Hawk War, there were still two senior Sauk chiefs that were not captured by the Americans. Ne-a-pope was a spiritual advisor to Black Hawk and sought to build a military alliance between various Indian tribes and the British against the United States. In contrast to Ne-a-pope was the Sauk chief Keokuk, who was friendly towards the U.S. and did not oppose white expansion. Keokuk was respected as a man of character and level-headed. He complied with U.S. demands to move west and shrewdly sought to gain as many privileges for his followers as he could. Keokuk trusted brevet Major Gustavus Loomis and admired the way Loomis showed concern and compassion to the refugee Indians under his control. On August 20, 1832, Keokuk captured Ne-a-pope and turned him over to brevet Major Gustavus Loomis at Fort Crawford.[179]

An image of the Sauk chief Keokuk, late 1840s.
A public domain image.

In September of 1832, Keokuk and other Sauk and Mesquakie leaders signed a treaty at Fort Crawford, with Gustavus Loomis and his wife Julia and his fifteen year old daughter Eliza present. The Sauk traded away six million acres in present-day Iowa in exchange for numerous financial and other amenities. The U.S. Government officially proclaimed Keokuk to be the civil chief of the Sauk and Fox, who were banished from Illinois and Wisconsin.

After a celebrity trip to Washington D.C. in the summer of 1833, Black Hawk and other tribal leaders were released into Keokuk's custody. The Sauk and Fox and others had moved to lands on the Des Moines River in Iowa.

---

179 *The Black Hawk War of 1832: Chase through Northern Illinois and Southern Wisconsin*, http://webs.rps205.com/departments/TAH/files/43BE35B3886E414390B8E ED720637B6E. Accessed September 6, 2009.

Here, under Keokuk's supervision, Black Hawk passed his last years in shame and bitterness until his death on October 3, 1838. Keokuk died well-respected by Indians and whites in 1848.

As the August 1-2, 1832 Battle of Bad Axe was the key event of the Black Hawk War, the official report of the battle, given by the senior U.S. Army officer in the region, Brigadier General Henry Atkinson, warrants our attention.

TO MAJOR GENERAL SCOTT, COMMANDING N.W. ARMY, CHICAGO, ILL.

Head Quarters 1st Army Corps, North-Western Army Fort Crawford, Prairie de Chien, Aug. 9.

Sir--I informed you on the 5th. Inst by a short official note, of the action on the morning of the 2d inst. between the troops under my command and the Sac enemy, on the bank of the Mississippi, opposite Ioway river.--Having received the reports of the officers commanding brigades and corps, I have the honor of reporting more in detail the events of the day.

After having pursued the enemy five days by forced marches, from his passage of the Ousconsin, we found ourselves at dusk, on the evening of the 1st inst. after a march of 25 miles, within a few miles of his position.

. . . After marching about three miles, the advance of Dodge's battalion came up with a small party of the enemy, and killed eight of them, and dispersed the residue. . . . The enemy was driven across several slucies down the river bottom, which was covered with fallen timber, underwood and high grass.

The regular troops, and Dodge at the head of his battalion, soon came up and joined in the action, followed by a party of Posey's troops, when the enemy was driven still farther through the bottom to several small willow islands successively, where much execution was done.

. . . *As soon as the enemy were slain or dislodged from the willow bars, the regular troops under Col. Taylor, and a company or two of volunteers, were thrown aboard of the steamboat "Warrior" that had just arrived, and were landed on the two adjacent islands to scour them of the enemy. Assisted by a detachment from Henry's and Dodge's commands on the river bank some three or four Indians were found and killed.*

Both the regular and volunteer troops conducted themselves with the greatest zeal, courage and patriotism, and are entitled to the highest approbation of their country. To Brigadier General Henry, of the 3d brigade of Illinois volunteers, Gen. Dodge, of the Michigan volunteers, and Col. Taylor, of the United States' Infantry, their greatest praise is due for the gallant manner in which they brought their respective corps in, and conducted them through the action. . . .

The enemy sustained a loss of about 150 men, killed--the precise number could not be ascertained, as a large proportion were slain in endeavoring to swim to the islands. Forty women and children were taken prisoners, seventy horses captured, &c. &c.

The loss on our part, was--of the U. States Infantry, 5 privates killed, and 4 wounded--Gen. Posey's volunteers, 1 private wounded--Gen. Alexander's, 1 private wounded--Gen. Henry's , 1 lieutenant and 5 privates wounded--Gen. Dodge's, 1 captain, 1 sergeant, and 4 privates wounded The steamer "Warrior," by the direction of Capt. [brevet Major] Loomis, had ascended the river, with a small detachment of the 4th U.S. Infantry, under the command of Lieut. Kingsbury, accompanied by Lieuts. Holmes and Torrence, on the day previous to the battle, to warn the Sioux of the approach of the Sacs:--in returning, near the battle ground, a party of Sacs was discovered, and fired upon, when a smart skirmish ensued. The Indian loss is since reported to be 23 killed--one now on board the steamboat, slightly wounded. Lieuts. Holmes, Kingsbury, and Torrence, as well as Captain Throgmorton, the commander of the boat, were conspicuous in the affair. A great advantage was derived from the presence of the steamboat, on this occasion, as it retarded the enemy in crossing the river.

I enclose herewith a list of the officers of the volunteers under Generals Henry and Dodge. A list of the officers of the other volunteer corps will be transmitted as soon as received, which I request may be placed on file in the War Office.

I have the honor to be, sir, With great respect, Your most ob't serv't

H. ATKINSON, Brig. Gen. U.S. Army To Maj. Gen. W. Scott, Commanding N.W. Army.[180]

A sketch of the steamboat *Warrior* in battle with Sauk and Fox Indians at the battle of Bad Axe, August 1-2, 1832. Public domain image.

---

180 Wisconsin Historical Society, www.wisconsinhistory.org/teachers/lessons/secondary/bh_badaxe.asp. Accessed August 29, 2009.

CHAPTER NINE

VARIOUS ASSIGNMENTS ON THE WESTERN FRONTIER

AFTER THE END OF THE Black Hawk War in August, 1832, brevet Major Gustavus Loomis and his family remained at Fort Crawford for six more months. With the cessation of hostilities with the Indians, white settlers flooded into the region. Some of the white settlers were pioneers looking to make a successful living by trading or farming. Others were vagabonds, ruffians intent on making a fast dollar. The combination of alcohol, greed and lawlessness created a dangerous subculture of white hooliganism that placed both Indians and whites in danger. At that time, itinerant missionary Rev. Cutter Marsh observed barroom brawling, "horrid oaths and blasphemies," and a spiritual void that he attributed to "the forces of darkness."[181]

From a military perspective, life at Fort Crawford after the Black Hawk War was somewhat predictable. After the remnant Sauk and Fox Indians were fed, clothed and shipped to reservation lands, the fort reverted again to its peacetime activities. Only an estimated one hundred and fifty members of Black Hawk's band survived. The Sauk and Fox remnants settled on reservation lands in Iowa, later relocated even farther west in Kansas Territory.[182] At Fort Crawford there were crops to plant, wood to cut, patrols to

---

181 "Historic Diaries: Marsh, 1834," www.wisconsinhistory.org/diary/002279. Accessed November 4, 2009. The date of this diary entry was July 18, 1834.

182 Daniel W. Howe, *What God had Wrought: The Transformation of America, 1815-1848*, (Oxford University Press, 2007), pp. 418-419.

perform, drills and ceremonies to conduct. Law enforcement duties were a constant burden, separating white alcohol sellers from
Indians, resolving feuds between land speculators and settlers, and
protecting settlers and farmers. Black Hawk remained dormant
the remaining years of his life. The Sauk and Fox Indians received
many offers from missionaries to come and teach them about
Christianity, but these offers were refused. Black Hawk maintained a neat and orderly lodge with well-maintained gardens off
to one side of their village in Iowa Territory.[183] He died in 1838
as an old man with broken and unfulfilled dreams.

The Gustavus Loomis family departed Fort Crawford on February 8, 1833. He had served at this fort for about three years. No
doubt it was an emotional farewell for the Loomis family, as they
departed the fort and said farewell to their Christian brethren at
the First Congregational Church in Prairie du Chien. Gustavus
was now forty-four years old. His wife Julia was thirty-six, and
their daughter Eliza was fifteen. For approximately the next four
months, brevet Major Loomis was placed on "detached service."
That meant he was on paid military leave.[184]

This was the first extended leave Loomis took from the army
since the end of the War of 1812. We have no record of where the
Loomis family visited during their four months of military leave.
A valid consideration is that the couple returned home to New
England. None of Gustavus's relatives in Thetford, Vermont had
met Julia or their daughter Eliza. Julia's relatives may have seen
Eliza as an infant but it had been far too many years of family
separation. In Thetford, Rev. Asa Burton, who led the boy Gustavus to faith in Jesus Christ, was older and semi-retired and still
ministering with an assistant at the First Congregational Church

---

183 "Historic Diaries: Marsh, 1834," entry dated August 30, 1834.
184 George W. Cullum, *Biographical Register of the Officers and Graduates of the U.S. Military Academy, at West Point, N.Y.,* (New York: 1868), p.118.

in Thetford. It must have been thrilling for the citizens of Thetford to hear the Christian testimony of their native born Gustavus, giving a report in the Congregational Church, with his wife and daughter present, about the goodness of the Lord. Gustavus left Thetford for West Point in 1808 and here he returned in 1833 as a brevet Major in the U.S. Army, a combat veteran of two wars, well established and successful as a Christian military officer. We can imagine the joy in Rev. Asa Burton, as his boy convert and disciple was still living for God many years after departing town.

On June 19, 1833, brevet Major Gustavus Loomis reported for "recruiting service."[185] He was now a middle aged man with over twenty-two years of army service. We have no record of where he served in recruiting, but we do know that he served in this capacity from June to the fall of 1833. A likely location for his recruiting activities was Saint Louis, Missouri. As with Loomis' previous two recruiting tours of duty (New York in 1820 and New Orleans in 1828-1830), Saint Louis was a town attracting thousands of migrants, settlers, fortune-seekers and rowdies. Many came west only to loose their finances. Bankruptcy was common, as was unemployment. Army recruiting in Saint Louis provided young, healthy men with steady work, fair pay and the opportunity to succeed. The army at that time consisted of less than ten thousand combined officers and soldiers. The entire army consisted of only infantry and artillery units. Militia units all over the country had horse cavalry units, but not the regular army. In 1833 mounted infantry, called Dragoons, were created to allow soldiers greater speed and mobility on the western prairies.[186] These new dragoon units needed recruits to fill in the ranks. Gustavus Loomis served on recruiting duty until he received orders for his next assignment, to Fort Snelling, in the Unorganized Territory north of Iowa Territory.

185 George W. Cullum, *Biographical Register,* p. 118.
186 Edward M. Coffman, *The Old Army,* (Oxford University Press, 1986), pp. 42, 55.

In the fall of 1833, the Loomis family steamed north on the Mississippi River to rural and isolated Fort Snelling. Built in 1825, Fort Snelling was an outpost in the wilderness. This vast remote territory inhabited by fur traders and Indians lay well beyond organized American settlement. After the War of 1812, the government took physical possession of this valuable northwest frontier by establishing a chain of Indian agencies and supporting forts from Lake Michigan to the Missouri River. Many of these forts are lost to history. These outposts denied non-citizens commercial use of American rivers. The U.S. Army kept Indian lands free of white encroachment until appropriate treaties were signed. The army also kept peace between rival Indians, apprehended outlaws, and protected law-abiding settlers, travelers and traders.

Sketch of Fort Snelling and surrounding areas. Source: www.mnhs.org/places-/sites/hfs/history.

The army built roads, constructed a gristmill and sawmill, planted hundreds of acres of vegetables, wheat and corn, cut hay for their livestock, felled trees for their fires, built hundreds of homes and made the first documented weather recordings in the area.[187] Out of wilderness a military community appeared on the banks of the Mississippi River near the meeting of the Minnesota River.

Fort Snelling was named after Colonel Josiah Snelling (1782-1828), who was the first Commander of Fort Snelling. The site was originally selected by Lieutenant Colonel Henry Leaven-

---

187 "Historic Fort Snelling," www.mnhs.org/places/sites/hfs/history. Accessed November 4, 2009.

worth, but Snelling was responsible for the design and construction of the fort. A Bostonian and a veteran of the War of 1812, Henry Snelling located the fort on a bluff above the junction of the Minnesota and Mississippi Rivers. The fort was designed like an elongated diamond. The eastern point of the diamond was designed with a half-moon battery. Two smaller batteries on the north and south sides were built for infantry and artillery. The western point of the diamond had a large round tower, about thirty feet high, with musket ports in the sides and a cannon on the top. Eight interior buildings of the fort were built from locally-quarried limestone, while two other buildings were built from wood cut locally. The army recognized the importance of fresh fruit and vegetables in a soldier's diet, and made post commanders responsible for establishing gardens. Colonel Snelling started cultivation in 1820 on about one hundred acres of land. By 1823, nearly 200 acres were being cultivated, about half of which were used for growing wheat. In order to deal peacefully with the Indians, Colonel Snelling partnered with local Indian Agents to build a council in 1823, where agents carefully distributed government food and supplies and provided other services to the Indians. This helped ensure good relations with rival tribes and helped to avert open hostilities between the Indians.

By 1823 steamboats could navigate the Mississippi River as far north as the Minnesota River, thus placing Fort Snelling at a key northern point in controlling river traffic. Relations with the Dakota, Sioux and Winnebago Indians made life at Fort Snelling tense. The fort was a central location for numerous Indian Agents, traders, trappers and pioneers. With the white people came diseases that caused great suffering among the Indians. Winter snows could accumulate to several feet in depth, killing the unprepared and paralyzing activities outside the fort. Communication between Fort Snelling and the outside world was dependent upon river traffic, which ceased during the winter months. It was not unusual for people to freeze to death or starve in the winter.

To counteract the monotony of wilderness life at Fort Snelling, some turned to alcohol. The illicit whisky trade was an ongoing source of frustration for officers like brevet Major Gustavus Loomis, who understood that many of the problems between whites and Indians could be attributed to the misuse of alcohol.[188] Occasionally, resupply riverboats heading to Fort Snelling were attacked by Indians acting like river pirates, shooting at the vessels and occasionally boarding ships and looting them of supplies. As early as 1829, Presbyterian missionaries saw Fort Snelling as a strategic location and attempted to develop a mission station. The fort was severely isolated but resembled other frontier military forts of that period.

In the fall of 1833, the Loomis family settled in to Fort Snelling. One element of life at this new assignment that thrilled the Gustavus Loomis family was the high interest in religion. Missionaries were frequently coming and going through Fort Snelling, seeking God's will about which Indian tribes they would serve. The senior Indian Agent, Major Lawrence Taliaferro, was a deacon in the Old School Presbyterian Church, a fact which brought much pleasure to Gustavus Loomis. A War of 1812 veteran, Major Taliaferro (1794–1871) was appointed by President Monroe in 1819 as permanent Indian Agent of what was to become the Minnesota Territory, a post he would hold for twenty years until his resignation in 1840. He was a devoted Presbyterian who, while doctrinally a rigid Calvinist, was a firm supporter of revivals. Indian Agent Taliaferro and Gustavus Loomis became good friends, both sincerely seeking the best for the Indians and both furious at the white people's vices

188 E.D. Neill, *Occurrences in and Around Fort Snelling, from 1819 through 1840,* (Minnesota Historical Society, 1845[?]), pp. 112-113.

which brought out the worst in the Indians.[189] The Indians first and critical need was spiritual, they asserted, not social or economic. Taliaferro and Loomis agreed that the Indians first needed Christianity and then civilization.[190]

Religious services were frequently held at Fort Snelling by a variety of ministers. Missionaries Samuel Pond and Gideon Pond arrived in 1833, the brothers devoting themselves to bringing the gospel to the Indians. Gideon Pond (1810-1878) stayed around Fort Snelling as a missionary to the Sioux Indians and preached at Fort Snelling. In the spring of 1835 Reverend Thomas S. Williamson, a physician and a missionary, arrived at Fort Snelling. Dr. Williamson (1800-1879) came to the northwest with his wife and young daughter to provide spiritual and physical ministry. T.S. Williamson brought the earliest medical care to the Dakota and to many soldiers, trappers and their families over the years. He, along with John Renville, Stephen Riggs and Gideon and Samuel Pond, created the first written alphabet and grammar of the Dakota language. Other missionaries came to start schools for Indian children and frequently visited the fort. An interesting event happened the winter of 1833-1834, when Major Gustavus Loomis was credited with initiating a "red hot revival" at Fort Snelling.

In the book, *Old Fort Snelling, 1819-1858*, it states, "During the winter Major Gustavus Loomis initiated a red-hot revival among the soldiers."[191] A contemporary of Gustavus Loomis and one who was present at Fort Snelling at the time was Henry H. Sibley. In his memoirs, Sibley comments on the intense spirituality of Gustavus Loomis and the stellar example his wife and

---

189 Wiloughby M. Babcock, "Major Lawrence Taliaferro, Indian Agent," *The Mississippi Valley Historical Review,* Vol.11, No. 3, (December 1924), pp. 358-375.

190 Marcus L. Hansen, *Old Fort Snelling,, 1819-1858*, (Cedar Rapids, Iowa: The Torch Press, 1918), p. 45.

191 Marcus L. Hansen, *Old Fort Snelling*, p. 46.

daughter were to others at the fort. Loomis was said to have his peculiarities, one of which was his "engrossing enthusiasm in the cause of religion." Again it was stated that he got up a "red-hot" revival among the soldiers.[192] What exactly did this mean?

In the mid-nineteenth century, local revivals were a manifestation of a national movement called the Second Great Awakening. This movement was Protestant and evangelical, meaning it supported the doctrines rediscovered by the Protestant reformers of the sixteenth century and was focused on a personal faith relationship with God through Jesus Christ. Men who served in the army at that time were mostly immigrants or working class men seeking to better themselves. Their officers were educated and typically from a more affluent social background. But according to proponents of revivals like Gustavus Loomis, both officers and enlisted soldiers need the same Lord. Both need salvation. All men and women are sinners who are in desperate need of forgiveness. A holy and righteous God, who is intolerant of sin, rejects all humanity. But in His grace and love and mercy, God has provided a way of salvation, one way for all. That way of salvation is through repentance from sin and acceptance of Jesus Christ as personal savior. This was the heart of the Second Great Awakening, that each person was condemned by God but that each one could be forgiven through the merits of Jesus Christ on their behalf. This was not a new message, as it came strait from the Bible. But for those who did not know the Bible, and for those who did, the message was life transforming.[193]

Upon his arrival at Fort Snelling in the fall of 1833, Gustavus Loomis did what he always did at every assignment. He reported to his superior officer, he settled his family in their home, he commenced his military activities, and he dedicated himself

192 Henry H. Sibley, *Autobiography of Henry Hastings Sibley*, (North Carolina, 1844), p. 32.
193 Bernard A. Weisberger, *They Gathered at the River: The Story of the Great Revivalists and their Impact upon Religion in America*, (Boston: Little, Brown & Company, 1958).

to the spiritual welfare of his family and sought ways to share his faith with others. There was nothing unusual about his actions at Fort Snelling but the spiritual results of his efforts were remarkable. Loomis gathered anyone who would listen as he read the Bible out loud. He taught others how to sing biblical psalms. He read sermons from preachers that were published in religious periodicals. At Fort Snelling there was an immediate favorable response.

Instead of a handful of participants, several dozen soldiers, officers and enlisted, attended his meetings. Parents eagerly brought their children to Loomis and his wife for Sunday School lessons. Those drawn to the meetings were the religious and the irreligious, the devout and the blasphemers. No doubt local missionaries such as Gideon Pond, J. D. Stevens and later Dr. Williamson helped to develop the spiritual climate that led to this religious awakening. On Sunday mornings Loomis led the meetings, encouraging others to give a testimony of faith, challenging the congregation to get right with God. He was not an ordained man, so as a Presbyterian he would not himself preach the Sunday sermon. That task was for the guest missionaries. If a missionary was not present, Loomis would read a published sermon. In speaking about Loomis' religious activities at Fort Snelling, one report credited Major Gustavus Loomis and Rev. Thomas S. Williamson with "bringing Presbyterianism from the east to Minnesota,"[194] while another report stated,

> DURING THE WINTER of 1834-1835, a pious officer of the army [Gustavus Loomis] exercised a good influence on his fellow officers and soldiers under his command. In the absence of a chaplain or ordained minister, he was accustomed... not only to drill the soldiers, but to

---

194 "Religion: Presbyterians in Saint Paul," *TIME,* June 3, 1929.

meet them in his own quarters, and reason with them "of righteousness, temperance, and judgment to come."[195]

The revival at Fort Snelling was enduring. It began slowly in 1833 and lasted through the winter of 1834-1835. In the spring of 1835, with the warmer weather and outdoor activities and the arrival of the whisky peddlers, numbers at the revival meetings decreased. Yet so many remained faithful that on June 11, 1835, when missionary Thomas S. Williamson arrived, a church was organized in one of the company rooms at Fort Snelling. The church was composed of soldiers, missionaries and fur traders and their families.[196] Rev. Williamson, an ordained minister and a physician, was sent to the Dakota peoples by the American Board of Foreign Missions, a joint missionary society of the Congregationalists and the Presbyterians. As an ordained minister Williamson could perform weddings, serve communion, conduct baptisms, and preach on Sunday mornings. The fledgling church at Fort Snelling began with twenty-two official members and many more supporters. Their church polity was Presbyterian. Four elders were elected, one of whom was Gustavus Loomis.[197]

In the summer of 1835 the church at Fort Snelling began to take shape. On Saturday June 13th lectures were conducted to prepare the people for the first official Sunday meeting of the new church, a meeting that would also celebrate the observation of the sacrament of communion. On Sunday morning, June 14th the excitement must have been intense, as the first organized church in the entire upper Mississippi Valley area met for worship. Sunday morning and afternoon preaching was shared between missionar-

---

195 Edward D. Neill, *History of Freeborn County: Including Explorers and Pioneers of Minnesota*, (Minneapolis: Minnesota Historical Society, 1882), p. 107.
196 Marcus L. Hansen, *Old Fort Snelling*, p. 46.
197 Edward D. Neill, *History of Freeborn County*, p. 108.

ies Thomas Williamson and J.D. Stevens. On July 31, J.D. Stevens was asked by the congregation to be the settled pastor, as long as his missionary labors with the Sioux permitted. As there had not been a chaplain at Fort Snelling, Stevens regularly preached on Sundays to this new Presbyterian Church in the fort. Gustavus Loomis was elected Stated Clerk of the Session, and they resolved to observe a monthly prayer meeting, led by Loomis, which would pray for the conversion of the world.[198]

Henry H. Sibley was an eyewitness to these events and was elected an elder in the church as was Loomis and others. Sibley wrote that Gustavus Loomis was an officer "distinguished for his piety" and who led Sunday services and read sermons when no minister was present. Sibley wrote about the forming of the church within the walls of Fort Snelling in a company room, where twenty white men (he did not count family members) stood up one at a time and swore a vow to maintain the church covenant. Elders were then ordained with a simple laying on of hands ceremony, a solemn ordination to the eldership that included Gustavus Loomis.[199] In 1838 the church at Fort Snelling was strengthened by the arrival of an official military chaplain, Rev. Ezekiel Gear, but this was after the Loomis family departed the fort. This fledgling congregation still exists today as the large First Presbyterian Church of Minneapolis, Minnesota.[200]

We have numerous glimpses into the personal life and characteristics of Gustavus Loomis while he served at Fort Snelling. He was now a career officer who exerted great influence upon

198 Edward D. Neill, *History of Freeborn County,* pp. 107-108. E.D. Neill, *Occurrences in and Around Fort Snelling,* p. 17.

199 Henry H. Sibley, *Autobiography of Henry Hastings Sibley,* p. 63.

200 Albert B. Marshall, *History of the First Presbyterian Church of Minneapolis, Minnesota, 1835-1910,* (Minneapolis: Minnesota Printing Company, 1910).

the military and civilians in the Upper Mississippi region. When people met Loomis they often wrote about it. For example, Rev. Cutting Marsh met the Loomis family on a routine steamboat ride on the Mississippi River. On July 4, 1834, Marsh wrote,

> IN THE EVE. the steamboat Warrior came up the river and they went on board to go to Rock Island. There I met with Capt. [brevet Major] Loomis, having his family on board bound to Prairie du Chien & from there to St. Peters, his place of destination. Had a very pleasant interview and after a short time bade them all adieu. The Lord bless and go with them.[201]

Another who met Gustavus Loomis at or around Fort Snelling was an Englishman named Mr. George W. Featherstonhaugh. In the 1830s many travelers, adventurers, authors, naturalists, and the wealthy with leisure time travelled along the beautiful Mississippi River. The Englishman Mr. Featherstonhaugh, a geologist, was a wealthy, prim-and-proper aristocrat who did not adjust well to rural and primitive living conditions on the American frontier. He appears to have been somewhat of a snob. In *Occurrences in and Around Fort Snelling*, it says of Mr. Featherstonhaugh, "On the 12th of September, the geologist, Featherstonhaugh, arrived. His actions were those of a conceited, ill-bred Englishman..."[202] The English guest was given a rearranged storeroom to use for his quarters and was fed by the Loomis family. It is somewhat comical to imagine the dainty Englishman sharing meals with the extroverted outdoorsman and outspoken Christian Gustavus Loomis. The rough wooden table in the simple Loomis home, with its variety of homey dishes prepared by Julia and Eliza Loomis, did not appeal to Mr. Featherstonhaugh. The homespun clothing of

---

201 "Historic Diaries: Marsh, 1834," entry dated July 4, 1834.

202 E.D. Neill, *Occurrences in and Around Fort Snelling, from 1819 through 1840*, p. 128.

Julia and Eliza appeared crude to the cultured Englishman. When Gustavus offered extended prayers of thanksgiving to the Lord for the food, and read and sung psalms after supper, it is not hard to imagine the Englishman's eyes rolling in his head and he squirming in his chair to get out of this unrefined and uncultured atmosphere. One account of Mr. Featherstonhaugh at Fort Snelling tells of his complaining about the dirty and foul-smelling living conditions and that he was bored with the spiritual exhortations and psalm singing which frequented the Loomis household.[203]

Missionaries Samuel and Gideon Pond served the Dakota Indians and frequented Fort Snelling. Samuel Pond dictated his memoirs to his son, memoirs that mention Gustavus Loomis. For example, speaking of the year 1835, "A new commandant, Major Gustavus Loomis, had arrived and assumed command at the fort the preceding summer. He was... a staunch Presbyterian and very friendly to the infant missionary enterprise." Loomis's presence at the fort made an immediate spiritual impact upon the soldiers and families and others at the garrison. Missionary Samuel Pond was thrilled to learn of a vibrant prayer meeting held weekly at the fort, led by Major Loomis. Pond stated there was a "revival of religion there," and that "Perhaps you have heard before now that an officer came here last summer who is a professor of religion, and there is no risk in saying that he is an active Christian. His wife and daughter too are Christians – three alone." Samuel Pond spoke of Loomis as follows;

> CAPTAIN LOOMIS, AT that time major by brevet, was a true friend of all the missionaries, and of Messrs. [Gideon and Samuel] Pond in particular, whom he ever aided with various counsel and influence. Lieutenant Ogden was their valued and familiar friend. The major's manner

---

203 Marcus L. Hansen, *Old Fort Snelling*, p. 49.

in prayer meeting was somewhat military. "Nutt, pray,"
"Ogden, pray," was his usual method of directing his subordinates to take part in the service.[204]

In the midst of religious excitement at Fort Snelling, the military missions of the fort were ongoing. There were disputes and
feuds between Indian tribes that needed mediation. There was the
ongoing mission of controlling navigation of the upper Mississippi
River against Canadian or European intrusions. Indian Agents and
government trading posts needed protecting. Major Loomis was
adamant in keeping away whisky peddling vagabonds who stirred
up trouble between whites and Indians. There were the routine
military drilling, parading, marching, patrolling, and scouting missions. In the winter there were rescue missions, as deep snowfall
stranded unprepared pioneers and settlers. In the warmer weather
there was farming and timbering and the maintaining of portage
facilities at the riverfront. In addition to all this, there were emigrants constantly arriving needing protection and provisions.[205]

At dawn the sounds of reveille awoke Fort Snelling. Like every
other army installation, life was regimented and could be monotonous. Formations of the troops and inspections were a daily occur-
rence. Various tasks of the day were completed based on the time of
the year. Meals were bland and predictable, making the arrival of a
steamboat at the fort a welcome site, as various spices and foods and
supplies could be bought. In 1832 the army exchanged its daily
liquor ration for coffee and sugar. Soldiers grew the wheat with
which the cooks baked fresh bread. A sutler's store provided small
luxuries for the soldiers and their families, at a cost regulated by the
government. The sutler was the authorized merchant at the fort,

204 Samuel Pond, Jr., *The Story of the Labors of Samuel and Gideon Pond,* (Boston:
    Congregational Sunday School Publishing, 1893), pp. 71-75.
205 E.D. Neill, *Occurrences in and Around Fort Snelling, from 1819 through 1840,* pp. 111-126.

every soldier at the fort contributing a small amount to allow the sutler to provide for widows, orphans and the wounded.

In the culture of that time, drunkenness and other violations of military discipline were swiftly and sternly punished. The severity of the punishment depended on the mood of the commanding officer. For example, Colonel Snelling, the founding officer of Fort Snelling, unmercifully flogged severe offenders who often begged him to stop. Other officers flogged delinquent soldiers by tying them to the flagpole, stripped to the waist, with drummers taking turns flogging the deviant trooper for the commander. Other officers used less painful methods. Major Loomis earned the name "Old Ring" for his disciplinary method of placing a log of wood upon a soldier's shoulder and compelling the soldier to walk around in a circle for hours

A sketch of Fort Snelling and surrounding Indian villages in the mid-1830s. Source: www.library.wisc.edu/etext/WI Reader/Images/WER1163.

under the watchful eyes of a sentinel. Another method of punishment was the Black Hole, a primitive solitary confinement chamber in which a delinquent soldier was placed for days at a time with no food or water. The fort had a stockade for the less severe offenders. In a fort with about three hundred and thirty soldiers, typically the stockade had from zero to about twenty-five under discipline at any one time.[206]

---

206 Marcus L. Hansen, *Old Fort Snelling*, pp. 27-29.

In addition to his many activities within Fort Snelling, brevet Major Gustavus Loomis and his family were very interested in supporting local missionaries to the Indians. Gustavus and his wife Julia and their daughter Eliza donated their time and sweat and finances to teach the Indians Christianity and civilization. Missionaries often ate at the Loomis home and were encouraged by this devout family. The opening of a mission school for the Indians was a celebratory event to which the Loomis's attended. For example, in the fall of 1836 the Loomis family and Lieutenant Ogden and others attended the opening of a Dakota Indian school sponsored by missionaries J.D. Stevens and Samuel Pond. This boarding school for Dakota girls was built with the intention of creating educated Christian women who could be effective wives and mothers in civilized society.[207] Several weeks later the Loomis family again was invited to an Indian school, this on Lake Harriet, located about ten miles northwest of Fort Snelling. The missionaries invited outside examiners to review lessons with the students in what was always a celebratory atmosphere. One report stated, "On the 30th of December there was an examination at the mission school at Lake Harriet. Henry H. Sibley and Major Taliaferro were appointed examiners. Among others in attendance were Major Loomis, Lt. Ogden, and their families, and Surgeon Emerson.[208]

The name of Lieutenant Edmund A. Ogden has recently but frequently appeared in this narrative. The Lieutenant was a resident of Catskill, New York and a 1831 graduate of the U.S. Military Academy at West Point. Edmund Ogden (1810-1853) was assigned to Fort Snelling and served under brevet Major Gustavus Loomis. Lieutenant Ogden was a full supporter of the revivals at Fort Snelling and frequently attended its prayer meetings and

207 William H. Folwell, *History of Minnesota*, (Minnesota Historical Society Press, 2006), vol. I, p. 195.

208 E.D. Neill, *Occurrences in and Around Fort Snelling, from 1819 through 1840,* p. 131.

religious services. He, like Major Loomis, eagerly supported local missionaries. It is not clear if Ogden was converted under Loomis' ministry or if he already was a devout Christian military officer before arriving at Fort Snelling. What we do know is that in 1834 the young officer was twenty-four years old and soon fell in love with the sixteen year old Eliza Loomis. The next year the seventeen year old Eliza Loomis married Lieutenant Edmund Ogden. As one account stated,

> On the twenty-seventh of this month [May 1835] the Rev. Dr. Williamson united in marriage at the fort Lieutenant Edward [Edmund] A. Ogden to Eliza Edna, the daughter of Captain [brevet Major] G. A. Loomis, the first marriage service in which a clergyman officiated in the present state of Minnesota.[209]

Eliza was the only surviving child of Gustavus and Julia Loomis. Every indication is that the Loomis family was happy and well adjusted. Eliza as an only child easily travelled with her parents to numerous military assignments. The hardships of such a life apparently did not affect her, as she happily married a military man. Most of her schooling was done at home by her parents. She was in no way rebellious to the faith of her father and mother. Numerous accounts speak of her piety and devotion to missionaries and her eager attendance at revival meetings. As a Christian young woman, her father would never allow her to socialize or be romantically involved with someone who was not a dedicated Christian. Lieutenant Ogden must have impressed Gustavus Loomis in both his spirituality and his military abilities.

It was a bittersweet event to see Eliza married and depart the Loomis home to live in a separate dwelling on Fort Snelling with

---

209 Edward D. Neill, *History of Freeborn County*, p. 108.

her new husband. As parents, Gustavus and Julia had done a good job. Eliza was a dedicated Christian military wife and mother. Edmund and Eliza Ogden had eight children, six that lived to adulthood. Their growing family travelled throughout the expanding west, as Edmund Ogden over the years was promoted from Lieutenant to Captain to Major. In 1853, at the young age of forty-three, Major Ogden died of cholera, he getting infected as he read the Bible and prayed with his sick soldiers in Kansas. Eliza was pregnant at the time and gave birth to their eight child, Edith, in 1854.[210]

In 1836 it was time for brevet Major Gustavus Loomis and his wife Julia to depart Fort Snelling. He received orders to report back to Fort Crawford, the place he departed in 1833 to enjoy military leave and to briefly serve in recruiting duty before coming to Fort Snelling. The Loomis' had many friends and a good church in Prairie du Chien and must have looked forward to the new assignment. This would be their first place of duty without their daughter Eliza, as she remained at Fort Snelling with her new husband. It must have been an emotional farewell between the parents and their only child, as Gustavus and Julia departed Fort Snelling on a steamboat, heading south to Prairie du Chien and Fort Crawford. The tearful parents could never have known when they again would see their eighteen year old newly married daughter.

When Gustavus and Julia Loomis arrived at Fort Crawford in 1836, they arrived at a fort that was in pristine condition under the watchful eye of Colonel Zachary Taylor. Fort Crawford retained a huge amount of military weaponry, everything from artillery canons to horse saddles to several tons of ammunition. The fort remained a vital center of Indian affairs between the

210 Elias Loomis, *The Descendants of Elias Loomis*, (New Haven: 1875), p. 287. Jonathan Mix, *A Brief Account of the Life and Patriotic Services of Jonathan Mix of New Haven*, (New Haven: 1886), p. 96.

always feuding Sioux, Winnebago, Sauk and Fox peoples. Fort Crawford was the location of settling disputes and signing treaties with the Indians. While the Loomis' were away from Fort Crawford in 1833-1836, Rev. David Lowry, a Presbyterian missionary, had opened and developed a missionary school for Winnebago children in Prairie du Chien. In 1835-1836 Fort Crawford troops were heavily engaged in constructing and maintaining a road from Fort Crawford to Fort Winnebago, a distance of about thirty miles to the northeast. Around this time the distinguished artist George Catlin visited Fort Crawford to paint Indian portraits and landscapes. In 1836 and 1837 there were no unusual Indian problems to increase activities in the fort. Gustavus Loomis was one of two hundred and sixty soldiers at Fort Crawford. Julia was one of thirteen women and the fort had twenty-three children.[211]

In October, 1836, Fort Crawford received an official inspection. The kitchens were clean and neat. Rations were properly prepared, cooked and served. The arms and ammunition of the men was in good condition. The barracks, clothing and bunks of the troops all passed inspection. Payroll and quartermaster books were examined and found to be accurate. No corruption, fraud or embezzlement was tolerated. The hospital did poorly on the inspection, but since there were no sick soldiers it was not taken seriously. The supply of stores, medicine and other provisions was abundant and neatly arranged. Sutlers at the fort were honest and provided what the people needed at fair prices. The drilling of the troops was inspected and there were no problems. Rations at this October inspection were enough to carry the fort through the winter and into May of the next year. The inspector declared, "No post, whether on the [eastern] sea board or the interior is provided with a better magazine and gun house than Fort Craw-

211 Bruce E. Mahan, *Old Fort Crawford and the Frontier*, (1926: reprinted by the Prairie du Chien Historical Society, 2000), pp. 201-211.

ford, nor at none can greater pains be taken to secure the article in store from waste or damage."[212] In the absence of Colonel Zachary Taylor, brevet Major Loomis was made commander of Fort Crawford from January to May, 1837.

Upon their arrival at Fort Crawford in 1836, Gustavus and Julia Loomis reunited with the brethren at the First Congregational Church at Prairie du Chien. Having been gone for three years there was much catching up to do. Many asked the status of the newly married Eliza, who remained at Fort Snelling. A significant change at Fort Crawford while the Loomis family was away was that a chaplain was appointed to serve the Fort Crawford community.

Rev. Richard F. Cadle became the military chaplain at Fort Crawford in 1836. Cadle was a tireless missionary with the Protestant Episcopal Church. A New Yorker with a master's degree education at Columbia College, Richard Cadle (1796–1857) was ordained in 1817 and first served churches in New York and New Jersey. In 1824 he was assigned as a missionary with the Domestic and Foreign Mission Society. His first missionary posting was to work with the Oneida Indians near Detroit. A very capable organizer and a good but not great preacher, Rev. Cadle ministered to his church in Detroit and did itinerant preaching throughout what would be later called Illinois, Michigan, Minnesota and Wisconsin. He helped found several churches and was famous in his day for the large Indian mission boarding school he founded in Wisconsin in 1827. While traveling in his itinerant ministry he frequently stopped at military forts to resupply and to preach. Around 1836 he accepted a position as an army chaplain at Fort Crawford. It was here that Richard Cadle and Gustavus Loomis first met.

---

212 Bruce E. Mahan, *Old Fort Crawford and the Frontier,* p. 211-212.

As chaplain at Fort Crawford, Rev. Cadle also started a Protestant Episcopal Church in nearby Prairie du Chien. At Fort Crawford he held Sunday services in the hospital, with attendance usually low. There were already a Presbyterian and a Methodist Church in Prairie du Chien, so competition for parishioners was noticeable. Later a room was designated for Sunday services at Fort Crawford for the chaplain, but many of the soldiers and their families, including the Loomis family, worshiped in Prairie du Chien. Chaplain Cadle was also the schoolmaster for the children at the fort, a responsibility that wearied him. As far as we can tell, brevet Major Loomis and Chaplain Cadle got alone fine. Cadle was esteemed for his "piety and integrity," was a tireless worker who travelled in all sorts of weather to preach, and had "the true spirit of Christian self-denial and singleness of purpose."[213] Theologically, Rev. Cadle was a supporter of the Anglican-Methodist revival preacher John Wesley and did not support the Oxford Movement, a trend at that time for the Church of England to incorporate rites and rituals of Roman Catholicism into its theology. While the less refined Gustavus Loomis would have snickered at Rev. Cadle's insistence that his cassocks be neatly cleaned and pressed and his liturgical articles be polished and properly laid out, Loomis would wholeheartedly agree with Cadle's profession of faith on his deathbed, "The blood of Christ is sufficient for all things."[214] After his work at Fort Crawford (1836-1840), Rev. Cadle, who never married, served churches in upstate New York, Vermont and Delaware. He died active in ministry in 1857, age sixty-one.

In 1837 Gustavus Loomis was ordered to duty at Jefferson Barracks near Saint Louis. He and Julia again said farewell to their friends at Fort Crawford. A few years earlier Loomis was on

---

213 Howard Greene, *The Reverend Richard Fish Cadle*, (Waukesha, Wisconsin: Privately published, 1936), pp. 43, 57, 91, 107.
214 Howard Greene, *The Reverend Richard Fish Cadle*, pp. 87, 92, 110.

recruiting duty, probably in Saint Louis. This was the first time brevet Major Loomis was assigned to Jefferson Barracks. The fort, built in 1826, was located on the Mississippi River at Lemay, Missouri, which is just south of St. Louis. The fort was a jumping off point for various explorers, scientists and adventurers. The fort held about two hundred and fifty soldiers, some with family members. The fort also served as a supply depot for numerous forts along the Mississippi River, and was a location from which U.S. troops deployed to hot spots along the frontier. The United States Regiment of Dragoons were formed and stationed at Jefferson Barracks.

Brevet Major Gustavus Loomis and his wife Julia were stationed here only a few months. The U.S. Army needed more soldiers in Florida, as the Seminoles were again acting up. Having served in Florida before, Loomis knew what to expect. What he could never have predicted was that he would be fighting in the Second Seminole War in Florida for the next five years.

Chapter Ten

The Second Seminole War, 1837-1842

In 1837, brevet Major Gustavus Loomis was sent to Florida with the 1st Regiment of Infantry. The Second Seminole War had begun, and the U.S. Army was sending hundreds and later thousands of soldiers into Florida to protect the white settlers; to enforce peace treaties with the Seminoles; and to eventually remove the Seminoles from Florida to western reservation lands. Loomis was no stranger to the Seminoles, as he was stationed at Fort Gadsden in northern Florida from 1820-21; he worked with the cousins of the Seminoles in the Creek Nation from 1825-1826; and he served at Cantonment Clinch in Florida from 1826-1827. Gustavus Loomis was now forty-eight years old, a seasoned and mature Indian fighter with experience in war and negotiations with the Winnebago, Sioux, Sauk, Fox, Creek and Seminole Indians. Not counting his cadet years at West Point, Loomis was at this time in the army with twenty-six years of service. With all his years of military experience, Loomis would be tested in the dismal swamps of Florida against a determined and belligerent enemy fighting on their home territory.

The conclusion of the First Seminole War in 1818 did not resolve the tension and hostilities in Florida between the remaining Seminoles and white settlers. Skirmishes between whites and Seminoles were routine through the early 1820s, as expansion minded whites sought the rich central Florida territory for settlement and commercial development. By 1822, Secretary of War John C. Calhoun determined that all Indians were to be deported west of the Mississippi River. In 1823 the Seminoles of Florida sent representatives to meet with Florida Governor William P. Duval and others to arrange for a more flexible treaty. On September 18, 1823 they met at Moultrie Creek, south of Saint Augustine, and there worked out an arrangement for a Seminole reservation in central Florida. The idea of the United States was to confine the Seminoles to lands distant from white settlers, where they could live in solitude and peace and still be monitored by the U.S. Army.[215]

The Treaty of Moultrie Creek did not last. Within a few months friction developed between Florida Governor William P. Duval and Seminole leader Neamathla, as the displaced and impoverished Seminoles began to roam into areas settled by whites, raiding for hogs and cattle and other supplies. By July 1824 Duval's patience with Neamathla had expired. He removed the Seminole from his leadership position and with the support of the Seminoles replaced him with the fifty year old Tuko-see-mathly, a name too cumbersome for the whites to pronounce, who simple called him John Hicks. To comply with the treaty approximately two thousand three hundred Seminoles began preparations to be displaced to reservation lands. Some were to travel westward to the Apalachicola River reservation, but the great majority were to move south to the central Florida reserve. The U.S. government provided monetary compensation to the Seminoles for their displacement expenses, in the form of currency acceptable to the Seminoles, silver coins.

The movements to the reservation lands were not well planned. Federal officials had little concern for how the Semi-

---

215 Joe Knetsch, *Florida's Seminole Wars, 1817-1858*, (Charleston, SC: Arcadia Publishing, 2003), pp.44-45; James W. Covington, *The Seminoles of Florida*, (University of Florida Press, 1993), pp.51-53.

noles would travel often hundreds of miles to the new Florida reservations, nor were the boundaries of the reservations clearly determined. In December 1825, Colonel George Brooke, stationed at Cantonment Brooke in northeast Florida, spoke of the Seminoles as follows.

> I CAN ASSURE you they are in the most miserable situation; and unless the Government assists them, many of them must starve, and others will deprecate on the property of the whites in the Alachua and St. John's settlements. It is impossible for me, or any other officer who possesses the smallest feelings of humanity, to resist affording some relief to men, women, and children who are actually dying for the want of something to eat.[216]

In Florida, the legislative council in 1827 passed a law forbidding Seminoles from leaving the reservation lands, with the threat of thirty-nine lashes for all violators. Gustavus Loomis was serving in Florida at that time. Skirmishes and local negotiations between whites and Seminoles continued through 1829, at which point the new President of the United States, the hero of the First Seminole War General Andrew Jackson, declared his intent to have all Indians removed promptly to reservation lands west of the Mississippi River. The new President had his way, and the Indian Removal Act of 1830 was adopted by Congress in a close vote. On the surface, the new law appeared humane, as Indians would receive financial compensation to move west and would own the lands they settled; policies which were only applicable with the consent of the Indians themselves.[217]

It was not until 1832 that the Seminoles were forced to

---

216 James W. Covington, *The Seminoles of Florida*, p.60.

217 Milton Meltzer, *Hunted Like a Wolf: The Story of the Seminole War*, (New York: Farrar, Straus and Giroux Publishers, 1972), pp.85–86.

respond to the Indian Removal Act of 1830. In January 1832 negotiations began with the Seminoles for their removal from Florida. On May 9, 1832, in a meeting at Payne's Landing on the Ocklawaha River, fifteen representative Seminoles signed the removal treaty. Immediately there was disagreement between the Seminoles related to the status of the removal agreement, with some saying it was binding while others insisted it was not binding until a designated group of Seminoles could travel west of the Mississippi River and see the proposed reservation home for the Seminole people. Thereafter seven Seminole leaders with the Negro interpreter Abraham and with white escorts traveled west to see the proposed reservation lands in Oklahoma Territory. This Seminole delegation on March 28, 1833 signed an agreement called the Treaty of Fort Gibson, which stated that the Seminoles agreed to relocate west three years after the U.S. Congress ratified the treaty. Accusations of fraud, manipulation, and deceit surrounded the treaty signed at Ft. Gibson,[218] but immediately whites in Florida began preparing for the deportation of the Seminoles and the acquisition of their lands.

The Treaty of Moultrie Creek in 1823, the Treaty of Payne's Landing in 1832 and the Fort Gibson Treaty of 1833 all helped the U.S. government to realize the issue was not if the Seminoles would be deported, but when and how it was to be done. In October 1834, Indian Agent Wiley Thompson called the Seminole chiefs and other leaders together to discuss the timing of their removal from Florida. Simultaneously Thompson was getting reports of large amounts of ammunition and weapons being acquired by the Seminoles, while white settlers and farmers con-

---

218 James W. Covington, *The Seminoles of Florida*, p.66; John K. Mahon, *History of the Second Seminole War, 1835-1842,* (University of Florida Press, 1985), p.83; Milton Meltzer, *Hunted Like a Wolf*, pp.88-89.

sistently complained about the Seminoles leaving the reservation and stealing their livestock.

The winter of 1834-1835 was unusually harsh and the Seminoles severely suffered. Simultaneously, General Duncan Clinch, the senior U.S. Army commander in southern Georgia, began to build up his military strength. In February 1835 Wiley Thompson read an ultimatum letter from President Andrew Jackson to one hundred and fifty designated Seminoles, imploring the Seminoles to relocate peacefully, with closing remarks stating that, "I have ordered a large military force to be sent among you...

An 1830's sketch of Seminoles and blacks attacking whites in Florida. Public domain image.

If you refuse to move, I have directed the commanding officer to remove you by force."[219] Now Wiley Thompson was able to get sixteen chiefs to sign a paper accepting the terms of the Payne's Landing Treaty, with others refusing to sign and compelled to fight the whites rather than be forced to relocate west of the Mississippi River. Internal strife now consumed the Seminoles, as General Duncan Clinch gave the Seminoles a January 1, 1836 date to accept the terms of relocation and begin the deportation process. As the deadline approached, hostilities erupted, and the Second Seminole War officially began in December 1835.

As the year 1835 came to a close, a sense of restlessness permeated the white plantation owners in Florida, as evidence began to surface that black slaves were in covert communication with Seminoles and that violence was imminent. Some of the Semi-

219 "Letter from President Andrew Jackson to the Seminoles," February 16, 1835, quoted in Meltzer, *Hunted Like a Wolf*, p.95.

nole chiefs became convinced that resistance was hopeless, and decided to succumb to the inevitable and move west onto reservation lands. A leading chief who advocated removal to the west was Chief Charlie Emathla, who was subsequently killed by the militant Seminole leader Osceola, with the followers of Emathla forced to join Osceola's band or be killed. Five peaceful Seminole chiefs and their followers fled to Ft. Brooke, seeking the protection of the U.S. Army against Osceola's war party. Meanwhile Osceola began raiding military baggage trains and Seminole chiefs King Philip and John Caesar raided valuable sugar plantations along the St. John's River. In response, Florida Governor John Duval recruited five hundred mounted horsemen as a roving militia while President Andrew Jackson, a man with no friendship towards the Seminoles, ordered the senior southern regional Army Commander General Duncan L. Clinch to inflict punishment for outrages so far unpunished. A major goal of the Seminoles was to kill the Indian Agent Wiley Thompson, an act that was completed on December 28 outside the gate of Ft. King. Coordinated with the murder of Agent Thompson on the same day was the ambush and massacre of over one hundred U.S. troops who were under the leadership of Major Francis L. Dade. [220]

As Osceola and his followers celebrated their victories, scouts informed them of a large U.S. Army force under General Clinch approaching Seminole locations on the Withlacoochee. The U.S. force was composed of two hundred and fifty regulars and five hundred Florida militia led by Richard K. Call. The Seminole scouts had effectively done their work, as it took three days for

---

220 Milton Meltzer, *Hunted Like a Wolf*, pp.102-103. The official U.S. military report of the Dade massacre was given by a survivor, Private Clarke, as dictated to the acting Inspector General in Florida, Major Ethan Allen Hitchcock. Major Hitchcock recorded his interview in his personal diary. See Ethan A. Hitchcock, *Fifty Years in Camp and Field: Diary of General Hitchcock*, W. A. Croffut, editor, (New York: The Knickerbocker Press, 1909), pp. 89-91.

General Clinch's troops to reach the Seminole locations on the Withlacoochee. Osceola entrenched his defensive positions as he commanded about two hundred and fifty Seminole warriors and at least thirty blacks. At this December 29, 1835 Battle of Withlacoochee, four U.S. soldiers were killed and twenty-five wounded, as the Seminoles withdrew into the dense swampy forests.

On January 1, 1836 the U.S. military nationwide had a total strength of around seven thousand soldiers led by six hundred officers, all scattered on small posts throughout the country and along the vast frontier. Navy strength was four thousand eight hundred sailors with seven hundred and fifty officers, with an additional force of one thousand four hundred Marines. In the entire vast southern military region there were only five ships. As 1836 began no formal declaration of war was initiated against the Seminoles, who had a total population of around four thousand men, women, and children, with approximately one thousand five hundred dedicated warriors and several hundred black men who served as warriors against the United States.[221]

In February 1836 General Winfield Scott arrived in Florida determined to sweep aside all Seminole resistance. He had a master plan of assault from three directions directly upon the Seminole positions near the Withlacoochee River between Ft. King and Ft. Brooke. This three-pronged attack was lead by General Duncan Clinch from the north, General Abraham Eustis from the east, and Colonel William Lindsey from the south. The intent of General Scott's strategy was to coordinate all three columns in attacking the Seminoles, pinning them against the Gulf of Mexico and thereafter shipping them to reservation lands west of the Mississippi River. This expedition was doomed by logistical problems, rivalries in leadership, and an ignorance of the impassability of the dense and

---

221 Milton Meltzer *Hunted Like a Wolf*, pp. 109, 111, 113.

swampy terrain. Some of the U.S. troops did participate in skirmishes, but the plan as a whole failed. Finally the exhausted troops arrived at Ft. Brooke, in a sad state, with multiple casualties and frustrated at the elusive nature of their enemy.[222] On May 21, 1836 General Winfield Scott gladly left a turbulent Florida that was harassed by random Seminole raids for reassignment in Alabama, thereby passing the senior leadership of U.S. troops in Florida to Governor and militia Brigadier General Richard Keith Call.

In 1836, General Richard K. Call devised a four-fold strategy for eliminating the Seminole problem in Florida. His troops were almost all militia from several states. Call's first attempt at a military campaign to drive the Seminoles south failed, as his troops succumbed to illness and poor supplies. The second attempt in September also failed, as the soldiers engaged the Seminoles but ultimately could not push the Indians south of the Withlacoochee River. His third campaign in September did cross the Withlacoochee River but only found abandoned Seminole villages. General Call's fourth and final campaign in November, 1836 did decisively engage the Seminoles at the November 21 Battle of Wahoo Swamp.

At the Wahoo Swamp several hundred Seminole men, women and children had gathered, General Call sending his entire combined force into the attack along a mile-wide front. With the Tennessee Brigade on the right, the regulars and Florida militia in the

---

222 A junior officer stationed in Florida at this time was Lieutenant John S. Hatheway, who vainly predicted a quick victory over the Seminoles. In his letters he stated, "It is thought we will march immediately for the Outhlacoochee, the sacred ground of the Seminoles. If we meet them there as we expect, you may soon hear of the last death struggle of the Seminoles… For them we strike and if secured, the submission of the Indians will follow in all probability." Lieutenant Hatheway was quickly proven wrong. See his recollections in *Frontier Soldier: The Letters of Major John S. Hatheway, 1833-1853,* (Vancouver, WA: Vancouver National Historic Reserve Trust, 1999), p. 27.

center, and allied Creek Indians on the left, the line moved forward under fire and held its own fire until about fifty feet from the entrenched Seminole positions. The U.S. troops fired in unison on command and then charged with bayonets. The Seminoles returned fire and slowly withdrew, while the advancing U.S. forces floundered in the dense swamp. After advancing over one mile through thick foliage and swamplands the troops under General Call reached a small open area in which passed a thirty-foot wide stream. From the far bank the Seminoles fired from a prepositioned area of felled logs and tree stumps, while the U.S.

An oil painting of the Seminole leader Osceola, painted in 1838.
Public domain image.

soldiers sought protection on the other side of the stream and re-turned fire. General Call's army outnumbered the Seminole force by almost three to one, yet the well fortified Seminoles and the unprotected stream crossing in open terrain forced the U.S. troops to withdraw and seek a resupply point. This encounter, called The Battle of Wahoo Swamp, was inconclusive for both sides.[223] Deeply disgruntled, General Call passed leadership of the U.S. military in Florida to a career regular army officer, senior quartermaster, and former Indian fighter named Major General Thomas Sydney Jessup. It was under General Jessup that brevet Major Gustavus Loomis re-ported to Florida in 1837.

General Thomas S. Jessup was reasonably successful in his turn as the senior U.S. Army commander in Florida. Jessup learned from his predecessors Major General Winfield Scott and Brigadier General Richard K. Call. Jessup saw no purpose in massing large

---

223 John Missall and Mary Lou Missall, *The Seminole Wars: America's Longest Conflict,* (University of Florida Press, 2004), p. 120.

numbers of troops in the virtually impassable swamps and bogs of central Florida. He rather sought out the Seminoles in their camps, capturing hundreds of older men, children, and women, destroying crops and buildings and seeking to force the Seminole warriors to agree to surrender and deportation. Throughout January 1837 Jessup's army successfully pushed the Seminoles farther and farther south and east, burning villages and taking hundreds of prisoners, but having little contact with the best of the Seminole warriors. On January 10, 1837 they attacked Osceola's headquarters located in a secluded village deep in a swamp, and though Osceola was able to escape, over fifty prisoners were taken.

It was shortly after this time that brevet Major Gustavus Loomis arrived in Florida. He was part of a larger strategy of increasing the American troop strength for a spring offensive against the Seminoles. Throughout 1837 various Companies within the 1st Infantry were transferred to duty in several locations in Florida. Loomis's immediate commander was Colonel Zachary Taylor and his senior commander was General Thomas Jessup. Throughout most of 1837 the U.S. Army pursued the Indian and black Seminoles towards the head of the Caloosahatchee River, catching up with their baggage train and taking prisoners. There were periodic skirmishes in and around the Great Cypress Swamp, with a few casualties on both sides, but no significant battles occurred nor were any of the elite Seminole warriors captured. Brevet Major Loomis and his men of the 1st Infantry were ordered to move in small groups in various directions to hunt down the Seminoles in their secluded hammocks, with minimal tactical success but with great achievement as far as upsetting the Seminoles, destroying food storage areas, forcing them to be socially disrupted, and not allowing them to plant crops or build permanent residences.

Simply put, the Seminoles were starving, homeless, and relentlessly pursued by a vastly numerically superior force.[224]

A significant military confrontation between the U.S. Army and the Seminoles occurred on December, 25, 1837 at the Battle of Okeechobee. In this battle, brevet Major Gustavus Loomis played a significant part with the 1st Infantry Regiment. The Battle of Okeechobee was one of the major battles of all the Seminole Wars. It was fought between troops of the 1st, 4th, and 6th Infantry Regiments and Missouri Volunteers against almost five hundred Seminoles led by chiefs Billy Bowlegs, Abiaca and Alligator. The Indian position was well prepared and carefully chosen. The warriors fought while the women, children, old men and other non-combatants were concealed and later fled. The advancing U.S. troops were forced to cross a waist deep saw grass swamp, open land, then a deep slough. Taylor's army came up to a large hammock with half a mile of swamp in front of it. On the far side of the hammock was Lake Okeechobee. Here the

saw grass stood five feet high. The mud and water were three feet deep. Horses would be of no use. It was plain that the Seminole meant this to be the battleground. They had sliced the grass to provide an open field of fire and had notched the trees to steady their rifles. Their scouts were perched in the treetops to follow

---

224 Kenneth E. Lawson, *Religion and the U.S. Army Chaplaincy in the Florida Seminole Wars, 1817-1858*, (Columbia, SC: Eastside Printing, 2006), p. 69.

every movement of the troops coming up.[225] Major Loomis and the other officers suspected a trap, and they were correct.

At about half past noon, the sun shining directly overhead and the air still and quiet, Taylor moved his troops squarely into the center of the swamp. His plan was to make a direct attack rather than encircle the Indians. All his men were on foot. Leading the attack was the Missouri Volunteers in the center of the line, with the 4th and 6th Infantry Regiments on each side. Major Loomis and the 1st Regiment were in reserve, ready to attack upon orders. While advancing the Missouri troops were decimated by fields of fire predetermined by the Seminoles. After exchanging fire with the Indians the Missouri Volunteers retreated and were replaced by regular army soldiers of the 6th Infantry. The 6th advanced under withering fire, the Seminoles intent on killing the officers and thus slowing down the advance. Then Colonel Taylor ordered the 1st Regiment and brevet Major Gustavus Loomis to attack the Seminoles on their right flank, to fire and then charge with fixed bayonets. This attack was fully successful, as the 1st Regiment forced the Seminoles to fire once and then flee the field of battle. The 1st Regiment fought hand to hand with the fleeing Seminoles before the Indians disappeared into the swamps of Lake Okeechobee.[226]

The entire Battle of Okeechobee lasted less than three hours, from just after twelve noon to three in the afternoon. United States casualties were twenty six killed and one hundred and twelve wounded, while Seminole casualties were estimated at twelve killed and less than twenty wounded. The Americans claimed a decisive victory. Technically, the U.S. Army did seize the field of battle and did cause the enemy to flee, so claims of vic-

225 John K. Mahon, *History of the Second Seminole War*, pp. 226-227.
226 John Missall and Mary Lou Missall, *The Seminole Wars, p. 143.* John K. Mahon, *History of the Second Seminole War*, pp.228-229.

tory at the Battle of Okeechobee are valid. Further, the Americans captured one hundred valuable ponies and six hundred Seminole cattle. Nevertheless, the U.S. casualties were very high and the majority of the Seminoles did survive the battle to fight another day. The American wounded were treated and taken to Fort Bassinger, Fort Gardner and Fort Brooke. Gustavus Loomis, as a dedicated Christian, spent considerable time comforting the wounded, meeting their physical and spiritual needs.

Colonel Zachary Taylor was deeply impressed with Loomis' courage under fire and his relentless pursuit of the Seminoles. Loomis was the type of soldier who thrived in a field environment. Although his staff and administrative capabilities were unquestioned, Loomis enjoyed the fight in the field. His men eagerly followed him and did not question his orders or his leadership. There is not even a hint of discontent mentioned by the soldiers or

The author by the historical marker for the 25 December 1837 Battle of Okeechobee.
Photo by Arthur Lawson.

other officers in the 1st Infantry Regiment related to brevet Major Loomis. Whenever he led patrols in the Florida wilderness or resupplied in the crude Florida forts, Loomis was noticed by soldiers. Perhaps it was his appearance, as his graying hair and his age at about fifty years old made him a father-like figure to the men. Perhaps it was his compassion for the ill and wounded that drew the notice of other soldiers. It might have been Loomis' technical competence as an officer with West Point credentials that impressed the men. As a dedicated Christian, Gustavus Loomis gained both the criticism of soldiers and the praise of soldiers, his lack of profanity, his abstinence from alcohol, and his daily Bible reading and hymn singing being routinely noticed by the troops. One example of Loomis being noticed is from the diary of U.S. Army Captain Electus Backus.

Leaving Detroit in November, 1837, Captain Electus Backus arrived in Florida on the eleventh of January, 1838. Captain Backus served in the 1st Regiment of Infantry, the same regiment as brevet Major Loomis. Captain Backus first mentions Loomis in a diary note dated January 21st, stating that Major Loomis was present and that "All well and in pretty good order." Captain Backus next mentions Major Loomis while both were on duty in the south Florida everglades, mentioning Loomis a total of ten times in his diary. The diary section related to the everyday activities of Loomis in the everglades is as follows.

MARCH 3RD — First Regiment ordered to return to Okeechobee, and build a bridge, road, &c. to Fort McRee. Major L [Loomis] to march in boats, with three companies... March 4th – Major Loomis embarked at 10 A.M... March 8th – Marched at 8 A.M.; and at nine, arrived opposite and in sight of Fort McRee, distant about one and a half miles. Encamped on low, wet ground; and commenced building the road. Major Loomis had arrived on the seventh; and sailed on the eighth, for the outlet. March 19th – Cool and windy, in the morning. Went over to Fort McRee. Saw smoke, supposed to be Major Loomis's fires South. Colonel Davenport sick. Some men sick, mostly from eating cabbage. Major Loomis arrived with boats, at six, P.M., having been detained three days with high winds. He had penetrated as far as Fish Creek; and ascertained that the lake had no distinct outlet, at low water. Captured two squaws and one child, sick, and fifteen canoes. The Indians will all come in, when they receive a white flag. They are very destitute and much scattered.   March 20th – A Beautiful, cool morning. Major Loomis ordered to return to Fish Creek for provisions, to supply this command...   March 26th – Marched at sunrise to Fort McRee... Major Loomis returned from Fish Creek with provisions, and had proceeded to Fort Basinger where we arrived at McRee...   March 30th – Major Loomis and command arrived. Assumed command. An express at twelve. But few letters and no papers. Major Loomis and three Companies came from Fort Basinger by water. Brought a cask of boots, and some sugar and tobacco, for this command...[227]

As the Commander of the First Regiment of Infantry in Florida, Colonel Zachary Taylor had a specific strategy for subduing the Seminoles. In command of three thousand, three hundred regular army troops and almost four hundred militia, Taylor intended to keep the Seminoles moving, not allowing them to plant their spring, 1838 crops for a later harvest. Gustavus Loomis and the other officers were responsible for leading the troops south into the Everglades, forcing the Seminoles to keep moving and thus unable to farm, build homes or adequately resupply. The Indians were starving and Colonel Taylor wished them to surrender for deportation to the western reservation lands. In February, 1838, Taylor ordered the 4th Infantry and the 1st Infantry to attack the scattered Seminoles in the northern everglades near

227 Electus Backus, "Diary of a Campaign in Florida, 1837-1838," *The Historical Magazine and Notes and Queries Concerning the Antiquities, History and Biography of America*,(Morrisania, NY: 1866), vol. X, pp. 279-285.

Lake Okeechobee. Major Loomis with the 1st Infantry scoured the shores of the gigantic lake, demolishing makeshift settlements and destroying Seminole canoes. Brief skirmishes ensued with dozens of famished Seminoles surrendering. The 4th and 1st Regiments reported to General Jessup that there were rumors that the Seminole leader Alligator wished to surrender. After intermediaries were sent, Alligator and three hundred and sixty of his followers surrendered.[228] In these dismal living conditions, always on the move, sleeping on moist ground, harassed by mosquitoes and snakes and other vermin, tracking an elusive enemy in thick forests, brevet Major Loomis performed admirably.

Gustavus Loomis was promoted to the rank of Major in the regular army on July 7, 1838. Loomis had served as a brevet Major since April 7, 1829. This was a direct result of Congress in 1821 reducing the size of the army, eliminating regiments and reducing the number of officers.[229]   For almost nine years Loomis was in the awkward position of holding a brevet rank, meaning he wore the rank of Major and he was treated as such, but he was not paid as a Major and could easily be reverted back from brevet Major to Captain. To hold a brevet rank for almost nine years was unusual but not unheard of. Simply stated, there were more officers in the army than there were positions. Promotions were typically few and far between. An aspiring officer had to wait for a senior officer to retire, resign or die before a vacancy was available and career progression was possible. Loomis had more than proven himself as a very capable officer. There is no record of Loomis ever complaining about his lack of promotion to his congressman

228 K. Jack Bauer, *Zachary Taylor, Soldier, Planter, Statesman of the Old Southwest,* (Louisiana State University Press, 1993), pp. 85, 89.

229 Allan R. Millett & Peter Maslowski, *For the Common Defense: A Military History of the United States,* (New York: The Free Press, 1994), p. 128. Maurice Matloff, *American Military History,* (Washington, DC: 1973), p. 154.

in Vermont or to his military chain of command. When a position opened up within the 2nd Regiment of Infantry in Florida, Loomis' superiors put him in for the promotion to Major in the regular army and it was granted.

The U.S. Army did not function well in the heat of the Florida summers. Typically the army operated against the Seminoles for eight or nine months of the year, using the summer months for detailed planning, rest, and provisioning of the troops. With the arrival of cool weather in November, 1838, the recently promoted General Zachary Taylor deployed the 2nd Regiment of Infantry and other regiments throughout almost the entire Florida peninsula. Major Gustavus Loomis and troops from the 2nd Regiment and a Georgia militia force were assigned to act against the Indians in the Okefenokee area. This region was a gigantic swamp along the north Florida border with Georgia. As settlers migrated into Florida, the U.S. Army was tasked with providing safety to the migrants. In the Okefenokee Swamp were several dozen or perhaps a hundred or more Seminoles and Creeks that evaded previous attempts for their resettlement or deportation. As one writer stated, "Major Gustavus Loomis with a mixed unit of infantry and dragoons drew the unenviable assignment of pacifying the Okefenokee Swamp and its surrounding region in conjunction with Georgia volunteers under Brigadier General Charles Floyd."[230] The overall objective of General Taylor's strategy was to force all Indians south of a line on his map parallel to Fort Brooke. The goal was to have all Seminoles above this line deported to western reservation lands or to have them resettled in the deepest southern everglades.

In the 1838-1839 military activities at the Okefenokee Swamp, the newly promoted Major Gustavus Loomis of the 2nd Regiment of Infantry was the senior regular army officer, working under

---

230 K. Jack Bauer, *Zachary Taylor*, p.89.

the command of a Brigadier General of Georgia militia. Loomis was completely isolated from his regular army chain of command. He was hundreds of miles from a convenient resupply depot. He was forced to work with Georgia militia, men who were not as disciplined as Major Loomis would have liked. Further, Loomis was required to respond to the orders of and coordinate his activities with militia General Floyd, something that many regular army officers would be reluctant to do.

In October 1838 General Charles Floyd was ordered to meet five companies of troops, about three hundred soldiers, on the southwestern side of the swamp in order to chase the Seminoles out of their secluded stronghold. In coordinating with Major Loomis, Floyd immediately set out to meet his troops and made his first foray into the Okefenokee in early November. During the campaign General Floyd faced an early mutiny, illicit alcohol use among the men, scattered Seminole bands that struck and ran, and the disorienting and sickening swamp. Loomis had no morale issues with his regular army troops but his soldiers did suffer from the miserable environment. General Floyd and his troops managed to traverse the Okefenokee Swamp a number of times in their search for the enemy, marching "through the most infernal places" and emerging from its vastnesses "worn down with fatigue, and many were without shoes, hats, & pantaloons, these articles having been destroyed by the obstacles in the swamp." Floyd's soldiers found only one abandoned village, which they burned, on an island. The soldiers named it Floyd's Island after their commander, an act that Floyd proudly reported in his diary. Soldiers under Floyd and Loomis did fight several times with small Seminole bands, with inconclusive results. General Floyd died a few months after his military service, probably as a result of a disease he acquired in the Okefenokee Swamp.[231] In his few months in the Okefenokee Swamp, into early 1839, Major Loomis again performed admirably.

An example of the appreciation Loomis received from his superior officers is in the July 20, 1839 report General Zachary Taylor filed with Colonel Roger Jones, the Adjutant General of the U.S. Army in Washington. In this six page report, read by all the senior military personnel in Washington and all the senior civilian military advisors to U.S. President Martin Van Buren, Brigadier General Taylor related in detail his military activities in Florida. In this fascinating analysis of the Seminole War by a senior military officer, Taylor mentions Major Gustavus Loomis twice. First, Taylor states that "Major G. Loomis, 2nd Infantry" was ordered to the Okefenokee Swamp with four companies of infantry and one company of dragoons, to work with the Georgia militia to secure the northern Florida border. In his second reference to Loomis, General Taylor summarized Loomis' success on this mission by saying, "The troops under Major Loomis, have succeeded in giving entire protection to the Georgia frontier."[232] This was high praise from the senior commander in all Florida, praise not readily handed out by the often stoic Zachary Taylor.

The year 1839 was not a good year for the U.S. Army in Florida. For example, in March Captain Russell of I Company, 2nd Regiment was killed in an ambush when his boat was fired upon by Seminoles who were hidden on the shore. In April and May the senior U.S. Army officer in the entire army, Major General Alexander Macomb, came to Fort King to negotiate a peace treaty with the

---

231 "Charles Reynaldo Floyd," *The New Georgia Encyclopedia*, www.georgiaencyclopedia.org/nge/Article.jsp?id=h-1098. Accessed January 5, 2010. John K. Mahon, *History of the Second Seminole War*, p. 253.

232 John T. Sprague, *The Origin, Progress and Conclusion of the Florida War*, (New York: 1847), pp. 222, 226.

Seminoles. While negotiations were ongoing, Lieutenant Martin of the 2ⁿᵈ Regiment was wounded in a Seminole attack, with two of his men killed. Of those soldiers who pursued the Seminoles, six troops were killed.[233] Nevertheless, on May 20 General Macomb declared that peace had been achieved and that the Seminoles would quietly move to a reservation south of the Peace River and west of the Kissimmee River towards the everglades.

As peace was declared in May, 1839, hostile bands of roving Seminoles were still dangerously at large. On June 5ᵗʰ, thirty Seminoles awaiting deportation escaped their modest confinement facility in Tampa and fled into the Florida wilderness. On June 17th the Chaires family near Tallahassee was massacred. While small scale deprecations by Seminoles against whites continued, a hopeful event occurred in the early summer of 1839, as Chief Arpeik (Sam Jones) near Ft. Lauderdale publicly stated his agreement with the Macomb peace plan and urged his clan to live up to the agreement. Meanwhile the Seminoles were pushed south as the region was carefully mapped by the army. Bridges, roads, and new posts were constructed at the cost of the lives of two officers and six enlisted men who were killed by marauding Seminoles.

In July 1839 the Macomb peace initiative completely collapsed. Under orders from General Macomb, General Zachary Taylor ordered Lieutenant Colonel William S. Harney and a small force of twenty-six men to establish a fort and a trading post on the Caloosahatchee River. At sunrise a surprise Seminole attack with a force of about one hundred and sixty warriors killed all but fourteen of the U.S. troops, departing with numerous weapons and supplies taken from the soldiers. Attacks by Seminoles occurred all over the Florida territory, ambushing wagon trains, scouting parties, and foraging details, to the point that any white person in central Florida

233 W. M. Wright, "The Second Regiment of Infantry," www.history.army.mil/books/ R&H/R&H-2IN. Accessed August 5, 2009.

who ventured outside a military fort was in grave danger. The Macomb peace plan totally failed, and General Taylor had an increasingly unstable and violent theater of operations to command. The use of bloodhounds to find the Seminoles in the swampy terrain was a failure and was widely criticized by American newspapers. In 1839, success remained elusive for the U.S. military, while Seminole raids and harassment increased.[234]

The Seminole War had become a federal embarrassment and a financial nightmare. Throughout 1839, brevet Major Loomis was in various locations throughout Florida commanding troops, coordinating supplies and reinforcements, caring for the injured, wounded and sick, and conducting endless administrative duties. Soldiers from his 2nd Regiment were literally all over Florida. At the end of 1839 and into 1840, Loomis was at the regimental headquarters at Picolata, west of Saint Augustine and performed courts martial duties at Pilatka, a few miles to the south. As General Zachary Taylor's time of command in Florida wound down, the critics of the army in Congress and the frustrations of the people of Florida pointed to the necessity of a change in senior command in the Seminole War. On April 21, 1840 Taylor joyfully received permission to resign from command in Florida and was reassigned to duty in Oklahoma and then Arkansas. On May 5th the new commander of U.S forces in Florida, brevet Brigadier General Walker K. Armistead assumed command.

General Walker Armistead was a career military officer with extensive experience who had served earlier in the Second Seminole War. In order to beat the oncoming summer heat and sickly season, Armistead immediately deployed troops to explore and patrol uncharted regions of Florida, set up his command headquarters at Fort King, and began communicating with territorial

234 Joseph Knetsch, *Florida's Seminole Wars*, pp. 120-123; John K. Mahon, *History of the Second Seminole War*, pp. 262-264.

officials in an effort to coordinate resources and tactics. Secretary of War Joel Poinsett ordered one thousand Florida militia to protect northern settlements. Later on July 14th he ordered the number increased to one thousand five hundred militia troops to be placed under the command of General Leigh Read of the Florida militia. Poinsett then ordered General Armistead to disband numerous established posts and to deploy mobile troops in groups of at least one hundred and twenty soldiers to seek out and engage the enemy.[235] Major Gustavus Loomis of the 2nd Regiment of Infantry was directly influenced by these orders. Using this strategy, army scouts continued to find secluded Seminole homesteads, large well-cultivated fields full of healthy vegetables, and multiple evidences that the Seminoles were not as far south as the U.S. leaders were led to believe.

General Armistead quickly divided Florida into two zones, separated by the Suwannee River, with the intent of removing or displacing the Seminoles from each zone. Before this plan could

be enacted the Seminoles struck, attacking a military detachment on May 19, 1840 under the leadership of Wildcat (Coacoochee), resulting in the death of one lieutenant and five soldiers. Shortly thereafter an unprotected civilian wagon train traveling from Picolata to St. Augustine was raided, mercilessly killing

---

235 Joseph Knetsch, *Florida's Seminole Wars*, p. 124.

most of the people and looting the caravan of goods and supplies. These deprecations propelled the U.S. military into a search and destroy mission, burning Seminole crops and destroying their secluded homes throughout the Wahoo Swamp, Chocochatti Hammock, and sites along the Ocklawaha River. Major Gustavus Loomis deployed numerous troops from the 2nd Infantry on such missions. Some of the Seminole villages discovered and destroyed were within fifteen miles of Ft. King, the headquarters for the U.S. Army in Florida and an area previously thought secure from Seminole influence.

On August 7, 1840 the Spanish speaking Seminole leader named Chakaika canoed with his band of warriors thirty miles along a string of small islands in extreme southern Florida. Between Ft. Dallas and Key West is the island called Indian Key. Here was located a small but successful civilian community with a rest home for invalids, a port for numerous marine salvage operations, a horticultural research facility, and a generally affluent and isolated white population. Thirteen whites were murdered by Seminoles, all civilians. Most of their buildings were destroyed; supplies were stolen, and were it not for the noise of the attack many of the defenseless whites would have been killed, the noise of the assault allowing many of the whites to flee to their boats for safety.[236]

A significant U.S. military victory was achieved under orders from General Armistead. Lieutenant Colonel William Harney was ordered to pursue the illusive Chakaika, who not only led the massacre at Indian Key but eighteen months earlier had successfully surprised and defeated Harney in an early morning attack. In early December 1840 Harney and his ninety men in sixteen canoes and with a reliable Negro guide stealthy traveled for twelve days through marshes, inland lakes and swamps infested

---

236 James W. Covington, The Seminoles of Florida, p. 99.

with dense undergrowth. The few Seminoles found on this covert operation were hung on the spot, allowing Harney's assault to take Chakaika and his warriors completely by surprise. Dressing themselves as Seminoles, the whites entered the Seminole camp undetected, Chakaika believing he was safe from any white detection. A fierce fight ensued, Chakaika was killed, and the soldiers prevailed, as Harney hung some captured warriors and even hung the corpse of Chakaika for public ridicule before Chakaika's wife and numerous prisoners. One U.S. soldier was killed in this action, four Indians were killed plus five hanged, several dozen Seminoles were made prisoners, while other Indians escaped into the swampy wilderness.[237]

While Armistead was commander in Florida there were numerous sharp engagements with the Seminoles, such as the June 1840 expedition lead by Captain Bonneville of the 7th Infantry, which probed deep into the Big Cypress Swamp and assaulted a group of one hundred Seminoles gathered to participate in the Green Corn Dance. That same month Captain Bonneville destroyed a Seminole stronghold at Chocachatti, endeavors which earned him a brevet rank of Colonel.[238] A significant attempt at peace was attempted on November 10, 1840, when Armistead met with the influential Seminole Chief Tiger Tail (Thlocklo Tustenuggee) who was of the Tallahassee can, and Chief Halleck Tustenuggee of the Mikasuki clan. After two weeks of delays while the Seminole delegation lived off U.S. food, supplies, and alcohol, the Seminoles departed without agreeing to a peace plan. General Armistead then ordered his four thousand five hundred regular Army troops and two thousand militia soldiers back to routine

237 James W. Covington, *The Seminoles of Florida*, pp. 99-100; John K. Mahon, *History of the Second Seminole War,* p. 283.
238 John K. Mahon, *History of the Second Seminole War* p. 278.

operations, beginning a period of dull and uneventful military service throughout the fall and winter of 1840-1841.

On September 22, 1840, a significant career milestone took place for Major Gustavus Loomis. On that date he was promoted from Major to Lieutenant Colonel in the regular army. This not a brevet promotion, Loomis was promoted remarkably quickly. Previously, on July 7, 1838 he was promoted to Major. That meant Loomis was promoted from Major to Lieutenant Colonel in twenty-six months. This was an amazing accomplishment, virtually unheard of the army at that time. The reasons for this quick rise to a senior officer position are several. First, army administrators may have understood the disservice done to Loomis from the nine years he served in the rank of brevet Major, and sought to make things right. Another consideration is the glowing reports about Loomis' service in Florida, especially the July 20, 1839 report from Brigadier General Zachary Taylor to the Adjutant General of the Army, a report that spoke well of Loomis' Florida service. Another factor in the quick promotion of Loomis from Major to Lieutenant Colonel was simply that he earned the promotion. At that time Loomis was fifty one years old and had a spotless military record. He had served in the miserable conditions of rural Florida since 1837 and had always performed ad-

A sketch of the Seminole Chief Coacoochee, a key antagonist in the Second Seminole War.
Source: The Seminole Tribe of Florida.

mirably. He was an excellent administrator and logistician. In a field environment he was an aggressive and fearless commander. He was loved by his men and respected by his superiors. With his promotion to Lieutenant Colonel, Gustavus Loomis was assigned to the 6th Regiment of Infantry in Florida.[239]

The 6th Regiment was an experienced unit with extensive service in Florida, a unit that welcomed Lieutenant Colonel Loomis. The 6th considered itself fortunate to have a seasoned and mature Lieutenant Colonel assigned to them and not some staff officer from Washington with no combat experience in the Florida swamps.

While much of Florida remained tense throughout the winter of 1840-1841, the removal policy of the U.S. government in deporting Seminoles to the west was gaining momentum. In February there were two hundred and seventy Indians held at Tampa awaiting removal, with small numbers being added to this all the time, the result of relentless scouting by U.S. troops. By this point in the prolonged Second Seminole War, U.S. soldiers had fully adapted to guerrilla warfare and were successful in using the swamps and hammocks of southern Florida to great advantage against the scattered Seminoles. The 6th Infantry under Lieutenant Colonel Loomis was no exception. The Seminole population in Florida was clearly declining. Along with the attrition of Indian forces from combat, the senior commander General Armistead offered financial rewards to Seminoles who voluntarily surrendered for deportation, a plan that had minimal results. The relentless pressure by roving U.S. patrols forced the minor chief Coacoochee (Wild Cat) in March 1841 to agree to surrender his clan in a few months time. General Armistead terminated his command on May 31, 1841, after almost thirteen months of command against the Seminoles. His record in Florida was relatively good. He had shipped four hundred and fifty Seminole Indians and Negroes west with two hundred and thirty six on the docks

239 George W. Cullum, *Biographical Register of the Officers and Graduates of the U.S. Military Academy, at West Point,* (New York: 1868), p. 62.

ready for deportation. As he departed command Armistead estimated that there were around three hundred Seminole warriors
and several hundred family members left in all of Florida.[240]

From 1841 through the end of the war in 1842, the 6th Regiment of Infantry under Lieutenant Colonel Loomis endured
predictable hardships. As a history of the Sixth Regiment stated,
Florida was a place "that was cold and wet in winter, and hot and
humid in summer; where only the Seminoles, alligators, snakes,
and mosquitoes knew how to survive; and where dysentery and
malaria were the primary rewards for Herculean efforts. There,
the regiment won Campaign Streamer - SEMINOLE - for its actions near Lake Okeechobee. The Regiment remained in Florida
until restoration of peace."[241]

Lieutenant Colonel Loomis had some morale and discipline
issues to address in his command of the 6th Regiment. For example, a lieutenant named William H.T. Walker caused Loomis a
few weeks of distraction in the spring of 1841. Lieutenant Walker
was wounded at the December, 1838 Battle of Okeechobee and
convalesced for almost two years. In November of 1840 he was
reassigned to the 6th Regiment. As commander, Loomis placed
Walker on duty under another lieutenant who had three months
less seniority than Walker. The impulsive Lieutenant Walker re-
acted poorly. As Walker's biographer stated, "In an amazing dis-
regard of military protocol, he [Walker] dashed off a hotheaded
letter, dated March 18, to the Regimental Commander, Lieutenant Colonel Gustavus Loomis, a fifty-three year old veteran of
the War of 1812." In the letter, Walker accused Loomis of neglect,
of violating his rights, and of slighting him. Walker's biographer

240 John K. Mahon, *History of the Second Seminole War* pp. 285-287. Kenneth E. Lawson, *Religion and the U.S. Army Chaplaincy in the Florida Seminole Wars*, pp. 86-87.
241 "The Regulars – A History of the 6th U.S. Infantry," www.fortatkinsononline.
org/6thInfyHistory. Accessed January 7, 2010.

remarked, "Loomis took this affront to his authority about as well as might be expected. He had Walker relieved from his company and placed in arrest, and he preferred charges against him to be resolved by court-martial." The court martial was in Tampa Bay. "After two days of this sham" and after offering "lame excuses," Walker was found guilty of one of the three charges.[242] He was reprimanded by General Armistead and was returned to duty with the 6th Regiment. All of this was a distraction to Loomis, but was part of the administrative responsibilities of serving as a regimental commander.

Lieutenant Colonel Loomis led the 6th Regiment in Florida until the illusive peace was achieved in August, 1842. The last senior U.S. commander in the Second Seminole War was the energetic Colonel William Jenkins Worth. He was a career military officer who served in the War of 1812, served as Commandant of West Point from 1820–1828, and served in the Black Hawk War and in numerous frontier assignments. At the time of his posting in Florida, military service against the Seminoles was considered a no-win situation, a graveyard for a commander's military reputation.[243] At this point Congress was fed up with the Florida Indians and began financial and troop cutbacks. Colonel Worth consolidated smaller commands and continued the use of roving well-armed patrols consisting of up to two hundred men which sought out illusive Seminoles from all directions. Worth also did something no other commander in Florida dared to do on a large scale, namely an extensive campaign in the tropical summer heat. This was with the intention of depriving the Seminoles of their summer planting season and thus increasing their chance of starvation over the winter months. This objective was relentlessly

---

242 Russell K. Brown, *To the Manner Born: The Life of General William H.T. Walker*, (Mercer University Press, 2005), pp. 14-16.

243 Joseph Knetsch, *Florida's Seminole Wars*, p. 129.

pursued by destroying hundreds of acres of crops and confiscating supplies, while capturing and deporting Seminole families as they labored on isolated family farms.[244]

Military patrols frequently departed from Forts Brooke, King and Dade, hounding the Seminoles and pushing them south, to either surrender or starve. The summer of 1841 campaign in Florida was highly successful for Colonel Worth's soldiers. The Seminoles were forced to flee hastily to the dense swampy morass of south central Florida. Soldiers were destroying Seminole homes and crops virtually unopposed. An exception to this successful U.S. military adventure was the inability to hunt down and capture the influential Seminole named Sam Jones (Arpeika). Excursions out of Ft. Dallas and Ft. Lauderdale into the everglades could not contact this clever Seminole leader.

The summer of 1841 campaign of Colonel Worth was called "a marvel of execution and planning."[245] Worth went against the medical corps' advice and executed a summer campaign in the sweltering and humid Florida tropics. Ordering Lieutenant Colonel Loomis and the 6th Regiment out of their comfortable quarters at Fort Harrison (Clearwater) Florida, Loomis divided his command into three coordinated columns. Loomis used Fort

244 Milton Meltzer, *Hunted Like a Wolf,* p. 187. A common soldier named Private James D. Elderkin was stationed in Florida at this time and wrote an insightful account of the tactics used by the evasive Seminoles and the harsh conditions experienced by the U. S. military. Of the Seminole tactics he stated, "They had penetrated the jungles deep… Concealing themselves under the dense foliage, covered with Spanish moss, they were indiscernible until they revealed their position by a rifle shot." Related to the disagreeable climate and terrain, Private Elderkin remarked, "Of all my experiences of hardship in three wars, that which I experienced in Florida was the worst" as he spoke of trails beset with thorns, razor sharp grass, poisonous snakes, horrible mosquitoes, saturated filthy clothing, and succinctly calling Florida a "dark and bloody ground." See James D. Elderkin, *Biographical Sketches and Antidotes of a Soldier of Three Wars as Written by Himself: The Florida, the Mexican War, and the Great Rebellion Together,* (Detroit: 1899), pp. 17-20, 32.

245 Joseph Knetsch, *Florida's Seminole Wars,* p. 130.

Cooper as his base. The first column headed up the Homosassa River and destroyed the lodgings and supplies of the Seminole leader Tiger Tail. The second column scoured the banks of the Withlacoochee River destroying dozens of Seminole campsites and farms. The third column searched the Withlacoochee and Lake Panasoffkee, destroying numerous planting grounds and small settlements. Loomis' planning, coordinating and execution of this three pronged search and destroy mission was masterful, as the surprised Seminoles were killed, captured or fled south.

The command philosophy of using larger, roving well-armed patrols coordinated by Colonel Worth successfully harassed Seminoles throughout all parts of Florida, resulting in large numbers of Indians surrendering for deportation. The 6th Infantry under Lieutenant Colonel Loomis captured dozens of Seminoles and forced scores more to surrender. In October 1841 almost three hundred Seminoles were deported, with a follow-on group of one hundred and sixty two Indians agreeing to surrender and relocation west of the Mississippi River, including the important leader Thlocko Tustenuggee. Early in February 1842 another two hundred and thirty Seminoles were shipped west, including sixty eight warriors.[246] For the first time, Seminoles knew that there was no place in Florida where they would be safe from the whites. The Indians were homeless, starving, and hiding from an enemy that was no longer ineffective in the marshy Florida wilderness. By early 1842 the U.S. military was in clear control of the Seminoles, with only isolated resistance from several groups of warriors and their families. Other Seminoles remained hidden. By the spring of 1842 there remained in Florida less than six hundred Seminoles, both males and females of all ages.

In January, 1842, Colonel Worth coordinated troops from the

---

246 Milton Meltzer, *Hunted Like a Wolf*, pp. 192-193.

4th, 6th and 7th Regiments to try and capture the illusive Halleck Tustenuggee and his band of followers. Halleck vehemently opposed the seizure of Indian lands by whites, and even killed his own sister by cutting her throat when she talked about surrender. He fought at the Battle of Lake Okeechobee on December 25, 1837, and was severely wounded by U.S. troops at a skirmish at Fort King in April 1840. After he recovered, Halleck Tustenuggee went on a bloody rampage in north Florida for two years, leading a series of raids and skirmishes. Lieutenant Colonel Loomis led the 6th Infantry into the Wacasassa Hammock in west central Florida, while the 4th and 7th Regiments searched elsewhere for Halleck Tustenuggee.[247] These efforts to search out for Halleck Tustenuggee kept him moving, hungry, homeless and in despair. His surrender was inevitable.

The last large confrontation between the Seminoles and the U.S. Army in this war occurred on April 19, 1842, and was directly led by Colonel Worth. Near Lake Apopka Halleck Tustenuggee and his forty warriors decided to make an entrenched stand against the nearly four hundred men under Colonel Worth's command from the Second, Fourth, and Eighth Infantry. Lieutenant Colonel Loomis and the Sixth Regiment were not in this engagement. The fight resulted in a total victory for the U.S. troops and the discovery that the Seminole families in hiding had no food, clothing, cooking utensils, or supplies of any kind.[248]

Seven years of financially wasteful, inefficient, and bloody war in Florida came to an official end in August 1842. President John Tyler and his military advisors prudently decided that a couple of hundred Seminoles isolated in virtually uninhabitable marshes in southern Florida were not worth the effort and expense it would

247 John K. Mahon, *History of the Second Seminole War* pp. 305-306.
248 James W. Covington, *The Seminoles of Florida*, pp. 105-106; Joseph Knetsch, *Florida's Seminole Wars,* pp. 131-132.

take to deport every last Indian. Colonel Worth suggested to the Secretary of War John C. Spencer that the Seminoles be allowed to settle peacefully in remote reservation lands far from white settlers. The recommendation was accepted. Secretary Spencer and the Commanding General of the entire U.S. Army, General Winfield Scott, both told Colonel Worth to end combat operations at an expedient time and location, and to pursue a peace treaty with the Seminoles.

On July 21, 1842 negotiations for peace and resettlement upon reservation lands in south central Florida began at Ft. Brooke, and were continued on August 5th at Tampa and on August 10th at Cedar Keys. Seminole chief Billy Bowlegs accepted the terms of peace, as did other Seminole representatives, but not all tribes were represented at the conference. Some Seminoles wanted to immigrate to the west to rejoin their families and were allowed to do so, while others desired to migrate south to the reservation lands. At this time no Seminole leader publicly stated that he wished hostilities to continue.

With the formal cessation of hostilities in Florida, Colonel Worth was promoted to Brigadier General for his efforts. Meanwhile many Florida residents still resented the fact that even one Indian remained in the peninsula.[249] White civilians attacked some of the south migrating Seminoles and the U.S. Army was called to protect the Indians and insure that the peace terms would be fulfilled. The war had decimated the Seminoles, as a population of over five thousand in Florida was reduced by immigration and war to less than six hundred men, women, and children. The U.S. casualties for the war were seventy four commissioned officers killed,[250] one thousand three hundred and ninety two regular Army non-commissioned officers or enlisted

249 Milton Meltzer, *Hunted Like a Wolf*, p. 197.
250 John K. Mahon, *History of the Second Seminole War*, p.321.

men killed; about 25 percent dying from direct combat and the rest killed by disease, infected wounds, suicides, or accidents. Sixty-nine total Navy men died, while casualty statistics for the numerous militia forces are incomplete. We do know that fifty five militia troops were killed in direct combat but we have no account of the hundreds who died of other causes in the Florida wilderness.[251]

The Second Seminole War had a distinct influence upon Gustavus Loomis. He entered the war in 1837 and remained on combat duty for the next five years, being in Florida in the summer of 1842 as combat operations ceased. Five years of drudgery in an inhospitable climate fighting a determined and elusive foe was a lot to ask of any man. Yet from every indication, Loomis thrived and excelled in this environment. He was a man of tireless energy, there being no record of him sick while hundreds of others succumbed to fever, dehydration, trench foot, malnutrition and various mosquito born diseases. He was mostly in the field with the troops, keeping the men well supplied, properly fed and with plenty of ammunition.

A drawing of Chief Micanopy, primary leader in the Second Seminole War.
Source: The Micanopy Historical Society, Micanopy, Florida.

He made the adjustment in military tactics to fight a guerrilla war and put away the Napoleonic tactics he learned at West Point which dominated the army at that time. In doing this he saved lives. As a devout Christian, Loomis sought

251 John K. Mahon, *History of the Second Seminole War*, p. 325.

to apply the Sabbath day rest for his soldiers whenever possible, a gesture tremendously appreciated by both the pious and the skeptic. Perhaps the most obvious evidence that Loomis thrived in his duties in the Florida wilderness was his rapid progression in military rank. He entered the war in 1837 as a brevet Major and was quickly promoted to Major and then to Lieutenant Colonel. He departed the Second Seminole War as a senior officer in the U.S. Army, one only a few dozen to hold such rank.

The religious zeal of Gustavus Loomis did not fade while he served in the Second Seminole War in Florida. Unfortunately for him the army did not assign chaplains to regiments at that time, but to large army installations. There were no army chaplains serving with Loomis in Florida. While he was stationed at Fort Brooke or Fort Harrison he had opportunity to attend civilian church services in nearby Tampa. When stationed near Saint Augustine at Fort Picolata or at Fort Pilatka, he may have attended a Protestant civilian church in the city. But the fact is that for Gustavus Loomis to maintain his spiritual fervor in the Florida swamps he largely had to do so on his own. Major and later Lieutenant Colonel Loomis dedicated himself to personal Bible study and prayer. He sang from the Psalms and memorized scripture. He read Christian books and newspapers. And he spoke to others about his faith whenever possible.

An example of Gustavus Loomis sharing his evangelical faith comes from the correspondence of two wealthy Floridians, one who was at Fort King in December, 1840. While visiting Fort King in north central Florida, Ms. Willo Brown wrote an interesting note to her sister, a note which mentions the religion of Lieutenant Colonel Loomis. The note says, in part:[252]

---

252 James M. Denham, Keith L. Hunetcutt, Corrina B. Aldrich, Ellen B. Anderson, *Echoes from a Distant Frontier: The Brown Sister's Correspondence from Antebellum Florida,* (University of South Carolina Press, 2004), p. 139.

DEAREST,

I should have written to you by the last mail, but in consequence of delaying to do so until the night before the express left, I lost my opportunity entirely; cause why, an express arrived from Tampa just as night set in & the Colonel's demand for my services was not to be refused. While Colonel Loomis was here, he blundered as usual upon the subject of religion at a most unreasonable time in the presence of Col. R & states to him that his duty to his God was paramount to all others & his duty to his country next. Col. R. replied "no – my duty to my country before all others" - & in saying so, I believe he was perfectly sincere…

I am now occupying my new quarters. The Colonel [Loomis] told me yesterday that he wished me to go to you about the 1st of next month, but I am somewhat in doubt about going until I can hear from you – as I could not remain many days in Newmansville – he goes at that time to Pilatka & on his return wishes me here to join him on a scout on the Ocklewaha… About transportation, I would say my dear Ell, that if I have not mentioned anything about it to you, it is because I did not give it a moment's thought – it is always at my command. I have rigged up an ambulance with four fine sorrel horses (in which the ladies ride out here every day, very imprudent by the bye at this time and I told them so) in which I intended to drive down in stile [style] with the Colonel's body guard, 20 horsemen, or part of it…

This is a very interesting insight into the personal life and habits of Lieutenant Colonel Gustavus Loomis. Here we see an officer and a gentleman providing hospitality and transportation to a wealthy socialite Floridian. Obviously this means that there were moments in the Second Seminole War when Loomis was not consumed with chasing Indians in the wilderness, that there were select opportunities for relaxation along with routine military duties. We also learn from this letter that during the war, white civilian women were allowed (with military escort) to travel throughout northern and central Florida. This shows us that the Seminole threat by the winter of 1840–1841 was confined to certain areas more to the south. The above letter from Ms. Willo Brown is also insightful as to the religious personality of Gustavus Loomis.

In her letter, Ms. Brown states, "While Colonel Loomis was here, he blundered as usual upon the subject of religion." Here Ms. Brown informs us that it was normal for Lieutenant Colonel Loomis to speak about religion, that it was typical for him to share his faith. She had heard him speak of the subject numerous times, and was likely present in Loomis' home when he sang Psalms after supper and read his Bible to his guests. It is interesting to read that Ms. Brown considered Loomis' religious expressions as "blundering". Obviously she was not a supporter of Loomis' outspoken Christianity.

Ms. Brown makes a second notation about the religion of Gustavus Loomis when she writes, "that his duty to his God was paramount to all others & his duty to his country next." For Loomis, the Lord was always first, above his career, above himself, above his marriage and daughter, above everything. This was not well received by Ms. Brown and by the other Colonel who was part of that conversation. Nevertheless, Loomis was on solid biblical and historical ground when he asserted that God was the first priority in his life.

Biblically, we are told in the Old Testament, in the first of the Ten Commandments, that a person is to put no god before the Lord (Exodus 20:3). In the New Testament, Jesus Christ taught that the first and greatest commandment is to love the Lord with all your heart, all your soul, all your strength (Matthew 22:36-38). From a historical perspective, as Loomis placed his service to God above all else, he was in full conformity to the first tenant of the *Westminster Shorter Catechism,* which asserts, "What is the chief end of man? Man's chief end is to glorify God, and to enjoy him forever." The *Catechism* continues and asks, "What is the duty which God requireth of man? The duty which God requireth of man, is obedience to his revealed will." In reference to the first of the Ten Commandments, the *Catechism* states, "What is required in the first commandment? The first commandment requireth us to know and acknowledge God to be the only true God, and our God; and to worship and glorify him accordingly… What is forbidden in the first commandment? The first commandment forbiddeth the denying, or not worshiping and glorifying, the true God as God, and our God; and the giving of that worship and glory to any other, which is due to him alone."[253] Gustavus Loomis learned this *Shorter Catechism* as a boy under the direction of Pastor Asa Burton in Thetford, Vermont. He never abandoned these teachings of his youth.

In 1842, Lieutenant Colonel Gustavus Loomis departed Florida for duty at Fort Gibson, Indian Territory, in modern Oklahoma. In the Second Seminole War there was about forty million dollars expended. Ten thousand U.S. Army troops and thirty thousand militia soldiers were called to duty sometime during this extended war. Few white Floridians were content with any Seminoles remaining in Florida, especially their new delegate in Congress, the Democrat David Levy, who stated, "Let us hear no more sympathy for these Indians. They know no mercy. They are demons, not men. They have the human form, but nothing of the human heart…. If they can not be emigrated, they should be

---

253 *Westminster Shorter Catechism*, www.reformed.org/documents/WSC. Accessed January 9, 2010.

exterminated."[254] Gustavus Loomis could have never known that thirteen years from this date he would be back in Florida fighting and relocating Seminoles. For now he was relieved to get out of the dismal Florida weather and inhospitable terrain to a new assignment in a comfortable garrison in the west.

---

254 Milton Meltzer, *Hunted Like a Wolf*, p. 197.

CHAPTER ELEVEN

INDIAN TERRITORIES, 1842-1848

IT IS NOT DIFFICULT TO imagine that Lieutenant Colonel Gustavus Loomis was relieved to depart Florida for his next assignment. He spent five years living in an inhospitable climate, sleeping in the wilderness or in ramshackle wooden forts hastily constructed. His time in Florida was mostly separate from Mrs. Loomis. They could be together occasionally when Loomis was at some of the larger forts, but for the most part Gustavus was separate from Julia. Now the happily married couple, beginning their twenty-fifth year of marriage in 1842, were able to be together again in the reasonably comfortable garrison assignment as commander of Fort Towson. Gustavus was fifty three years old, in excellent health, spry and active and typically exuberant about his work.

For the next several years Gustavus Loomis would be sent from fort to fort, traveling with the command headquarters of the Sixth Regiment of Infantry. Specifically, he served at Fort Towson from 1842-1843; Fort Gibson from 1843-1844; again at Fort Towson from 1845-1846; and again at Fort Gibson from 1846-1848. Additionally, soldiers under his command were also assigned to Fort Washita and Fort Smith.

Fort Towson, along the Texas border in Oklahoma Territory, was a small part of the national expansion of the United States. The country at that time was rapidly increasing its geography, settling in areas such as Texas, Oregon, and Florida. Millions of settlers poured into the vast prairies of the Midwest. In this surge of nationalistic development the army served as explorers, law enforcement, security, and engineers, helping to develop infrastructure. The army coordinated with scientists and explorers to help discover the hidden geographic and geological wonders of America. The military escorted anthropologists and Indian agents to insure their safety. The army built roads, canals and railroads with the engineering help of West Point graduates. In addition to routine military duties, soldiers spent much of their time farming, improving their barracks, or cutting firewood. A military post in any area meant an economic boom to the civilian community. Soldiers spent their free time and money in local communities while the fort depended upon civilian contractors to supply such things as building materials and tools. Local farmers supplies fresh meat and supplemented whatever the soldiers grew in their gardens.[255] In the 1840s life in a frontier fort was safe, the biggest threats coming from drunken gunfighters rather than bands of Indians or invading Mexicans.

Beginning in 1824 the United States saw the need for a military fortification at a strategic location on Gates Creek along what is today the Oklahoma-Texas boundary. This rural outpost was built to keep peace between Indians and to protect white settlers. Cantonment Towson was named after Nathan Towson, Paymaster General of the U.S. Army. Connected to the east by a good road, what became Fort Towson served as a landmark for settlers bound for the Republic of Texas. By the time Lieutenant Colonel Gustavus and Julia Loomis arrived in 1842, the fort was in disrepair. As the army reinforced its southwestern forts due to the instability with Mexico and the Republic of Texas, a reconstruction program commenced to replace wooden forts with stone structures. The fort had a strategic location, not only related to Texas and Mexico, but as an army quartermaster depot along the Indian frontier.

---

255 Allan R. Millett and Peter Maslowski, *For the Common Defense: A Military History of the United States of America*, (New York: The Free Press, 1994), pp. 137-138.

With the threat of war with Mexico, a detachment from the 6th Infantry was sent to Fort Towson with orders to strengthen its defenses. In 1842 Lieutenant Colonel Loomis began a reconstruction campaign which replaced many of the dilapidated wooden structures with stone and plank buildings. The stone was quarried from a bluff behind the officer's quarters. The new buildings were constructed from locally quarried limestone and walnut logs sided over with plank boards. The construction program designed the garrison buildings in a "U" shape opening southerly towards the sun. The fort stood on a bluff overlooking Gates Creek to the north. All of the buildings were painted sky blue. Along the north side of the parade ground were three officers' quarters. The commanding officer's quarters was in the center, flanked by barracks housing the officers of the garrison. Gustavus and Julia Loomis were comfortable in their quarters. On both sides of the parade ground running south of the officer's quarters were storerooms. The east side of the parade ground was bounded by a storeroom, a guard house, and two barracks for enlisted personnel. The west side of the grounds was defined by a storeroom, a combination laundresses' quarters, a school and two enlisted barracks. There was no chapel building and no military chaplain.

Located on the Fort Towson parade ground were the flagpole and two wells. At the far south end of the parade ground, once approached by a broad avenue, was the hospital and post commissary. The fort's shop buildings, including a bakeshop, carpenter and blacksmith shops, and the stable complex, were located in a line east of the officers' quarters. The post powder magazine, a large brick structure, was in the northeast corner of the parade ground between the east officers' barracks and the east storeroom.[256] For Lieutenant Colonel Loomis and his wife this was a familiar scene.

256 "History of Fort Towson," www.civilwaralbum.com/indian/towson_history. Accessed January 12, 2010.

They had lived in such forts for years, the difference now being that Loomis was the commander and therefore had the best housing accommodations.

Gustavus and Julia Loomis stayed at Fort Towson for less than one year. Then, when the headquarters for the 6th Infantry moved north about one hundred and seventy five miles to Fort Gibson, the Loomis's made the move to their new assignment.

Fort Gibson, like Fort Towson, was located in Indian Territory in what would later be the state of Oklahoma. First built in 1824, Fort Gibson was a part of a chain of military installations that protected the western frontier running from Fort Snelling in modern Minnesota to New Orleans in Louisiana. The location for Fort Gibson was strategically situated near the confluence of the Grand, Arkansas and Verdigris Rivers. Log buildings were constructed to house the soldiers and military supplies, surrounded by a strong wooden fence. Fort Gibson maintained communication with the outside world by means of transportation on the Arkansas River over which keelboats brought men and supplies to the fort. Later, steamboats that supplanted the keelboats came up to the fort with military supplies and merchandise for the sutler at the post and for merchants in that vicinity. The fort was also reached by the famous thoroughfare known as the Texas Road, which came through southwestern Missouri, southeastern Kansas, and following the course of the Grand River passed Fort Gibson and continued on to Texas. For many years an amazing number of emigrants, freighters, and traders passed over this road.[257]

The year 1832 was a notable one in the history of Fort Gibson. A commission had been created by Congress for the purpose of locating in Indian Territory the Indians about to be removed from the East. It was necessary for the commission to make its

---

257 Grant Foreman, "Fort Gibson – A Brief History," www.freepages.genealogy.rootsweb. ancestry.com. Accessed January 12, 2010.

headquarters at Fort Gibson and to negotiate treaties with the local prairie Indians to prepare them for the impending changes in their neighbors. Many of the new Indians migrating to the west were Seminoles and Creeks, tribes which Lieutenant Colonel Loomis knew quite well from his time in Alabama and Florida. In 1843, as the commander of Fort Gibson, Loomis spent much time settling disputes between Indians, as tribes unknown to each other were forced to coexist on reservation lands. Loomis was responsible to protect and support the Indian Agents and to insure the safe and dignified treatment of thousands of displaced Indians.

A typical example of an Indian deportation to Fort Gibson and the western reservation lands occurred after the conclusion of the Second Seminole War. On December 12, 1842 Captain Ethan Allen Hitchcock sailed down the Apalachicola River in Florida, intending to pick up Seminoles who came out of hiding and agreed to a peaceful relocation out west.[258] Messengers went ahead to the minor Seminole chief named Pascofa and agreed to conduct a ceremony requested by Chief Pascofa to signify the importance of his migration out of Florida. The vessel moved out of the Apalachicola River, sailed along the coast, then headed inland along the Ocklocknee River thirty miles to the predetermined pick up point. After some delays, the entire clan of Chief Pascofa, composed of twenty one warriors, nineteen women, and ten children, departed Florida for Fort Gibson, never to return home again. Along the way the Seminoles were well fed, were allowed some liberties, and were given blankets, shirts, turbans, and dresses for the women. At their final destination at Ft. Gibson they were organized, rationed, equipped, and sent to their designated homestead locations. In 1844, while Lieutenant Colonel Gustavus Loomis was in command, there were over three

---

258 Edwin C. McReynolds, *The Seminoles*, (University of Oklahoma Press, 1972), pp. 236–237.

thousand Seminoles in the Ft. Gibson area, with a few thousand Indians from other tribes.

The day to day routine of garrison life at Fort Gibson was predictable. Soldiers of the fort were awakened each morning as the bugler sounded reveille at daybreak to rouse a sleeping garrison. The flag was run to the top of the pole with a gun salute as the troops stood at attention. After an early breakfast the soldiers went about their routine duties. Details worked in the garrison garden among the vegetables. The oxen, horses, and mules were fed and cared for. Troops were put through their drills by the sharp commands of non-commissioned officers. Soldiers worked distributing food and supplies to the Indians. The end of the day of toil or boredom was announced by the drums sounding retreat, followed by the evening canon salute and the ceremony of lowering the flag at sunset. This routine repeated day after day, month after month, and year after year, made life at the post a dull experience. Fort Gibson was an isolated station in the western wilderness, far from civilization and white settlements of consequence.[259]

The officers and men, exiled as they termed it to this remote garrison, wearied of its limited possibilities for entertainment. Trifling incidents varied the dull routine of their lives. Important events were of absorbing interest. Serene cheerful diversions were available, such as fishing and hunting. A billiard room furnished entertainment. Plays were written and presented in the "theater," the building used on occasions for Indian councils and religious services. Lieutenant Colonel Loomis was a firm advocate of church services and began coordinating Sunday morning meetings. When a missionary was present, the missionary would preach a sermon. When no ordained minister was available, Loomis led the service with psalm singing, reading of scripture and an exhortation typically from a printed sermon in a religious periodical. One distraction for the men at Fort Gibson was horse racing. As one account stated,

> A COURSE WAS laid out and every year there were exciting horse races for high stakes with entries from all divisions of the fort's population officers, traders, and Indians. Indian ponies, that hardly had time to rest up from running buffalo, were entered against the horses of the post. And there were crooked race horse owners who came up the river to the fort for the sole purpose of making what money they could by their peculiar methods. This situation become so demoralizing that Colonel Loomis issued an order barring these people from the reservation.[260]

The religious life at Ft. Gibson was greatly enhanced by the presence of Lieutenant Colonel Gustavus Loomis, who assumed command of the fort in 1844. At this time the post was without a chaplain, but this did not prevent various religious activities being conducted at Ft. Gibson, all with the enthusiastic approval of Loomis. Before his assignment to Ft. Gibson, Loomis had extensive experience in dealing with the Florida Seminoles. Loomis was stationed in Florida shortly after the First Seminole War, where he served in combination with duties at Baton Rouge, Louisiana from 1819 to 1825. He then spent 1826–1827 again in Florida, followed by his extensive and noteworthy service in the Second Seminole War in which Loomis fought in Florida from 1837–1842. Loomis knew the Seminoles well, and many of the Indians now under his care were combatants against him in Florida.

---

260 Grant Foreman, "Fort Gibson - A Brief History," p. 3.

Lieutenant Colonel Loomis was known as "the Christian commander of Fort Gibson."[261] When Loomis arrived at Ft. Gibson the post was surrounded by homeless Seminoles who refused to be settled on lands adjacent to the hostile Creek Nation. It must have been an interesting experience for Loomis to now be in charge of the safety, nurture and relocation of the very same Seminoles that he fought a few years earlier in the Florida swamps. Loomis took command at Ft. Gibson of four companies of Infantry and two companies of Dragoons, as well as numerous soldiers temporarily assigned to the fort in conjunction with other missions. Loomis immediately made his influence as a devout Christian known in several ways to the Ft. Gibson community. Before he had an assigned chaplain, Loomis was a firm supporter of the religious services provided on Ft. Gibson by the local civilian missionaries. He was influential in getting Chaplain David McManus assigned to the fort a few years later. When temperance meetings were planned for whites and also for the Indians, Loomis gave his unqualified support, even to the point of approving of a soldier's choir which would travel and sing religious songs at the temperance meetings. And Gustavus Loomis approved of the construction of a new combined chapel building and schoolhouse to be built at Ft. Gibson.[262] The schoolhouse and chapel building was completed after Loomis departed Fort Gibson early in 1844.

The construction of a designated chapel at Ft. Gibson was a controversial event. Previously soldiers at Ft. Gibson worshiped at the small wooden building constructed in 1824, known as the Council House. For most of the week this structure was used for

---

261 Carolyn T. Foreman, "Gustavus Loomis: Commandant Fort Gibson and Fort Towson," *Chronicles of Oklahoma*, vol. 18, no.3. September, 1940, p. 222.

262 Carolyn T. Foreman, "Gustavus Loomis: Commandant Fort Gibson and Fort Towson," p. 222.

secular purposes and was swept out and simply decorated for religious events. Loomis desired a separate building solely dedicated for religious purposes. In 1844 Loomis approved a construction plan for the new chapel, with the building completed in June of that year. A problem quickly surfaced related to financing the construction costs of the chapel. Loomis simply sent a bill to the government, which was refused payment due to the fact that there was no funding available to build military chapels. Loomis paid the construction costs himself. When Chaplain David McManus arrived at Ft. Gibson in 1845 he had the supervision of a brand new chapel. To appease critics of Loomis in relation to him funding the construction of the chapel from his private resources, the building was also used as a schoolhouse, which therefore allowed government funds to be spent for the maintaining of the building.[263]

Gustavus and Julia Loomis were at Fort Gibson from late 1843 to mid-1844. They were then transferred back to Fort Towson with the headquarters of the Sixth Infantry. Arriving at Fort Towson after a year and a half away, Lieutenant Colonel Gustavus and Julia Loomis found many improvements in the infrastructure of the fort. The building projects begun under Loomis were continued while he was away and many were completed. Meanwhile, Fort Towson was gaining visibility and prominence in direct proportion to the escalation of tensions with Mexico. As commander of Fort Towson, Loomis was responsible for receiving millions of dollars of supplies and munitions and thousands of soldiers temporarily assigned to the fort. Fort Towson was a staging area for troops headed for Mexico, the last stop in the United States before entering the Mexican region of Texas.

War was declared with Mexico on May 13, 1845, a direct result of the 1845 U.S. annexation of Texas, which Mexico consid-

---

263 Interview with David Fowler, Oklahoma Historical Society, July 8, 2004.

ered part of its territory in spite of the successful 1836 Texas Revolution. The territorial expansion of the United States to the Pacific coast was foremost in the minds of President Polk and his associates in their support of the war. Expansion-minded Americans wanted all the land in dispute with Mexico, and were willing to fight for it. This meant that Lieutenant Colonel Gustavus Loomis was in command of the closest U.S. military installation to Mexico. If Mexico attacked the United States, their first assault would be at Fort Towson. Loomis was on the front line, the first line of defense against a Mexican invasion of the United States.

At Fort Towson, Lieutenant Colonel Loomis fortified his defenses and trained and supplied the thousands of soldiers who temporarily came to his fort. Loomis also trained and equipped his own soldiers from the 6th Regiment of Infantry, men who would eventually fight in Mexico.

It was uncertain if Gustavus Loomis would serve in Mexico during the Mexican-American War. His assignment was as the garrison commander of Fort Towson. It became clear that the United States would be the aggressor and that Mexico would not invade the United States. That meant the strict maintaining of a border fortification for the 6th Infantry at Fort Towson became less necessary. Therefore the headquarters of the 6th

A Sketch of Fort Towson at the start of the Mexican War, 1845.
Source: www. digital.library.okstate.edu/ encyclopedia/entries/F/FO044.html

Regiment of Infantry were sent not closer to Mexico, but about one hundred and seventy five miles farther away from the war, back to Fort Gibson.[264] It appeared that Gustavus Loomis, at age fifty six, would not serve as a combatant in the war.

On the date that war was declared with Mexico the 6th Regiment was at Fort Gibson, Indian Territory, in the current state of Oklahoma. At Fort Gibson was the headquarters along with Companies A, E, G and H. Companies B and C remained at Fort Towson. Companies I and K were at Fort Washita, about a hundred miles away. Companies D and F were at Fort Smith, southeast of Fort Gibson about fifty miles.[265] Loomis had administrative command over all these Companies, and his supervisory responsibilities were immense.

Previously, Gustavus Loomis had served at Fort Gibson from December, 1843 to June, 1844. Now he would serve as the commander at Fort Gibson from March, 1846 through February 1848. Life at Fort Gibson for the Loomis family during the Mexican-American War was frantic. Loomis was responsible for support missions to the Mexican War; for settling disputes between thousands of relocated Indians on nearby reservations; for the protection of white migrants; and for keeping often disorderly soldiers in line with military regulations.

Frequent reports came to Fort Gibson of the hostilities of the Plains Indians against the mostly white American people of Texas, along with rumors that the Mexicans were aiding and abetting them. Requests were made for the authorities at Fort Gibson to aid in making peace with these Indians. The Secretary of War William Marcy directed this to be done and in March, 1843, Cherokee

---

264 George W. Cullum, *Biographical Register of the Officers and Graduates of the U.S. Military Academy, West Point, N.Y.,* (New York: 1868), p. 62.
265 Charles Byrne, "The Sixth Regiment of Infantry," www.history.army.mil/books/R&H/R&H-6IN. Accessed January 14, 2010.

Agent Pierce with an escort attended a council on Tawakoni Creek in Texas, but nothing definite was accomplished. Another effort was made in the fall when Indian Agent Butter was accompanied by eighty men commanded by Colonel William Harney. Again the Indians were elusive and non-committal. The next summer in 1844, another effort was made when Captain Nathan Boone, with a company of the First Dragoons, left Fort Gibson on September 25 and went to the rendezvous in Texas. But the Indians had left when Boone arrived and he returned to Fort Gibson unsuccessful, after an absence of six weeks. A fourth attempt was made in January, 1846, when a large detachment of troops departed Fort Gibson with a company of hunters and adventurers and representatives of the Creek, Cherokee, Chickasaw, and Seminole tribes. Agent Butler was finally successful, and on May 15, 1846, at Council Springs, Texas, he negotiated a peace treaty with the Comanche, Anadarko, Caddo, Wichita, Waco, and other western tribes that brought a sense of security to the frontier settlers of Texas. Lieutenant Colonel Gustavus Loomis was the commander at Fort Gibson when this May, 1846 treaty was signed.[266]

Like all military installations at that time, Fort Gibson had its share of trouble-makers. There were gamblers, loafers, prostitutes, black market liquor dealers, and the destitute that came out west to find their fortune but instead went bankrupt. The thievery of government supplies was a constant problem. Colonel Richard Mason, commander at Fort Gibson immediately before Gustavus Loomis arrived, was "greatly exasperated by the conduct of the enlisted men in frequenting disorderly houses outside the reservation, ordered the guards doubled, the gates of the post were closed at retreat, and the rolls called at unexpected hours." Nevertheless, civilian missionaries and eventually a military chaplain conducted

---

266 Grant Foreman, "Fort Gibson – A Brief History," p. 6.

popular religious services at Fort Gibson, services which demanded the construction in 1845 of a twenty two by forty feet building for church and for a schoolhouse for the children.[267]

When Gustavus and Julia Loomis arrived at Fort Gibson in the spring of 1846, Chaplain David McManus was already assigned to the fort. Ford Gibson had a military chaplain from 1840-1841, but that chaplain was not asked to stay. The post council at Ft. Gibson was unsatisfied with the ministry of the former chaplain, so much so that they did not appoint another chaplain until 1845. Displaying considerable caution, the post council was impressed with the application for the chaplain position that came from the Rev. David McManus. A Protestant Episcopal, Chaplain McManus was a career missionary in the Indian Territories, an articulate teacher and respected preacher who previous to his assignment as chaplain at Ft. Gibson was a missionary pastor and an instructor at the Van Buren Seminary, Arkansas.[268] Because of the fallout from the previous chaplain's ministry, McManus was accepted on a probationary period for one year. David McManus was an excellent choice for a frontier Army chaplain, the Ft. Gibson community being so satisfied with his ministry that he was continually reappointed through 1857, when the post closed. Furthermore, when the U. S. Congress authorized a salary increase for chaplains, the Ft. Gibson council resolved to award McManus an extra twenty dollars a month, an almost 50% increase in pay.[269]

267 Carolyn T. Foreman, "General Richard Barnes Mason," *Chronicles of Oklahoma*, (vol. 19, March, 1941), p. 29.

268 *Arkansas Intelligencer*, July 29, 1843. Rev. McManus was the principle instructor at the Van Buren Seminary, teaching male students in twenty-two week sessions such courses as Greek, Latin, Grammar, Geography, Arithmetic, and other primary lessons. The school was in Crawford County, Arkansas, and was sponsored by the Protestant Episcopal Church.

269 R.D. Gamble, "Army Chaplains at Frontier Posts," *Historical Magazine of the Protestant Episcopal Church*, (XXVII, December, 1958), pp. 300-301.

Chaplain McManus arrived at Ft. Gibson in 1845, at a time when great progress was made for the relocation of the Seminoles and other Indians to reservation lands. For the prior several years the Seminoles were adamant in their refusal to relocate on lands surrounded by their antagonists the Creeks. In a vain attempt to force the Seminoles to relocate, rations provided by Ft. Gibson were temporarily withheld. This only led to the Seminoles raiding the produce and herds of neighboring tribes, which raised tensions in the region. In 1845 Seminole Chief Alligator negotiated the exact location of Seminole relocation to the point where he was satisfied, and the Seminoles disbursed from their lodgings around the perimeter of Ft. Gibson.[270] During the 1845-1857 ministry of Chaplain McManus at Ft. Gibson the Seminoles that arrived in spurts were a broken and impoverished people. Some of the migrant Indians arrived virtually naked, sickly, and depressed from the rigors of deportation and their long struggle to resist deportation ending in failure. The soldiers who called David McManus their chaplain attended to the needs of the Seminoles with professional-

These photographs, taken after Ft. Gibson closed in 1857, show two locations frequented by Lieutenant Colonel Gustavus Loomis, the hospital (above) and the Post Chapel (below), which was also designated as the Council House. Source: Grant Foreman, "The Centennial of Ft. Gibson," *Chronicles of Oklahoma*, Vol.2, No. 2, June 1924, p. 119.

270 Brad Agnew, *Fort Gibson: Terminal on the Trail of Tears*, (Norman, OK: University of Oklahoma Press, 1980), p. 176.

ism and courtesy, there not being a single registered complaint from the Seminoles from 1845 until the fort closed in 1857.

Specifically, the Rev. David McManus, an Episcopal clergyman, served as chaplain at Ft. Gibson from September 3, 1845 through June 1, 1857.[271] Chaplain McManus was present at the fort during the so-called "Roman Catholic Controversy" of 1847.[272] This controversy was based on the attempts of a local Roman Catholic missionary named Rev. P. W. Walsh desiring to perform Roman Catholic religious services in the new Ft. Gibson chapel. An officer at Ft. Gibson named Lieutenant Cave J. Couts, without full knowledge of the facts and ignoring the chain of command in processing complaints, wrote a letter of protest directly to the Adjutant General of the Army. In his letter he stated inaccurately that Lieutenant Colonel Gustavus Loomis was discriminating against the Roman Catholic soldiers at Ft. Gibson by not allowing a Roman Catholic priest on the post to perform the Mass. In fact Loomis did object to the civilian priest using the church building for the Roman Catholic Mass, but he objected only for the times which the building was prescheduled for other religious uses. When Chaplain McManus was approached about the issue, he simply responded that the use of the chapel was coordinated with the approval of the post Commandant and that he had no control over the overall scheduling of the usage of the building. Loomis felt that much ill feeling could have been avoided if Lieutenant Couts' letter had been sent through proper command channels.

The truth was that Lieutenant Colonel Loomis did in fact offer the use of the chapel to the Roman Catholic priest, but the

271 Carolyn T. Foreman, "Gustavus Loomis: Commandant Fort Gibson and Fort Towson," p. 222.
272 Tensions between Roman Catholics and Protestants at that time in America were very tense. See Mark A. Knoll, editor, *Eerdman's Handbook to Christianity in America,* (Grand Rapids: Eerdman's Publishing, 1983), p. 413. Sydney E. Ahlstrom, *A Religious History of the American People,* (Yale University Press, 1972), p. 559.

priest desired rather to have another area for religious services, he being not too comfortable conducting Mass in a Protestant church building. From June through October 1847 a series of letters were exchanged between the Adjutant General of the Army, Lieutenant Colonel Loomis, and Roman Catholic priest P. W. Walsh. The issue terminated when Father Walsh wrote to Loomis, excerpts of which are as follows:

> MUCH RESPECTED SIR Yours of the 7th inst I received this morning… Before touching the question you put before me, I must beg you to accept my sincere thanks for the kind and gentlemanly hospitality you tendered me on my visit to Fort Gibson… You referred me to the Quarter Master and you did further state, that the church was at my service when not required for post purposes… I feel quite sorry that my visit should have been the occasion for any misunderstanding or misconception… I am your Obedient Servant, P. W. Walsh.[273]

As the commander at Fort Gibson, Gustavus Loomis ran a disciplined fort. His attention to detail was exact. His respect for military customs and protocols was unquestioned. The garrison under his command was clean, orderly and professionally maintained. Yet Loomis also found time to express his Christian faith through numerous benevolent activities. His support of local missionaries was well known. His founding of temperance societies encouraged moral behavior among the men. An eyewitness account of Lieutenant Colonel Loomis and his charitable activities comes from the pen of Hannah W. Hitchcock, daughter of missionary Rev. Samuel A. Worchester. Missionaries such as Samuel Worchester came out west to minister to displaced Indian

---

273 Carolyn T. Foreman, "Gustavus Loomis: Commandant Fort Gibson and Fort Towson," p. 226.

tribes on reservation lands. Frequently the missionaries assisted the army in providing care for the Indians.[274] Hannah Worchester Hitchcock spoke of Loomis as follows:

> WE WENT TO many temperance meetings in different parts of the [Cherokee] Nation; some in the woods on the banks of the beautiful, clear-running streams, or near some of the fine springs so plentiful in our Nation. The people gathered from near and far; meat was barbequed; bread, cakes and pies for all. Through the courtesy of the Christian commander at Fort Gibson, Col. Gustavus Loomis, my father was permitted to have the attendance at some of his meetings of the finest band in the United States Army then stationed at Fort Gibson; and once a choir of nineteen soldiers sang temperance songs, and more delightful singing I never heard in all my long life. Great was our consternation and grief when that fine band was ordered to march with the regiment to the Mexican War, and left Fort Gibson, never to return.[275]

The Christian devotion of Gustavus Loomis was evident for all to see at Fort Gibson. Loomis had a firm belief in the Bible. In his scriptures he read that God created all people from Adam and Eve. The human race thereafter fell into sin in the Garden of Eden. The result was that all people are sinners. God expressed his displeasure at humanity by flooding the world in judgment in the days of Noah. The surviving human race therefore are all descendants of Noah and his sons. This meant to Loomis that both Indians and blacks had the same inherent dignity as white people. All humanity was created in the image of God and were therefore

---

274 Kenneth E. Lawson, *Religion and the U.S. Army in the Florida Seminole Wars, 1817-1858,* (Columbia, SC: Eastside Printing, 2006), p. 236.
275 Grant Foreman, *The Five Civilized Tribes,* (University of Oklahoma Press, 1982), p. 387.

of great value. All people, blacks and Indians included, had a soul for which Christ died. Therefore all people were to be treated with dignity and respect. And all people needed to believe in Jesus Christ as savior to be redeemed from their sins. An eyewitness of Lieutenant Colonel Loomis at Fort Gibson in 1844 spoke of the miserable conditions of the displaced Indians, how they gravitated towards various vices and were apathetic for their own improvement. Tirelessly working with the Indians were "four companies of infantry and two of dragoons stationed there under the command of Liet. Col. Loomis, a devout Christian."[276]

The benevolent Christianity of Gustavus Loomis towards Indians and blacks was not always appreciated by his fellow officers. Some officers resisted Loomis' efforts since it meant that soldiers could no longer illegally trade whiskey to the Indians. Other officers, particularly those from southern states, adamantly opposed Loomis as he taught blacks to read in small classes in which they studied from *The New England Primer,* the *Shorter Catechism* and the Bible. Meanwhile unscrupulous whites infiltrated Fort Gibson to manipulate the Indians to sell their black slaves. Other whites arrived as slave catchers with dubious paperwork seeking runaway slaves from southern plantations. The unethical behavior of whites and Indians towards blacks was unconscionable. For example, some Indians would sell blacks from their tribes for alcohol or increased rations. Seminole Indians around Fort Gibson had for decades accepted blacks as full members of their tribe, but were willing to sell their brethren to the highest bidder. In some cases, black children were sold for a bottle of whiskey.[277]

276 "Journal of a Tour in the Indian Territory, by N. Sayer Harris in the Spring of 1844," edited and annotated by Carolyn T. Foreman, *Chronicles of Oklahoma*, Vol. X, p. 219. Quoted in Grant Foreman, *The Five Civilized Tribes*, p. 231.
277 Daniel F. Littlefield, *Africans and Seminoles: From Removal to Emancipation*, (University of Mississippi Press, 2001), p. 112.

As the commander of Fort Gibson, Gustavus Loomis had an ongoing controversy with Indian Agent Marcellus Duval. Appointed in 1844, Duval was an ardent slave holder from South Carolina. Duval clashed continually with the officers at Fort Gibson, particularly Lieutenant Colonel Loomis. When Agent Duval learned that Loomis was leading Sunday school classes and teaching black Seminoles to read, he said simply, "Every sensible man can see the evil of it."[278] Duval complained all the way to the President of the United States that Loomis was protecting blacks from their white owners too zealously, and that Loomis gave blacks certain privileges not allowed in slave states or territories.[279] Indian Agent Marcellus Duval's interests were not just ideological. Within a year of his arrival he was rumored to own illegally captured black Seminoles on his plantation in Van Buren, Arkansas. It later became known that he and his brother secretly and illegally contracted with Indians to secure title to over two hundred and sixty of the racially mixed black-Indians called maroons. In exchange, the Duval brothers were slated to personally receive one-third of the blacks -- a potentially huge economic windfall.[280]

Indian Agent Duval dedicated himself to stirring up political outrage in Washington about the liberties granted blacks on the frontier at Fort Gibson. A prolific writer, he fired off angry letters to anyone who would listen, such as newspaper editors, southern politicians, and government bureaucrats. In his letters to President James Polk he ominously warned against any attempt to classify the blacks as free and firmly resisted emancipation. Meanwhile, the Fort Gibson commander and other officers were personally teaching blacks how to read and write, facts that infuriated Agent Duval. Loomis began a Sunday School for

---

278 "Marcellus Duval," www.johnhorse.com/trail/03/b/27. Accessed January 18, 2010.
279 Daniel F. Littlefield, *Africans and Seminoles*, p. 111.
280 "Marcellus Duval," p. 3.

blacks at Fort Gibson, angering southern officers and soldiers and Agent Duval. Yet Loomis kept his superior officer, Brigadier General Matthew Arbuckle fully informed of all his activities with the blacks and Indians and he had the full support of General Arbuckle, a native Virginian.[281]

Under Lieutenant Colonel Gustavus Loomis' command, Fort Gibson became a haven for blacks seeking their freedom. Some blacks were maroons, of mixed Indian race. Others were full members of Indian tribes. Some were slaves of the Indians seeking their freedom. And some were simply runaway blacks from southern plantations who came west to escape slavery in the southern states. Loomis was passionate about protecting blacks from illegal or immoral behavior from whites or Indians. He insisted that all paperwork related to returning blacks to

A reconstruction of the commanding officer's quarters at Fort Gibson. Lieutenant Colonel Gustavus and Julia Loomis lived in such a building from 1843-1844 and again in 1846-1848. Source: Fort Gibson Historic Site.

slavery be in perfect order or he would not cooperate. He forbid the selling of blacks for alcohol or other trade goods. While resisting the aggression of slave catchers and others seeking to re-enslave all blacks regardless of their status, Loomis continued to educate blacks at Fort Gibson about reading, writing and Christianity. As one author stated,

281 Daniel F. Littlefield, *Africans and Seminoles*, p. 112.

LOOMIS HAD NOTHING but praise for the blacks. During the preceding summer, they had raised large amounts of corn and rice on the reserve. For the past two or three months, some of them had assembled every Sunday for a Sabbath School, at which Loomis tried to give what instruction as would tend to make them better men and women. Some of them were trying to read the Bible. Loomis wanted the government to pay for their removal or persuade some benevolent society to transport them to Africa.[282]

The 1846-1848 command of Lieutenant Colonel Gustavus Loomis at Ft. Gibson occurred at a time when there were no major clashes between the Indians and the whites. While there were several occasions of war hysteria, nothing came of them. The Army-Indian relations at Ft. Gibson showed considerable restraint on both sides and a genuine desire to cooperate and understand each other. Indeed, the entire history of the post can be summarized by ongoing frustrating attempts to arrange truces between feuding tribes, to pressure the warlike Plains Indians to abandon their desire to exploit the relocated Indians, to resolve conflicts within individual tribes, and to enforce legal standards related to black slavery. Although these mundane peacekeeping activities were not glamorous and were monotonous for most soldiers, the army restrained the anger of tens of thousands of frustrated Indians and acted as good will agents for the best interests of these displaced peoples. Simultaneous to all these operations, the war in Mexico continued. Unpredictably, in 1848, the fifty nine year old Gustavus Loomis would be deployed from Fort Gibson to combat duty in Mexico.

---

282 Daniel F. Littlefield, *Africans and Seminoles*, p. 121.

CHAPTER TWELVE

THE MEXICAN AMERICAN WAR

THROUGHOUT THE EARLY 1800S TENSIONS increased between Mexico and the United States. With the U.S. acquisition of the Louisiana Purchase in 1803, Mexico and the United States shared an enormous boundary. Certainly part of the tensions between the two nations related to religion and racism, as the mostly Protestant United States had cultural and ideological differences with the Latino Roman Catholics of Mexico. There were also stark political differences between the democratic United Stated and the dictatorship of the Mexican General Antonio Lopez de Santa Anna. But the most contentious issue related to the Mexican province of Texas, as thousands of white Americans were encouraged by Mexico to settle this rural land and become citizens of Mexico. The thousands of U.S. settlers came but their allegiance to Mexico was superficial at best. The Texans began an independence movement from Mexico and were ultimately successful. From 1836 to 1845 the Republic of Texas existed as an independent nation, with whispers in Washington related to how Texas could be annexed to the U.S. as a new state. In 1845, Texas became the twenty eighth state of the United States. Soon after, war was declared between the United States and Mexico.[283]

---

283 For more details see Kelly K. Howes, *Mexican American War*, (Farmington Hills, MI: Thomson Gale Publishers, 2003), pp. 17-56. Daniel W. Howe, *What God Hath Wrought: The Transformation of America, 1815-1848*, (Oxford University Press, 2007), pp. 731-743. Maurice Matloff, *American Military History*, (Washington, DC: Office of the Chief of Military History, 1973), pp. 161-164.

On May 13, 1846, war was declared. At that time Lieutenant Colonel Gustavus Loomis was assigned as a senior officer within the Sixth Regiment of Infantry, a regiment scattered among several forts in the Indian Territory of what would eventually become the state of Oklahoma. Loomis was with the headquarters of the 6th Regiment at Fort Gibson when war was declared. The ten companies which composed the 6th Regiment were located at Fort Smith, Fort Gibson, Fort Washita and Fort Towson. By July, 1847 the entire 6th Regiment, with the exceptions of Company G and Company I, deployed to Mexico under Major General Winfield Scott. The fifty-seven year old Lieutenant Colonel Loomis was designated to remain as the commander of Fort Gibson and to serve as a conduit for resupplies and new recruits to fill the ranks of the 6th Regiment. Simultaneously he was responsible for protecting white settlers and pioneers and handling the many issues related to Indians and blacks on the frontier.

The deployed 6th Regiment of Infantry in Mexico fought at Contreras, San Antonio, Churubusco, Molino del Rey and Chapultepec (Mexico City). The regiment performed remarkably well and dominated the Mexicans. The regiment suffered several hundred casualties, many to combat but many more to the infernal Mexican weather and to diseases from poor camp sanitation. The defeated Mexican General Santa Anna resigned his presidency on September 12, 1847. On November 11 a new Mexican congress was elected, which helped initiate the Treaty of Guadalupe Hidalgo on February 2, 1848, officially ending the war. On July 4, 1848, the United States received official notice that the Mexican government had ratified the treaty of Guadalupe Hidalgo. Meanwhile back at Fort Gibson, Lieutenant Colonel Gustavus Loomis was recruiting and training over one thousand soldiers and preparing to take them to Mexico. When

Loomis departed Fort Gibson in February, 1848, news of the cessation of hostilities had not reached him. Between the February 2 signing of the treaty and the May 30 ratification of the treaty by Mexico, the United States was still technically at war. At that time Lieutenant Colonel Gustavus Loomis arrived from Fort Gibson to Mexico. Loomis had missed all the major battles of the Mexican War, but he would be gainfully employed in Mexico in peace keeping and rebuilding the nation for the next few months.

When Loomis departed Fort Gibson in February, 1848 he was fifty-nine years old. He was in excellent health, trim and spry for his age. He wore a long grey beard and was beginning to slightly bald in the top of his head. He was easily old enough to be the father of the majority of his troops, perhaps even a grandfather to the younger soldiers. As one account stated, "Officers and men went from Fort Gibson to take their places in the war with Mexico; the veteran commander Colonel Gustavus Loomis was the last high ranking officer to leave, when he deported in February, 1848, for his post in Mexico City."[284] Loomis led these fresh troops of the 6th Regiment from Fort Gibson to the nearby Arkansas River. It must have been quite a scene as over one thousand soldiers led by the grey bearded Gustavus Loomis embarked on dozens of vessels of all sizes waiting to take them downriver on the Mississippi to New Orleans. This enormous flotilla arrived safely in New Orleans and reloaded supplies, personnel and equipment onto ocean going vessels destined for Mexico. We have no account of the voyage of Loomis and his troops across the Gulf of Mexico. But we do know that Loomis and his flotilla arrived at Vera Cruz, Mexico on March 6, 1848.[285]

284 Grant Foreman, "Fort Gibson – A Short History," www.freepages.genealogy. rootsweb.com. Accessed January 18, 2010, p. 7.

285 Carolyn T. Foreman, "Gustavus Loomis: Commandant of Fort Gibson and Fort Towson," *Chronicles of Oklahoma,* vol. 18, no. 3, (September, 1940), p. 227.

Why was the elderly Loomis deployed to Mexico? There were many reasons. First, even at fifty-nine years old, Loomis was known to be energetic, in excellent health and was physically able to endure the rigors of a sea voyage and a tour of duty in an inhospitable climate. Second, Loomis was a more than capable officer, experienced and mature and administratively skilled. Simply stated, he was needed. Further, the length of the war, about twenty months long when Loomis deployed from Fort Gibson to Mexico, had decimated the ranks of the 6th Regiment of Infantry. Hundreds of men from the 6th Regiment fell to injuries, illness or death in combat. The unit was exhausted and was in desperate need of reinforcements. Loomis recruited over one thousand soldiers, trained them and deployed with them to Mexico. Another reason for Loomis to deploy to Mexico was the soon expiration of militia enlistments for soldiers assigned to support the 6th Regiment. Twelve month militia volunteers were serviceable soldiers but when their enlistments expired they departed.[286] Major General Winfield Scott needed regular army soldiers to complete the conquest and pacification of Mexico, and Loomis provided what he needed. It is not difficult to imagine the euphoria within the 6th Regiment of Infantry when Lieutenant Colonel Loomis arrived in Mexico with one thousand one hundred fresh troops for the regiment.

Map of the major campaigns of the Mexican American War, 1846-1848. Source: www. media-2.web.britannica.com/eb-media/61/64961-004-0FCD63B1.gif

---

286 Allan R. Millett and Peter Maslowski, *For the Common Defense: A Military History of the United States of America*, (New York: The Free Press, 1994), p. 155.

Gustavus Loomis served in Mexico for less than five months. His official West Point biographical summary simply states that Loomis served "in the war with Mexico, 1848."[287] As a lieutenant colonel with eight years in that rank, Loomis' arrival in Mexico made him one of the senior officers under Major General Winfield Scott. Loomis arrived about four weeks after the Treaty of Guadalupe Hidalgo was signed on February 2. Large combat operations between opposing armies was over, but the country was in shambles. There was an almost six month's period of tense peace as politicians worked out the details of the surrender and subsequent peace negotiations. Loomis became part of an army of occupation, with Mexicans hating the Americans for their victory and the resulting loss of huge amounts of land.[288] The country was in disorder, with bandits and rouge militias robbing both Mexican civilians and United States wagon trains. The American military had to work with the new fledgling Mexican government to overcome the chaos. As one author stated, "The war was over, but now the difficult work of peace would begin."[289]

There were three basic missions that Gustavus Loomis performed for his months in Mexico. First, he coordinated the deployment of soldiers to fight bandits and other rouge groups which harassed the U.S. Army. These guerrilla forces infested certain areas, terrorizing civilians and raiding U.S. supplies. Major General Winfield Scott wrote about these renegades as those who stabbed, stole and shot for personal gain and who robbed churches and took sniper shots at U.S. troops.[290] Loomis deployed squads company

287 George W. Cullum, *Biographical Register of the Officers and Graduates of the U.S. Military Academy, at West Point, N.Y.*, (New York: 1868), p. 62.

288 John E. Weems, *To Conquer a Peace: The War between the United States and Mexico*, (New York: Doubleday Books, 1974), p. 451.

289 Kelly K. Howes, *Mexican American War*, p. 103.

290 Winfield Scott, *Memoirs of Lieutenant General Winfield Scott*, (1864: Reprinted in 1970), p. 541.

level and below (from a few dozen men up to one hundred) to scour the countryside seeking out these renegade forces. Although the Mexican army was defeated in direct combat with the United States, the rouge forces in the countryside were formidable opponents to dispersed U.S. troops. The Mexicans were superb horsemen and were expert snipers and quite skilled with a rope. A *norte americano* soldier that wandered away from his formation could be shot or caught in a *lasso,* paying for his carelessness with his life.[291]

A second mission that Lieutenant Colonel Loomis achieved upon his arrival in Mexico was the detailed reorganization of soldiers within the 6th Regiment. The over one thousand new soldiers Loomis brought to Mexico had to be assigned specific units, resupplied by unit quartermasters, and assigned to specific companies. This allowed the wearied veterans of the 6th Regiment some time for rest, a few months of relaxation while the new soldiers pulled guard duty, went on patrols, provided security, and chased bandits in the wilderness. The typical teasing went on between the veteran troops who fought the big battles and the replacement soldiers. For Lieutenant Colonel Loomis, however, such teasing did not exist. Loomis had fought way too many battles and served in the army too many years to be the butt of jokes from junior officers. One exception to this is from the young and immature Lieutenant Winfield Scott Hancock, who referred to his senior officer in private as "Old Loomis" and who thought that Loomis' conservative lifestyle was a bit archaic, as Hancock sought amorous encounters with various Mexican women.[292]

A third mission Loomis completed while on duty in Mexico was the needed assistance he provided in administrating the temporary U.S. military government in Mexico City. The headquarters of

---

291 John E. Weems, *To Conquer a Peace, p. 167.*

292 David M. Jordan, *Winfield Scott Hancock: A Soldier's Life,* (Indiana University Press, 1995), p.20.

the U.S. Army in Mexico was surrounded by rebellious and dissatisfied Mexicans. For several months, as peace negotiations continued, Mexico City remained a dangerous place. On April 21 Lieutenant Colonel Loomis entered Mexico City in command of a huge wagon train, to resupply the soldiers and relieve the troops with replacement soldiers. Loomis brought into the city a field artillery battery just in case it was needed to keep the peace. Loomis' troops were then disbursed throughout Mexico City while others were sent to Pachuca, Toluca and Cuernavaca.[293] The U.S. military government in Mexico City under Major General Winfield Scott attempted to maintain the peace during the transition of power. Not until May 30 were ratifications exchanged between the Mexican and U.S. governments. Then preparations began immediately to evacuate American soldiers from Mexico, Loomis taking an active part in this gigantic administrative endeavor. On

June 12, Loomis and the occupation army marched out of Mexico City, and on August 1, 1848 the last U.S soldiers departed Mexico at the port of Vera Cruz.[294]

While Lieutenant Colonel Gustavus Loomis of the Sixth Regiment of Infantry served in Mexico only about five months, there were several eyewitness accounts of his activities before and

293 Carolyn T. Foreman, "Gustavus Loomis: Commandant of Fort Gibson and Fort Towson," p. 227.

294 Maurice Matloff, *American Military History*, p. 179.

during his Mexico deployment. For example, in May 1846 Lieutenant William H. T. Walker observed Lieutenant Colonel Loomis involved in breaking apart various companies within the 6th Infantry to fill up those under strength companies which were deploying to Mexico. Lieutenant Walker then observed that Loomis was successful in sending new recruits from Fort Gibson to Mexico, stating, "At Perote, on May 2, the 6th Infantry was joined by several officers, the regimental band, and 180 recruits from Fort Gibson who had come to Vera Cruz from New Orleans and then marched up [to Perote] to join the army."[295] Walker also made a comment that he knew Lieutenant Colonel was still back at Fort Gibson in command of the fort and active in Indian affairs.

For a brief time while stationed in Mexico, Lieutenant Colonel Loomis had the valued company of a fellow Vermonter. Stephen W. Shaw was born in Windsor, Vermont in 1817. After a common school education and work as a mechanic he became a self taught portrait painter. He worked as a painting and drawing teacher at Norwich, Vermont before setting out to paint throughout the American south and west as an itinerant artist. As a civilian he was allowed to travel with Lieutenant Colonel Loomis in order to paint the portraits of the significant U.S. senior military commanders. We can only wonder about these two Vermonters reminiscing about the beauty of their home state as they travelled through dry and barren Mexico. The city of New Orleans commissioned Stephen Shaw to paint a portrait from life of their native son, General Persifor Smith, who was then military governor in Mexico City. Shaw travelled with Gustavus Loomis from Vera Cruz to Mexico City to fulfill his commission of a portrait of General Smith. During the weeks Smith and Loomis travelled together there is no evidence of them not getting along. Actu-

---

295 Russell K. Brown, *To the Manner Born: The Life of General William H.T. Walker*, (Mercer University Press, 2005), pp. 25, 38, 40.

ally, Stephen Shaw became a volunteer aid-de-camp to Gustavus Loomis and travelled with him, Shaw grateful for the military protection offered him through his friendship with Lieutenant Colonel Loomis.[296]

One lieutenant that had a confrontation with Gustavus Loomis was Winfield Scott Hancock. At the time of their confrontation in the summer of 1848 in Mexico, Hancock was an extroverted, profane and lighthearted twenty-four year old junior officer two years out of West Point, who had a love for Mexican ladies and Mexican whiskey, called julep. After the Treaty of Guadalupe Hidalgo was signed and eventually ratified, the army moved back toward the coast. It camped in the hills around Jalapa until the transports were ready. Here they waited for transportation for the Sixth Infantry, while Lieutenant Hancock was given a provisional appointment as regimental quartermaster directly reporting to Lieutenant Colonel Loomis. Hancock got himself into some trouble when the orders came to move out from Jalapa to the boats at Vera Cruz. Hancock was directly responsible for moving the troops in an orderly fashion to the coast. However, Hancock was drunk on julep whiskey, as were many of his men. And the road, as might be expected, quickly became congested with traffic hopelessly snarled. The dialogue between Loomis and his junior officer was recalled as follows:

> LIEUTENANT COLONEL GUSTAVUS Loomis, newly arrived to command the Sixth Infantry, came along, saw the jumble, mainly of Hancock's quartermaster wagons, and became very angry. In the presence of some officers of the regiment he exclaimed: "This is all Hancock's fault; if he had attended to his duty, this blockage would not have occurred; he has shamefully neglected his duty."

296 Peter E. Palmquist and Thomas R. Kailbourn, *Pioneer Photographers of the Far West*, (Stanford University Press, 2001), p. 491.

Hancock, hearing of this outburst, corralled [Lieutenant Harry] Heth and dragged him off for a confrontation with Loomis, whom they found in his tent, reading his Bible. Heth did not realize just how much of the dragoon's whiskey Hancock had consumed.

Hancock said: "Colonel Loomis, you said today in the presence of several officers that I had shamefully neglected my duty. Now, sir, by ---------I will not permit anyone to say I neglected my duty."

Loomis replied: "Don't swear in my presence, young man"; to which the irate young lieutenant sputtered: "I will be God damned if I don't swear."

Loomis put an end to the interview: "Go to your tent, sir, under arrest." Heth took his friend back to his tent and put him to bed, where he soon fell fast asleep.

The next morning Heth related what had happened, and Hancock realized an apology was urgently needed. When Loomis said he would accept Hancock's apology, it was quickly made and the incident ended.

Chastened and with, no doubt, an aching head, Winfield Scott Hancock moved onto the transport at Vera Cruz that would take him and the Sixth Regiment to New Orleans. His less than glorious departure, however, could not obscure the fine record he had make in Mexico.[297]

For a brief time in the spring of 1848, Gustavus Loomis served as commander of a temporary base camp called Camp Washington. This temporary staging, communication and logistics encampment was located one mile outside Mexico City. Lieutenant Daniel H. Hill was in Mexico at that time and observed Loomis

---

297 David M. Jordan, *Winfield Scott Hancock: A Soldier's Life*, p. 19.

as commander of Camp Washington. Loomis was consumed with administrative details, personnel accountability, logistical inventory of supplies, and care for the sick. As Lieutenant Hill recorded on March 21, 1848,

> I YESTERDAY RECEIVED several letters from my friends at home and one from my Mother, the first that I have received from her in eight months. Today I went a mile beyond the walls of the city to Camp Washington to visit Capt. Shover… There are about three thousand Volunteers and Recruits at this Camp under the command of Lt. Col. Loomis, I believe of the 6th Infantry. There is a great deal of sickness in this Camp but so much as was last month at the City of Mexico. I understand that in [the] last month alone a thousand died or were discharged at Mexico.[298]

The Mexican American War was the first war fought by the fledgling U.S. Army completely on foreign soil. During this conflict the U.S. successfully moved over one hundred thousand men, as well as huge amounts of equipment and supplies over land and sea. The Americans overcame a vast number of problems, including inhospitable weather, extended supply lines, rugged terrain, a language barrier, and the coordinated efforts of a determined enemy fighting on his home soil. Pestering the U.S. troops at all times were guerrilla fighters, sniping and robbing and harassing soldiers at every opportunity. The U.S. Army defeated, with occasional help from the Navy, a much larger Mexican army. Territorial gains for the U.S. included vast lands that would eventually become the states of Arizona, New Mexico and California as well

---

298 Nathaniel C. Hughes and Timothy D. Johnson, *A Fighter from Way back: The Mexican War Diary of Lieutenant Daniel Harvey Hill, 4th Artillery, USA*, (Kent State University Press, 2002), pp. 179-180.

as parts of other states. The country spent one hundred million dollars to finance the war, an incomprehensively high amount of money in the 1840s. Over one hundred and four thousand U.S. service men fought in Mexico, with almost fourteen thousand casualties, most from illness or disease. The resulting thirteen percent mortality rate remains the highest of any U.S. war.[299]

The war with Mexico also provided a training ground for a whole new generation of American military officers. Lieutenant Colonel Gustavus Loomis was senior to all of these officers, some of whom served directly or indirectly under his command at some time in their early careers. For example, at the end of the Mexican War, Ulysses S. Grant was twenty-six years old; George Meade was thirty-three years old; George McClellan was twenty-two years old; Jefferson Davis was forty years old; George Pickett was twenty-three years old; Thomas (later nicknamed "Stonewall") Jackson was twenty-four years old; and Robert E. Lee was a forty-one year old Captain in the Corps of Engineers. All these men would come to fame in the U.S. Civil War. The oldest of this selected group, Robert E. Lee, was almost twenty years younger than the aged Lieutenant Colonel Gustavus Loomis.

The Mexican War was over in 1848. Gustavus Loomis was eager to return to his beloved wife Julia at Fort Gibson. None could have expected that Loomis would still be wearing the uniform of his country almost twenty years from this date.

---

299 Kelly K. Howes, *Mexican American War*, pp 105-106.

Chapter Thirteen

Assignments in the West and Northwest

THE CESSATION OF THE MEXICAN War meant that Lieutenant Colonel Gustavus Loomis had to make a decision. At the end of the War in 1848 Loomis had served in the army for thirty seven years. All indications are that he was physically healthy and mentally alert. Being in good health, he could easily have left the army, having completed a successful career, and transitioned to civilian life. There is no doubt that he missed New England. This would have been an ideal time for him to take military leave and return to his hometown in Thetford, Vermont, or to visit his wife's relatives in Connecticut. Nevertheless, at age

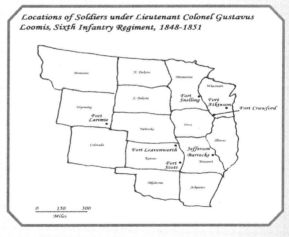

Locations of Soldiers under Lieutenant Colonel Gustavus Loomis, Sixth Infantry Regiment, 1848-1851

fifty nine, Gustavus Loomis did not take leave and he remained in the army. He was reassigned from Mexico with the rest of the 6th Regiment of Infantry to Jefferson Barracks near Saint Louis.

Over the next couple of years Gustavus Loomis was moved to several locations. Specifically, he was at Jefferson Barracks near Saint Louis immediately after returning from

Mexico. In late 1848 he was assigned to Fort Crawford. In 1849 Loomis was again reassigned to Fort Snelling and Fort Laramie into 1851.

The stay at Jefferson Barracks was only temporary for the 6th Regiment. They were billeted there in transition, as senior army commanders figured out how to disburse the 6th throughout various forts on the American frontier. Husbands and wives were joyfully reunited. Mexican War widows sought out information related to their deceased husbands and whatever military benefits they were entitled. Over the next few months the various Companies within the 6th Regiment were assigned to Saint Louis, Missouri; Fort Snelling, in what would later be Minnesota; Fort Crawford, Wisconsin Territory; Fort Atkinson, Wisconsin Territory; Fort Leavenworth, in what would be the state of Kansas; Jefferson Barracks near Saint Louis; and Fort Scott, Kansas Territory.[300] While awaiting reassignment orders, the troops at Jefferson Barracks had idle time. The soldiers were exhausted from their deployment in Mexico, and English speaking merchants with American goods and English speaking women were all a welcome sight. An account of single young Lieutenants Winfield Scott Hancock and Harry Heth in Saint Louis at this time is narrated in *Winfield Scott Hancock: A Soldier's Life,* an account which mentions Gustavus Loomis.

> THE EXCITEMENT, THE strangeness, the danger of fighting and loving in Mexico was over. The Sixth Infantry shipped out for New Orleans arrived there without incident, and then moved upriver by steamer to Jefferson Barracks, south of Saint Louis… Everyone knew that in a very short time the regiment would be split up and scattered over the western frontier, their brief existence

300 T.F. Rodenbough, *The Army of the United States: Historical Sketches of Staff and Line with Portraits of Generals-in-Chief,* (New York: 1896), p. 488.

as actual units ended except on paper in the war Department. A Company here, a Company there, and the thrill of fighting a real war would fade, living only in the memories of the battles with Santa Anna's force. In the meantime, however, each of the regiments gave a ball for its officers and the ladies of Saint Louis, a final fling before the deadening routine of the peacetime army fastened its grip again. Hancock, as acting regimental quartermaster, had to spend a lot of time in Saint Louis, making arrangements for the ball. Harry Heth recalled that Hancock would say to him, "Heth, get permission from old Loomis, and let us go to St. Louis and make some calls." The colonel usually gave Heth a difficult time but eventually relented. The two young officers maintained an active social life in St. Louis as they had done in Mexico, though Heth, when he fell in love with a beauty in the city, had to scheme for ways to see her alone – without Hancock. "I knew," Heth said, "if Hancock accompanied me, my cake would be all dough; she would never look at me."

Eventually, of course, the regimental balls came and went, and the time came for the Sixth Infantry to move north. With a portion of the regiment shipping out on a Saturday afternoon, the headquarters contingent remained in St. Louis for the night to take on supplies. Heth cooked up a plan to take the regimental band into town "to serenade our sweethearts." When Colonel Loomis understandably refused permission, Heth persisted until Loomis yielded on the condition that Hancock had to be with the party. Since Hancock was included from the beginning, of course, Heth got his band, and all the young officers still in town spent the evening marching around with the band, serenading young ladies.[301]

While stationed at Jefferson Barracks for a few months, Lieutenant Colonel Gustavus and Julia Loomis had access to a military chaplain. Loomis had no chaplain support for his five months in Mexico, so the fact of having a military chaplain readily available must have been a comfort to the Loomis family. Chaplain John E. McCarty was assigned to Jefferson Barracks from sometime in 1848 through December 31, 1852.[302] Chaplain McCarty was a New Yorker who joined a volunteer unit during the Mexican American War. He saw extensive combat in Mexico and was appreciated by his men. At the end of the Mexican War he resigned his commission, two months later reapplying again as an army chaplain. He was assigned to Jefferson Barracks and was briefly the pastor for Lieutenant Colonel Loomis and his wife Julia.[303] Chaplain McCarty was Protestant Episcopal, a former navy chaplain and a civilian pastor in New York and New Jersey. He was an honorary member of the Aztec Club, a Mexican American War veterans group to which he served as chaplain. After he departed Jefferson Barracks Chaplain McCarty served as a chaplain at various other forts in the far west and Pacific regions, he being appointed by the Domestic and Foreign Missionary Society as a missionary in 1852. He reached Portland, Oregon, on Jan. 19, 1853, to begin his ministry. He was also active in starting a church in Vancouver, Washington. McCarty did extensive missionary work throughout the Pacific Northwest. He retired from

---

301 David M. Jordan, *Winfield Scott Hancock: A Soldier's Life,* (Indiana University Press, 1995), p. 20.

302 Lorenzo D. Johnson, *Chaplains of the General Government,* (New York: 1856), p. 68.

303 Herman A. Norton, *Struggling for Recognition: The United States Army Chaplaincy, 1791-1865,* (Washington, DC: Department of the Army, 1977), pp. 74-76.

the army in 1867 but remained active in civilian ministry until his death in Washington, D. C. in 1881.[304]

After the war with Mexico, the U.S. Army on the western frontier in the 1840s and 1850s was a small force responsible for an enormous geographical area. The fiscal concerns of the U.S. Congress, and not military strategy, dictated the size and composition of the frontier army. The army was mostly scattered at tiny outposts throughout the west, rarely with enough personnel to do more than monitor relations with Indians and serve as a forward deployed sign of American power. In addition to low levels of manpower, commanders had to deal with desertion, furloughs, death, disease, alcoholism, the black market and numerous other problems. It was obvious that the army's greatest need on the frontier was for cavalry, but Congress was often stingy in providing funds for horses, cavalry supplies and feed for the animals. Bewildered commanders on the western frontier saw Indians mounted on horses while their own troops were either on foot or were under supplied with the necessary amount of horses to accomplish their missions.[305] An example of infantry foot soldiers being deployed to the western frontier was the 6th Regiment of Infantry under Lieutenant Colonel Gustavus Loomis, the on-foot regiment scattered without appropriations for horses to forts in the vast western prairies.

The regular army that manned the frontier forts was a mix of the good and the bad, the motivated and the lethargic, the capable and the incompetent. Young West Point officers had done well in the Mexican War and were more than capable junior officers on the frontier. Some older officers became too set in their ways and were disconnected from their soldiers. Some garrison command-

304 "John McCarty," *An Episcopal Dictionary of the Church*, www.episcopal-life. org/19625_12828_ENG_HTM. Accessed 25 January, 2010.

305 Robert M. Utley, *Frontiersmen in Blue: The United States Army and the Indian, 1848-1865,* (University of Nebraska Press, 1967), pp. 18-20.

ers became petty tyrants within the walls of their forts.There were many issues which drained the motivation of soldiers. Frontier service frequently offered abominable food and desperate living conditions. Severe weather in winter and in summer drained the body.The monotony and isolation frequently encouraged depression which was a major source of alcohol abuse.Added to this was the unpredictability of contact with the Indians, whether or not they were friends or enemies often uncertain until the last moment. Some officers and sergeants excelled under these pressures while others gave in to lethargy and incompetence, deadbeats holding down their rank only for the pay and job security.[306] Numerically, the army was smaller than its allotment in 1812.

From Jefferson Barracks near Saint Louis, Lieutenant Colonel Gustavus Loomis was assigned to Fort Crawford, now in the state of Wisconsin. Loomis was there almost twenty years prior, during the Black Hawk War of 1831-1832. Loomis was assigned to Fort Crawford from September 6, 1848 through April 25, 1849.[307] Not all of that time was he at Fort Crawford, as he had multiple Companies scattered on various forts throughout the frontier. For the brief time Loomis was at Fort Crawford his duties were typical of a frontier fort at that time. He and Mrs. Loomis resided in a log cabin designated for the garrison commander.The last military chaplain at Fort Crawford departed in 1845, meaning that Loomis took the responsibility of providing religious activities for the fort. Militia units came and went through the fort seeking provisions while on Indian patrols. Regular army troops on steamboats frequently stopped at Prairie du Chien to see friends at Fort Crawford and to resupply. Missionaries passed through

306 Maurice Matloff, *American Military History,* (Washington, DC: Office of the Chief of Military History), pp. 180-181. Robert M. Utley, *Frontiersmen in Blue,* pp. 28-32.

307 Peter L. Scanlan, *Prairie du Chien: French, British, American,* (Menasha, Wisconsin: Collegiate Press, 1937), p. 247.

the fort and spoke on Sundays. There were no local troubles with the Indians, as relocation of Indians or the maintenance of treaties made for peace. The fort had past its prime and was designated for closure, which was no surprise to those restless and idle soldiers stationed at the fort.

Like Fort Crawford, many of these northern frontier forts were closing, as the army's interest shifted to points further west and southwest. Fort Crawford, no longer needed, was evacuated in April, 1849. The 6th Infantry was divided between various forts, the headquarters with Lieutenant Colonel Loomis, his staff, the regimental band, and others removing north to Fort Snelling.

In 1849, Julia Mix Loomis died. As records were poorly maintained at that time, or are missing, we do not know many details related to her death. Her exact death date is unknown, as is the location of her death. The official Mix family genealogy simply states that she died in 1849.[308] Gustavus and Julia Mix Loomis began 1849 in Fort Crawford, having departed Saint Louis. There is no record of Julia's death or burial in Saint Louis records or in the Jefferson Barracks National Cemetery. Gustavus Loomis was at Fort Crawford, Prairie du Chien, Wisconsin, until April, 1849. There is no record of Julia Loomis' death at Fort Crawford and she is not buried, as are other military wives, at the Fort Crawford National Cemetery. Nor is Julia Loomis buried in a civilian cemetery at Prairie du Chen. Julia may have been buried at the Fort Crawford Cemetery, now a National Cemetery, but records were poorly kept and the fort and cemetery were abandoned and neglected after the troops departed in 1856. After service at Fort Crawford, Gustavus Loomis was stationed at Fort Snelling, Minnesota from 1849-1850. As at the Jefferson Barracks National Cemetery in Saint Louis; and the Fort Crawford National Ceme-

---

308 "Jonathan Mix," *Descendants of Thomas Mix,* www.reocities.com/Colosseum/ Court/8705/mix. Accessed February 15, 2010.

tery in Wisconsin; so also there is no record of Julia Loomis' death and burial in the Fort Snelling National Cemetery. The weekly newspaper, *Minnesota Pioneer,* for the years 1849–1850 makes no mention of the death of Julia Loomis, a notable fact since the newspaper was printed near Fort Snelling in the growing city of Saint Paul.[309] If Julia Loomis had died while she was the wife of the Fort Snelling commander, there definitely would have been an obituary notice and a summary of the funeral.

We can speculate as to the location of the death and burial of Julia Loomis. She died either at Fort Crawford, Wisconsin; or on the way from Fort Crawford to Fort Snelling, Minnesota; or she died at Fort Snelling. It is unlikely that she died at Fort Snelling since there would have been an obituary notice for such an influential person in the local newspaper, but there was none. Therefore she probably died at Fort Crawford or on her way to Fort Snelling. If she died at Fort Crawford there is no reason she was not buried in the Fort Crawford Cemetery, as were other officer's wives. However, records from Fort Crawford at that time are scant. Perhaps Julia died on the Mississippi River on her way north to Fort Snelling from Fort Crawford. This is possible, and could explain why she was not buried in either fort's cemetery. To make things more complicated, we must remember that Gustavus Loomis commanded troops from the 6th Regiment scattered from Wyoming to Kansas, from Missouri to Minnesota. The simple fact is that we do not have enough information to accurately describe the death and burial of Julia Loomis.

Around May of 1849, Gustavus Loomis arrived at Fort Snelling. Gustavus and his family were at Fort Snelling before, in 1834–1836. At that time Gustavus was forty-four years old, Julia was thirty-six, and their daughter Eliza was fifteen years old. Now

---

309 "Minnesota Pioneer," *Minnesota Historical Society Holdings*, 4-2-1849 through 1-9-1850.

at the beginning of another tour at Fort Snelling, Lieutenant Colonel Loomis was sixty years old and a recent widower. In 1835 their only daughter Eliza married Lieutenant Edmund Odgen. The marriage of Eliza to Lieutenant Odgen was a happy marriage, the couple eventually giving eight grandchildren to Gustavus Loomis, one which died shortly after birth. By his 1849 arrival at Fort Snelling, Lieutenant Colonel Loomis had four grandchildren with another one on the way. Two more were born in 1852 and in 1854. His oldest grandchild was almost ten years old.[310]

The Fort Snelling that Gustavus Loomis entered in 1849 was much more developed and advanced than he remembered. Sturdy stone buildings and a dignified parade field dominated the fort. In 1841 settlers developed land nearby which eventually become the city of Saint Paul, Minnesota. The ideal location and proximity to Fort Snelling caused Saint Paul to grow quickly. The town swarmed with settlers, trappers, pioneers, businessmen, Indians, vagabonds and ruffians. Throughout the 1840s a close relationship developed between Fort Snelling and Saint Paul. The Territorial government was weak and frequently used Fort Snelling troops for support. The military jail was used by the civilian town until a suitable jail could be constructed in Saint Paul. The soldiers were overjoyed to have a developing town nearby to break the monotony of military life on the frontier. As the commander of Fort Snelling, Lieutenant Colonel Loomis insisted that his troops act respectfully in the town or there would be severe consequences. In the warmer months activities between the civilians of Saint Paul and the soldiers of Fort Snelling were friendly, as picnics and riverfront activities were common. In the winter months, sledding parties on the frozen rivers and lakes was a common pas-

---

310 Jonathan Mix, *A Brief Account of the Life and Patriotic Services of Jonathan Mix of New Haven: Being an Autobiographical Memoir*, (New Haven, Connecticut: 1886), p. 96.

time, with huge bonfires and singing and food for all. The 6th Regiment military band was always present at such activities and was very popular. There were no major problems with the local Sioux or Chippewa Indians. Tourists came in the summer months on steamboats to enjoy the natural beauty of the area. While there were typical issues related to a few soldiers' drunkenness or immorality, overall Fort Snelling around 1850 was a pleasant military assignment.[311]

The always religiously minded Gustavus Loomis was pleased to have the services of a career military chaplain at Fort Snelling. Rev. Ezekiel Gilbert Gear (1793-1873) arrived at Fort Snelling in 1838. Gear was a New Englander, born and ordained in the Protestant Episcopal Church in Connecticut. As a young minister he labored among whites and Indians in New York State. In 1836 he was appointed by the Board of Missions to work in the areas that became northern Illinois and southern Wisconsin. Gear was the first Christian minister in this area. In late 1838 Rev. Gear arrived near Fort Snelling and began missionary work with the Sioux and Chippewa Indians and became the official Army chaplain at Fort Snelling. When Lieutenant Colonel Gustavus Loomis arrived at Fort Snelling in 1849, Rev. Gear had served as the garrison chaplain for eleven years. It was the stability of a military chaplaincy that drew Gear to Fort Snelling. Chaplain Ezekiel Gear conducted religious services at the fort and at nearby Saint Paul for civilians.[312] Very early in his chaplaincy ministry Ezekiel Gear was severely injured by a fall from a one horse sled onto the ice. His broken hip caused him difficulties the rest of his long life. Thereafter he was forced to preach from a sitting position, with the power of his voice and his commanding presence making up

311 Marcus L. Hansen, *Old Fort Snelling, 1818-1858,* (Cedar Rapids, Iowa: The Torch Press, 1918), pp. 56-57.

312 Herman A. Norton, *Struggling for Recognition,* pp. 54, 58.

for his physical limitations. Chaplain Gear conducted a school at Fort Snelling and was said to be "faithful and efficient" in his ministrations at the fort. Of his character it was stated;

> To be the first Christian minister to officiate regularly in the English language among the white settlers of Minnesota is proud enough title for any man. But when we add to this that in personal character, in missionary zeal, in intellectual ability, in far-seeing plans, as well as in commanding physical presence, here was a man of all together exceptional force and power, and one whose influence as a force for righteousness counted more than that of any other one man in those earliest days of Minnesota's history.[313]

After Fort Snelling closed in 1858, Rev. Gear stayed a few years to minister to the families until he accepted a chaplain position at Fort Ripley, Kansas, where he served the Union Army throughout the Civil War. Retired from ministry in 1867, he died in 1873 in Minneapolis.

As commander of Fort Snelling, Gustavus Loomis resided in a very nice home. The Commanding Officers' Quarters was the scene of receptions and award ceremonies, a welcome haven for travelers, and a place for Gustavus Loomis to hold bible studies and evening psalm singing activities. Here regimental business was

The Rev. Ezekiel Gilbert Gear, D. D., army chaplain at Fort Snelling, 1838-1858. Source: www.//anglicanhistory.org/usa/mn/edsall_gear.

---

313 "The Rev. Ezekiel Gilbert Gear, D.D. Chaplain at Fort Snelling, 1838-1858," *Minnesota Historical Society Collections,* 1908, www.anglicanhistory.org/usa/mn/edsall_gear. Accessed January 27, 2010.

conducted in the basement headquarters, government policy for a vast region was administered and formal dinners were prepared in the spacious kitchen. Yet the home must have seemed empty without his recently deceased wife Julia. Lower enlisted soldiers met Loomis' domestic needs. Chaplain Ezekiel Gear frequently ate at the Loomis dinner table in this home.

Outside Fort Snelling, Minnesota was a vast wilderness. Around six thousand whites inhabited the entire region in 1850. The mostly German and Scandinavian immigrants created neat and efficient farms and villages. In 1851 the few Sioux Indians that remained signed a treaty and removed from the area.[314] This meant that shortly after Loomis departed Fort Snelling in 1850, the new Territory of Minnesota was open to settlement, pushing the frontier farther west. Newer forts such as Ridgely, Ripley and Abercrombie took over frontier duties while Fort Snelling was demoted to a supply depot. The need for a forward frontier military post at Saint Paul had diminished and the fort was sold to a civilian in 1858 for ninety thousand dollars.

By 1850 the United States was beginning to noticeably divide over the issue of slavery. As early as 1808 Congress banned the importation of slaves from Africa. In 1820 The Missouri Compromise banned slavery north of the southern boundary of Missouri. Slave revolts under Denmark Vesey in Charleston in 1822 and under Nat Turner in Virginia in 1831, led to stricter slave laws. In 1831 William Lloyd Garrison began publishing the *Liberator*, a weekly paper that advocated the complete abolition of slavery. He became one of the most famous figures in the abolitionist movement. In 1846 The Wilmot Proviso, introduced by Democratic representative David Wilmot of Pennsylvania, attempted to ban slavery in territory gained in the Mexican War. The proviso was blocked by south-

---

314 Robert M. Utley, *Frontiersmen in Blue*, p. 262.

erners but continued to enflame the debate over slavery. By that time the Underground Railroad was in full operation, smuggling escaped slaves into northern states or into Canada. There was much fear that new lands captured from Mexico after 1848 would all become slave states, causing national instability.[315] The continuing debate whether territory gained in the Mexican War should be open to slavery was decided in the Compromise of 1850: California was admitted as a free state, Utah and New Mexico territories were left to be decided by popular sovereignty, and the slave trade in Washington, DC was prohibited. It also established a much stricter fugitive slave law than the original law passed in 1793.

Officers throughout the U.S. Army resided from both northern and southern states. After 1850 the topic of slavery was frequently discussed among officers, typically in a responsible manner. As a Vermonter, Lieutenant Colonel Gustavus Loomis despised slavery as a civil injustice. As a dedicated Christian, Loomis rejected slavery as an offense to God who created all people in his image. The controversy over the expansion of slavery into western lands after the Mexican American War sharpened the sectional identities of both northern and southern soldiers. Few in the early 1850s could have imagined the horrors of the Civil War only ten years away. In discussing the various views of slavery within the U.S. Army officer corps, one author stated;

> CAPTAIN BRAXTON BRAGG hoped that the South would take a firm stand in 1848; although he feared a confrontation, Lieutenant William M. Gardner affirmed his willingness to support the South. However, Lieutenant Colonel Gustavus Loomis probably came closer to expressing the views of the majority of the officer corps in a letter to Minnesota's Territorial delegate in 1850:

'What a spectacle would be presented by our country
being in a state of civil war!! The most enlightened
country in the world quarreling because one part of
you shant take the niggers *there* & the other saying I will,
not only *there,* but where I please. I hope Old Zach will
have firmness enough to bring up those who become
obnoxious to the laws without regard to party.'[316]

While serving as the commander of Fort Snelling in the 6th
Infantry Regiment, Gustavus Loomis was required to travel to
visit soldiers of the Regiment at their various locations. If Lieutenant Colonel Loomis made an extended visit of several weeks
or a few months, he would move the 6th Regimental Headquarters with him. This happened in 1850, as Loomis was required to
depart Fort Snelling for a few months to accomplish duties at
Fort Laramie, in the current state of Wyoming. A few Companies
from the 6th were located at Fort Laramie but actually were scattered for hundreds of miles in the vicinity of the fort. Negotiations with several Indian tribes were ongoing in 1850, and Loomis
needed to make an appearance with a show of force and authority. Loomis' preparatory work eventually resulted in the the Fort
Laramie Treaty of 1851, signed on September 17, 1851 between
United States treaty commissioners and representatives of the
Sioux, Cheyenne, Arapaho, Crow, Shoshone, Assiniboine, Mandan,
Hidatsa, and Arikara nations. Loomis had already departed when
this treaty was signed but he helped lay the foundation for it. The
treaty set forth traditional territorial claims of the tribes between

---

316 "Lt. Col. Gustavus Loomis to Henry H. Sibley, January 9, 1850," *Henry H. Sibley
Papers,* Minnesota Historical Society. Quoted in William B. Skelton, *An American
Profession of Arms: The Army Officer Corps, 1784-1861,* (University of Kansas
Press, 1992), pp. 551-552. The reference to "Old Zach" is U.S. President Zachary
Taylor, under whom Loomis served in the Second Seminole War.

themselves, while guaranteeing safe passage for white settlers on the Oregon Trail. In return the Indians got an annuity of fifty thousand dollars for fifty years. The Indians also allowed roads and forts to be built in their territories. The United States Senate ratified the treaty, adding Article 7, to adjust compensation from fifty to ten years, if the tribes accepted the changes. Acceptance from all tribes, with the exception of the Crows, was procured. However several tribes never received the payments. The treaty produced a brief period of peace but was broken by the mass emigration during the Pike's Peak gold rush of 1858 into the territory set aside for the Indians.

A fanciful 1858 painting of Fort Laramie, by Alfred J. Miller.
Source: www.historyglobe.com/ot/ftlaramie

Fort Laramie was founded in 1849 when the army purchased the old Fort John trading post for four thousand dollars and began to build a military outpost along the Oregon Trail. The fort was a significant nineteenth century trading post and diplomatic site. It was a primary stopping point on the Oregon Trail and the Mormon Trail and was an economic hub of commerce in the region. For many years the Plains Indians and the travelers along the Oregon Trail had coexisted peacefully. As the numbers of emigrants increased, tensions between the two cultures began to develop. To help insure the safety of white travelers, the U.S. Congress approved the establishment of forts along the Oregon Trail and a special regiment of Mounted Riflemen to man them. Fort Laramie was the second of these forts to be established.

The popular view of a western fort is that of an enclosure surrounded by a wall or stockade. Fort Laramie, however, was never enclosed by a wall. Initial plans for the fort included a wooden fence or a thick structure of rubble, nine feet high, which would enclose an area five hundred and fifty feet by six hundred and fifty feet. Because of the high costs involved, however, the wall was never built. Fort Laramie was always an open fort that depended upon its remote location and riverfront and its garrison of troops for security. In the 1850s one of the main functions of the 6th Infantry Regiment troops stationed at the fort was patrolling and maintaining the security of a lengthy stretch of the Oregon Trail. This was a difficult task because of the small size of the garrison and the vast distances involved. The fort was commanded by a captain who reported to Lieutenant Colonel Loomis. Here was the gateway to the Rocky Mountains, a critical stop for travelers moving in all directions.

In the early 1850s Fort Laramie maintained a vigorous trade with thousands of Indians from different tribes, the whites exchanging manufactured good for furs and produce. It took intensive efforts to keep the Plains Indians peaceable, but the U.S. Army was generally successful. The fort was also a stopping point for trappers, pioneers, artists and celebrity tourists. Local Indians, specifically the Kiowas and the Comanches, showed restraint. Congress complained about the high cost of maintaining an army in an area where there was no threat of war, and drastically cut back troop strength after 1851.[317]

Although Lieutenant Colonel Gustavus Loomis of the 6th Regiment was stationed at Fort Laramie for only a few months, while there he had the benefit of meeting Chaplain William Vaux. Rev. Vaux arrived at Fort Laramie around 1850 as a Methodist Episcopal chaplain. He was born in England around 1808 and immigrated to the U.S. in the late 1840s. He does not appear

---

317 Robert M. Utley, *Frontiersmen in Blue,* pp. 62, 69, 112-113.

in the 1850 U.S. Census but he is listed in the 1860 Census as "Chaplain-Episcopal" at Fort Laramie. In 1850, Chaplain Vaux was the first chaplain at Fort Laramie. He quickly began religious services on Sunday, opened a school for children, initially living with his wife and children in "a decrepit three room adobe shack covered with a mud roof."[318] While Chaplain Vaux was at Fort Laramie, including the time he overlapped with Gustavus Loomis, the fort strictly observed the Sabbath, so much so that negotiations with the Indians were not held on Sundays. At Fort Laramie from 1850 to 1860, Chaplain Vaux performed the normal duties of a military chaplain. Activities expected of all chaplains were performing weddings, teaching children in a day school, conducting funerals, assisting with good relationships with the Indians, and speaking out against soldier's vices such as alcohol abuse, stealing, slothfulness, and immorality.[319] There is no doubt that Lieutenant Colonel Loomis and Chaplain Vaux were likeminded and supported each other.

In addition to Lieutenant Colonel Loomis' work as commander of Fort Snelling and as a senior officer in the 6th Regiment, in October, 1850 Loomis was given the additional responsibility of serving as the Superintendant of the General Recruiting Service. He had this additional responsibility from October 1, 1850 to July 15, 1851.[320] Any army needs to replenish itself through recruiting entry level soldiers to fill the ranks and to rise in career progression, replacing others who retire, resign, are killed, or are unable to continue their duties. Loomis' new responsibilities included coordinating recruiting efforts on the frontier. The ideal candi-

318 Douglas C. McChristian, *Fort Laramie and the U.S. Army on the High Plains*, (National Park Service Historic Resources Study, 2003), pp. 61-62.

319 Kenneth E. Lawson, *Religion and the U.S. Army in the Utah War, 1857-1858*, (Printed in Puerto Rico, 2009), pp. 44-46.

320 George W. Cullum, *Biographical Register of the Officers and Graduates of the U.S. Military Academy, West Point, N.Y.*, (New York:1868), p. 62.

date for the army was a native born American male who grew up on a farm. This was because such young men knew the value of hard work, were physically fit, understood English, and were able to acclimate to outdoors living. However, most of the recruits on the frontier were foreigners who spoke little English, many who were physically under strength and used to city living. Of all the foreigners who enlisted in the army, Irish immigrants supplied more than half the force, followed by German speakers and those who spoke Scandinavian languages.[321] Many of these new recruits, American born or foreign born, were destitute and in need of a way to make a living. For those who could handle the physical rigors of military life, the army was a reliable way to make it in America. As Superintendant of the General Recruiting Service, Loomis travelled a lot and coordinated the efforts of recruiters throughout the frontier, sending reports back to Washington.

While stationed either at Fort Snelling or at Fort Laramie, the widower Lieutenant Colonel Gustavus Loomis again found marital love. In February, 1851 Gustavus was married to a widow named Mrs. Mary Anne T. Panton. Gustavus Loomis enjoyed his thirty two or so years of marriage to his first wife Julia. He was the type of man who wanted to be home with his wife, a man who enjoyed the quiet life of reading his Bible or singing psalms by the fire with his family. At age sixty two, Lieutenant Colonel Loomis took his new wife "Annie" into the Commanding Officer's Quarters at Fort Snelling.

We do not know much about his second wife Annie Panton. Her birth name was Mary Ann Tomasina Codrington. We do not know for certain how they met or how they fell in love. It is likely that Gustavus Loomis met the widow Annie Panton while he was Superintendant of the General Recruiting Service, as this posi-

---

321 Robert M. Utley, *Frontiersmen in Blue*, pp. 39-40.

tion required Loomis to travel to various military installations on the frontier. One of the locations Loomis visited in this position was Fort Leavenworth, Kansas. At Leavenworth, Gustavus Loomis was able to visit his daughter Eliza Ogden and her husband and his several grandchildren, as brevet Major Edmund Ogden was assigned to Fort Leavenworth. Certainly such visits to family were significant to the recent widower Loomis. In the Leavenworth community, the Panton family name was prominent in civic positions. How Gustavus Loomis and Annie Panton met and fell in love we do not know. Did his daughter Eliza and her husband introduce Loomis to the widow Annie Panton?

We can be sure that Loomis would never get involved with a woman who did not share his evangelical Christian zeal. One account states that Mrs. A. T. Panton (Annie) was born in Fairfield, Connecticut around 1793, making her about fifty eight years old at her marriage to Gustavus Loomis.[322] A more likely report states that she was born in 1806 in the West Indies, making her forty-five years old at the time of her marriage to Lieutenant Colonel Loomis.[323] However the 1860 U.S. Census says that she was born in 1815 in the West Indies.[324] The records are contradictory and incomplete. Since both the 1860 and the 1870 U.S. Census state that she was born in the West Indies, that much is confirmed. Her maiden name was Mary Anne T. Codrington. She was from a maritime family from the New Haven, Connecticut area. She may have been born in 1806 and married to her first husband, George Panton, around 1825. She had at least two children, one of whom was George B. Panton. Mary Anne Panton was a widow when she married Gustavus Loomis in 1851. Being from the West Indies, Mary Anne was Anglican by religion, called Prot-

322 "Mrs. A.T. Panton," www.familysearch.org. Accessed November 14, 2009.
323 "Mary Anna Loomis," *U.S. Census for Stratford, Connecticut, 1870.*
324 "Annie Loomis," *U.S. Census for Stratford, Connecticut, 1860.*

estant Episcopal in the United States. U.S. Census records show a variety of families with the Codrington and Panton names in southern Connecticut in the mid-1800s.

Loomis and Annie Panton were married on February 24, 1851.[325] They were married at the Saint Thomas Episcopal Church in New Haven, Connecticut. At the time of his wedding, Lieutenant Colonel Gustavus Loomis was stationed at Fort Snelling, Minnesota, meaning a long trip east was necessary to have the wedding ceremony. Gustavus was sixty two years old and Annie was around forty-five. No one could have predicted that the elderly Gustavus and his younger bride Annie Loomis would have a long and happy marriage that lasted twenty one years, until Gustavus' death in 1872.

We can get a glimpse into the religious life of Gustavus and Annie based on the location of their wedding ceremony. The ceremony was conducted at Saint Thomas Episcopal Church in New Haven, Connecticut. This church was thoroughly consumed with the awakening that swept through southern Connecticut in the 1850s. The minister of the church, Rev. Eben E. Beardsley (1808-1891), arrived in 1847. Within twelve years the congregation had a new gothic style stone church building and dramatic increases in attendance. Hundreds made professions of faith and were baptized and confirmed according to the Protestant Episcopal Church liturgies. The Loomis' were married in a temporary brick chapel which was in use before the large stone church structure was complete. Rev. Beardsley was a thoughtful, articulate minister who embraced the awakening. He allowed the Loomis wedding ceremony to be performed in his church but he was not the officiating minister.[326]

---

325 Elias Loomis, *The Descendants of Joseph Loomis in America,* (published by the author in 1875: 1908 edition), p. 320.

326 "Gustavus Loomis Folder," Stratford Historical Society. "History of Saint Thomas Episcopal Church," www.stthomasnewhaven.org/history. Accessed April 3, 2010.

In the early spring of 1851 Gustavus Loomis received word of his promotion to Colonel. His last promotion, to Lieutenant Colonel, was on September 22, 1840. To be promoted to the senior rank of Colonel was a lifetime accomplishment. Only a small fraction of all military officers ever earned the rank of Colonel. On March 9, 1851, Gustavus Loomis became a full Colonel in the U.S. Army. His rejoicing and thankfulness to God must have been profound. Having been remarried only two weeks and now with a promotion to one of the most senior ranks in the army, Gustavus Loomis was not going to retire. But with his promotion there was a requirement to move. Colonel Loomis became the Commander of the 5th Regiment of Infantry, he and his new wife Annie departing with the regiment to service in the rugged frontier of Texas.[327]

327 "History of the Fifth Infantry Regiment,: www.bobcat.ws/history. Accessed January 20, 2010.

CHAPTER FOURTEEN

TEXAS, 1851-1856

THE NEWLY REMARRIED AND NEWLY promoted Colonel Gustavus Loomis departed for Texas in March, 1851. He had never been to Texas before. As commander of the 5th Regiment of Infantry, Loomis and his troops relieved the 7th Regiment. Soldiers from the 5th Regiment were scattered at various locations throughout Texas, primarily at Fort Belknap, Fort McIntosh and Ringgold Barracks. Loomis stayed in Texas for the next five years.[328] All indications are that the aging Colonel Loomis retained his energetic personality, his devout Christianity, and his enthusiasm for his work.

In the early 1850s, Texas had an economy dependent upon agriculture, concentrated first on subsistence farming and herding cattle and then on cotton as a cash crop. Thousands of migrants and immigrants descended to Texas in the 1850s, some from northern states, but most of the new settlers were from southern states that supported black slavery. In March, 1850 the Texas legislature was defending "slavery and southern rights."[329] The 1850 U.S. Census recorded over two hundred and twelve thousand white and black people in Texas (Indians were excluded). About ninety-five percent of this population lived in the eastern regions of Texas, safe from Indian attacks. As the population within Texas moved westward, so did slavery. The fertile soils of the Blackland Prairie

---

328 "The Old Army: History of the Fifth United States Infantry," www.theoldarmy.com/usarmy/5us. Accessed January 16, 2010.

329 "Antebellum Texas," *The Handbook of Texas Online*, www.tshaonline.org/handbook/online/articles/AA/npal1. Accessed August 13, 2009, pp. 2-3.

and the Grand Prairie produced millions of bales of cotton, all of which was picked and processed with slave labor. As one author stated, "The cotton frontier of antebellum Texas constituted a virtual empire for slavery."[330] King Cotton ruled the agricultural economy and supported urban industries in the central and eastern Texas cities. Within Texas, one family in four owned a slave, an astounding twenty-five percent of all white Texas families being slave owners. The majority of black slaves were in servitude to larger farms or plantations which could have dozens or hundreds of slaves. In the 1850s the black population was growing faster than the white population.[331]

The Texas to which Colonel Gustavus and Annie Loomis entered was in every way a frontier state. As a new member of the United States, the Texas state government was in its infancy. Pioneers and settlers expanded west and populated new lands, in frequent clashes with the Comanche Indians. Federal troops, many under the command of Colonel Loomis of the 5th Regiment of Infantry, were responsible for protecting the frontier. In his five years of duty in Texas, Loomis had much success in his dealings with the Comanche, but the troops were never able to completely remove the Comanche threat from the frontier. Indeed, even after the 1861-1865 Civil War, the U.S. Army was in operations in the southwest against the Comanche. With the lack of water and timber in western Texas, as well as the Comanche threat, white settlers did not advance much past a string of U.S. Army forts scattered throughout Texas in the 1850s.

The movement of the 5th Regiment of Infantry to Texas under Colonel Loomis was a result of the reasonably peaceful relations between the Sioux and Cheyenne Indians after the Fort Laramie

330 Antebellum Texas," *The Handbook of Texas Online*, p. 5.
331 Daniel W. Howe, *What God Hath Wrought: The Transformation of America, 1815-1848),* (Oxford University Press, 2007), pp. 670-671.

Treaty of 1851. Residing peacefully along the Arkansas River and vicinity, the Indians allowed U.S. troops to move to the more volatile area of Texas. Peaceful relations with the Sioux and the Cheyenne Indians did not last, perhaps partly because most of the U.S. Army moved out of that area. There were proposals to close Forts Kearney, Laramie and Atkinson, ideas that went unheeded. After Loomis took the 5th Regiment to Texas, each of these three forts were maintained by a skeleton team composed of only one Company at each installation from the 6th Regiment.[332]

Meanwhile in Texas, tensions with the Indians remained high. From the beginning of the Republic of Texas in 1838 through the annexation of Texas to the United States in 1846, Texans and Comanches were constantly skirmishing. The Republic of Texas built a series of frontier forts that ran along the frontier, forts intended to separate the Comanche from the whites. Throughout 1840 there were meetings between whites and Comanches, with both sides disingenuous in their intentions.[333] Meanwhile Comanche raids upon civilian settlements resulted in the tortuous deaths of hundreds, with Texas Rangers seeking out retribution. Texas became part of the United States in 1845, but federal troops were not readily available to protect Texans from the Comanche until after the Mexican American War in 1848. Meanwhile, Texans produced an incredible amount of corn and cotton per acre, supplying much of the United States.[334] When federal troops arrived in Texas in late 1848 they agreed with the Texans who had build a line of forts to protect their frontier. From 1848 to the summer of 1849 the U.S. Army built eight more forts to provide a

---

332 Robert M. Utley, *Frontiersmen in Blue: The United States Army and the Indian, 1848-1865,* (University of Nebraska Press, 1967), p. 112.

333 Odie B. Faulk, *Crimson Desert: Indian Wars of the American Southwest,* (Oxford University Press, 1974), p. 94.

334 David Nevin, *The Old West: The Texans,* (New York: Time Life Books, 1975), p. 148.

barrier between the Comanche and the whites. The soldiers sent to garrison these forts were infantrymen, not the much needed cavalry. The mounted Comanche had little difficulty slipping past these forts and raiding white settlements.[335]

On December 10, 1850, a few months before Colonel Loomis and the 5th Infantry arrived in Texas, John H. Rollins, Superintendant for Indian Affairs in Texas, met with thirty-four chiefs of the Comanche and other smaller tribes to sign a treaty. The Indians were intimidated by the arrival of the federal troops and the rapid increase in construction of forts on the frontier. This treaty, which was never validated by the U.S. Congress, allowed thousands of whites to settle on former Comanche lands. This led to more skirmishes and political uncertainty. Another treaty was then agreed upon on October 28, 1851. Gustavus Loomis was in Texas at that time and his troops provided security for the meeting. The Comanche were not united on the results of this treaty and began squabbling among themselves. Meanwhile the U.S. government built seven new forts farther west in strategic locations. One of these new forts was Fort Belknap, to which Colonel Loomis and his wife Annie reported in the spring of 1851.

When the Loomis family arrived at Fort Belknap the garrison was almost ready for its official opening. The fort was officially opened in late June, 1851. Lieutenant Colonel Loomis was not the commander of the fort. This responsibility fell to a junior officer, Captain C.L. Stephenson. Loomis was the commander of the 5th Regiment of Infantry which was scattered among several Texas forts. Fort Belknap had no defensive fortifications. Shelters at first were wood and mud but were quickly replaced with stone. Loomis' troops of the 5th Regiment pursued raiding bands of Indians and mounted offensive expeditions to take the battle

---

335 Odie B. Faulk, *Crimson Desert*, p. 99.

to the Indians on the prairies on occasion as far north as Kansas. The fort housed four companies of soldiers and was the northern anchor in a chain of forts protecting the Texas frontier. The presence of the fort drew migrants who enjoyed the protection of the fort. The fort was on the overland stage route from Saint Louis to San Francisco, so contact with the outside world was a bit more frequent than at other Texas forts. Loomis was not bogged down with infrastructure repairs on the fort, as his mission was to command troops in the field, taking the fight to the illusive and belligerent Indians in the area. Beginning in 1854, Loomis had the additional responsibility of ensuring the safety of the Brazos Reservation and the Comanche Reservation. The Brazos Reservation was located about twelve miles from Fort Belknap at a bend in the Brazos River. The two thousand or so Brazos Indians and others who lived there were thankful for their protection by the United States against the Comanche. Also that year a Comanche Reservation was opened about forty miles west of Fort Belknap, with almost five hundred Comanche Indians residing there, the majority of Comanche resisting the move to agricultural life on the reservation.[336]

Commanding the 5th Regiment from Fort Belknap meant that Colonel Loomis was responsible for guarding part of the heavily travelled overland route to El Paso, a major link in the fledgling transcontinental route. Loomis was also partially responsible for supplying and coordinating the efforts of Texas Rangers and militia units that roamed the area in defense of white settlements. Further, Fort Belknap was the starting point for an exploratory mission led by Captain Randolph B. Marcy and Lieutenant George B. McClellan. This exploratory adventure mapped the Canadian River in the Texas panhandle and

336 "Brazos Indian Reservation" and "Comanche Indian Reservation," *Handbook of Texas Online,* www.tshaonline.org/handbook/online/articles. Accessed January 10, 2010.

discovered the headwaters of the Red River, the last section of the southern plains to be explored.[337]

Like life at other frontier forts, military duty at Fort Belknap could become monotonous. The thrill of patrols meeting un-friendly Comanches or Kiowas was overwhelmed by the routine and unin-teresting life within a military garrison. As the commander of the 5th Regi-ment of Infantry, Colonel Loomis was responsible for holding court martials for a wide variety of offenses. For ex-ample, on March 25, 1851, Lieutenant Thomas O. Davis was before a court martial chaired by Colonel Loomis. As commanding officer, Loomis literally had the power of life and death over his soldiers. Punishments from a court martial included confinement, flog-ging, hard labor, ball and chain, for-feiture of pay and allowances, or even

The Fort Belknap powder magazine, built around 1852, as it appears today. This was the storage area for ammuni-tion utilized by Colonel Loomis and his soldiers.
Source: www.texasescapes. com/TexasTowns/Fort-Belknap-Texas.

death.[338] Loomis was no more or no less a disciplinarian than his fellow commanders in other regiments. True, Loomis had a lifelong intolerance of alcohol abuse and strove hard to remove its abuses from Fort Belknap. At the same time, Colonel Loomis displayed Christian benevolence to the needy and was polite and respectful to his subordinates.

---

337 Robert G. Ferris, *Soldier and Brave: Historic Places Associated with Indian Affairs and the Indian Wars in the Trans-Mississippi West,* (Washington, DC: National Park Service, 1971), pp. 315-316.

338 Quoted from a April 3, 1851 Letter from the General-in-Chief of the Army, Winfield Scott. See *Orders of General Courts Martial, Courts of Inquiries and Letters Commenting on Said Courts (1838-1852)*, www.vialibri.net/item_pg1927583-1838-john-quincy-adams-united-states-orders. Accessed June 6, 2009.

In December, 1851 *The New York Times* newspaper ran an article called "The Texas Frontier – Army Movements." The purpose of this article was to inform readers of the whereabouts of soldiers on the Texas frontier. News from Texas was scarce and readers were interested in the location and status of loved ones. Colonel Gustavus Loomis at Fort Belknap is mentioned in this news story.[339]

Texas Frontier 1852-1861

Colonel Gustavus Loomis served with the 5th Regiment of Infantry in Texas, 1852-1856. He was assigned to Forts Belknap, McIntosh and Ringgold Barracks. Source: www.txarch.org/pdf/academies/2004-hadbourneFinalFigures.pdf

AT OUR LATEST dates from Texas all was quiet throughout the length and breadth of its extensive frontier, and the measures adopted by General [Persifor] Smith to insure tranquility can hardly fail of success. Small marauding bands of Comanches may slip through the chain of posts at times, but their deprecations must be of minor consequence, and ample punishment will almost certainly follow the commission of any overt act on the part of the savages. As it may be interesting to many who have friends in the army, and along the Texas frontier, we will give a statement of the composition of the forces and the positions at present occupied by our troops...Five companies of the Fifth Infantry, under Colonel [Carlos] Waite, are at the post at Phantom Hill, on the clear fork of the Brazos, and five companies of the same regiment, under Col [Gustavus] Loomis, at Fort Belknap, a post on

---

339 "The Texas Frontier –Army Movements," *The New York Times,* December 10, 1852.

the salt fork of the same stream. The above force forms
the exterior line of encroachments of the Indians on the
upper frontier of Texas, and as scouting parties from the
different posts are kept continually out, the most ample
protection is afforded in that quarter.

In early 1853, Fort Belknap received a U.S. Army chaplain,
Rev. David W. Eakins. Gustavus and Annie Loomis overlapped
with Chaplain Eakins only a few months, as later in 1853 Colonel
Loomis took his 5th Regiment headquarters to Fort McIntosh.
Chaplain David Eakins (1814–1876) was a Presbyterian minister from Philadelphia, ordained by the Philadelphia Presbytery in
1848. He then served as a missionary to the Creek Indians before
becoming the U.S. Army chaplain at Fort Belknap, Texas. Rev.
Eakins was a graduate of the College of New Jersey at Princeton in 1844 and Princeton Theological Seminary in 1847.[340] As
a seminary student, David Eakins had the privilege of studying
under such theological giants of Protestant theology as Archibald
Alexander, Samuel Miller, Charles Hodge and others. It is easy to
imaging Colonel Loomis and Chaplain Eakins in deep theological discussions related to sin, salvation, election, predestination and
the like, Loomis smiling ear to ear as he discussed the Bible with a
knowledgeable and like-minded chaplain. In February, 1853 Rev.
Eakins arrived at Fort Belknap. His arrival would seem almost
comical if it were not so dangerous. A news report stated;

> A POST CHAPLAIN was sent out some few weeks since
> to Camp Belknap, on the Brazos – Rev. David Eakins,
> who for some time resided as a missionary near the
> Creek Agency. The night previous to his reaching the
> post he was surrounded and chased by a party of Co-

---

340 *General Catalogue of the Theological Seminary, Princeton, New Jersey, from 1812-
1881*, (Trenton, NJ: 1882), pp. 145-146.

manches, who were prowling around the post on foot, in order to steal horses and mules. Mr. Eakins was on horseback, and had in company a very light baggage wagon. One of the Indians came up near him without exciting any suspicion, and Mr. E. handed him some paper or trifle he had in his hand, when the Indian gave a war whoop and raised the party, who immediately gave chase, pursuing some six or eight miles. Mr. E. being on a small pony came very near falling into their hands. The horses in the baggage wagon outran Mr. E. and also escaped. The driver of the wagon informs me that the Indians had stolen about forty mules from the post a few days previous, when the soldiers killed one of the party and captured a Chief, who was still in custody at the time of Mr. E.'s arrival, the 29th ult. An escort came in with the wagon to this settlement.[341]

A close relationship between Chaplain Eakins and Colonel Loomis was just developing when sometime in 1853, Loomis was ordered to move the headquarters of the 5th Infantry Regiment south to Fort McIntosh.

Fort McIntosh was founded on the banks of the Rio Grande in 1849, shortly after the Mexican War. Located at Laredo, the fort watched the international boundary with Mexico and defended settlers from hostile Comanches and Apaches.[342] The fort was a complex of stone, brick and wood buildings formed in a star shaped earthwork built by army engineers and troop labor. The fort was a key link in the chain of forts that lined the Rio Grande

---

341 "Indian Foray – The Van Buren *Intelligencer* publishes the following extract from a letter dated North Folk, Cherokee Nation, Feb. 19" [1853], *The New York Times,* March 21, 1853.

342 Robert G. Ferris, *Soldier and Brave*, p. 331.

and the Texas frontier. Its isolated location, lack of rainfall, poor soil, and summer heat made the fort an undesirable place to be stationed. This may not have been the ideal location for Colonel Loomis and his wife Annie to live, but they made the best of it and were content.

The Loomis' lived at Fort McIntosh from 1853 to 1854. Although the post was small and the weather was typically dusty and hot, the physical accommodations of the fort were adequate. The Loomis' had a nice stone home to live in, quite comfortable for them. There was no chapel and no chaplain, so Colonel Loomis did what he had done for decades – he led Sunday church services by singing, testimonies and reading a published sermon. When a missionary or a military chaplain was in the area they were invited to preach. Loomis' activities as the commander of the 5th Regiment at Fort McIntosh consisted of routine drills, patrols, formations and the like. Added to this were the always present Indians who were notorious thieves, able to steal almost anything not carefully protected. Animals sent out to feed had to be carefully watched by numerous armed guards. Supplies delivered to the post were under constant threat of ambush. And with the international boundary of the Rio Grande nearby, illusive Indians simply crossed the river and were therefore out of the jurisdiction of the U.S. Army. As one account stated, "Colonel Loomis at Fort McIntosh, Texas reported that small parties of Indians were crossing the [Rio Grande] river at various places, and committing robberies and murders."[343]

While stationed at Fort McIntosh, Gustavus and Annie Loomis expanded their family. Annie's son George B. Panton died in 1857 in Leavenworth, Kansas. His wife Adele (or Adeline) Clarissa Blake preceded him in death, she dying at Leavenworth in 1854.

343 Albert G. Brackett, *History of the United States Cavalry*, (Bibliolife Publishers, 2009), p. 132.

The couple had two small daughters, Adele (b.1853) and Emma (b. 1854). The parentless children went to live with their grandmother, Annie Loomis and her new husband, Colonel Gustavus Loomis.[344] In the 1860 and 1870 U.S. Census, both girls were still at home under the guardianship of Gustavus and Annie Loomis.

Much of Fort McIntosh experienced by Colonel Gustavus Loomis remains today as part of the campus of Laredo Community College. The old guardhouse, warehouse, living quarters, infirmary, commander's house and commissary remain in use as college facilities and housing for faculty and students. The original earthen fort is now an educational institution and home to the Paso del Indio Trail. The fort was abandoned by Federal troops at the outbreak of the American Civil War. The Civil War Battle of Laredo took place near the fort on March 19, 1864, when seventy-two Confederates repelled three attacks from a force of two hundred Federal soldiers sent from Brownsville, Texas. On October 23, 1865, the post was re-occupied by Federal troops when a company of the 2nd Texas Cavalry occupied the fort. Later in the nineteenth century, Fort McIntosh was used by several African-American units including the Tenth Cavalry, the famous "Buffalo Soldiers." The fort was also utilized in the Army expeditions against the Mexican Poncho Villa around 1916. The old layout of Fort McIntosh is easily discernable today, including the home in which Colonel Gustavus Loomis and his wife Annie resided.[345]

After his 1853-1854 tour at Fort McIntosh, Colonel Loomis was again transferred with the headquarters of the 5th Regiment of Infantry, this time farther south to Fort Ringgold, often called Ringgold Barracks. This is one of Texas' best preserved old military posts, named for Major David Ringgold, the first army offi-

---

344 *New York Evening Post,* February 25, 1857.

345 www.wikimapia.org/1762221/Laredo-Community-College-Fort-Mcintosh-Campus.
   Accessed February 4, 2010.

cer killed in the Battle of Palo Alto in the Mexican War. It was established in 1848 immediately after the Mexican War for protection against Mexico and to assure the Rio Grande as a national boundary. This was the southern most U.S. fort along the Mexican border, the site chosen to protect the area from Indian and Mexican attacks. Gustavus Loomis would serve here from 1854 through much of 1856.

Initially Fort Ringgold was of flimsy wooden construction. However, the home that Gustavus and Annie Loomis lived in is still standing. The fort brought stability and financial resources to an isolated part of Texas and assured residents of safety from border violence. Eventually Fort Ringgold held the areas first telegraph office while waging protracted opposition to smugglers, cattle rustlers, Indians and insurrectionists who plagued the area. As a visitor to Fort Ringgold stated in the early 1850s,

Among the distinguished landmarks at Fort Ringgold is the Lee House, once occupied by Col. Robert E. Lee when he commanded U.S. troops in Texas before the Civil War. Before Robert E. Lee lived in this house, it was the home for Colonel Gustavus Loomis and his wife Annie.
Source: www.texasescapes.com /TOWNS/Rio_Grande_City/ FortRinggoldRT1George-Benoit061506

THE MILITARY POST of Ringgold barracks rose before us on a high sandy bluff, its rows of long, low, whitewashed modern buildings, placed at regular intervals around a level ground, in the center of which rose the flag-staff, with its colors hanging droopily, unstirred by the sultry air. These buildings were the government storehouses, barracks, and officer's quarters... There were no signs of vegetation around; not even a blade of grass was to be seen. The sentinels monotonously walking guard gave unmistaken token of a military post.[346]

Fort Ringgold did not have a military chaplain. The region was destitute of Protestant Christianity, the few whites in the area being mostly irreligious. Those of Mexican ancestry inevitably followed Roman Catholicism with various degrees of commitment. One officer's wife noted that, "There are but few religious observances kept in this part of the world." One religious procession she observed outside Fort Ringgold around 1851 displayed a syncretism of Roman Catholic and Native Indian spirituality, as European-looking images dressed in native clothing and local feathers were paraded through the dusty streets. Mrs. Teresa Viele stated, "There are hundreds of intelligent souls ripe for instruction." Shortly before the Loomis family arrived, there was only one man in the region known to own a Bible.[347]

While at Fort Ringgold, Colonel Gustavus Loomis had a supporting role in the establishment of Indian reservations for the Comanche and other tribes. In 1854 the Texas Legislature desired to give the Comanche people a designated land of their own. About fifty thousand acres of land were taken from the public domain of the state and redesignated as Indian Reservations. One site was on the Brazos River for the sedentary tribes of central and east Texas who were driven west by the whites and were homeless. The other location was on the Clear Fork of the Brazos River, designated for the Comanche. Initially over one thousand Comanche migrated to the reservation, but false rumors of a trap and slaughter of the Indians by the U.S. Army scattered the Comanche. Only after the U.S. cavalry was sent to the region were

346 Teresa G. Viele, *Following the Drum: A Glimpse of Frontier Life,* (New York: 1858), p. 130.
347 Teresa G. Viele, *Following the Drum,* pp. 161-163.

the Indians rounded up and sent to the reservation lands.[348] Colonel Loomis supported these efforts by sending troops from his 5th Infantry Regiment to support the Indian Agents and by resupplying cavalry soldiers who passed through Fort Ringgold.

In 1855 Gustavus Loomis suffered deep sorrow from the loss of his beloved son-in-law brevet Major Edmund Ogden. Major Edmund and his wife Eliza Loomis Ogden were happily married, Eliza taking easily to the life of an officer's wife, a lifestyle she enjoyed as the daughter of Gustavus and Julia Loomis. The couple met at Fort Snelling in 1834 and fully supported the revivals that surrounded Gustavus Loomis' efforts at Fort Snelling. Edmund and Eliza were married in 1835 and had eight children, seven that lived beyond birth. The Ogden family endured numerous family separations, as Edmund was a veteran of Indian campaigns and served in the Mexican War. Brevet Major Edmund Ogden died at Fort Riley, Kansas on August 3, 1855, age forty-four.[349] At that time a cholera epidemic swept through Fort Riley. Ogden was infected while he spoke about God to those in the hospital. When news of his son-in-law's death reached Gustavus Loomis in Texas, the news must have been devastating. His only child Eliza was now a

This monument honors brevet Major Edmund A. Ogden, who oversaw the construction of Fort Riley. He died in the cholera epidemic which occurred at Fort Riley in July and August 1855.
Source: www.riley.army.mil/documents/DPT-MS.../090429100408.doc

348 Odie B. Faulk, *Crimson Desert*, pp.101-102.

349 "Edmund A. Ogden," Corpus Christi Public Libraries, www.cclibraries.com/local_history/MexicanWar/ogdenea. Accessed January 29, 2010.

widow at age thirty-seven with seven children to provide for, a terrible circumstance which unfortunately was not that unusual on the American frontier.

Fort Ringgold was not an ideal location for Colonel Gustavus and Annie Loomis. Food was frequently awful, with resupply dependent upon steamboats on the Rio Grande arriving at infrequent times. There was always dust, hot winds, little rain and very poor soil for farming. Without resupplies from the steamboats, Fort Ringgold would starve. There was never any fresh cold water to drink, as the warm and silty water of the Rio Grande had to be strained before drinking and was often suspended in clay jars in the evenings to try and make the water cooler to drink. The nearest town was Rio Grande City, a pitiful outpost of about one thousand Americans and Mexicans who struggled in the dust of southern Texas to survive. Fresh meat was often displayed for purchase at open markets, meat that was frequently covered with ants or flies and was unsanitary. There was no church for the Loomis family to attend, as the only church in the area was Roman Catholic. The citizens of Rio Grande City were observed to be mostly lazy and alcoholics, living in a land unfit for humans. As one observer stated, "There never was a country more unfitted by nature to be the home of civilized man, than this lower region of the Rio Grande in Texas. It seems to hate civilization."[350] Yet the soldiers and civilians tried to make the best of it, laughter frequently heard at the banks of the Rio Grande as people bathed and swam and washed laundry. Everyone rejoiced at the arrival of the steamboats, as fresh supplies, interesting people and news from the outside world put local residents in a jovial mood.

On December 6, 1854, the twenty-one year old Lieutenant Stephen D. Lee arrived at Ringgold Barracks. His biogra-

---

350 Teresa G. Viele, *Following the Drum*, p. 151.

pher mentions that Colonel Loomis was the commander of the Fifth Regiment and was the post commander. In total there were twenty officers and five hundred and seven men under Loomis. Life for Lieutenant Lee at Ringgold Barracks was routine and uneventful. There were some health issues among the men but nothing remarkable.[351]

With the arrival of U.S. cavalry units in Texas around 1855, the role of the 5th Infantry in Texas was diminished. The 5th Regiment was an experienced unit full of career military officers and non-commissioned officers, an exceptional unit that performed well in a wide variety of assignments and locations. As the role of the cavalry increased in Texas, the role of the infantry diminished. By 1855, a new mission had developed for the U.S. Army. Again, there was trouble in Florida with the Seminoles. There were reports of whites being killed and property stolen. Previous treaties had not withstood the test of time. All of white Florida nervously observed the rising fury of the Seminoles. The Florida militia, capable but overwhelmed, sought out federal troops to help suppress the Seminoles. Throughout 1856, Colonel Loomis detached various Companies from the 5th Regiment of Infantry for duty in Florida, he also departing Texas with Annie for the 5th Regimental headquarters in Fort Meyers.[352] By November 2, 1856 the last of Loomis' troops boarded the steamer *Ranchero* destined for western Florida.

---

351 Herman Hattaway, *General Stephen D. Lee,* (University of Mississippi Press, 1976), pp. 10-11.

352 "The Old Army: History of the Fifth U.S. Infantry." George W. Cullum, *Biographical Register of the Officers and Graduates of the U.S. Military Academy, at West Point, N.Y.,* (New York: 1868), p. 62.

CHAPTER FIFTEEN

THE THIRD SEMINOLE WAR

THROUGHOUT LATE 1856 THE TIRED 5th Regiment of Infantry was relieved in Texas, transferred to duty in Florida. The headquarters for the 5th Regiment was at Fort Meyers, along the Gulf coast of Florida. The regiment remained reasonably intact in Florida for about six months, after which a large portion of the regiment was diverted for duty in Utah Territory for what history calls the Utah War against the Mormons.[353] In 1855-1856 the senior army commander in Florida was Colonel John Munroe. In 1856 senior command was given to Brigadier General William Harney. When Harney departed for the Utah expedition, the senior commander in the Third Seminole War became Colonel Gustavus Loomis of the Fifth Regiment of Infantry, headquartered at Fort Meyers, Florida.[354]

Built on the banks of the Caloosahatchee River in 1850, the Fort Myers known to Colonel Loomis in 1857 was located in the same strategic location twice chosen by the United States Army for a military fort. Even before the Army had come the Seminole Indians had chosen the spot for their villages. Before the Seminoles the ancient Calusa Indians had built earth and shell mounds along the south side of the river. The Caloosahatchee

---

353 Kenneth E. Lawson, *Religion and the U.S. Army in the Utah War, 1857-1858*, (San Juan, Puerto Rico: 2009).

354 Robert M. Utley, *Frontiersmen in Blue: The United States Army and the Indian, 1848-1865,* (University of Nebraska Press, 1967), p. 119. John & Mary Lou Missall, *The Seminole Wars: America's Longest Indian Conflict*, (University of Florida Press, 2004), p. 219.

area remained a desired location through the years. The weather was nice and fish and game abounded. From its mouth near San Carlos Bay, the wide river broadened to a width of almost two miles. Visibility was good in both directions, and there were plenty of creeks that served the Calusa and Seminole as watery escape routes into the vast Everglades. From there, the Indians could easily travel east to the Atlantic Ocean, or south to the islands of the Florida Keys.

Renewed skirmishes against the Seminoles in 1850 caused a reoccupation and extensive reconstruction of what became Fort Meyers. The post was named in honor of Colonel Abraham C. Myers, who was soon to wed the daughter of Major General David E. Twiggs, then commanding Fort Brooke at Tampa. Fort Myers was built as a military fort to fend off Seminole Indians that were massacring the area's few white settlers. Fort Myers was one of the first forts built along the Caloosahatchee River as a base of operations against the Seminoles. The expanded fort eventually became an impressive base. At its peak, it featured a one thousand foot wharf used by army quartermasters and more than fifty buildings constructed of rugged yellow pine. But when Loomis arrived the fort was still a humble military post of rough built buildings, with other more permanent buildings under construction. The cleared ground around the fort was for farming and grazing cattle and horses and to serve as open firing lanes against Seminole attacks. This was a comfortable place to live for the sixty-seven year old Colonel Gustavus Loomis with his wife and two small granddaughters.

At the formal completion of the Second Seminole War in August 1842, there remained numerous unsettled issues that prevented a true celebration of peace in Florida. Indians confined to reservation land would often wander harmlessly outside of their boundaries to the fright of whites. Some whites were disgusted that even one Seminole remained in Florida and were vocal in their contempt towards all Indians. Meanwhile the Territory of Florida prepared for statehood, that being achieved on March 3, 1845. The new state of Florida decided to try to solve its own economic problems created by the Second Seminole War while accepting that federal troops would address the Seminole issue. Throughout the 1840s the peace treaty facilitated by Colonel William J. Worth came to be considered a temporary agreement to allow the Seminoles time to attend to their affairs before deportation. The position of the Army was that the combination of restricted activities, white expansion, and encouragement by the U.S. government would eventually persuade the Seminoles to peacefully depart Florida for reservation lands out west.

Throughout the late 1840s there were numerous small confrontations between whites and Seminoles, keeping the issue of Seminoles residing in Florida a constant irritation to both white settlers and politicians. Unsubstantiated rumors of Indian ambushes and raids whipped the whites into a passionate call to deport the Seminoles completely. One substantiated Seminole raid occurred in early January 1847, as a white family sought the U.S. Army's help after a raid

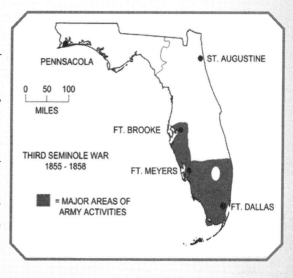

on their Charlotte Harbor farm.[355] The majority of Seminoles were content to reside on their reservation lands and remain distant from the whites, yet numerous influential and greedy whites strongly desired the Indian lands for personal profits to be gained from cattle ranching, farming, real estate transactions, and by deporting large numbers of Seminoles to lands west of the Mississippi River.

While there was virtual unanimity by whites to have every Indian deported from Florida, a series of violent actions by roving Seminoles created such widespread outrage that a substantial number of U.S. troops were deployed to Florida in what is called The Seminole Uprising of 1849. In January 1849 a white man fishing in the Indian River encountered a party of wandering drunken Seminole men who promptly killed him and stole his gun and his boat.[356] The vast majority of Seminoles resided peacefully on reservation lands until an internal dispute at a Green Corn Dance caused a Seminole clan of twenty to roam off reservation lands. Upset at the white men's laws that restricted them to the reservation, the group planned raids against isolated white settlements on both coasts of Florida. On July 12, 1849 four of these disgruntled braves visited a small town on the Indian River four miles from Fort Pierce, and after being fed by the James Russell family opened fire upon the family, killing and wounding some and then burning homes in the town. Another outbreak of violence occurred on July 17 when a small group of Seminoles appeared at a trading post near the Peace River on Paynes Creek, subsequently attacking Captain George Payne, Dempsey Whiddon, and the William McCullough family while they ate super, killing or wounding all the white men present and robbing the store and then burning the building and adjoining structures.[357]

355James W. Covington, *The Seminoles of Florida*, (University of Florida Press, 1993), p. 112.

356 Edwin C. McReynolds, *The Seminoles*, (University of Oklahoma Press, 1972), p. 264.

357 James W. Covington, *The Seminoles of Florida*, pp. 115-116.

White Floridians, many of whom profited from military operations against Seminoles, or sought fertile Indian lands for personal financial gain, magnified deprecations by the Seminoles. When the constant friction between Seminoles and whites in Florida intensified there was typically blame to be shared on both sides. The event called The Third Seminole War was no exception.[358] While the white newspapers were merciless towards Seminole violations, little was said about wayward and abusive whites in Florida that trespassed on Seminole lands, stole Negroes from Seminole clans, illegally sold alcohol to the Indians, or provoked altercations with the Seminoles. Army or militia patrols were constantly on the lookout for Seminole violations and threats or signs of Seminoles trespassing, even exploring into pre-designated Seminole lands and seemingly looking for excitement in provoking the Seminoles.

In August 1854 Secretary of War Jefferson Davis had waited long enough, and imposed measures upon the Seminoles designed to cause them to respond with violence and thus provoke the U.S. military into large-scale operations for Seminole removal. Features of Secretary Davis' plan included imposing a trade embargo on the Seminoles; the topographical survey and sale of land in southern Florida; the opening or renovating of forts along the frontier; and an increase of Army patrols; all for the expressed purpose of peacefully or forcefully removing the Seminoles from

---

358 Edwin C. McReynolds, *The Seminoles*, p.264. An Army officer in Florida named Lieutenant Oliver O. Howard was fully aware of the devious intentions of many whites who could financially profit from another major conflict with the Seminoles. Lieutenant Howard stated, "The Indian raids were, of course exaggerated, but the fear of them was widespread. Undoubtedly, greedy land owners and many unscrupulous village traders took advantage of the situation to magnify rumors and to call for troops, with a view principally of furnishing abundant supplies. They insisted upon raising volunteers, which, after being mustered in, had to be furnished with arms, ammunition, and food." Oliver O. Howard, *My Life and Experiences Among Our Hostile Indians*, (New York: Da Capo Press, 1972), p. 75.

Florida once and for all.[359] By November 1855 there were eighty-one U. S. troops at Fort Capron, two hundred and forty-seven at Fort Brooke, one hundred and sixty-eight at Fort Dallas, and two hundred and seventeen at Fort Myers.

It was on one of the topographical surveys ordered by Secretary of War Jefferson Davis that provoked an incident normally considered the first event of the Third Seminole War. First Lieutenant George L. Hartsuff, an experienced Florida soldier, was ordered to patrol, measure, and survey lands around the Big Cypress Swamp, observing the Seminoles but with orders not to provoke them. His patrol of two noncommissioned officers and eight privates left Fort Myers on December 7, 1855 and patrolled through swamps, marshes, hammocks, and cornfields, observing abandoned Seminole villages and long since deserted U.S. forts from the Second Seminole War. On December 19, nearing the end of their patrol near Bonnet Pond sixty miles from Fort Myers, the small group camped for the night without posting a guard. Early in the morning of December 20, forty Seminoles lead by Chief Billy Bowlegs attacked the small camp. Lieutenant Hartsuff and the men returned fire but were quickly overwhelmed, with Hartsuff severely wounded, he having to crawl to a small pond to conceal himself from the scalping and looting Seminoles. Of the eleven soldiers in the camp, four were killed, four were wounded and three were uninjured, the wounded and uninjured making it to Fort Meyers to sound the alarm.

In 1856, Lieutenant Oliver O. Howard was a recent graduate of the U. S. Military Academy at West Point when he was ordered from an assignment in Maine to fight in the Third Seminole War.

---

359 James W. Covington, *The Seminoles of Florida,* p.127; Joe Knetsch, *Florida's Seminole Wars, 1817-1858,* (Charleston, SC: Arcadia Books, 2003), p.149.

He reported to Colonel William S. Harney at Tampa and then at Fort Meyers. Howard wrote that Fort Meyers was nothing but a humble military post, with roughly constructed quarters for men and officers, and a few log buildings for storehouses. This was the headquarters for the 5th Regiment of Infantry and the residence of Colonel Gustavus Loomis and his family. Lieutenant Howard remarked of the drudgery of endless patrols with little contact with Seminoles, of failing to negotiate a peaceful relocation plan for the Indians, and of his empathy for the impoverished Seminole women, children, and elderly who were no longer able to evade the U. S. soldiers and were deported.[360] Even though Howard had little contact with hostile Seminoles during his 1856-1857 tour in Florida, violent Seminole raids did continue in locations away from his troops. Colonel Loomis and Lieutenant O.O. Howard would develop a very close relationship.

A photograph of Chief Billy Bowlegs taken around 1858. Public domain image.

Colonel Gustavus Loomis knew the Florida Seminoles well. In 1820-21 he was assigned at Fort Gadsden in the Florida panhandle. In 1826-1827 Loomis was assigned to Cantonment Clinch near Saint Augustine, Florida. From 1837 to 1842 Loomis fought in the Second Seminole War. In the late 1840s Loomis was assigned to forts on the western frontier, locations which housed thousands of displaced Seminoles. Now in late 1856, Gustavus

---

360 Oliver O. Howard, *Autobiography of Oliver O. Howard,* (New York: The Baker and Taylor Company, 1908), vol. I, pp. 81, 91, 94.

Loomis was again in Florida fighting the children and grandchildren of the Seminoles he first confronted in the 1820s.

The undisputed leader of the Seminoles in the 1855-1858 Third Seminole War was Chief Billy Bowlegs (c.1810-1859).[361] For his entire life Billy Bowlegs was in conflict with whites in Florida. As a boy he and his family were pushed south into Florida from the campaign of General Andrew Jackson in the First Seminole War. Coming from the Mikasuki clan of Seminoles, his English name was believed to be Billy Bolek, which was corrupted into the name of Billy Bowlegs. As an intelligent man who could speak Spanish, English, Mikasuki, and perhaps another Seminole dialect, Billy Bowlegs rose to prominence in the Second Seminole War as a minor chief and warrior. He saw treaties with the whites violated and his people deported and fought in the Second Seminole War beside many of the Seminole's greatest warriors.

In December of 1855, when Lieutenant George L. Hartsuff's group was attacked and the Third Seminole War was initiated, Billy Bowlegs personally led the Seminole forces. The Seminoles under Bowlegs waged a guerilla war, attacking the U. S. military's weak points to limit the Seminole's loss of life and property. There was no master strategy for defeating the whites in Florida. Instead, Bowlegs led or endorsed a series of raids, ambushes, and skirmishes when the opportunity presented itself. Whites were routinely murdered in their homes, on the roads, or at their farms, the Indians then retreating into the swamps to hide in their remote hammocks. The U. S. troops had trouble locating the Seminoles and moving their clumsy equipment in the Florida marshes. In August 1856, Seminoles in western Florida finally reached a deportation and compensation agreement with the U. S. govern-

---

361 Charles H. Coe, *Red Patriots: The Story of the Seminoles,* (University of Florida Press, 1974). James W. Covington, *The Billy Bowlegs War,* (Chuluota, FL: Mickler House Publisher, 1981).

ment, but Bowlegs and his ever decreasing group of followers remained in Florida and continued their resistance. It was in this context that Colonel Gustavus Loomis in early 1857 assumed command of all U.S. Army forces in Florida.

In December, 1856 Colonel Loomis assessed the situation in Florida. In January 1857 he began combat operations. In January, 1857 Private Joel A. Delano served under Loomis with the Fifth Infantry out of Fort Meyers. Later in life Delano recorded his experiences in the Third Seminole War.

> IN MY YOUNGER days I desired to become a soldier, so went to Buffalo June 20, 1856. The next morning was at recruiting office of Uncle Sam's, enlisted for 5 yrs. donning the blue June 21, 1856. I was sent to Newport Barracks, Ky drilled and then to Ft. Myers Fla some 28 miles above the mouth of the Caloosahatchee River.
>
> Assigned to Capt Randolph B. Marcys Company D 5th U.S. Infantry, Gustavus Loomis Colonel. Jan 1857 active operations began against Seminole Indians under leadership of Chief Billy Bowlegs. The Regt continued to scout during spring and summer until June 1857, engaged in several skirmishes. One in particular which occurred in Billy Bowlegs garden March 5, 1857 in which the writer acted, our loss was 2 killed and 7 wounded.[362]

As the commander of the 5th Infantry, Colonel Loomis maintained operational command while delegating direct command of troops in the field to his subordinate commanders. Loomis was responsible for the overall strategy and operations of the Third Seminole War. He deployed dozens of company level units in tac-

362 Joel Andrew Delano, *The Genealogy, History and Alliances of the American House of Delano*, (New York: 1899), pp. 357-358.

tical operations throughout most of central and southern Florida. Loomis received dispatches from his company commanders and coordinated the war effort from his headquarters at Fort Myers or at Fort Brooke near Tampa. Loomis' overall strategy was to deploy company level units or smaller to relentlessly harass and engage the Seminoles, forcing them to fight or surrender. Loomis and his command staff tracked the movements of his units on a large map board. Loomis issued orders which his staff implemented. Communication to company commanders in the Florida wilderness by messengers on horseback was slow but Loomis was effectively able to coordinate the overall strategy of the war. A report of a fight between a small unit of Loomis' troops and Seminoles was recorded as follows;

> LIEUTENANT EDMUND FREEMAN, 5th Infantry, reconnoitering with a small party in the Big Cypress Swamp, near Bowleg's town, Florida, was attacked by the Seminoles, March 5, himself and three of his men severely wounded and one man killed. Captain Carter L. Stevenson, 5th Infantry, called by express from Fort Keats 20 miles distant, came rapidly to the relief of Lieutenant Freedman's party, attacked the enemy, and, after a gallant skirmish, put them to flight, with an evident loss to the Indians, the extent of which could not be ascertained, owing to the density of the hummock.[363]

A common soldier in the Third Seminole War was Private Andrew P. Cordova of Palatka, Florida. Private Cordova was quite literate and provided an almost weekly letter to his hometown newspaper in Palatka named the *Southern Sun*. These letters were accumulated over Cordova's three years of duty in the Florida

---

363 *The Old Army: History of the Fifth U.S. Infantry*, www.theoldarmy.com/usarmy/5us. Accessed January 16, 2010.

militia and were compiled into a book in 1885. Upon enlisting in the militia to protect the interests of his home state, he
spent 1856 in uneventful service. In 1857 he was mustered into a
unit at Fort Brooke and sent on numerous patrol missions in the
Everglades. He wrote of the splendor of Lake Okeechobee, the
murderous insects, sharp saw grass higher than their heads, waist
deep mud, and the capture of several Seminole Indians and blacks,
they being mostly females, children, and older people. Private
Canova writes vividly of the torment he and the other soldiers
experienced from infections in their feet from the acidic water,
how wagons used to transport captured Seminoles from the wilderness to Colonel Loomis at Fort Myers for deportation were
often stuck in the boggy soil, and that the sea grass around Lake
Okeechobee was so thick and tall that men had to climb trees just
to see the path ahead of them. Cordova only wrote of the death
of one soldier, who ate a scavenger bird for dinner and became so
ill he died in spite of the best efforts of medical people.[364]

By the end of 1857 the Third Seminole War was coming to a
conclusion. Scouting activities came mostly out of Fort Dallas, Fort
Lauderdale, and Fort Capron. Under Colonel Loomis, Lieutenant
Colonel Justin Dimick was in charge of many of these operations
for most of the war. While the U. S. efforts to peacefully relocate
the Seminoles out of Florida had limited results, simultaneous
negotiations in Washington and with Seminoles in the Oklahoma
Indian Territory attempted to agree on the geographic displacement of the Seminoles and their financial compensation. The last
notable operation in the Third Seminole War occurred on New
Year's Day 1858, when Colonel S. George Rogers led a combined
army and militia unit of almost three hundred soldiers into the

---

364 Andrew P. Canova, *Life and Adventures in South Florida*, (Palatka, FL: 1885),
    pp.16-36.

Big Cypress Swamp, dividing this formable patrol into three parts, destroying numerous Seminole villages, farmlands, dwellings, and supply locations. With the whites using horses, foot patrols, and boats, the Seminoles were no longer able to hide for lengths of time in the swamps and hammocks.

As 1858 began, Billy Bowlegs and his few dozen male followers were one of the last bands still fighting. Most other groups had surrendered and moved out west. Financial rewards for Seminoles who surrendered produced minimal results. The U. S. military tried to open peace negotiations by bringing Seminole Chief Jumper and other leaders back from Oklahoma to Florida to talk with Billy Bowlegs, but he was not yet ready to surrender his homeland and be deported. In February 1858 there was another group of Seminoles from Oklahoma that returned to Florida to try to persuade Bowlegs to surrender, with some success. Billy Bowlegs' band was further reduced now to a scattered few warriors in several locations, with a few dozen women and children, all fighting starvation and exhaustion. While the senior U. S. commander at this time, Colonel Gustavus Loomis, ordered a drastic reduction in military activities, the Superintendent for Southern Indian Affairs named Elias Rector continued aggressive negotiations with several small Seminole bands. Billy Bowlegs and his followers finally succumbed to the inevitable, and on May 4, 1858 boarded the U. S. vessel *Grey Cloud* for deportation west.

The face-to-face meeting between the two enemy senior commanders must have been a memorable event. Gustavus Loomis had been the enemy of Billy Bowlegs since the Indian leader was a child. When Bowlegs was a boy Loomis was stationed in northern Florida, partially responsible for displacing Bowlegs and his family into central Florida. During the Second Seminole War,

Bowlegs was a warrior who fought against Loomis. Now at the termination of the Third Seminole War, Chief Billy Bowlegs was defeated. Colonel Gustavus Loomis was about twenty-three years older than Chief Bowlegs, old enough to be his father. In 1858 Loomis was a stately older gentleman sixty-nine years old, with white hair and a long white beard. Loomis was in good health while Bowlegs was ill from a combination of dehydration, malaria, exhaustion and starvation. The next year Billy Bowlegs was dead. In late April, 1858, Loomis and Bowlegs met for the first time, Loomis as commander of the Fifth Regiment and commander of Fort Myers, Bowlegs as a sick and defeated prisoner in rags and chains. On May 4, Billy Bowlegs and his followers left Florida.

Lieutenant O. O. Howard was a keen observer of military activities in Florida. His 1856-1857 service in Florida was physically demanding but not militarily efficient. Howard stated;

> DURING MY YEAR... [IN Florida] I do not recall an important engagement between the Indians and the regular troops. The regulars disliked the Indian service... but the volunteers were very active. They had good captains and lieutenants, but the rank and file were made up for the most part from the roughest white population of the South. Sometimes orders did not restrain them; they chased the Indians from place to place and shot them down mercilessly, men, women, and children – taking very few prisoners.[365]

In 1857-1858, Captain Abner Doubleday had little contact with the Seminoles in his incessant patrolling activities. He wrote vividly of him and his troops being breathless in their attempts to prevent themselves from sinking in the mire, of

---

365 Oliver O. Howard, *Autobiography*, pp. 88-89.

scanty accommodations, of ever present vermin, and of near starvation, stating that he found plenty of snakes and alligators but no Indians.[366]

After Chief Billy Bowlegs was deported in early May, 1858, the spirit of the Seminoles was broken. Further, the exhausted U.S. Army was very willing to use the departure of Chief Bowlegs as a symbolic point at which to cease military operations against the Seminoles in Florida. The U.S. military had no problem leaving a hundred or so homeless and desperate Seminoles in the Florida Everglades, as the troops were eager to depart Florida before the summer sickly season. On May 8, 1858, Colonel Gustavus Loomis declared the war to be officially over.[367]

A photograph of Colonel Gustavus Loomis taken around 1858.
Source: www.lincoln.lib.niu.edu/fimage/lincolnimages/mb-gustavusloomis.

Shortly after the Third Seminole War ceased, Fort Myers, the senior headquarters for the war and the home of Colonel Gustavus Loomis, was abandoned. In 1863 a small number of Union troops re-occupied the fort during the Civil War. In 1865 the fort was attacked unsuccessfully by a small band of Confederates. After the Civil War the fort was again deserted. The first white civilian settlers arrived in 1866, but it was not until 1882 when the city experienced significant growth.

At the conclusion of the Third Seminole War, Colonel Gustavus Loomis became a nationally known figure. His name was printed in newspapers throughout the country, as the commander who finally resolved the Seminole problem in Florida. For

---

366 Abner Doubleday, *My Life in the Old Army*, ([1873?] Edited by Joseph E. Chance. Fort Worth: Texas Christian University Press, 1998), pp. 180-185.
367 Joe Knetch, *Florida's Seminole Wars*, p. 156.

example, *The New York Times* newspaper reported the following about Colonel Loomis; [368]

> COLONEL G. LOOMIS, 5th Infantry, has exhibited zeal, ability and good judgment in the arduous duty of bringing to a successful close the late Indian hostilities in the Peninsula of Florida; and the officers, non-commissioned officers and soldiers – both regular and volunteer – and employees under his command, have ably supported him by their active and unremitted exertions in all seasons, and at all times, in a country where military operations are difficult, and where but little occurred to relieve the dangers and heavy drudgery of the campaign. The Commander, and those who served under him, have deserved well of their country. After closing up the affairs of the Department, Colonel Loomis will report, in person, at the Headquarters of the Army for further orders.
>
> By command of Brevet Lieutenant General Scott.
>
> Irvin McDowell, Assistant Adjutant-General

In the same issue of *The New York Times* there was a reference to Loomis in the "Latest Telegraph from Washington" section. Here it states that the Department of Florida will be broken up and that troops will be reassigned to garrisons throughout the army. It further commends Colonel Loomis and those who served under him in bringing the Seminole issue to a resolution.[369]

Colonel Loomis had done his job well. He transformed local militia units that were reluctant to patrol too far from home into effective combat units far from home in pursuit of the Seminoles. Loomis made good use of the local Florida militia, he confidently

---

368 "Reinforcements for Utah Withdrawn – The Department of Florida Broken Up," *The New York Times,* July 22, 1858.

369 "Latest telegraph from Washington," *The New York Times,* July 22, 1858.

deploying them with success in various skirmishes with the Indians.[370] The integration of militia units with regular army units in
combined operations was always tricky, but Loomis pulled it off
well. At sixty-nine years old the aged Colonel displayed amazing
flexibility in his tactics and revealed creative solutions in utilizing
his troops to force the surrender of the Seminoles. His reputation as a combat leader was unquestioned. However, for Colonel Loomis there was another priority that guided his actions in
Florida. As a devout Christian, Loomis sought to share his faith
with others at Fort Myers, Fort Brooke and throughout the Third
Seminole War campaign.

At Fort Meyers there was not a civilian church until many
years after the Loomis' departed. Further, there was no regular
army chaplain assigned in all of Florida. Gustavus Loomis and
his wife and granddaughters frequently went to Fort Brooke near
Tampa for both military reasons and to attend religious services
at the Methodist Church. The First Methodist Church in Tampa was a hot-bed for revivals and biblical preaching, facts which
greatly attracted the Loomis family. The church was founded in
1846 by a few white families and had slowly grown over the years.
Gustavus Loomis assisted the church in a variety of ways, including leading services, public Bible reading and prayer, recruiting members, and attending services whenever he was able. One
soldier who was deeply influenced by the religion of Gustavus
Loomis was Lieutenant Oliver O. Howard of Maine. At the end
of his long military career, then Major General Howard (1830-
1909), a veteran of the Civil War and later numerous Indian wars
on the Great Plains, wrote his life memoirs. His extended narrative is an invaluable insight into the Third Seminole War, and
gives numerous illustrations of the military and personal life of

---

370 Joe Knetch, *Florida's Seminole Wars*, p. 153.

Colonel Gustavus Loomis. The relevant section of Howard's narrative begins as follows;

> BY NOON OF January 9, 1857 we were on board *The Fashion*, which we found ready at the mouth of the river. Our return journey was very pleasant, and the next morning we anchored close to the city of Tampa, running into shore with a small boat... That afternoon I was assigned to ordinance duty at the Tampa depot. The depot consisted of two rough main buildings and a separate office far from the garrison of Fort Brooke, but on its grounds. One of the buildings was a small magazine where powder and mixed ammunition were stored, and the other held everything that belonged to the equipment of the troops... From the time I left home till June 1st my duties of receiving ordinance supplies and issuing them to the troops were constant, though not very onerous. At that time I was taking great interest in books, especially in religious reading. I cannot tell for what reason, but after considerable activity in operations in every direction from Tampa as a center, [Brigadier General] Harney asked to be relieved, and Colonel [Gustavus] Loomis, of the Fifth Infantry, became the commander of the department. This was a very helpful change to me. Colonel Loomis, a member of the Presbyterian Church, soon showed great interest in whatever concerned me. As often as he could he would converse with me and give me books, booklets and tracts, for he said, "Howard, you have an inquiring mind." I absorbed all these books with great avidity. About this time my brother Rowland became a pronounced Christian, gave up his law studies and went into the ministry. He naturally wrote

me accounts of his Christian experiences and sent me well-selected books. Among them was the life of Captain Hedley Vicars of the British Army. I had a small office building near those of the arsenal, which I fitted up for use and made my sleeping room. In that little office, with my Bible and Vicar's Life in my hands, I found my way into a very vivid awakening and change, which were so remarkable that I have always set down this period as that of my conversion. It was the night of the last day of May, 1857, when I had the feeling of sudden relief from the depression that had long been upon me. The joy of that night was so great that it would be difficult to attempt in any way to describe it. The next morning everything appeared to me to be changed – the sky was brighter, the trees more beautiful, and the songs of the birds were never before so sweet to my ears. Captain Vicars, who had been a good man and a Christian in the Crimea, and a consistent member of the Church of England, afterwards, under the influence of a single verse of the First Epistle of John, "The blood of Christ cleanseth us from all sin," had experienced a wonderful change, so that his influence over his comrades in arms was more marked and his Christian work in the hospitals among the sick and wounded so increased and so enthusiastic as to leave a striking record. My own mind took a turn like that upon reading an account of it: What was it that made him such a different man from what he had ever been before? Later, the influence of the same scripture produced that strong effect upon me and caused me ever after to be a different man, with different hopes and different purposes in life.

There are always epochs in the lives of young people, and surely this was an epoch in my own career. There was only one church of any activity in Tampa – the Methodist. The clergyman, Mr. Lynde, had been at one time a Catholic priest, and was a very earnest preacher. He showed me so much kindness that I have always remembered him as just the kind of a friend that I needed at that time. One night I was sitting in the back of his church, when, after the Methodist fashion, amid continual singing, he called people to come forward to the altar. Quite a number arose and worked their way down to the front; among them was a poor hunchback woman whose gait in walking was very peculiar. I noticed some young men on the other side of the church, that I knew, laughing at her grotesque appearance. I asked myself, "Which would you rather be, on the side of those who were trying to do God's will, or on the side of the scoffers?" I instantly rose and went to the front and knelt at the altar. Mr. Lynde, in tears, put his hand upon my head and prayed for me. I was not conscious of any particular change within myself, but I had taken the public stand, which caused quite a sensation in our garrison. Some of the officers said that I had disgraced the uniform; others that I was half crazy; but a few sympathized with me and were my friends then, and, in fact, ever after...Our new Department commander in Florida [Colonel Gustavus Loomis] was very active in his operations with a view to close out the war with the Seminoles, but there was no great battle. The regulars had little faith in the war itself. It was a frequent remark by our regular officers: "We haven't lost any Indians." Of course, however, they did their duty, but without much adore or

enthusiasm. It was not the case, however, with the volunteers. They usually had well-selected officers, but the
majority of the companies were made up of the roughest
element...One day in June Colonel Loomis sent for me
and told me that he wanted me to go as a peace com-
missioner to the Indians in the Everglades, and explain to
them how easy and advantageous it would be for them to
submit to the government and end the war. If possible I
was to find Chief Billy Bowlegs and use all the influence
I could with him to get him to take his tribe and join
the remainder of his people in the far west...We went
towards Lake Okeechobee... The forests through which
we made our way, the sweet open glades within which
we encamped for the night, and the easy marches of every
day, I have never forgotten. All this experience was new
and fresh to me and everything in nature filled me with
an enthusiasm which much amused my companion...On
arriving at Lake Okeechobee a wonderful transformation
took place in our Seminole woman... She promised us
so faithfully that she would bring us into communication with her people that with some reluctance I gave
her instructions and let her go... I hoped almost against
hope that Mattie, as we called the Indian woman, would
prove true and bring about a meeting with her tribe, but
I was to be disappointed. I could not, after many trials, get
an interview with any chief. My mission was, to all ap-
pearances, a failure. Still, it is probable that the news the
woman carried helped to bring about the peace which
was secured by Colonel Loomis soon after I had left his
department – a peace which has lasted without interrup-
tion from that day until today...After my peace expedi-

tion into the interior I hastened back as quickly as possible to Tampa and found on my desk a bundle of letters which greatly delighted me. The first one I opened was from my mother, giving me news of the birth of our second child, whom we subsequently named *Grace Ellen*. She was born June 22nd in our home at Leeds, Maine; I myself that day was at Fort Deynaud, Fla. One evening, July 15th, found me at the Methodist prayer meeting. Our department commander, Colonel Loomis, with his white hair and beard, was leading the meeting when I entered. He was reading a portion of scripture, after which he spoke in his quiet, confident style, making remarks very edifying to the people, and then, standing erect and looking up, he led in a simple prayer. It was a great comfort to me at that time to find a commanding officer so fearless and exemplary and so sympathetic with every Christian effort...That remarkable summer when there was so much sickness and death and such faithful preaching, with our commander [Colonel Loomis] sympathizing with every Christian effort, influenced most of the officers and many of the men to change the character of their lives. Our experience there constituted an epoch in the religious history of Tampa...[371]

Lieutenant Oliver O. Howard was thoroughly converted to evangelical Christianity in Florida, greatly influenced by Colonel Gustavus Loomis. The old man Loomis must have appeared like a biblical prophet, with his white hair and beard; or perhaps he was looked upon as a John the Baptist who pointed people to the Lord Jesus. The sixty-nine year old Loomis was respected by his

---

371 Oliver O. Howard, *Autobiography*, vol. I, pp. 73-89.

men for his tactical and military abilities as well as for his genuine Christian compassion and sincere interest in the best for his troops. The newly converted Oliver Howard remained in the military for about thirty more years. Throughout his long career which culminated with him at the rank of Major General, Oliver O. Howard was known as "The Christian General." At the end of his long life, Oliver Howard wrote a large two-volume autobiography in which he states the defining moment of his life was his religious conversion in Florida during the Third Seminole War.[372]

Sometime towards the end of May, 1858, Colonel Loomis and his wife Annie made the trip, probably by boat, from Florida to Washington. Colonel Loomis reported directly to the General in Chief of the Army, Major General Winfield Scott. The careers of these two elderly men (Scott was about three years older than Loomis) had frequently overlapped. The aging General Scott was comfortable in a nice office in the bustling city of Washington while Loomis had been living in sparse conditions in the miserable Florida wilderness. This must have been an interesting meeting, both men old veterans of the War of 1812, numerous Indian wars and the Mexican War. Colonel Loomis may have inquired about a next assignment. Since he was promoted to Colonel in 1851, Loomis might have been considered for promotion to Brigadier General. The fact was that Loomis was getting older and there was no war. He was holding a Colonel position in the 5th Regiment of Infantry that junior officers needed for career advancement. Gustavus had not taken any extended military leave since the end of the Black Hawk War in 1832. He had accrued years of military leave with Colonel's pay. Gustavus decided to temporarily hang up his uniform and return to New England on paid military leave.

---

372 Oliver O. Howard, *Autobiography*, vol. II, pp. 578-579.

Chapter Sixteen

In Connecticut on Paid Leave from the Army, 1858-1861

In the summer of 1858, Gustavus Loomis was, for the first time in his adult life, living as a civilian. At age sixty-nine, he had given the best years of his life to the army. While on military duty he had buried one wife, one son-in-law and two infant children. He fought the British in Canada, fought Indians throughout the United States and its territories and states, and fought Mexicans in the Mexican American War. He served in areas of extreme cold and in areas of terrible heat and humidity. He was a prisoner of war by the British and he suppressed a mutiny on board a military vessel in the Atlantic. In his over forty-five years of military service he had accumulated several years of time away from his family while deployed, his wife and daughter not having him home. Now all of that would change. Throughout his career Colonel Gustavus Loomis earned a huge amount of military leave. The Army General in Chief Winfield Scott placed Loomis on indefinite paid military leave. That meant Gustavus and Annie were free to live wherever they chose, with Gustavus receiving military pay while on official leave. The Loomis family chose to reside in Stratford, Connecticut.

We can speculate why Gustavus and Annie chose to reside in Stratford. First, Gustavus was a through-and-through New Englander, proud of his family heritage. It is hard to imagine him choosing to live outside New England. Second, there was not much for Gustavus in his hometown of Thetford, Vermont. The community was still very rural, with farming the main economic force. Loomis was too old to be a farmer and even as a boy he never liked farming. Third, the genealogy of the Loomis family was from southern Connecticut. Gustavus had literally hundreds of relatives in southern Connecticut but very few relations still alive in Thetford. Particularly in Stratford, in the 1860 U.S. Census there was recorded four Loomis households.[373] Also, Gustavus' wife Annie had many family relations in southern Connecticut. It was a natural choice for Gustavus to take his family back to his family roots in Connecticut.

One relative that Gustavus Loomis sought out was his influential distant cousin James C. Loomis. As an attorney and a businessman in Bridgeport next to Stratford, James Loomis (1807-c.1875) was the type of man that provided numerous financial, business and community service opportunities for his cousin Gustavus.[374] Colonel Loomis had plenty of free time and his mind and body were still vigorous as he approached seventy years old. James Loomis was very well-connected in Connecticut and was a helpful resource for Colonel Loomis. Living on a Colonel's salary in Stratford did not make the Loomis family wealthy. Army pay was notoriously low in the nineteenth century. Soldiers were compensated for low pay through allowances for clothing, food and housing. Gustavus was living in a civilian home and experiencing financial obligations unknown to him in over forty years of military service. According to the 1860 U.S. Census, Gustavus Loomis has three thousand dollars of real estate and one thousand dollars in his personal estate. This placed him at the same financial

373 *Stratford, CT U.S. Federal Census 1860.*

374 Samuel Orcutt, *A History of the Old Town of Stratford and the City of Bridgeport, Connecticut,* (Fairfield County Historical Society, 1886), pp. 545, 683, 736, 737.

level as lower middle class laborers such as well diggers, machinists, peddlers and gardeners.[375]

Before Mary "Annie" Loomis married Gustavus Loomis she was a widow. From her previous marriage she had a son named George B. Panton. George and his wife had at least two children, daughters. The girls, Adele and Emma, were born in 1851 and 1853. Shortly thereafter their mother died, followed by the death of their father. The family was living in Kansas at that time. The two orphaned girls were accepted into the home of their grandmother Annie Loomis in Texas and later in Stratford, Connecticut. While Gustavus Loomis had no biological connection to these young girls, he readily accepted them into his home and raised them as his own daughters, a significant event for a man almost seventy years old. The girls were to be raised in Stratford.

A handwritten note in the Stratford Historical Society states that, "Gen. Loomis lived in the Marshall Tavern that stood [illegible] of Stratford Ave & Main St. Stratford about 1860."[376] This was the location Gustavus and Annie and their two granddaughters lived while they made the adjustments to civilian life. In May of 1859 Gustavus and Annie negotiated for a loan to purchase a home at the corner of Main Street and Bridgeport Road in downtown Stratford. The property had an average sized house and was on about one acre of land. Gustavus and Annie co-signed for the loan of three thousand dollars to buy the land and house at a six percent interest rate. The home was one block from the Christ Episcopal Church and about the same distance to the Stratford Academy, where their grandchildren Adele and Emma went to school. The railroad station was north about three blocks away. Riverfront ac-

---

375 *Stratford, CT U.S. Federal Census 1860*. The vast majority of Gustavus Loomis' relatives in Stratford were of similar financial status.

376 "Gustavus Loomis File," Stratford Historical Society.

tivities were three blocks to the east.[377] Overall this was an ideal location for the aging Gustavus Loomis and his family to live.

While living in Stratford the Loomis family attended the Christ Episcopal Church. Throughout his military career Loomis worshipped in a variety of denominational settings and supported a variety of military chaplains. He was raised Congregational, but after departing New England for his military career it was difficult to find a Congregational minister. Loomis and his family supported churches and military chapels that were Congregational, Presbyterian, Dutch Reformed, Methodist Episcopal, and Protestant Episcopal. The unifying theme of all these denominations was revival. Loomis enjoyed fiery preaching with an evangelistic emphasis. Another unifying theme of these denominations (excepting Methodism) was the theology from the Protestant Reformation. Loomis was a lifelong Calvinist and supporter of revivals. When Loomis could find a church that preached sound biblical doctrine and had evangelistic fervor he was happy. Denominational titles were not important to him.

The Loomis family attended the Protestant Episcopal Church of Stratford, Connecticut. The church traces its roots to 1707 as the first Anglican Church in Connecticut. In 1724 the congregation had grown enough, in spite of their puritan neighbors, to erect a simple wooden building. During the American Revolution the church was seen as pro-British and was closed for the duration of the war, the minister placed under house arrest.[378] Throughout the 1800s, periodic revivals came and went from the church, evident by surges in church attendance, by an increase of the number of meetings held, and by the increase of those who sought church

---

377 Records of the Stratford Historical Society, Book 35, pp. 620-621. 1867 "Map of Stratford, Connecticut," courtesy of the Stratford Historical Society.

378 "History of Christ Episcopal Church, Stratford," www.christchurchstratford.org/history_5. Accessed April 5, 2010.

membership. Gustavus Loomis and his family worshipped at the church in a brand new stone building completed in 1858. The minister of the church was Rev. John Stearns, who first appears in ministerial records in 1844 as a Protestant Episcopal minister in the Diocese of New York. Rev. Stearns came from Saint Peter's Episcopal Church in Brooklyn, New York and served in Stratford from 1855-1862. Stearns was a longtime member of the American Bible Society.[379] Much of Gustavus Loomis' life centered on the Protestant Episcopal Church in Stratford. He was always at church meetings and was respected for his age and his piety as well as for his lengthy and successful military career.

Colonel Loomis and his family were thrilled to be members of the Protestant Episcopal Church in Stratford. The church building was a short walk north from their house along Main Street. This church in particular and similar churches in general all benefited from the New York Fulton Street Prayer Meetings and the subsequent revivals. Loomis' wife Annie was born into the Anglican Church in the West Indies and she enjoyed the rituals and liturgies of Anglican or Episcopalian worship. Loomis, raised a Congregationalist with strong puritan roots, was not a big supporter of such rituals, although in later life he seemed to mind it less and less. In 1858 the Connecticut Council of the Protestant Episcopal Church met in Stratford. This dignified council of fifty Protestant Episcopal clergymen and their associates met in the new church building in Stratford.[380] On a quite night the Loomis' could hear the singing from their home a few blocks away. Religiously, the Loomis family was very happy in Stratford.

While living in Stratford from 1858 to the beginning of the Civil War in 1861, Colonel Gustavus Loomis had free time. His

---

379 "The American Bible Society," *The New York Times,* May 17, 1878.
380 Eben E. Beardsley, *History of the Episcopal Church in Connecticut,* (1868: reprinted 2009 by Cornell University Press), vol. II, pp. 406-407.

finances were consistent, as he was still on the payroll of the army. He was by no means wealthy, but he was reasonably comfortable. His eager and active mind and his still healthy body demanded challenges. When not helping out at the Protestant Episcopal Church in Stratford, what could he do with his time? He attended abolitionist meetings and supported the Stratford Anti-Slavery Society. As Stratford was a small but bustling maritime town, Loomis' interests naturally leaned towards the sea.

Stratford maintained an active maritime community. Throughout Gustavus Loomis' years in Stratford there were numerous wooden vessels constructed and launched from Stratford. This industry gave birth to various other industries, such as joiners, carpenters, cabinetmakers, caulkers, and wheelwrights, all who were skilled in various trades to produce the numerous items needed to fit out a ship. Stratford built fishing and trading schooners produced huge revenues for the community. Vessels constructed in Stratford varied from one hundred tons or less to vessels over three hundred tons.[381] After 1850 the railroad took away much of the maritime coastal trade, Stratford mariners adjusting to the shift by focusing on lumber, stone, coal or brick distribution for local consumption. Trade with the West Indies had died down as steam boats replaced the larger trading vessels in Stratford Harbor. In 1858 Colonel Loomis saw the largest ship he had ever seen, as the gigantic seven hundred and thirty-four ton steamboat *Bridgeport* frequented Stratford Harbor. Oyster fishermen in Stratford had a thriving business, harvesting tons of oysters, shucking them and packing them on ice for distribution by railroad throughout the United States. By around 1860 it was not unusual to see wealthy yachtsmen on elegant specially made vessels plying the waters around Stratford.[382]

381 Lewis G. Knapp, *Stratford and the Sea,* (Charleston, SC: Arcadia Publishing, 2002), pp. 44-45.
382 Lewis G. Knapp, *Stratford and the Sea,* pp. 213, 243

Gustavus Loomis did not have much money to invest in the diverse maritime activities in Stratford. But his image and prestige as a Colonel in the U.S. Army immediately elevated him to the highest levels of society in Stratford. He was good friends with the wealthy and the influential in the community, businessmen and investors eager to befriend the pious and respected elderly military officer. Having Gustavus Loomis as a public sponsor for any maritime interest made sound business sense. His good name lent credibility to various investment ideas and maritime opportunities.

When Loomis saw a viable business opportunity he took it, his reputation of more value to investors and businessmen than his meager finances. There is no record of Loomis profiting very much from these interludes into the business world, but neither did he lose money. He hobnobbed with the elite and wealthy based on his reputation and experience, not on his personal wealth.

These Stratford citizens in 1859 were all connected with the sea. Standing are Captain Pulaski Benjamin, General Loomis, Captain Thomas Austin, geographer Jesse Olney, merchants Henry Plant and T.B. Fairchild. Seated are Admiral Joshua Sands, William Benjamin, Captain John Sterling and his son John, mill owner Edwards Johnson, and James Olney, plus their children

The above photograph from the Stratford Historical Society shows the influential people Gustavus Loomis associated with in Stratford and how his good name was helpful for various maritime and business adventures. Captain Pulaski Benjamin was a lifelong Stratford resident and a naval veteran of the War of 1812. He made his fortune as a captain of trading vessels in the East Indies and China. He attended the Episcopal Church in Stratford but spent most of his life at sea.[383] Captain Thomas Austin served on gigantic three-masted ships of well over one thousand

---

383 "An Old Sea Captain Dead," *The New York Times,* October 30, 1883.

tons as a merchant sea captain, circling the globe and away from Stratford sometimes for years at a time. Jesse Olney was a world-class geographer and educator. A native of Connecticut, Olney settled in Stratford in 1854. His geography books sold by the millions worldwide and were treasured by sea captains and explorers. Jesse Olney was Unitarian and had service in the Connecticut legislature. Henry Plant was born in Branford, Connecticut and worked his way up from a common seaman on local steamboats to a merchant executive. After the Civil War he made a fortune in railroads in the south. Merchant T.B. Fairchild was from a Stratford family but he eventually settled with his family in New York City. Admiral Joshua Sands was, like Gustavus Loomis, a veteran of the War of 1812, the Mexican War and the Civil War. Admiral Sands sailed as a naval officer worldwide, even helping to lay the transatlantic telegraph cable in 1857. In the Civil War he served as a Lighthouse Inspector for the Union. His funeral in 1883 caused the U.S. Navy to pause in respect.[384] William Benjamin was from a wealthy Stratford family involved with maritime and merchant activities. Captain John Sterling was a naval veteran of the War of 1812 who later sailed merchant clipper ships from New York City to South America and the orient. When Captain Sterling met Gustavus Loomis in the 1850s, Sterling was retired from the sea and was a successful businessman and banker in Stratford until his death in 1866.[385] Edwards Johnson was the son of prominent Stratford residents William and Susan Johnson. Johnson inherited a prosperous mill and granary from his father where ships could tie up directly at the mill and be loaded with grain for sale worldwide.[386] James Olney was related to the geographer Jesse Olney and was a prominent member of Stratford's society.

384 "Funeral of Admiral Sands," *The New York Times,* October 5, 1883.
385 Lewis G. Knapp, *Stratford and the Sea,* p. 189.
386 Lewis G. Knapp, *Stratford and the Sea,* p. 118.

An interesting observation from the above photograph is the two young girls at the right of the picture. These girls are about the same age as Loomis' granddaughters Adele (b.1853) and Emma (b.1854). It is more than likely that these two girls were the granddaughters of Annie and Gustavus Loomis.

The home of Gustavus Loomis and his family in Stratford, Connecticut was about sixty miles away from New York City, connected by train and by a good strait road. A spirited carriage ride could make the trip in less than four hours; a train ride was about an hour and a half. In 1857, shortly before the Loomis' arrived in Stratford, a religious revival broke out in New York City that quickly spread along the southern Connecticut coastline, then throughout much of the United States. This revival directly affected the community of Stratford.

The Fulton Street Prayer Revival in New York City began as a one-man ministry of seeking others to meet for prayer. Jeremiah C. Lanphier (1809-1890) was a layman who canvassed neighborhoods around the Old Dutch North Church at Fulton and Williams streets in lower New York City. In September, 1857, Mr. Lanphier's intention was to encourage people to pray, hoping that revival would result. He was not disappointed. At first a handful of people attended, but interest quickly grew. The weekly prayer meetings began to meet daily. There was nothing spectacular or sensational. People were encouraged to attend for as long or as short a time as was possible. The meetings started promptly and ended promptly so to allow businessmen and others to meet their obligations. All types of people attended the meetings, from messenger boys to wealthy executives, from wealthy women to poor women who worked in factories. Rules were drawn up for participation, the most important rule being that no person was allowed to speak for longer than five minutes. Within six months there were ten thousand gathering daily for prayer in New York City. In 1858 news of the Fulton Street Revival spread throughout America. In various cities unoccupied theaters during the day were opened up for prayer meetings.[387] The revival quickly spread along the southern Connecticut coastline and influenced religious attitudes in Gustavus Loomis' hometown of Stratford, Connecticut.

The revival of 1858 swept through much of New England. East of Stratford, the campus of Yale University was overwhelmed by the revival. The largest church in New Haven could not hold all the Yale students and others affected by the revival, with two daily prayer meetings necessary to accommodate all the people.[388] As the seventy year old Gustavus Loomis observed this revival of Christianity in Connecticut, he was elated. For over four decades Loomis had encouraged revival and participated in revival meetings. The revival or awakening in 1858 and thereafter was of the nature and design exactly as Loomis had been encouraging all his adult life. Namely, the revival was a laymen's movement; it was nonsectarian and inter-denominational; it was based on prayer and scripture; it had no emotionalism; and it led to genuine and enduring religious conversions.[389]

The 1858-1860 revival within the Protestant Episcopal Church of Stratford, Connecticut was marked by additional meetings, increase in attendance, and a surge in applications for church membership. It was not an excitement predicted or prearranged. There were remarkable answers to prayer, public confession of sins, repentance from bad habits, and striking cases or religious conversions. The revival in Stratford affected all classes of people,

---

387 "Revival Born in a Prayer Meeting," *Knowing & Doing,* Fall, 2004, pp. 1-7.

388 "Revival Born in a Prayer Meeting," pp. 3-4.

389 Samuel Prime, *The Power of Prayer: The New York Revival of 1858,* (Carlisle, PA: The Banner of Truth Trust, 1991).

from very wealthy merchants to very poor day laborers. Outward prosperity was exposed as insufficient to satisfy the desires of the heart, as hundreds came to Jesus Christ for salvation or for sanctification. Like the Fulton Street Old North Dutch Church in New York City, the Protestant Episcopal Church in Stratford was opened during the day for prayer meetings, at which Gustavus Loomis was a regular attendee. People were compelled to pray for one another and confess their sins and repent. Others rededicated themselves to the Lord. Throughout New England the revival commenced almost simultaneously in many cities, towns and small villages.[390] Through the use of the telegraph and newspapers, the revival spread within a few months to all parts of the United States. From Boston to New Orleans to Saint Louis, revival in churches was common. This movement was not denominationally centered, but prayer centered. Sectarian jealousies were diminished before the power of the Holy Spirit called down by prayer among the people. Gustavus Loomis, with his puritan roots and his Calvinistic theology, rejoiced in the revival as an outpouring of the sovereign grace of God upon a needy people.

While Gustavus Loomis was dabbling in business adventures and participating in the revival in Stratford, he was also still in the service of the U.S. Army on paid leave with the rank of Colonel. The fact that Gustavus Loomis was still being paid by the army while on indefinite leave meant that the army could recall him at any time. An example of this happening was in August, 1859, as Loomis was ordered to serve as an officer on a court martial board. Colonel Loomis put back on his army uniform, in his closet for the past year or so, and reported to New York City. The presiding officer for the court martial was Colonel J.K.T. Mansfield, with Loomis as second officer, there

390 Samuel Prime, *The Power of Prayer: The New York Revival of 1858*, p. 27.

being twelve army officers in all. *The New York Times* printed a summary of the court martial as follows:[391]

COURT MARTIAL OF MAJOR OSBORN CROSS

Investigation of charges of embezzlement and misapplication of public money. A general Court-Martial was convened Wednesday morning, by order of the War Department, at the United States Army quarters in State Street, to try Major Osborn Cross for alleged misapplication and embezzlement of the public money while he held the office of Quartermaster at San Francisco, California. [Presiding Officers] Col. J.K.T. Mansfield, Inspector General, Col. Gustavus Loomis, Fifth Infantry...

While Gustavus Loomis and his wife Annie and their young granddaughters enjoyed life in Stratford, Connecticut, larger national issues plagued the United States. The tension of a slave-owning South against an anti-slavery North made conflict almost inevitable. President Abraham Lincoln did not propose federal laws against slavery where it already existed, but in his 1858 "House Divided" speech he expressed a desire to "arrest the further spread of it [slavery], and place it where the public mind shall rest in the belief that it is in the course of ultimate extinction."[392] Much of the political battle and civil unrest in the 1850s focused on the expansion of slavery westward and into Florida. "Bloody Kansas" was an iconic expression of that time. Most of the organized territories were likely to become free-soil states, outlawing slavery, which increased the Southern movement toward secession and independence. Southern states chaffed under pressure from the federal government over the extent of federal law within individual states.

---

391 "Law Reports: Court Martial of Major Osborn Cross," *The New York Times,* August 5, 1859.

392 Abraham Lincoln, *House Divided Speech,* Springfield, Illinois, June 16, 1858.

In early March, 1860 Abraham Lincoln campaigned for President in southern Connecticut. On March 6 Lincoln was in New Haven and on March 10 he was in Bridgeport. The train carrying Lincoln passed through Stratford, a few blocks from the Loomis home. At each stop several hundred people heard Lincoln speak. It is more than likely that Gustavus Loomis heard Abraham Lincoln speak in Bridgeport, a couple of miles from Loomis' house.[393] Up to this point the two men had never met, although Abraham Lincoln was a common militia soldier while Loomis was a Major in the U.S. Army as they fought in the 1832 Black Hawk War. But their paths would soon cross as the nation prepared for a civil war.

A definitive event from which the nation descended into a civil war was the April 23, 1860 National Convention of the Democratic Party assembled at Charleston, South Carolina. Here the Southern Democrats withdrew from the Northern Democrats over the issue of congressional control over slavery. The pro-slavery Southern Democrats created their own convention, the first interstate government formed against the federal union. In the 1860 presidential election the democrats were divided between northern and southern presidential candidates, insuring that the Republican candidate, Abraham Lincoln, would be elected President of the United States. After the November, 1860 election of Abraham Lincoln, ominous and foreboding political and military movements was apparent. On December 6 Congress created a committee to take measures to insure the perpetuity of the Union. On December 10 the Secretary of the Treasury, Howell Cobb of Georgia, resigned. On December 20 South Carolina became the first state to adopt an ordinance of secession. Fearing an attack, the vulnerable U.S. Army troops at Fort Moultrie covertly transferred to Fort Sumter in the Charleston, South Carolina Harbor. The next day Fort Moultrie was seized

393 Sharon B. Smith, *Connecticut's Civil War*, (Milford, CT: Featherfield Publishing, 2010), pp. 97, 101-102.

by troops from South Carolina. On December 27 the U.S. Revenue cutter *William Aiken* was seized by South Carolina. On December 30, the United States Arsenal in South Carolina was seized by South Carolina officials.[394] At the end of 1860 it appeared the United States might lose South Carolina as a state. No one could imagine that these events were only a prelude to a full-fledged Civil War in the United States.

As 1861 began, the first twelve days of the year were representative of the hostilities soon to follow. In these days Fort Johnson in South Carolina was seized by state authorities, as was Fort Pulaski in Georgia and the U.S. Arsenal at Mount Vernon, Alabama. Fort Morgan and Fort Gaines in Alabama were then seized, as was the U.S. Arsenal at Apalachicola, Florida and Fort Marion, Florida. In North Carolina local citizens seized Fort Johnston and Fort Caswell. In Louisiana the Arsenal and Barracks at Baton Rouge were seized by state authorities, while Fort Jackson, Fort Saint Philip and the U.S. Marine Hospital were all taken in Louisiana. These dreadful twelve days for the Union in early January concluded with Florida state authorities taking the Barrancas Barracks, Fort McRee and Fort Barrancas, and the Navy Yard in Pensacola. By January 12, 1860, the federal union was in shambles. In anticipation of the military rebellion of Southern States, President Lincoln called to Washington the senior officer in the U.S. Army, brevet Lieutenant General Winfield Scott. Scott arrived on December 12, 1860 and was in Washington as numerous U.S. military facilities were overtaken by Southern States. An ominous sign was the resignation of the Secretary of War, John B. Floyd, a Virginian, on December 29.

In the first twelve days of January 1860, General Scott responded to the seizure of federal military properties. On January

---

394 *Battles and Leaders of the Civil War,* (1887: Reprinted by Castle Books, Edison, NJ,) p. xxiii.

5th Scott authorized the first relief expedition for the threatened Fort Sumter, an expedition that was blocked in Charleston Harbor on January 9th by South Carolina troops and forced away. This is often considered the first combat of the U.S. Civil War. On January 10th General Scott authorized a relief expedition from Boston, Massachusetts to Pensacola, Florida. On January 12th the Governor of Florida demanded the surrender of Fort Pickens, Pensacola which Scott refused to do. Meanwhile Jacob Thompson, a Mississippian, resigned as Secretary of the Interior, while Florida, Alabama and Mississippi voted for secession. In his memoirs, Winfield Scott initially refused to believe that the South would take up arms against the federal government, a belief in which he was bitterly disappointed.[395]

In January of 1861 Connecticut Governor William Buckingham issued an order calling for the state militia to begin preparations for an emergency.[396]

It is significant to note that Colonel Gustavus Loomis made out his will on January 9, 1861. Apparently Colonel Loomis could see that his beloved nation was spiraling into a Civil War in which he would serve and potentially be killed. Those early days of January, 1861 were disheartening to Loomis. Local newspaper editorials were rabid in their denunciations of southern slavery and bloodshed over slavery in the western territories. To prepare his family for his possible death, Loomis wrote a legal Last Will and Testament which was filed before the court in Stratford. Everything that Gustavus Loomis owned he left to "my beloved wife Mary Ann T. Loomis." He left his wife "Eight shares of Little Miami Railroad Stock of Fifty dollars each." He left his wife land which he had purchased in Wisconsin in 1855. He also left Annie all his household furniture and personal property and appointed her to be the Executor of his Last Will and Testament. The three page handwritten document is signed, "G. Loomis, Col. 5 Infantry." It is interesting to note that Gustavus' only surviving child from his first marriage, the widow Eliza (Loomis) Ogden, was present as a witness for the signing of this legal document.[397] This speaks of the Christian home life that Gustavus Loomis practiced with his extended family. Loomis loved his first wife Julia and he adored his only child Eliza. When Julia died, Gustavus remarried and had a blessed marriage with Annie. In his home as an older man he welcomed two step-granddaughters to whom he showered his love. At the same time, his adult daughter Eliza and his several biological grandchildren were still an active part of his life. Gustavus Loomis was a type of benevolent patriarch, the older man affectionate, kind, generous and godly in all his ways. His family adored him.

In the November presidential election of 1860, the Republican Party, led by Abraham Lincoln, campaigned against the expansion of slavery beyond the states in which it already existed. Most Southerners voted Democrat and pro-slavery. There was no talk from Lincoln of outlawing slavery in the U.S. or of the emancipation of the slaves. The Republican presidential election victory in November, 1860 resulted in seven Southern states declaring their secession from the Union even before Lincoln took office on March 4, 1861. Both the outgoing and incoming U.S. administrations rejected the legality of secession, considering it rebellion and treason. Eventually eleven Southern slave states declared their secession from the United States and formed the Confederate States of America. Led by the former U.S. Secretary of War Jefferson Davis, they fought against the United States which was supported by all the free states and the five border

---

397 "Last Will and Testament of Gustavus Loomis," Stratford, Connecticut Historical Society.

slave states. Although skirmishes had been going on for months, the April 12-14, 1861 bombardment and surrender of the federal facility at Fort Sumter, South Carolina is considered the official start of the U.S. Civil War.

On April 8, 1861 Colonel Gustavus Loomis prepared legal documents providing for the care of his wife Annie's granddaughters. In 1861, Adele and Emma were both less than ten years old. The girls had lived with Gustavus and Annie since around 1857 when both parents had died. Gustavus had no biological connection to these girls, but he welcomed them into his home and showered them with Christian love. But nothing legal related to guardianship of the girls had yet been drafted. With the coming of the Civil War, Colonel Loomis knew that he needed to provide legal guardianship for his granddaughters. Although finances were very tight, Loomis gladly paid the three hundred dollar fee for this transaction. This provided a legal bond for the girls and insured that should Gustavus be killed in the war, guardianship of Adele and Emma would be retained by his wife Annie.[398] The seventy-two year old patriarch of his family, while consumed with the details of preparing for a Civil War, did not forget about his vulnerable granddaughters.

Why did Loomis choose to serve in the Civil War? He had nothing to prove to anyone. He had served admirably for over forty years in the army holding the rank of colonel. He had faced various enemies over the years in combat and he had served well. His leadership and integrity were unquestioned. At the beginning of the Civil War Gustavus Loomis was seventy-two years old. He could have sat this war out and nobody would have given it a second thought. The General in Chief of the U.S. Army Winfield Scott was a couple of years older than Loomis and was in poor

---

398 "Gustavus Loomis File," *Probate Court Records, April 8, 1861*. Courtesy of the Stratford Historical Society.

health. War is for the young and vigorous, not for the old. Yet Colonel Loomis was compelled, even driven to contribute to the cause of the Union against the Southern Rebellion.

There were two driving forces that compelled Colonel Loomis to retain his commission and serve in the Civil War. One factor was Loomis' abhorrence of slavery. Locally in Stratford there was an active anti-slavery society founded in 1837 and there was a stop in town for the Underground Railroad.[399] If it took military force to contradict the belligerence of the South over slavery, then so be it. But the removal of Southern slavery was not the primary motive for Loomis in serving with the Union.[400] Loomis was a patriot, firmly dedicated to the United States of America. With his Vermont heritage and his West Point education, combined with his over forty-five years of military service, Gustavus Loomis was fervently pro-Union. Loomis was a professional soldier. He understood how the military works. He was excellent at drilling troops, he being noticeably proficient in army tactics, customs, protocols, traditions and administration. At age seventy-two he was too old to take the field. But his contributions to the Union could still be significant. He could pass on to new recruits, most old enough to be his grandchildren, what he had learned through multiple combat experiences and over four decades of military service.

---

399 "Christ Episcopal Church, Stratford," www.christchurchstratford.org/history_5. Accessed March 3, 2010.

400 For a study of why men fought in the Civil War, see James M. McPherson, *For Cause and Comrades: Why Men Fought in the Civil War*, (New York: Oxford University Press, 1977).

Chapter Seventeen

Recruiting and Training Union Troops in CT and RI

War fever overtook Colonel Loomis' adopted state of Connecticut. The state played an important role for the Union, manufacturing arms, producing supplies and furnishing manpower. Only a small minority in Connecticut opposed the war. The state had consistently voted against the expansion of slavery into the western territories and had a long history of abolitionism and support of the Underground Railroad. Further, Connecticut was very devoted to the preservation of the federal union. Governor William A. Buckingham eagerly urged Connecticut's citizens to support the Union cause by raising and recruiting regiments to fight for the defense of Washington and the preservation of the Union. Connecticut residents assumed the righteousness of their cause and believed they fought for their flag and their national preservation. The assault upon the federal government by Southern rebels could not stand.[401] By the end of April, 1861, Connecticut raised three regiments for three months duty, which was all the time expected to end the Southern rebellion. Some joined out of patriotism. Others enlisted out of a sense of adventure. Still others joined the cause because everyone else was doing it and it seemed like the right thing to do. Some were unemployed and were happy to be provided meals and a paycheck.[402] In Washing-

---

401 James McPherson, *Battle Cry of Freedom,* (New York: Oxford University Press, 1988), p. 308

402 James McPherson, *For Cause and Comrades: Why Men Fought in the Civil War,* (New York: Oxford University Press, 1997), pp. 5-6, 8.

ton, General in Chief Winfield Scott expressed complete confidence in the Union victory, acknowledging that war fervor on both sides could lead to a short but bloody conflict.[403] The popular excitement in Connecticut was immense. Colonel Gustavus Loomis of Stratford, Connecticut was one of the senior U.S. Army officers within all six New England states. As the commanding officer on paid military leave from the Fifth Infantry Regiment, Loomis' exact role in the war was yet to be determined.

At the start of the Civil War, the 5th Infantry Regiment was still stationed on the western frontier. When Loomis left the regiment for paid military leave in 1858 the soldiers were scattered throughout Texas and Utah. In the fall of 1860 the 5th Regiment transferred to various posts in New Mexico. At the outbreak of the Civil War in April, 1861 the regiment was concentrated in Albuquerque and at Fort Defiance, New Mexico. Elements of the 5th Regiment fought three small battles in New Mexico. On February 21, 1862 various companies from the 5th fought Confederates at the battle of Valverde. On March 28, 1862 several companies within the 5th fought Confederate rebels at Apache Canon. Elements of the regiment also fought at Perala, New Mexico on April 15, 1862. The 5th Regiment of Infantry stayed in New Mexico for the remainder of the war and saw no further combat. After the war in 1866 the regiment was redistributed to various western posts. The 5th Regiment was not called upon to fight in any of the major campaigns of the war.[404]

Colonel Gustavus Loomis retained his rank within the 5th Infantry but was assigned to recruiting duty near his hometown in southern New England. In Loomis' official biographical summary from West Point, it states that at the beginning of the Civil

---

403 Bruce Canton, *The Coming Fury*, (New York: Doubleday & Company, 1961), p. 325.
404 "History of the 5th U.S. Infantry," *The Old Army*, www.theoldarmy.com/usarmy/5us.
  Accessed January 16, 2009.

War he was "Mustering Connecticut and Rhode Island Volunteers into service, April 18 to August 19, 1861."[405]

The mustering and training of volunteers was difficult work. The methods by which these companies and regiments were raised were various. In 1861 a common way was for someone who had previous military service to take the initiative and circulate an enlistment paper for signatures. His chances were good for obtaining a commission as captain in the company. Men who had been prominent in assisting him would likely secure key positions.[406] In the first wave of volunteering there grew the practice of permitting individuals to take the initiative in raising regiments, and thus overnight to become colonels, with brigadier-generalships thereafter easily attainable. From a strictly military standpoint this was madness. Independent regiments formed in order to please friends of the politically prominent. The authority of state governors was driven against the federal government insuring clashes of authority. Another mistake was permitting the troops to elect their officers. Though this was not the usual method, this election practice for officers below the rank of colonel was widespread and was accepted by both state and federal authorities. By July, 1861, this unmilitary method was written into federal law. For the filling of vacancies in the new volunteer forces it was allowed that each company should vote for officers as high as captain. More senior vacancies were to be filled by the votes of the commissioned officers.[407] Thus progress in military rank could become a popularity contest and not based of tactical proficiency. A man prominent in

405 George W. Cullum, *Biographical Register of the Officers and Graduates of the U.S. Military Academy, at West Point, N.Y.*, (New York: 1868), pp. 62-63.

406 "Enlisting in a Civil War Army," www.civilwarhome.com/enlisting. Accessed February 13, 2010.

407 "The Administration of the Union Army," www.civilwarhome.com/armyadmin. Accessed February 13, 2010.

civilian life might be voted as a senior officer in a new unit, with disastrous results.

General Benjamin F. Butler, briefly the commander of the short-lived Department of New England, appointed Colonel Gustavus Loomis as the senior mustering officer for Connecticut and Rhode Island. This meant that Loomis had to make sense and order out of the recruiting and volunteering chaos. There was initially no standard for training. Companies formed, drilled and then presented themselves to their state governor for approval and for further orders. Some troops had weapons, most did not. Other troops had uniforms while some wore homespun clothing. Some units had capable leadership while others were led by incompetents, political hacks seeking fame in battle. The turmoil and disorder caused by the initial wave of enthusiastic volunteers was aptly described as follows:

> FROM THE HOUR the call for troops was published, enlistments began, and recruits were parading the streets continually. At the capital the restless impulse to be doing something military seized even upon the members of the Legislature, and a good many of them assembled every evening upon the east terrace of the State House to be drilled in marching and facing by one or two of their own number who had some knowledge of company tactics. Most of the uniformed independent companies in the cities of the State immediately tendered their services and began to recruit their numbers to the hundred men required for acceptance. There was no time to procure uniforms, nor was it desirable; for these companies had chosen their own, and would have to change it for that of the United States as soon as this could be furnished. For some days companies could

be seen marching and drilling, of which part would be uniformed in some gaudy style such as is apt to prevail in holiday parades in time of peace, while another part would be dressed in the ordinary working garb of citizens of all degrees. The uniformed files [rows of soldiers] would also be armed and accoutered [equipped], the others would be without arms or equipments, and as awkward a squad as well could be imagined.[408]

From April to August, 1861, Colonel Gustavus Loomis travelled by train and by horse drawn carriage throughout southern New England as a mustering officer for the federal government. This meant that Loomis was responsible in one way or another for the organization, training and certification process by which volunteer units were declared ready for federal service. Loomis then gave the federal oath of office to the troops and swore in the unit as a federal force.

In his adopted home state of Connecticut, Colonel Loomis helped to muster, train and swear into federal service five infantry regiments. The 1st Regiment of Infantry was organized in Hartford on April 22, 1861. After almost a month of training they departed Connecticut on May 18th for Washington. This was a three month unit which defended Washington and then served in operations in northern Virginia including the disastrous July 21st battle of Bull Run. The unit mustered out on July 31, 1861. The 2nd Regiment of Infantry was organized in New Haven on May 7, 1861. With only twelve days of organization and training they departed Connecticut on May 19th for duty defending Washington. Throughout June and July the unit was involved in picket duty and security missions. The regiment served in the

---

408 *Battles and Leaders of the Civil War: The Opening Battles,* (1887: reprinted by Castle Books, Edison, NJ in 1956), vol. I, p. 91.

battle of Bull Run and was mustered out on August 7, 1861. The 3rd Regiment of Infantry was organized in New Haven and mustered in on May 14, 1861. Like the 1st and 2nd Regiments from Connecticut, this regiment served in the defense of Washington and in various duties in northern Virginia, including the humiliation of the battle of Bull Run. The 3rd Regiment was mustered out on August 12, 1861.[409]

In addition to the three month regiments Loomis mustered and helped train, he was influential in the creation of the three year 4th Regiment of Infantry. The unit served in Pennsylvania and in Maryland and then was assigned to defend Washington. In January, 1862 the unit converted to the 1st Connecticut Heavy Artillery consisting of twelve companies of one hundred and fifty men each. The unit saw extensive combat in such famous battles as the battle of Fredericksburg; the battle of Chancellorsville; the battle of Gettysburg; and several others. The 4th Regiment fought as far south as North Carolina and was mustered out of service in Washington on September 25, 1865, with six officers dead and two hundred and twenty-one soldiers' dead from combat or illness.[410]

The last Connecticut unit that Colonel Gustavus Loomis helped muster in was the 5th Regiment of Infantry. The regiment was organized in Hartford on July 26, 1861. After brief service in the defense of Washington the regiment moved throughout northern Virginia and participated in a series of raids and skirmishes. In 1862 the 5th Regiment fought at Cedar Mountain and the second battle of Bull Run, then fought at Chancellorsville and at Gettysburg. The regiment was later assigned as part of the Atlanta campaign, participating in the siege of Atlanta and

---

409 "Connecticut – Union Regimental Histories," *The Civil War Archive*, www.civilwararchive.com/Unreghst/unctinfl. Accessed February 12, 2010.

410 "Connecticut – Union Regimental Histories, *The Civil War Archive*, www.civilwararchive.com/Unreghst/unctarty. Accessed March 16, 2010.

General Sherman's famous march to the sea in November and December, 1864. The 5th then participated in the siege of Savannah and then fought a series of battles heading north through the Carolinas. The regiment was present when Confederate General Joseph E. Johnston surrendered the last rebel forces in the east, on April 17, 1865.[411]

What must it have been like for these Connecticut young men and adults to be mustered into federal service by the elderly Colonel Gustavus Loomis? All indications are that Loomis at age seventy-two was still vigorous. The aged senior officer in all six New England states was certainly a sight to behold, his white hair and thick white beard giving him the look of a biblical patriarch. This experienced combat veteran with almost fifty years of military service must have seemed like a figure larger than life to the young men who were his new recruits. It is not difficult to imagine Colonel Loomis with his deep, commanding voice issuing orders to intimidated volunteers. Loomis trained the recruits with the standard textbook of that time, *Hardee's Rifle and Light Infantry Tactics*. Published in 1855, the revised 1861 version was the standard military handbook for both sides during the Civil War. Volume one consisted of training for the individual soldier as well as operations at the company level. Volume two covered larger unit tactics and formations. The author was Lieutenant Colonel William J. Hardee, a Georgian, who served as a Major General for the Confederacy in the Civil War. The Union, not wanting to use a textbook written by a Rebel, issued a copy of Hardee's work published by a Union officer, General Silas Casey in 1862.

The Connecticut Governor William A. Buckingham fully supported the Union cause. In his correspondence with Secretary of War Simon Cameron, the Governor pledged his full support

---

411 "Johnston's Surrender in North Carolina April, 1865," www.sciway3.net/proctor/ marion/military/wbts-/Johnston_surrender. Accessed March 16, 2010.

for the call of troops into federal service. Governor Buckingham conferred directly with General in Chief Winfield Scott as well as with Secretary Cameron. The Governor knew he needed a senior military officer to muster, train and swear in his volunteers into federal service. The most qualified person for these duties was Colonel Gustavus Loomis of Stratford, Connecticut. Both the Secretary of War Cameron and General in Chief Scott approved of Loomis to assume this position. Governor Buckingham was obviously thrilled to have such a senior active duty army officer in his state available to muster and train his volunteers.[412]

In addition to his recruiting, mustering and training duties in Connecticut, Colonel Gustavus Loomis had the same military responsibilities in Rhode Island. Tiny Rhode Island furnished over twenty-five thousand men to the war, of which about one thousand six hundred died of various causes. In addition, the industrial capability of Rhode Island supplied the Union with tons of supplies and equipment.

In May, 1861 the U.S. Naval Academy moved from Maryland to Newport, Rhode Island out of fear of a Confederate takeover. One day after President Lincoln called for seventy-five thousand volunteers to serve the Union, Rhode Island Governor William Sprague on April 16, 1861 responded to the call by supporting the state's quota of one infantry regiment

The Stratford, CT Civil War memorial was dedicated to local men like Colonel Gustavus Loomis who served during the war.
Source: www.hmdb.org/marker. asp?marker=25782

412 Samuel G. Buckingham, *The Life of William A. Buckingham, the War Governor of Connecticut*, (Springfield, MA: 1894), pp. 163-164.

plus an additional field artillery battery. The first wave of Rhode Island volunteers was mustered into service with the assistance of Colonel Gustavus Loomis.

The initial soldiers mustered from Rhode Island were artillery and infantry troops on three months orders. On May 7, 1861 Governor Sprague ordered an artillery battery to be formed, designated Battery A of the 1st Regiment Light Artillery. The regiment served in the defense of Washington and in Northern Virginia and in Maryland and fought in the July 21 battle of Bull Run. In September, when the three month enlistments expired, the unit was in Virginia, replenished by other Rhode Islanders. The initial three month volunteers were mustered, trained and sworn into federal service by Colonel Gustavus Loomis. Other volunteers were enlisted for three years orders. The same was true for the men of Battery B of the 1st Regiment Light Artillery. Colonel Loomis was a school trained artilleryman with a West Point education and took seriously his responsibility of insuring these volunteers understood basic artillery procedures. The recruits would learn more when they arrived at their deployed location. Battery B was mustered into service on August 18th and departed Rhode Island shortly thereafter. The battery served along the Potomac River, throughout northern Virginia and into Maryland when the three month soldiers were released from federal service, replaced by other Rhode Island men.

Colonel Loomis' influence on Battery B was immediately apparent. As one account stated,

> IN AUGUST 1861, knowing they would soon be called up for service, the men who had signed up for Battery B commenced drilling at the Benefit Street Arsenal in Providence. The men began to become proficient in artillery drill and they soon received their uniforms… On August 10 the battery horses arrived and the mounted

drill began… At 3:30 pm on August 13, after success-fully completing a medical examination, four commis-sioned officers and one hundred and thirty-seven men were mustered into government service for three years as the First Rhode Island Light Artillery, Battery B, by Colonel Loomis of the United States Army.[413]

Artillery troops mustered and trained by Colonel Loomis depart from the Provi-dence, RI train station in July, 1861 for duty in Washington.
Source: www.batterybri.org/V2/providence.

Just as Loomis was influen-tial in mustering, training and swearing into federal service Rhode Island artillerymen, so he also helped provide troops for Rhode Island infantry regi-ments. Loomis helped muster in the 1st, 2nd and 3rd Regiments of Rhode Island Infantry. The 1st Regiment of Infantry was mustered in April, 1861 as a three month regiment. They served in the defense of Wash-ington and in northern Virginia and in the battle of Bull Run. They were mustered out of service on August 2nd with one officer killed and twenty-four soldiers dead from combat or from disease. The 2nd Regiment of Infantry was organized in Providence in June, 1861 as a three year regiment. The 2nd saw extensive combat throughout Virginia and Pennsylvania and participated in such major battles as Fredericksburg, Chancellorsville Gettysburg and Spotsylvania. The enlistments for the 2nd Regiment expired in 1864 but many enlisted for another year. The regiment repulsed an attack on Washington by Confederate General Jubal A. Early on July 11-12, 1864 and chased

---

413 "Providence to Washington," www.batterybri.org/V2/Providence. Accessed March 17, 2010.

General Robert E. Lee in April, 1865. The unit lost one hundred and ninety-six soldiers to combat or disease. The 3rd Regiment of Infantry from Rhode Island organized at Providence in August, 1861. They deployed to New York Harbor and then to Washington and then back to New York. By October, 1861 the 3rd Regiment was in South Carolina fighting Confederates around Port Royal. By the end of the year the 3rd Regiment of Infantry was redesignated as the 3rd Heavy Artillery Regiment and engaged in combat operations in South Carolina and in Florida until the end of the war.[414]

An interesting eyewitness account of Colonel Gustavus Loomis as a mustering and training officer in Rhode Island is provided by Private Elisha H. Rhodes of the 2nd Regiment of Infantry. Loomis made sure the volunteers were properly recruited, mustered and indoctrinated into military life with uniforms and essential equipment. As Private Elisha Rhodes recorded in his diary,

> JUNE 5, 1861 – Today our Company marched to a building on the east side of Eddy Street near Clifford Street and was mustered into the U.S. Service by Colonel Loomis, U.S.A. The scene was a solemn one and the impression made upon our minds will last a long time. We marched back to the Armory, and during the evening I was fitted out with a uniform. It consisted of a blue flannel shirt worn with the flaps outside of the pants, fatigue or forage cap and shoes. It was after dark, donned my new rig and receiving permission I walked to Pawtucket, five miles distant, reaching there about nine p.m. Now I was an object of curiosity to my school friends. My mother shed many tears but was willing that I should go. That was my last visit home before leaving for the war.[415]

414 "Rhode Island – Union Regimental Histories," *The Civil War Archive,* www.civilwararchive.com/Unreghst/unriinf. Accessed February 16, 2010.

415 Elisha Hurt Rhodes, *All for the Union: The Civil War Diary and Letters of Elijah Hunt Rhodes,* (Vintage Civil War Library Edition, 1992), pp. 6-7.

Colonel Gustavus Loomis was an excellent recruiter and was well-admired for his tenacity as a mustering officer for the federal government. The old warhorse was venerated by his subordinates, greatly esteemed for both his experience and his administrative capabilities as a senior U.S. Army officer in New England. Loomis was zealous for the cause of maintaining the Union. He was adamant that slavery was a great evil, a curse upon America. The old white haired colonel with the bushy white beard was also a calming Christian influence upon all he met. Not given to emotional outbursts or spur of the moment decisions, the steady Loomis amidst the chaos of the first months of the war was noticed by his superiors in Washington. With the approvals of President Abraham Lincoln, General in Chief Winfield Scott and Secretary of War Simon Cameron, in August, 1861 Colonel Gustavus Loomis was made Superintendant of the General Recruiting Service for the entire United States.[416] This was a huge vote of confidence upon Colonel Gustavus Loomis by his superiors. There was a very real possibility of promotion to Brigadier General. On August 19, 1861, Colonel Loomis and his wife and two young granddaughters arrived at Fort Columbus on Governor's Island in New York Harbor, to assume his new responsibilities as the senior recruiting and mustering officer in the United States Army.

A series of sketches drawn in 1861 depicting U.S. Army recruiting efforts.
Source: *Harper's Weekly,* September 7, 1861.

416 George W. Cullum, *Biographical Register of the Officers and Graduates of the U.S. Military Academy,* pp. 118-119.

Chapter Eighteen

Fort Columbus, New York

FORT COLUMBUS, ON GOVERNOR'S ISLAND in New York Harbor, had many pleasant memories for Colonel Gustavus Loomis. Here his military career began fifty years earlier, when Loomis in 1811 was a naïve young second lieutenant of artillery fresh out of West Point. Here he brought his young bride Julia and here their only surviving child, Eliza, was born. There were wonderful memories of picnics with his bride along the shore and walks with their infant daughter along the fort's perimeter. Now Julia had been dead for over ten years, Loomis had remarried, and his only daughter was widowed with a large family. Colonel Loomis was now a seasoned veteran of four wars – the War of 1812; the Black Hawk War; the Mexican War; and the Seminole Wars. In 1861, upon assuming command at Fort Columbus, Colonel Loomis had recently turned seventy-three years old, one of the oldest active duty soldiers in the entire army.

Fort Columbus had changed a lot since Loomis departed the fort in the 1820s. While the facility retained its basic original design from the early 1800s, improvements in artillery and defenses were noticeable. The fort still had a dry moat and a five-point star design surrounded by a sloping grassy area which provided no cover for attacking troops. Housing for officers had improved and many of the comfort items found in New York City were also available at Fort Columbus. Improvements were made in the gun mounts. Wooden platforms were discarded for concrete or iron. Improvements in cut stone, concrete and brick work was noticeable. Exte-

rior stairways were replaced with interior stairways wherever possible. After 1852 the fort was a primary recruiting station, meaning
that vast improvements in housing facilities (barracks) were made,
including new roofs and kitchen facilities. The actual artillery canons at Fort Columbus were older but adequate for defending New
York Harbor. In July, 1861, several weeks before Colonel Gustavus
Loomis arrived at Fort Columbus, the canons at the fort were described as "older" and as "87 old guns."[417]

By January, 1861 the military activities at Fort Columbus
dramatically increased. As an article in *The New York Times* stated,
"The six hundred troops quartered at Fort Columbus, on Governor's Island, are daily drilled, and are being prepared for active service should they be called for. A considerable portion of
them are raw recruits, but they are fast being broken in and will
make efficient soldiers." The article continued, "They appear very
observant of every movement which indicates an intention to
draft them into active service, - a feeling being prevalent in the
garrison that they will, sooner of later, be required to proceed to
southern forts."[418]

Even before the Civil War officially began in mid-April, 1861,
Fort Columbus was actively involved in suppressing the Southern
rebellion. In addition to its routine duties as the largest fortification protecting New York Harbor, Fort Columbus twice in 1861
secretly dispatched supplies and troops to relieve the besieged
garrison at Fort Sumter, South Carolina. The first effort failed on
January 9 when the relief ship was fired upon by cadets from The
Citadel military academy. The second effort also failed on April
9 when South Carolina forces fired upon the relief ship, forcing
it away. For the duration of the Civil War, Fort Columbus was a

---

417 Barbara A. Yocum, *Fort Jay: Historic Structure Report,* (U.S. National Park Service,
    2005), pp. 69-72, 87.
418 "The Troops at Fort Columbus," *The New York Times,* January 15, 1861.

defensive facility with various important administrative and logistic responsibilities. The fort was never attacked by the Confederates, but it was attacked by frustrated anti-draft and pro-Southern New Yorkers during the New York City draft riots in 1863.[419]

Fort Columbus contributed to the Union cause in various ways. The fort was a defensive structure protecting New York City. Fort Columbus was also a huge recruiting and mustering location, a place to in-process many tens of thousands of men for service in the Union Army. The fort was also a location for numerous military court martial cases and several executions. There was also a military hospital and facilities for training army band members. A primary mission of Fort Columbus was as a prisoner of war camp for Confederate soldiers and officers.

Colonel Gustavus Loomis arrived at Fort Columbus in August, 1861. His first official title at the fort was as Superintendant of the General Recruiting Service. This meant that Loomis was responsible for the orderly recruiting, mustering and initial training of many thousands of new recruits from New York and New England. As one report stated,

> EVERY DAY FROM 25 to 50 men arrive at Governor's Island from the various recruiting offices in New York and elsewhere, and are immediately drilled in squads, until they are fit to be formed into companies and drafted into regiments. Every afternoon the troops are marched out upon the grassy slope to the rear of the southeastern battery, and are drilled in every conceivable movement for the space of about one hour... A staff of officers usually occupy the rising ground.[420]

---

419 Edmund B. Smith, *Governor's Island: Its Military History under Three Flags,* (New York: 1913), p. 82.

420 "Governors Island Prisons," www.correctionhistory.org/civilwar/governorsisland/frame_main1. Accessed March 27, 2009.

As the senior recruiting officer in the United States Army, Colonel Loomis set policy for recruiting and implemented procedures for mustering in raw recruits. His policies were the standard nationwide for all Union recruiting. If this was his only responsibility at Fort Columbus, he would have made a significant contribution to the overall war effort. However, Fort Columbus provided many leadership challenges and opportunities for Gustavus Loomis.

Colonel Loomis had no experience as a warden or administrator of a prison camp. Nevertheless, this additional responsibility was imposed upon him early in the war. Union deserters as well as political prisoners were held at Fort Columbus, but the largest prison population was from captured Confederate soldiers and officers. Part of the fort became a "dungeon for Confederate prisoners of war, large numbers being confined there during the war and several executions taking place."[421] Various diseases ravaged the prison population, such as measles, typhus, smallpox, pneumonia and various fevers. About one thousand five hundred Rebel prisoners stayed at Fort Columbus for various lengths of time, with Colonel Loomis serving as the Commandant of the prison camp.[422]

As a defensive structure protecting New York Harbor, Fort Columbus was impressive. Colonel Loomis, a trained artilleryman with a West Point education, insured that the fort was in ready condition to defend the harbor from Confederate attacks. Loomis was upset that a few buildings were constructed on the island over the years which hindered clear lanes of fire for the artillery. In June, 1863 the Corps of Engineers wrote that numerous buildings had to be removed or destroyed but no action was taken. A congressional appropriation was made in July, 1864 for one hundred thousand dollars to be spent on upgrading the defense of

---

421 Edmund B. Smith, *Governor's Island: Its Military History under Three Flags,* p. 82.
422 "Governors Island Prisons," p. 2.

New York Harbor, including Fort Columbus.[423] Obtaining ammunition for artillery practice was not a problem. Colonel Loomis drilled the artillerymen at Fort Columbus with live rounds fired into the sea and drilled the troops in military formations on the parade field. As Loomis had done throughout his long army career, he demanded orderliness, military bearing and discipline, and cleanliness.

Fort Columbus was not designed as a prisoner of war camp. Confederate officers were held in the reasonably comfortable barracks at Fort Columbus while the enlisted prisoners were held at Castle Williams, a part of the Fort Columbus defense of Governors Island. The first prisoners arrived in late August and early September, 1861, a few days after Colonel Loomis arrived. Loomis thought he was coming to Fort Columbus to serve as Superintendant of Recruiting for the United States. This was correct, but many additional duties confronted him at Fort Columbus. One such additional duty was to serve as the commandant for the Confederate prisoners of War sent to the fort for safe keeping.

Civil War era photographs of Castle Williams, part of the Fort Columbus defensive system.
Source: www.correction-history.org/civilwar/governorsisland/index.

An August, 1861 Union victory at Cape Hatteras, North Carolina meant that several hundred confederate prisoners were sent to Fort Columbus. Prisoners from the Washington Grays, a Confederate unit from North Carolina, arrived on August 29. On September 4 Colonel Gustavus Loomis wrote to the Adjutant

---

423 Barbara A. Yocum, *Fort Jay: Historic Structure Report*, p. 88.

General's Office in Washington, "I have received the whole of the prisoners of war upon this island. The officers are quartered in Fort Columbus and the men at the castle."[424] These prisoners were housed at Fort Columbus for several weeks until they were transferred to a more healthy prison at Fort Warren in Boston Harbor. While under Loomis' supervision at Fort Columbus these Confederate soldiers suffered from deplorable hygiene conditions. The facilities were not designed to house so many personnel. The fort was greatly overcrowded with the resulting problems of sanitation, hygiene, feeding, sleeping and toilet facilities. As Doctor William J. Sloan, Medical Director for the Union stated after a visit to Colonel Loomis at Fort Columbus,

> THE PRISONERS ARE crowded into an ill-ventilated building which has always been an unhealthy one when occupied by large bodies of men...There are now upwards of eighty cases of measles amongst them, a number of cases of typhoid fever, pneumonia, intermittent fever, etc....Every building on the island being crowded with troops, with a large number in tents. I know not how the condition of these prisoners can be improved except by a change of location.[425]

Colonel Loomis was placed in an impossible situation. Fort Columbus was bursting with Confederate prisoners who were ill and poorly clothed. Accommodations for the soldiers were atrocious, a little better for the officers. As fall and then winter cold approached Governors Island all feared the worst. Colonel Loomis was a compassionate commandant for the prisoners, doing all he could to make them safe and reasonably comfortable in

---

424 Barbara A. Yocum, *Fort Jay: Historic Structure Report,* p. 92.

425 Lonnie R. Speer, *Portals to Hell: Military prisons of the Civil War,* (Mechanicsburg, PA: Stackpole Books, 1997), p. 4.

a difficult situation. One author commended Loomis as follows: "Everything necessary in a sanitary point of view has been urged upon them but is only carried out by the persistent effort of the officer in charge of the castle" [Colonel Loomis]. Loomis' Christian compassion and aggressive advocacy for the vulnerable and despondent prisoners is illustrated as follows:

> COLONEL GUSTAVUS LOOMIS, the commander of all facilities on the island, concurred with [Dr. William J.] Sloan's assessment that conditions in the two prisons were dehabilitating. He also agreed with the surgeon's warning that with the onset of the frigid New York winter the number of deaths would spiral out of control, and he [Loomis] notified his superiors in Washington that there were only two coarses of action that would avoid this catastrophe. Either they authorized him to construct suitable barracks for all the prisoners, or they allowed the prisoners to be removed before cold weather comes. Wishing to avoid the trouble and expense of constructing new housing for hundreds of prisoners, the war department selected the second option.[426]

In October, 1861 the Confederate prisoners were moved from Fort Columbus. The next wave of Confederate prisoners arrived at Fort Columbus in April, 1862. Colonel Loomis wrote that about five hundred prisoners were at Fort Columbus in May, and another five hundred and thirty-nine arrived in June. This impossible situation did not last long, as Loomis reported in late June that his prisoner population had decreased to slightly less than five hundred. By July all the prisoners were gone, relocated to other facilities throughout the north. For the remainder of

---

426 Charles W. Sanders, *While in the Hands of the Enemy: Military Prisons of the Civil War*, (Louisiana State University Press, 2005), p.58.

1862 there were no prisoners at Fort Columbus, except in September when five were noted.[427]

In 1863 Fort Columbus held fifteen prisoners in June and July, fourteen in August and thirteen prisoners in September. At that time there were also Union deserters and other offenders held at the fort. Obviously the War Department understood that Fort Columbus was not an appropriate place to house large numbers of Confederate prisoners of war. Nevertheless, in 1864 the fort was again utilized to hold hundreds of Confederate prisoners. For example, in January there were eight prisoners; February had seventy-eight prisoners; three hundred and one in September; three hundred and three in October; three hundred and sixteen in November; and thirty four in December. In the last months of the war the fort was still used to house Confederate prisoners of war. In January, 1865 there were one hundred and thirty-five prisoners; February had one hundred and twenty-six; in March there were nine prisoners; and by the end of April, the last month of the war, there were no prisoners at Fort Columbus. Colonel Loomis wrote that on April 1st he held nine prisoners. During that month five prisoners were added. These fourteen total prisoners were transferred out so that on April 30, 1861, Loomis recorded that there were no prisoners at Fort Columbus.[428]

There is abundant correspondence that has survived related to Colonel Loomis' various activities as the commander of Fort Columbus. Most of this correspondence relates to the status of the prisoners held at Fort Columbus on Governors Island. Loomis corresponded with senior U.S. Army officials and others in working out the legalities, privileges allowed, and general care and safety of his few thousand Confederate prisoners. This was all new to the U.S. Government, how to treat prisoners of war in a Civil

427 Barbara A. Yocum, *Fort Jay: Historic Structure Report,* p. 87.
428 Barbara A. Yocum, *Fort Jay: Historic Structure Report,* p. 87, 104.

War. For example, on September, 1861 Loomis received approval from the General in Chief, Winfield Scott, related to certain liberties to be granted Confederate officers who were prisoners. The next day the Adjutant General's Office in Washington gave Colonel Loomis guidance related to prisoner's clothing, comfort items, visitations and the amount of money the prisoners could possess. Loomis also had to address issues of privileges to senior Confederate officers who were his prisoners, such as Confederate Navy Flag Officer Samuel Barron, who questioned Loomis' policy related to hiring civilian cooks for the Confederate officers and boys to hire to take care of cleaning and firewood and other needs. Other correspondence related to deaths of prisoners at Fort Columbus, as dozens of men died of illness, disease, injury or wounds from battle.[429] There are hundreds of short letters to and from Colonel Loomis that give numerous details about his heavy administrative duties as the commander of Fort Columbus.

Briefly in 1862, the Confederate prisoners at Fort Columbus did have one advantage. Confederate Army Chaplain Peter Whelan was imprisoned at Fort Columbus from April to August, 1862. Peter Whelan (1800-1871) was born and initially educated in Ireland and volunteered as a Roman Catholic priest to missionary duty in the United States. He completed his seminary training in Charleston, South Carolina and was ordained a priest in 1830. His itinerant work took him throughout eastern North Carolina, then northeastern Georgia. At the beginning of the Civil War Rev. Whelan was a senior priest in the Archdiocese of Savannah. He volunteered as a Confederate chaplain and travelled extensively throughout coastal Georgia ministering to troops. Chaplain Whelan was at Fort Pulaski, Georgia when the fort was attacked and surrendered to the Union forces. The Confederate prison-

---

429 Official Records of the Union and Confederate Armies, Series II, volume III, pp. 35, 39, 43, 46.

ers were sent to Fort Columbus under the command of Colonel Gustavus Loomis. As one author stated, "On April 13, two days after Pulaski surrendered, the captured Confederates were divided into groups for transportation north. Whelan, now a prisoner of war, endured the rigors of the voyage with the men and, after arriving at Governor's Island, New York, he shared their prison life as well. This place of detention, under the command of an elderly colonel, Gustavus Loomis, was one of several Atlantic forts pressed into use by the Commissary General of Prisoners."[430]

Colonel Loomis was a devout protestant, a dedicated Christian with an evangelical zeal and in full agreement with the Protestant Reformation. Loomis did not like Roman Catholic theology, but he was a keen evaluator of a person's character. The Roman Catholic Chaplain Peter Whelan caught Loomis' attention. Whelan was a man Loomis could admire, as the chaplain relentlessly comforted the sick, buried the dead, and sought to make life more comfortable for other prisoners. Colonel Loomis placed no restrictions on Chaplain Whelan's ministry. In fact, Loomis allowed Chaplain Whelan to be designated the official chaplain to the Confederate prisoners at Fort Columbus, and he allowed Whelan to conduct daily Mass in Castle William next to Fort Columbus.[431] One report of Chaplain Whelan at Fort Columbus is as follows:

> IN APRIL 1862, when the Montgomery Guards manning Fort Pulaski at the mouth of the Savannah River were captured by Union forces and about to be shipped north as POWs, Fr. Whelan was offered his freedom but he elected to remain with the men he served as chaplain. He and all but a few too seriously wounded to travel were loaded onto a sea steamer to Governors Is-

430 Peter J. Meaney, "The Prison Ministry of Father Peter Whelan, Georgia Priest and Confederate Chaplain," *The Georgia Historical Quarterly*, vol. LXXI, Spring 1987), pp. 7-8.

431 Peter J. Meaney, "The Prison Ministry of Father Peter Whelan," p 8.

land. Chaplains are ranked officers and therefore Whelan was lodged with the other Confederate officers in a Fort Columbus barracks. But the priest spent most of his time with the enlisted men in damp, dark and dismal Castle Williams. The rebel prisoners there were in such desperate need for adequate food and clothing that he appealed to the pastor of the oldest Catholic Church in New York State, St. Peter's on Barclay St. in Lower Manhattan, for help. The pastor, Fr. William Quinn, was most responsive, even writing federal authorities to parole Whelan to St. Peter's for the war's duration. Though Washington approved, Whelan again declined to leave the men. On June 20 when the Montgomery Guard officers were taken to Ohio for exchange, Whelan also chose to stay with the enlisted troops. Finally, when these regulars were exchanged in August, the priest accepted release too.[432]

In addition to his role as a commandant of a prison camp, Colonel Loomis was tasked by the Secretary of War to conduct court martial duties at Fort Columbus. Desertion was a huge concern for the Union, especially as the war dragged on year after year. Also military discipline needed to be enforced to support the chain of command and the proper utilization of military supplies and equipment. On March 10, 1863 President Abraham Lincoln issued a "Proclamation Respecting Soldiers Absent Without Leave." In this decree, President Lincoln stated that "all soldiers enlisted or drafted in the service of the United States, now absent from their regiments without leave, shall forthwith return to their respective regiments... on or before the first day of April, 1863."

432 "Chaplain to POWs at Governors Island and Andersonville," www.correctionhistory. org/civilwar/governorsisland /frame_main3. Accessed March 23, 2010.

President Lincoln stated that these wayward troops "may be restored to their respective regiments without punishment, except the forfeiture of pay and allowances during their absence; and all who do not return within the time above specified shall be arrested as deserters, and punished as the law provides." There were thirty-six such locations for deserters to reintegrate into the military, scattered as far away as Maine to California. One of the locations for these soldiers absent without leave to report to was "At Governor's Island, New York, to Colonel G. Loomis, U.S. Army."[433] This was a potential administrative nightmare for Colonel Loomis. There were already large numbers of troops frequently encamped on Governor's Island either coming from or going to the front lines.[434] Even without the Confederate prisoners of war that occasionally were held at Fort Columbus, the fort was crowded. Added to this were deserters who sought to reintegrate into the army, hospital operations, mustering activities, and the defense of New York Harbor. It is quite remarkable that Gustavus Loomis, now approaching his mid-seventies in age, so capably and professionally handled these multiple responsibilities. Loomis had the full confidence of President Lincoln, the General in Chief of the Army, and the Secretary of War.

The penalty for desertion from the Union Army or Navy was death. Specifically, the *Lieber Code of 1863* stated,

> DESERTERS FROM THE American Army, having entered the service of the enemy, suffer death if they fall again into the hands of the United States, whether by capture or being delivered up to the American Army; and if a deserter from the enemy, having taken service in

433 "Important to Deserters; A Proclamation by the President. An Amnesty to Deserters who will Return Before the 1st of April. A Warning to those Who Promote Desertions," *The New York Times,* March 11, 1863.

434 Edmund B. Smith, *Governor's Island: Its Military History under Three Flags,* p. 82.

the Army of the United States, is captured by the enemy, and punished by them with death or otherwise, it is not a breach against the law and usages of war, requiring redress or retaliation.[435]

Colonel Gustavus Loomis at Fort Columbus implemented the federal laws against desertion and put soldiers to death. For example, in a report dated July 30, 1863, Colonel Loomis served as President of a court martial at Fort Columbus. Corporal Michael McGarvey of Company G, 4th U.S. Infantry, was charged with "Desertion" from his unit near Fredericksburg, Maryland in September, 1862. Corporal McGarvey pled guilty. The court deliberated and sentenced him "To be shot to death, at such a time and place as the General Commanding may direct."[436]

The administrative paperwork and legal procedures necessary to hold a court martial were daunting. Nevertheless, Colonel Loomis served as President of numerous court martials while the commander at Fort Columbus. For example, In February, 1863 Colonel Loomis served as President of a court martial for 1st Lieutenant James W. Weir of the 14th U.S. Infantry. Lieutenant Weir was charged with neglect of duty; absence without leave; conduct unbecoming an officer and a gentleman; and disobedience of orders. Specifically, Lieutenant Weir was accused of improper processing of new recruits, sloppy paperwork, poor financial accountability, not being present at his place of duty, and refusing to provide accountability of his whereabouts and his financial records as a recruiter. He pled "Not Guilty" to all charges but after the court

---

435 "The Lieber Code of 1863," *Correspondence, Orders, Reports and Returns of the Union Authorities from January 1 to December 31, 1863*, www.civilwarhome.com/liebercode. Accessed February 13, 2010.

436 *General Orders of the War Department, Embracing the Years 1861, 1862, 1863*, (Washington: U.S. War Department, 1864), p. 306.

deliberations he was found guilty to almost all charges and was dismissed from the service.[437]

In May, 1863, Colonel Loomis presided on the court martial for a musician named Private Ambrose Hall, who was accused of stealing one hundred dollars from another private at Fort Columbus. Private Hall pled guilty and was sentenced to jail for the remainder of his enlistment and then to be dishonorably discharged.[438] Colonel Loomis again served as President of a court martial in June, 1863 for Lance Corporal John Clary, who was charged with "Conduct prejudicial good order and military discipline." The corporal worked as a quartermaster at Fort Columbus and was accused of stealing large quantities of various items for resale in New York City. He pled guilty and was dishonorably discharged and given a five year prison sentence.[439] A final example of Colonel Loomis serving on court martial duty is from November, 1863, when Captain Joab Wilkinson of the 12th U.S. Infantry was charged with "Conduct prejudicial to good order and military discipline." Specifically, the issue was that Captain Wilkinson as an officer was drinking alcohol in a public place with enlisted men. He pled "Not Guilty" but the court found him guilty and sentenced him to a two year suspension without pay from the army.[440]

Under Colonel Loomis' command there were various executions at or near Fort Columbus of federal lawbreakers and of Confederate spies. Two notable executions witnessed by Loomis are worthy of further discussion.

Captain Nathaniel Gordon (1826-1862) was a resident of Portland, Maine and a career mariner. The unscrupulous Captain Gordon was engaged in acts of piracy in the Caribbean and was

---

437 *General Orders of the War Department, Embracing the Years 1861, 1862, 1863*, p. 28.
438 *General Orders of the War Department*, pp. 166-167.
439 *General Orders of the War Department*, pp. 235-236.
440 *General Orders of the War Department*, pp. 17-18.

a notorious scoundrel. On August 7, 1860 Captain Gordon loaded almost nine hundred slaves aboard his slave trading ship at the mouth of the Congo River in West Africa. The U.S. Piracy Law of 1820 forbid the transporting of slaves from Africa by American vessels. The next day he was captured by the USS *Mohican* fifty miles from port. After one hung jury and a new trial, Captain Gordon was convicted of slave trafficking and was sentenced to death by hanging on February 7, 1862. Shortly before his execution, President Lincoln gave a stay of execution for two weeks. Captain Nathaniel Gordon was hung to death on February 21 before a large civilian and military crowd.

A sketch of the execution of Captain Nathaniel Gordon, February 21, 1862. Notice the soldiers in the sketch dispatched by Colonel Loomis to insure the execution took place properly.
Source: www.blackhistory.- harpweek. com/7Illustrations /Slavery/ExecutionOf-Slavetrader. Accessed March 24, 2010.

Colonel Gustavus Loomis, as the senior military officer in the New York City area, provided the military detail which insured crowd control and the enforcement of federal law. The execution took place in New York City and not on Governor's Island.[441] Nathaniel Gordon was the only American citizen ever executed for violation of the U.S. Piracy Law of 1820.

Captain John Y. Beall (1835-1865) was a Confederate soldier and later a naval officer. In his service as a Confederate soldier he was severely wounded. After his convalescence he became a mas-

---

441 "Nathaniel Gordon: American Pirate and Slave Trader," www.thepirateking.com/bios/gordon_nathaniel. Accessed March 24, 2010. "The Execution of Nathaniel Gordon," *The New York Times,* February 22, 1862. Ron Soodalter, *Hanging Captain Gordon,* (Washington Square Press, 2007).

ter in the Confederate Navy who successfully completed numerous covert raids upon Union ships. Beall was eventually caught and imprisoned for piracy, which later was changed to prisoner of war. In May, 1864 Beall was exchanged and went to Canada to look for more opportunities to continue his partisan activities. He devised a plan to free Confederate prisoners of war in prison camps in Ohio along Lake Erie. While in civilian clothes as a Confederate naval officer, Beall planned to capture two Union ships on Lake Erie and use the vessels in his attempt to free the Confederate prisoners. The plan eventually failed and Captain John Y. Beall was arrested and imprisoned first at Fort Lafayette and then at Fort Columbus, both in New York. On January 17, 1865 Beall was tried by a military court and found guilty of being both a spy and a guerrilla and was sentenced to be hanged.[442] He was hung on gallows at Fort Columbus, with Colonel Gustavus Loomis in attendance.

Colonel Gustavus Loomis lived an almost frantic existence at Fort Columbus. He was pulled in many different directions simultaneously and had severe demands upon his time. He was not in a combat assignment. Nevertheless the stress and pressure of his responsibilities would overwhelm a lesser man. He was in a militarily important assignment with high political visibility. The life and death of soldiers depended upon his wise decisions. Gustavus Loomis was deeply committed to his Protestant evangelical faith. In his religion he found stability and courage and inner peace. Through his personal faith in Jesus Christ, Loomis was content through the ups and downs of everyday life. He lived for another world. Loomis was fortunate to have assigned with him at Fort Columbus military

---

442 "John Yates Beall," www.wtv-zone.com/civilwar/jbeall. Accessed March 24, 2010. "The Execution of John Yates Beall, CSN" www.tfoenander.com/beall. Accessed March 24, 2010. John Y. Beall, *Memoir of John Yates Beall: His Life, Trial, Correspondence and Diary,* (Cornell University Press, 2009).

chaplains. Chaplain John McVickar served at Fort Columbus from 1844 to 1862; Chaplain Joseph Scudder served from 1862-1865; then Chaplain James A.M. LaTourette came to Fort Columbus and served as an army chaplain from 1865 to 1890.

Chaplain John McVickar (1787-1868) came to serve the military at Fort Columbus in 1844. His first religious services were held in the open air or in various sheltered locations in poor weather. McVickar had a close relationship with Trinity Episcopal Church in New York, a wealthy congregation which donated funds for the construction of a chapel on Governor's Island. The General in Chief of the Army, Winfield Scott, approved the idea and allotted land on the south side of the island for the location of the chapel. The wooden chapel was dedicated on April 19, 1847 and was still in good repair when Colonel Loomis arrived on the island in 1861. Before the scholarly Chaplain McVickar arrived, civilian clergy rowed out to the island or later took a ferry boat to the island to conduct church services. A Roman Catholic priest and an Episcopal minister provided Catholic and Protestant services for the soldiers and their families.[443] Colonel Gustavus Loomis was not one to miss a Protestant church service, and he fully supported the efforts of Chaplain McVickar. The Colonel was always at church meetings with his wife and grandchildren. Loomis with his serious reformed Protestant faith was always happy to discuss theological intricacies with an ordained minister. From all indications, Colonel Loomis and Chaplain McVickar were friends.

Chaplain McVickar served Fort Columbus in times of peace and war. In his long tenure as post chaplain he ministered to soldiers, families, civilians and to prisoners of war. When Fort Co-

443 "Chapels on Governors Island," www.correctionhistory.org/civilwar/governorsisland/frame_main4. Accessed January 9, 2007. John W. Brinsfield, William C. Davis, Benedict Maryniak, James I. Robinson, Faith in the Fight: Civil War Chaplains, (Mechanicsburg, PA: Stackpole Books, 2003), p. 177.

lumbus was overwhelmed with Confederate prisoners, Chaplain McVickar provided spiritual and physical support to the prisoners and assisted prisoner of war Confederate Chaplain Peter Whelan in his ministry. McVickar also had an active hospital ministry on Governors Island, in times of peace and war ministering to sick family members, women delivering babies, and sick, injured or wounded soldiers.[444]   For Sunday church services, military regulations then in order forced soldiers to attend divine services. At the sounding of church call troops were marched to the chapel and seated towards the front of the building. Troops excused were only those on duty or those who objected based on religious principles. Officers and their families, civilians and others all had designated sections for seating.[445]

John McVickar served as a chaplain at Fort Columbus while teaching at Columbia College.
Source: www.correctionhistory.org/civilwar/-governorsisland/frame_main4.

In 1862 the army saw the need to have a chaplain living at Fort Columbus, not visiting weekly as did Chaplain McVickar. The chaplain was fully employed at Columbia College and lived on their campus. McVickar could not justify living on Governors Island, so he resigned his position as chaplain at Fort Columbus in 1862. Trinity Episcopal Church in New York then provided Protestant civilian clergy to come and minister to the soldiers and families. A Roman Catholic priest also visited weekly. Another full-time military chaplain was assigned to Fort Columbus later in 1862, Rev. Joseph Scudder of the Dutch Reformed Church.[446]

---

444 Edmund B. Smith, *Governor's Island: Its Military History under Three Flags*, p. 83.
445 Edmund B. Smith, *Governor's Island*, p. 136.
446 Edmund B. Smith, *Governor's Island*, p. 140.

Rev. Joseph Scudder (1826-1911) served as chaplain at Fort Columbus from 1862-1865.[447] Previously he served for one year with 59th New York Volunteer Regiment, ministering to soldiers around Washington and then in the Shenandoah Valley of Virginia. On November 7, 1862 he resigned his chaplaincy with the 59th Regiment to become the chaplain at Fort Columbus.[448] A Dutch Reformed clergyman, Chaplain Scudder was born in Ceylon, India as the child of missionaries. Before going to the mission field his parents were from New Jersey. Joseph returned from Ceylon to attend college in America, graduating from Rutgers College in 1848 and New Brunswick Theological Seminary in 1851. That same year he was licensed to preach, and he was ordained in 1853. Immediately after his ordination he returned to Ceylon with his wife and they assisted his parents as missionaries from 1853-1859. His wife died in Ceylon and he had to return to the United States for medical reasons. In 1860 the following newspaper account mentioned Rev. Joseph Scudder; [449]

IT WILL PLEASE our readers to know that the health of Rev. JOSEPH SCUDDER is so far restored as to enable him to preach once more with something of his usual power. A service of about eight years in India, under an unfavorable climate, rendered his return to the United States necessary. He remained in England and France three months, where he consulted high medical authorities respecting the nature and treatment of his disorder. At present he is staying at West Farms, Westchester County, where, with judicious care, we trust his ener-

447 Edmund B. Smith, *Governor's Island,* p. 140.

448 *Official Army Register of the Volunteer Force of the United States Army for the Years 1861, 1862, 1863, 1864, 1865, New York and New Jersey, (*Washington: Adjutant General's Office, 1865), p. 512.

449 "Religious Intelligence: Religious Services Tomorrow," *The New York Times,* November 3, 1860.

gies will be recruited. He is to preach next Sabbath in Dr. ELMENDORF's church, Brooklyn. If earnestness of manner, and power in delineating with graphic fervor the theme of discourse, are desirable in a preacher, then will it be easily confessed that in these particulars few preachers equal Mr. SCUDDER.

In 1861, Joseph Scudder volunteered to serve as the chaplain for the 59th Regiment of New York Volunteers. He served in this unit for about one year and then became the chaplain at Fort Columbus in New York City. In this capacity Chaplain Scudder had daily interaction with Colonel Gustavus Loomis. Scudder was a Calvinist who loved the doctrines of the Protestant Reformation and who had an evangelistic zeal. He and Colonel Loomis were perfectly compatible. An interesting anecdote about Chaplain Scudder relates to the death of his cousin Lieutenant William H. Pohlman who died at the battle of Gettysburg. Lieutenant Pohlman's body was sent to Albany, New York.

HIS COUSIN, JOSEPH Scudder, did not receive the news in time to attend the funeral. He came in the evening. He said if he had known Willie was dangerously wounded, he would have gone on immediately. He referred to a satisfactory conversation he had with Willie after his visit home, in February, on his way to join his regiment. He went from home to Governor's Island. Chaplain Joseph Scudder is now stationed at Governor's island, and was formerly chaplain of the 59th New York State Militia, with which Lieutenant Pohlman was connected at the time of his death. Mr. Scudder remarked that as they parted, he said, "Willie, live for Jesus." He answered, "Yes, I will." Mr. Scudder says that he has not the least doubt that the precious one is now happy, and he is as perfectly assured of this as if he had been with him at the last, and heard from his own mouth that he was going to Jesus.[450]

With full approval from Colonel Gustavus Loomis, Chaplain Joseph Scudder conducted numerous Bible studies, temperance meetings, revival sermons, Sunday preaching, and was a very positive influence upon the soldiers at Fort Columbus. As Colonel Loomis already passed the military mandatory retirement age of forty-five years active service, Chaplain Scudder did all he could to retain Colonel Loomis at Fort Columbus, even to approaching President Lincoln. As one report stated;

> COLONEL LOOMIS, WHO was commandant of Fort Columbus, Governor's Island, in New York Harbor, reached the age at which by law he should be put on the retired list. He was a very religious man, and his influence was so marked that the chaplain and some others, determined to appeal to the President to have him continued at the post. The Reverend Dr. Duryea of Brooklyn was sent to Washington to prefer the request. "What does the clergyman know of military matters?" inquired the President. "Nothing," was the reply. "It is desired to retain Colonel Loomis solely for the sake of his Christian influence. He sustains religious exercises at the fort, leads a prayer-meeting, and teaches a Bible class in the Sunday School." "That is the highest possible recommendation," replied the President. He approved the request, and the Christian officer was retained there until imperative military duty called him elsewhere.[451]

450 Rufus W. Clark, *The Heroes of Albany: A Memorial of the Patriot Martyrs of the City*, (Albany: 1866), p. 493.

451 Henry Ketcham, *The Life of Abraham Lincoln*, www.authorama.com/life-of-abraham-lincoln-42. Accessed August 5, 2009.

Colonel Gustavus Loomis would need spiritual help in the many issues facing him at Fort Columbus. Up to this point in his Civil War service, Loomis faced bureaucratic complexities and relentless administrative issues in his multiple activities at Fort Columbus. Typically his attention was focused within the walls of Fort Columbus and within the boundaries of Governors Island. However, Colonel Loomis faced additional challenges, namely Confederate maritime activities threatening New York; an 1863 labor strike; local draft riots; and a Confederate plot to burn New York City.

CHAPTER NINETEEN

FORT COLUMBUS, NEW YORK AND THE END OF THE CIVIL WAR

IT MUST HAVE BEEN VERY rewarding for Colonel Gustavus Loomis to still wear his military uniform into his seventies. He was too old for combat operations in the field but he could definitely contribute to the Union war effort through his various operations at Fort Columbus.

The service of Colonel Gustavus Loomis to the Union at Fort Columbus was at times frustrating and at other times humorous. An example of Loomis' frustration comes from the fact that in September, 1862 the seventy-three year old Loomis was arrested over the confusion related to an army recruit who was actually underage that apparently bluffed his way through the recruiting and mustering process. Loomis was in the custody of the sheriff while this situation was worked out. In October the boy was still not found and Loomis was in contempt of court. Loomis made every attempt to find the boy through messengers sent to Washington, but the scattered regiment made it difficult to find the boy. Loomis was then discharged from custody of the sheriff, paid his fees and was released from custody.[452] Then in June, 1863 Loomis was summoned by the New York Supreme Court

---

452 "The Traphagan Habeas Corpus case – The Boy not Produced," *The New York Times,* September 12, 1862. "Traphagan vs. Colonel Loomis," *The New York Times,* October 4, 1862.

to produce in court a recruit that enlisted illegally, underage and without parental consent. There was confusion about the young man's enlistment, his age, his physical limitations and his medical evaluation.[453] With thousands of troops moving rapidly in and out of Fort Columbus it was probable that a few recruits could sneak into the army underage or bluff their way through physical examinations. All of this was a headache to Colonel Loomis, details and administrative bureaucracy that required his full attention. Nevertheless, mistakes were made.

One humorous anecdote from Loomis' time at Fort Columbus was his reception of orders appointing him as Superintendant of the General Recruiting Service. Loomis began this duty in August, 1861, but his official orders did not arrive until June, 1863.[454] The inefficiency of military bureaucracy was astounding, almost laughable. It is not difficult to picture the elderly Colonel with the bushy white hair and thick white beard snickering over just receiving orders for his assignment that he began almost two years earlier.

Colonel Loomis could control the various military duties performed within the walls of Fort Columbus and on Governor's Island. What he could not control were Confederate maritime activities around New York; a labor strike in New York which directly impacted the operations of Fort Columbus; local draft riots; and Confederate plots to burn New York City.

Beginning in March, 1862, fear of Confederate maritime activities swept through northern port cities. Both Union and Confederate engineers and shipbuilders designed iron clad vessels which revolutionized naval warfare worldwide. These slow, low riding steam powered ships were designed to attack both coastal

---

453 "Government Habeas Corpus Case: Henry A. Smith vs. Col. Loomis, Commandant of Governor's Island," *The New York Times,* June 23, 1863.

454 *Special Orders, War Department, Adjutant General's Office,* Numbers 244, June 1, 1863. Source: www.ehistory.osu.edu/uscw/library/or/124/0242. Accessed January 3, 2007.

fortifications and enemy shipping. On March 8, 1862 the Confederate iron clad *Virginia* (often called the *Merrimack*), commanded by Franklin Buchanan, steamed into Hampton Roads, Virginia to attack the Union blockading squadron. She rammed and sank the *Cumberland*, destroyed the *Congress* after running her aground, and scattered the remaining Union ships. The *Virginia* took numerous direct hits but sustained virtually no damage. The next day the *Virginia* was challenged by the Union iron clad *Monitor*. The ships engaged in a four hour duel which ended in a draw. The senior U.S. Army commander, Major General George B. McClellan, understood the vulnerability of Union cities to Confederate iron clad ships like the *Virginia*. General McClellan quickly wrote a note to Colonel Gustavus Loomis, commander of Governors Island in New York Harbor. General McClellan was concerned that the *Virginia* was steaming north to attack New York City. On March 9, 1862, McClellan wrote by telegraph to Loomis and Loomis quickly replied. Loomis' reply is as follows;[455]

UNITED STATES MILITARY TELEGRAPH

Received March 9, 1862

From New York 9th

To Maj Gen McClellan

Have received your dispatch & have notified the Navy yard & Fort Hamilton & am taking every precaution & using every exertion to meet your wishes.

Gustavus Loomis

With orders from the senior U.S. Army Commander in hand, Colonel Loomis anticipated the worst. He and others expected a Confederate attack on New York City. The senior military com-

---

455 "Telegraph from Colonel Gustavus Loomis to General George McClellan, March 9, 1862," *The Abraham Lincoln Papers at the Library of Congress,* letter # 14908.

manders in New York at that time were Governor Edwin D. Morgan, who had the rank of a two-star General, and Chester A. Arthur, who was a Brigadier General serving as the Adjutant General and Inspector General for New York troops. An interesting account recalled by Brigadier General Arthur related to Colonel Gustavus Loomis.

IT WAS WHILE Inspector General that he had an exciting and amusing experience. One Sunday in March, 1862, there came hurrying into his office, almost breathless, and flushed a deep red, Colonel Gustavus Loomis, the oldest regular infantry officer in the service. "What in the world has happened, Colonel? said General Arthur, offering the aged officer a chair. "The rebel ram Merrimack! The rebel ram Merrimack," faintly said Colonel Loomis. "Well, what about her?" "I have a dispatch from General McClellan saying that she has sunk two United States ships – that she is coming to New York to shell the city – may be expected at any moment – I'm so out of breath running to tell you the news that I can hardly speak." "*Running* to tell me the news! Why on earth didn't you hire a carriage?" "Hire a carriage," answered Loomis with apparent horror; "hire a carriage! why that would cost me $2.50. I can't afford to spend so much out of my own pocket, and if I made such an extraordinary expenditure on account of the Government it would take all the rest of my official life to explain why I did so." General Arthur thought that Colonel Loomis did not realize "that time was worth a million an hour at such a time," and sent out for several carriages while reading the dispatch from General McClellan.[456]

---

456 E.V. Smalley, *The Republican Manual with Biographical Sketches of James Garfield and Chester A. Arthur*, (New York: 1880), pp. 317-318.

General McClellan, General Arthur and Colonel Loomis had no idea that there was no real maritime threat to New York City from any Confederate ironclad. The iron clad ships from both Union and Confederate shipyards were notoriously poor navigating in the open sea. No ironclad Rebel ship ever came near New York City. Nevertheless, at that time there was panic by civilians and urgent actions by the Union army to defend New York Harbor. Colonel Loomis told his superiors that the forts protecting New York were filled with new recruits who were not proficient in using artillery. This was because when Loomis received new recruits he trained them on the artillery, only to have them reassigned as fillers in units that came and went through Fort Columbus. This situation was resolved as Loomis accepted the use of local militia artillery units, who were proficient in the use of the guns at Fort Columbus.[457]

The maritime threat to New York City from iron clad vessels never materialized. However, other Confederate maritime activities did have a direct impact on New York and the soldiers at Fort Columbus under Colonel Loomis' command.

The mission of the Confederate Navy in the Civil War was simple: harass the vastly superior Union Navy, avoid the loss of any vessels, and cause the Union Navy to divert ships from the southern blockade by covertly raiding northern civilian shipping. At the beginning of the war the Confederate Navy consisted of three hundred and twenty-one men and ten ships, a pitiful fraction of men and ships available to the Union. The South, with few exceptions, would wage a defensive fight. The Confederates planned to offset their deficit in ships by creating a privateer fleet of large, fast vessels that would raid northern shipping.[458] Mostly built in Eng-

457 E.V. Smalley, *The Republican Manual*, pp. 316-319
458 Kenneth E. Lawson, *Essex Vessels in Times of War: A Study of the Wooden Ships of Essex, Massachusetts in the Revolutionary War, the War of 1812, the Mexican*

land, these Confederate ships terrorized northern trading, whaling and general commerce. Shipping in and out of the busy New York Harbor was directly affected by the privateer (some say piracy) activities of the Confederate vessel *CSS Alabama*.

In the fall of 1862 the *CSS Alabama* was harassing northern shipping around Long Island, New York and southern New England. Captained by the capable Rear Admiral Raphael Semmes, the *Alabama* skillfully evaded attempts at her capture while attacking northern commerce vessels. The ship was built in England and Raphael Semmes was her only Captain. The *Alabama* was propelled by both steam and sail and had at least eight large cannons. Departing Liverpool, England in late August, the *Alabama* began terrorizing northern trading and whaling vessels around the Azores and the west coast of Africa. On October 3, 1862 the *CSS Alabama* was near Long Island, New York, capturing northern ships, removing their cargoes, releasing the civilian sailors and either burning the ships or allowing a few to limp back to northern ports.

Throughout the month of October, 1862 the *CSS Alabama* successfully raided eleven northern ships off Long Island and Connecticut. Most of these ships were either sailing to New York or from New York. Colonel Loomis at Fort Columbus could only watch as numerous civilian ships sailed past the protection of his fort, some never to return. For example, on October 7th the merchant ship *Dunkirk*, sailing from New York to Lisbon, Portugal, was captured and sunk. The *Manchester* was sailing from New York to Liverpool, England when she was captured on October 11th by the *CSS Alabama,* looted and burned at sea. The bark *Lamplighter* was sailing from New York to Gibraltar, Spain and was captured on October 15th. She was burned and sunk. The *Lafayette* was sailing from New York to Belfast, Ireland

War, the Civil War, the Spanish American War, World War I, and World War II, (Essex, MA: Essex Historical Society, 2001), p. 82.

when she was captured on October 23rd and sunk. The schooner *Crenshaw* was sailing from New York to Glasgow, Scotland when she was captured by the *CSS Alabama* on October 26th, set on fire and sunk. The bark *Laurietta* was sailing from New York to the Madeira Islands when she was captured, burned and sunk on October 28th.[459] Colonel Loomis despaired of his inability to do anything about local Confederate raiding activities. Something he could help control, however, were the labor strikes and draft riots in New York City in 1863.

In early 1863 tensions were raising between civilian longshoremen and the wealthy ship owners who paid their wages. Affluent ship owners who did not suffer losses to the *CSS Alabama* or other Confederate raiders made a lot of money during the war. At the same time the wages for laborers, longshoremen and others, were cut due to the higher inflationary costs of doing business in wartime. Laborers who worked on the docks refused to work and went on strike. Such activity in a time of war was critical. Hundreds of ships every week departed New York Harbor in support of the war effort. A labor strike on the docks eventually affected soldiers in battle. The federal government sent mediators to New York but they were unsuccessful. Supplies headed to the front were sitting unloaded on the piers. With authorization from the President of the United States, Colonel Loomis implemented a brief but successful plan. Loomis ordered one hundred and fifty Union Army deserters held at Fort Columbus and sixty-five walking wounded Union soldiers convalescing in the area to work on the docks. A detachment of Loomis' soldiers from the fort watched the laborers with fixed bayonets while New York

---

459 *The New York Times*, November 11, 1862. For a full treatment of this subject see Stephen Fox, *Wolf of the Deep: Raphael Semmes and the Notorious Confederate Raider CSS Alabama,* (Vintage Press, 2008).

City police patrolled the docks.[460] The standoff eventually ended and the longshoremen returned to work. This brief incident
was quickly overshadowed by the much more violent and deadly
New York City draft riots on July 11-13, 1863.

New York City was a hotbed of anti-Republican sentiment.
The Democrat Governor Horatio Seymour of New York openly
opposed the Republican President Abraham Lincoln. The city was
divided between radical abolitionists, those generally opposed to
slavery, and those wealthy New Yorkers who were Southern sym-
pathizers that made a lot of money from plantation slavery. At the
beginning of the Civil War, New York provided thousands of soldiers, far exceeding their quotas. But as the war dragged on, New
Yorkers began to doubt the wisdom of Generals who ran the war.
New recruits for the war effort from New York were declining.
On March 3, 1863 Congress passed the unpopular Enrollment
and Conscription Act, a law which meant that all eligible males in
the U.S. were to participate in a military draft. Yet the Enrollment
and Conscription Act had several exemptions, the most odious
being the payment of a "commutation fee" which allowed those
who could afford it to pay their way out of military service. The
poor immigrants of New York were outraged at this exemption
for the wealthy. By the time the names of the first draftees were
drawn of July 11, 1863, the Union had earned remarkable military victories at Vicksburg and Gettysburg. The war appeared to
be drawing to a conclusion. Many thought the draft was unfair
and unnecessary. Some whites in New York feared that free blacks
would come to the city and take their jobs. There was a overall
feeling in the city of restlessness and discontent.

On June 11, 1863 the first names for the conscription were
publically read. The next day the names were in the local newspa-

460 "Governors Island Prisons," www.correctionhistory.org/civilwar/governorsisland/
    frame_main1. Accessed March 29, 2010.

pers. Within hours, irate white citizens banded together and began random acts of vandalism. Numerous black citizens were beaten or hung. Many working men resented having to fight for the emancipation of slaves who may come north and take away the unskilled jobs on which they and their families depended. Over the next days the mobs numbered about fifty thousand people, many committing acts of trespassing, assault, desecration of property, and even murder. As one author stated, "It would seem from the facts that those who started the movement had no idea at the outset of proceedings to the length they did. They simply desired to break up the draft in some of the upper districts of the city, and destroy the registers in which certain names were enrolled."[461] Much of the New York militia had previously been moved to Pennsylvania to defend against a Confederate invasion. New York City police were overwhelmed at the aggressive looting, rioting and vandalism. Angry crowds assaulted army recruiters. Recruiting offices were burned to the ground. Mobs shouted, "Kill the rich!" "Kill the niggers!" and "Down with the black republican nigger lovers!" Mobs attacked various targets, notably the Colored Orphan Asylum on Fifth Avenue between 43rd and 44th streets. Two hundred orphans were evacuated by courageous neighbors before they could be harmed, but the building was destroyed and blacks throughout the city were assaulted and killed. New York City Hall was overrun. Stores were sacked. By the end of the riot over one thousand people were killed and many thousands more injured. President Lincoln sent federal troops from Pennsylvania to restore order, the soldiers staying several weeks in and around the city. But before federal troops arrived, soldiers in New York under the supervision of Colonel Loomis were called to protect lives and property in the city.[462]

461 Joel T. Headley, *The Great Riots of New York City,* (Scholarly Publishing Office, University of Michigan Library, 2006), p. 131.

462 "Political Events," www.answers.com/topic/1863. Accessed March 29, 2010. For

The senior U.S. Army commander overseeing New York was Major General John E. Wool. General Wool was commander of the Department of the East and was responsible for all military operations in several eastern states. General Wool was five years older than Colonel Loomis, making him the oldest military officer on either side in the Civil War. He was widely considered one of the most capable officers in the army and a superb organizer. Both General Wool and Colonel Loomis were War of 1812 veterans. The headquarters for the Department of the East was in New York City but not near the location of the riots. Once the riots began, General Wool was immediately informed and began to issue orders to protect lives and property and to squelch the riot. One of the first orders issued by General Wool through his adjutant was to Colonel Loomis, as follows:[463]

HEADQUARTERS DEPARTMENT OF THE EAST

New York City, July 13, 1863

Col. G. Loomis Commanding Governor's Island

Colonel: The major-general commanding directs that you send immediately to this city for special service all the troops, regulars and volunteers, that you now have under your command, to report to Col. Robert Nugent, acting assistant provost-marshal-general, No. 106 Leonard Street. The men will have 40 rounds of ammunition each with their arms.

By command of Major-General Wool; C. T. Christensen Assistant Adjutant-General

---

further study see James McCauge, *The Second Rebellion: The New York City Draft Riots of 1863*, (DoubleDay Publishers, 1968). Adrian Cook, *The Armies of the Streets: The New York City Draft Riots of 1863*, (University of Kentucky Press, 1982).

463 *Reports of Maj. Gen. John E. Wool, U.S. Army, Commanding Department of the East, with Orders, & etc. July 13-16, 1863*, www. Civilwarhome.com/woolor. Accessed June 9, 2009.

Colonel Loomis quickly deployed his men by boat from Governors Island across the harbor to New York City. The troops conducted patrols, skirmished with rioters, and confiscated hundreds of guns of various sizes. Soldiers in some cases had to conduct house to house searches for the leaders of the riots and were engaged in firefights with looters and anti-military renegades. Meanwhile, the observant looters knew that Fort Columbus on Governors Island deployed its soldiers into the city. Therefore the rioters sought to attack Fort Columbus and rob the fort of munitions and supplies.

Colonel Loomis remained at Fort Columbus during the riots. His replacement, Colonel G.N. Bumford, had either not yet arrived or had arrived but was too new to the command to begin his duties during the riot. Loomis was senior to him and therefore Colonel Loomis retained command. Loomis' troops deployed to downtown New York City and were responsible for protecting the Treasury on Wall Street. Meanwhile the fort was under-staffed. Typically several hundred soldiers were stationed on Governors Island, but during the riots there was fewer than one hundred men, mostly quartermaster troops and civilians, who stayed behind while the majority of soldiers deployed to the city. These quartermaster soldiers and civilians were supply clerks, laborers and administrative support personnel that stayed with Colonel Loomis in the fort. The rioters decided to attack the undermanned fort and were repulsed under fire by orders of Colonel Loomis. It must have been a sobering moment when Loomis ordered his small number of ragtag defenders to open fire with cannon and then with rifles against armed civilians, residents of New York City who advanced with hostile intent towards Fort Columbus. These were the last orders Colonel Loomis ever gave to open fire. As one report stated;

DURING THE DRAFT riots of that year the troops stationed on Governors Island were guarding the Sub-
Treasury on Wall Street. Their absence was seized by the
rioters as a time for attacking the island and capturing ammunition, rifles and stores. The City authorities,
hearing of this movement, withdrew all ferry boats from
their slips. The rioters, however, secured other boats and
soon were on their way to the island. Eighty employees
of the Ordinance Department hurriedly armed themselves with muskets, trained some canon on the invaders
and succeeded in repulsing the attack.[464]

During the July 13-17, 1863 draft riots and the deployment of troops from Fort Columbus into New York City, Colonel Loomis was involved but he was technically no longer
the senior commander of Fort Columbus. He had reached the
mandatory retirement age and on June 1, 1863 he was retired
from active duty in the army. In Loomis' official biographical
summary from the U.S. Military Academy at West Point, it
says that Colonel Gustavus Loomis was "Retired from Active
Service, June 1, 1863 Under the Law of July 17, 1862, Having Been Borne on the Army Register More Than 45 Years."[465]
This retirement order was also a bit odd, in that Loomis had
at that time served in the army since 1811, for a total of fifty-
two years to that point. The administrative procedures, retirement paperwork and change of command responsibilities for
Loomis to retire all took several weeks to perform, so Loomis
continued his duties.

---

464 Edmund B. Smith, *Governor's Island: It's Military History under Three Flags*, (New
York: 1913), p. 82.

465 George W. Cullum, *Biographical Register of the Officers and Graduates of the U.S.
Military Academy, at West Point, N.Y.*, (New York: 1868), p. 119.

Colonel Loomis' retirement was only an administrative procedure. Immediately upon his retirement he was recalled to active duty. He had no break in service and he did not miss a day wearing his uniform. In the capacity of a retired officer recalled to active duty, the army was able to place an active duty officer in command of Fort Columbus while retaining the valuable services of Colonel Loomis. The new commander at Fort Columbus was Colonel G.N. Bumford. Colonel Bumford was a native New Yorker who was serving with the 42nd New York Volunteer Infantry Regiment. In battle at Sharpsburg, Maryland a horse was shot out from under Bumford, causing him serious injury when he was partially crushed by the horse.[466] This may be why he was reassigned to a garrison position at Fort Columbus, in that he was a New Yorker and that he was injured and could no longer aggressively serve in the field.

Colonel G.N. Bumford and Colonel Gustavus Loomis served together at Fort Columbus through the end of the war. There is no evidence of friction between the two men. Colonel Bumford was the commander at Fort Columbus and commandant of all military activities on Governors Island. No longer would Loomis drill new recruits from General Silas Casey's *Infantry Tactics*. No longer would the seventy-four year old senior colonel train artillerymen on the guns. Instead, Loomis was now fully devoted to duties which he had performed on a part-time basis for the last few years. Colonel Loomis was now dedicated, by direction of the Secretary of War, to devote his time fully to recruiting duty and to serving as a senior officer for court martial duties.

By 1863 recruiting duty was difficult work. Hundreds of thousands of casualties weakened morale and the urge to enlist. As the war dragged on, fewer and fewer men wanted to join. The

---

466 "Safety of Lieutenant Colonel Bumford," *The New York Times*, October 19, 1862.

March 3, 1863 Enrollment and Conscription Act was unpopular
and only slightly helped replenish Union forces. As 1863 began
the State of New York was almost thirty thousand recruits short
of their requirement from the federal government.[467] Loomis
served as Superintendant of the General Recruiting Service for
the entire United States from August 19, 1861 through August 10,
1864.[468] There is little doubt that the aging Colonel Loomis was
happy to have completed his tour of duty as the senior recruiting
officer for the Union.

Colonel Loomis continued his work as a senior officer on
court martial duty through 1867. This was emotionally draining
work, as he had to hear often pitiful accounts of poverty, des-
peration, immorality, theft, murder, cowardice in battle, desertion,
disobedience to orders, and the like. Some of those found guilty
of the most serious crimes were executed. An example of an execution from a court martial supervised by Colonel Loomis was
the case of Private James Devlin, who was executed by firing
squad on February 3, 1865 at Fort Columbus. Devlin repeatedly
enlisted and deserted in order to collect the enlistment bonuses. A
newspaper summary of the execution is as follows;

> YESTERDAY AFTERNOON, GOVERNOR'S Island was
> the scene of a solemn and imposing tragedy. JAMES
> DEVLIN, a deserter from the army, was executed, in the
> presence of a thousand persons, in accordance with the
> findings of a court martial... He first entered the army
> under his right name, and deserted. He then entered the
> army under the name of Patrick Dimond, and having de-
> serted a second time, entered the army under the name
> of Patrick Sully... The sentence having been approved,

467 "The 1863 Draft Riots," www.mrlincolnandnewyork.org/print.asp?ID=91&subjectID=4.
Accessed June 9, 2009.
468 George W. Cullum, *Biographical Register*, p. 119.

the time of execution was fixed between the hours of twelve and two o'clock yesterday… At one o'clock the firing party, consisting of twelve men belonging to the Twentieth New York Volunteer Artillery, entered the sallyport of Fort Columbus, preceded by a drum… The entire garrison of the island, together with the recruits, numbering in all about four hundred men, were drawn up in double lines… At three minutes to two o'clock the white handkerchief was placed over his eyes, and he knelt in front of his coffin… For three minutes the wretched man knelt motionless, awaiting the order to send him to eternity. To the spectators it seemed an age, so dreadful was the suspense. At precisely two o'clock Capt. Ryer gave the order, in a loud, firm voice. "Ready," when the muskets were pointed with steady arms, at the breast of the doomed man. The command "Aim," was given, and at a flourish of his sword, ten balls sped upon their deadly errand, passed through his body, and sank into the bay… His death must have been instantaneous… The execution took place under the direction of Col. Bumford, Commandant of the island, whose arrangements were excellently planned.[469]

Colonel Gustavus Loomis was fully employed in his court martial duties at Fort Columbus, New York Harbor, when in November, 1864 there was an attempt by Confederate spies to burn New York City. On November 2 Mayor C. Godfrey Gunther of New York City received a telegraph from U.S. Secretary of State William H. Seward warning the mayor of a Confederate plot to burn the city. The suspected date was around Election Day, No-

469 "Military Execution at Governor's Island: Tragic End of a Bounty Jumper," *The New York Times*, February 4, 1865.

vember 8. Union soldiers by the thousands came to New York City to prevent any major incidents and were successful. On November 25, ten days after the Union troops departed, eight Southern conspirators armed with firebombs attempted to burn down dozens of buildings in the city. From around 7:30 to 9:30 pm the arsonists threw their fire bombs into theaters, museums, shipping facilities and hotels. These were not military targets. The arsonists were armatures. The numerous fires caused some smoke and fire damage but no lives were lost, thanks to the quick response of firefighters and volunteers. From Governors Island, Colonel Loomis could see the flames against the night sky. The Confederate plot to burn down New York City failed. The Confederate arsonists fled New York by train to Toronto, Canada. Eventually only one of the arsonists was caught, Captain Robert Cobb Kennedy.[470]

Trying to sneak back into the United States, the arsonist Confederate Army Captain Robert C. Kennedy was caught in Michigan and returned to New York City for trial. Robert Cobb Kennedy (1835-1865) was from a wealthy plantation family in Louisiana. He attended the U.S. Military Academy at West Point in 1854 but could not pass the academics and was forced to withdraw. He worked on his family plantation supervising numerous slaves until the start of the Civil War. He was wounded in the thigh in April, 1862 at the battle of Shiloh and was a prisoner of war. He escaped into Canada and joined a Confederate spy ring in Toronto. In Toronto he was part of the detailed planning to burn New York City. As a Confederate Army officer in civilian clothes planning to torch New York, Captain Robert C. Kennedy was acting as a spy. By military and civilian law, a spy who was tried in court and found guilty was to be executed. Kennedy be-

---

470 "The Plot," *The New York Times,* November 27, 1864.

lieved he was merely repeating the behavior of General Sherman who led Union troops in their destructive march to the sea.[471]

The trial of Confederate Army Captain Robert Cobb Kennedy was held in a military court at Fort Lafayette in New York Harbor. Kennedy did not deny the charges against him, defiantly wearing his chains and shackles in the courtroom. We do not know exactly what relationship Colonel Loomis had to Captain Kennedy. Loomis was the senior officer supervising and scheduling court martial cases in New York, so he was certainly involved in some way. The military trial for Captain Kennedy did not last long. He was found guilty and was sentenced to death by hanging on March 25, 1865 at the Fort Lafayette courtyard.

For Colonel Loomis, he had seen too many Southerners die this way. As he watched the executed prisoner die, the aged Colonel must have wondered how much longer the war could last. When would this madness cease? When could he return to his home in Stratford, Connecticut and enjoy the retired life of an army Colonel with his wife and granddaughters? Captain Kennedy was the last Confederate soldier executed by the Union. The end of the war was close. As an aging Colonel with over fifty year's military experience, something happened to Gustavus Loomis that was long overdue and greatly appreciated. By order of President Andrew Johnson, Colonel Gustavus Loomis was promoted to the brevet rank of Brigadier General.

On July 17, 1866, Secretary of War Edward M. Stanton requested to President Andrew Johnson that Colonel Loomis be promoted to brevet Brigadier General. The promotion would be backdated with retroactive pay to March 13, 1865. The note from Secretary Stanton to President Johnson stated, "Sir: I have the honor to propose for your approbation the following named officers

471 Lawrence L. Hewitt, *Louisianans in the Civil War*, (University of Missouri Press, 2002), pp. 164-174.

for appointment by brevet in the Army of the United States: To be brigadier-generals by brevet… Colonel Gustavus Loomis, of the United States Army, for long and faithful services in the Army, to date from March 13, 1865." In Loomis' official West Point biographical summary it simply states, "Bvt. Brig-General U.S. Army, March 13, 1865, for Long and Faithful Service in the Army."[472]

To become a brevet Brigadier General was the culmination in rank of a stellar military career. Gustavus Loomis had served admirably in five wars. There was never a formal reprimand in his records. His administrative and logistical skills were superior. In his combat experiences he was fearless. Although there were isolated instances where fellow officers thought his devout Christianity was a bit odd, the soldiers who served under Loomis loved him. At every step in his career, from second lieutenant to Colonel, Gustavus Loomis was a professional soldier with an admirable record. His promotion to brevet Brigadier General took place a little more than a year after the end of the Civil War. Loomis wore his new rank with dignity and experience from his seventy-six years of life and fifty-five years of military service. For the last year of his extensive military career he was known as General Loomis. He had exceeded all his U.S. Military Academy classmates from his class of 1811 in both rank and longevity of service. Including his time as a cadet at West Point, almost his entire life was devoted to military service. Then, in 1867, his military career was over. His work with court martial duty at Fort Columbus was complete.

Throughout his long and distinguished military career, brevet Brigadier General Gustavus Loomis had numerous military chaplains. For his last years as a retired brevet Brigadier General still in uniform on special duties at Fort Columbus, Loomis was ministered to by Chaplain James A.M. LaTourrette. A Protestant

---

Episcopal minister, Chaplain LaTourrette (1826-1891) was a native New Yorker. He was a graduate of the University of New York City and Princeton Theological Seminary around 1849. He served from 1851-1855 as pastor at the Reformed Protestant Dutch Church of Westfield on Staten Island, New York. In 1855 he changed his denominational affiliation from Dutch Reformed to Protestant Episcopal. He then moved to Ohio to serve Protestant Episcopal churches in Columbus and Cincinnati. From 1860-1865 Rev. LaTourrette came back to New York and served as rector at Trinity Church in Potsdam, New York. On February 6, 1865 LaTourrette was elected to be the chaplain at Fort Columbus by the council of administration at the fort.[473] On March 12, 1865 LaTourrette resigned his church position in Potsdam to join the army chaplaincy and become the chaplain at Fort Columbus, New York. It was at this time that the brand new to the military thirty-nine year old minister met the seasoned veteran seventy-six year old brevet Brigadier General Gustavus Loomis.

Chaplain LaTourrette served at Fort Columbus from March, 1865 to sometime in 1867, when the post-Civil War activities of Colonel Loomis came to an end. It took over two years after the end of the war for all of the legal, administrative and bureaucratic issues to be resolved. There were absent without leave cases to consider; dereliction of duty cases to resolve; various inventory and warehouse controversies related to war supplies; desertion charges to be resolved; the downsizing of the army and relocation of troops; the legal status of prisoners of war; and a host of other administrative, legal and bureaucratic issues to address. Chaplain LaTourrette served with General Loomis and other soldiers as

---

473 "U.S. vs. LaTourrette, 151 U.S. 572 (1894)," Supreme Court Records, February 5, 1894, p.2. Charles W. and William T. Davis, *Staten Island and Its People,* 1609-1929, (New York: Lewis Historical Publications, 1930), pp. 441-442.

Fort Columbus slowly lost its vitality, its Civil War service the last significant duty the old fort would ever provide.

General Loomis and Chaplain LaTourrette shared the same evangelical zeal in their Protestant reformed faith. Loomis and his family faithfully attended chapel services provided by Chaplain La-Tourrette on Governors Island. After departing Governors Island in 1867, Chaplain LaTourrette became a career military chaplain. After 1868 he was serving at army forts in Colorado and New Mexico and spent the next thirty-three years as a chaplain in the American West. He retired from the army in 1890 and died while associated with Grace Cathedral in Indianapolis, Indiana in 1891.[474]

The post-Civil War army in which Gustavus Loomis served for two years as a Colonel and then as a brevet Brigadier General was a military in demobilization. From over one million soldiers, the Union had about eighty thousand soldiers one year after the war. Two years after the war, when Loomis finally retired, there were only about twenty seven thousand troops in the peacetime army.[475] During these years the fractured nation sought to heal, while confusion remained as to the legal status of free blacks and uncertainty and hesitation prevailed in Southern states related to rejoining the United States. Over six hundred thousand men from both sides lost their lives in the war, all of whom had families with some type of claim to benefits. On May 15, 1865 Loomis' friend and convert to Christianity, Major General Oliver

A photograph of Rev James A.M. LaTourrette around 1865.
Source: *A Historical Sketch of Trinity Church, Potsdam, NY*, p. 125

---

474 William Berrian, *A Historical Sketch of Trinity Church, Potsdam, New York*, (privately published, 1896), pp. 124, 128, 179. "U.S. vs. LaTourrette, 151 U.S. 572 (1894)," p.2.
475 James McPherson, *Battle Cry of Freedom*, (Oxford University Press, 1988), p. 853.

O. Howard, began his work with the Bureau of Refugees, Freedmen and Abandoned Lands. Loomis led Howard to personal faith in Jesus Christ during the Seminole Wars and Howard never wavered from that decision. Throughout the remainder of Howard's long military career he was known as the "Christian General," a title he readily accepted.[476] On May 29th President Lincoln issued an amnesty proclamation to all Confederate military who served in the war. Issues related to the national debt, the federal government assuming the Confederate debt, the civil rights of freed blacks, the restoration of trade between the North and South, the reinstitution of Southern congressmen and senators into the federal government, and a host of other issues beset the nation. Meanwhile at Fort Columbus, brevet Brigadier General Loomis did his part. He completed his backlog of court martial duties and happily retired to Stratford, Connecticut with his wife and grandchildren in 1867.

While stationed at Fort Columbus, Colonel and later brevet Brigadier General Loomis' name and reputation was continually before President Lincoln and later President Johnson. President Lincoln agreed to the posting of Colonel Loomis at Fort Columbus in 1861 and was constantly aware of Loomis' results as a court martial officer and as the Superintendant of the General Recruiting Service. President Johnson was aware of the fine reputation of Colonel Loomis and approved of his promotion to brevet Brigadier General. President Lincoln was so impressed with Loomis' work as commander at Fort Columbus that upon the mandatory retirement age for Loomis, President Lincoln immediately recalled Loomis onto active duty as a retired Colonel. Lincoln understood that Loomis was a Christian example to the soldiers, recruits and prisoners of war at Fort Columbus. The President

476 John A. Carpenter, *Sword and Olive Branch: Oliver Otis Howard,* (Fordham University Press, 1999), pp. 86-87.

understood Loomis was an excellent soldier. Lincoln also knew that Loomis led prayer meetings, conducted Bible studies, taught Sunday School, and was an outspoken evangelical Christian. President Lincoln admired him for it.[477]

An 1866 photograph of brevet Brigadier General Gustavus Loomis.
Source: www.brevetbrigadier-generals.com.

477 *Thetford, Vermont Historical Society Newsletter*, Spring 2009, p.2. Henry Ketcham, *The Life of Abraham Lincoln*, www.authorama.com/life-of-abraham-lincoln-42. Accessed August 5, 2009.

CHAPTER TWENTY

RETIREMENT AND DEATH, 1867-1872

GUSTAVUS LOOMIS FIRST PUT ON a military uniform as a cadet at the United States Military Academy in 1808. Now the year was 1867 and it was time to hang up his uniform once and for all. Including his cadet years, brevet Brigadier General Loomis served his country in the army for fifty-nine years. At age seventy-eight he was not only ready to retire; he had far exceeded the average life expectancy for men of that time. He was the oldest officer in the U.S. Army. We can only speculate what it was like for Loomis to take off his blue dress uniform for the last time, as he gazed upon the star on his shoulder boards which displayed his brevet rank of Brigadier General. No doubt the uniform was wrapped in a protective covering and carefully stored away. The work of a lifetime was over.

Gustavus and Annie Loomis had planned well for retirement. In 1858 they purchased a home at the corner of Main Street and Bridgeport Road in downtown Stratford, Connecticut. When Loomis was called back to active duty in 1861 for Civil War service, Annie and their granddaughters travelled back and forth to Stratford. The girls walked to school at the Stratford Academy. How often Gustavus was able to take the train from his assignment in New York City to visit Annie and the girls we do not know. We do know that Gustavus and Annie were diligent related to their personal finances. In April of 1866 they renegotiated their mortgage payments for their home in Stratford, preparing for

Gustavus' reduction in wages as he went from active duty pay to lower pay as a retired soldier.[478]

In the 1870 U.S. Census for Stratford, the Gustavus Loomis household is listed as follows: He was an eighty year old white male with employment as a retired Colonel in the U.S. Army. His birthplace was Vermont. His wife is listed as Mary Anne, a sixty-four year old white female who was employed as "keeping home." Her birthplace was the West Indies. Their two granddaughters are listed as Adel Panton and Emma Panton, ages seventeen and sixteen, both white females "at home," both born in Kansas. It is interesting to note that the elderly retired Colonel Loomis transferred all of his monetary assets to his younger wife. Under the census headings "Value of Real Estate" and "Value of Personal Estate," Gustavus had zero, while Annie had five thousand dollars value in real estate and one thousand dollars in her personal estate. This amount of money was about average for a tradesman of that day.[479] The thoughtfulness and kindheartedness of the elderly Gustavus is evident in his providing for his wife and granddaughters after his death.

A close up view of downtown Stratford, Connecticut in 1867. Notice the Loomis home at the corner of Main Street and Bridgeport Road, and the Protestant Episcopal Church a block north of their house.
Map courtesy of the Stratford Historical Society.

A visitor from New York City came to Stratford in 1866 and called the town "a quiet, refreshing retreat." He commented on

---

478 Bank Records courtesy of the Stratford Historical Society. Transaction dated April 26, 1866.
479 *U.S. Census*, Stratford, Vermont, 1870.

the wagons and oxen on Main Street, along with horses, carriages and pedestrians. Specifically he mentions the positive influence of the Congregational, Protestant Episcopal and Methodist churches in the town. He observed that Stratford had no factories or large commercial activities, the town supporting itself through smaller businesses. This was the hometown of the Gustavus Loomis family. The writer stated that the children in Stratford appeared intelligent and the women were modest and beautiful. With a population of three thousand people, Stratford was to him an ideal place to live. He commented;

> THE PRINCIPLE STREETS of the town are well shaded with magnificent, tall, friendly elms. At brief intervals the residences of the inhabitants appear, somewhat in the background on either side of the streets. Not a few of these belong to gentlemen whose business relations are in New York, but who evince no small amount of common sense in choosing such a place for their dwellings.[480]

The community of Stratford was at that time, like many American towns, still adjusting from the trauma of the Civil War. Nevertheless life went on. The railroad connected Stratford to New York City and was a boom for the local economy. In 1870 there was a lot of activity on the northeast side of Stratford as a new railroad bridge was constructed over the Housatonic River, taking two years to complete. The glory days of Stratford's shipbuilding and maritime activities had past, but the riverfront was nevertheless a busy place with various vessels coming and going. Some schooners were still being built at the waterfront and steamships frequented Stratford. It was only a ten minute walk for the elderly Gustavus Loomis from his home to Shelby's Pond or the Ferry Bridge Creek,

---

480 "Stratford, Conn. One of the Oldest and Best of the New England Settlements," *The New York Times,* July 20, 1866.

where fishermen filled their nets with shad.[481] At that time Stratford had the very wealthy, the very poor, and a large middle class of
workers, tradesmen and laborers. Financially the Loomis' were on
the lower end of the middle class, as a retired Colonel's pay was not
overwhelming. Nevertheless, Gustavus and Annie had a home and
a small piece of land, they had some savings, and remained young at
heart from the presence of their teenage granddaughters.

The Loomis family was actively involved with the Protestant
Episcopal Church in Stratford. When Colonel Loomis departed
Stratford for his Civil War duty in 1861, the Episcopal minister
was Rev. John Stearns. Pastor Stearns departed in 1862 and was
replaced in 1863 by Rev. Daniel C. Weston, who served the Stratford church from 1863 to 1873. Daniel Weston was from Maine. In
1850 he was a candidate for ordination and throughout the 1850s
he served churches in Saco, Bath and Augusta, Maine. He then
went to Connecticut, and in 1863 departed a church in Stonington,
Connecticut to become the minister at the Protestant Episcopal
Church in Stratford.[482] Rev. Weston was, like his predecessor Rev.
Stearns, a supporter of balanced revivals and doctrinally precise theology. Shortly after his arrival, Rev. Weston understood that a new
Sunday School room was needed because of the overflow of chil-
dren in the church.[483] The new stone church building constructed
under Pastor Stearns was typically full for Pastor Weston's sermons.
An eyewitness account of the revival in the Protestant Episcopal
Churches in Connecticut around that time is as follows:

> MANY PROOFS OF steady and continuous growth were
> now visible in many parts of the Diocese… Daily prayer

---

481 Lewis G. Knapp, *Stratford and the Sea,* (Arcadia Publishing, 2002), pp. 32, 128-
129, 206-207.

482 *Journal of the Annual Convention of the Protestant Episcopal Church, Diocese of
Maine,* (Portland, 1876), pp. 6, 22.

483 "The History of Christ Episcopal Church of Stratford," www.christchurchstratford.
org/history. Accessed April 6, 2010.

meetings and the ordinary instructions of the pulpit on Sundays, and occasionally on other days, were followed by the conversion of many sinners, and their pursuit of a new and better life... The quiet and earnest work of the pastors seemed to be producing the blessed fruits for which some of them had patiently waited.[484]

The Loomis family was faithfully served at the Protestant Episcopal Church in Stratford by Rev. Daniel Weston. Shortly after the Civil War there were one hundred and twenty families that attended the church, for an average of about four hundred weekly attendees. This is remarkable in a town of only three thousand residents. There were one hundred and nineteen communicants, meaning those who were confirmed in the faith and partook of the sacraments on a regular basis. The church had about one hundred children in Sunday School and gave generously to a fund for wounded and sick Civil War veterans.[485] Both Rev. Weston and his wife were very devoted to their ministry and had a reputation as scholars with an evangelical zeal.[486] The pastor earned a salary of eight hundred dollars a year plus use of the rectory and the adjoining land. The church blossomed under Rev. Daniel Weston.[487]

In 1872, Gustavus Loomis was eighty-three years old. His granddaughters were becoming young adults. Shortly after 1870, the oldest granddaughter, Adele at age eighteen moved to North Carolina. We do not know why she moved south. We do know

---

484 Eben E. Beardsley, *History of the Episcopal Church in Connecticut,* (1868: reprinted 2009 by Cornell University Press), pp. 398-400.

485 *Journal of the Annual Convention of the Protestant Episcopal Church the Diocese of Connecticut, 1864-1866,* (Hartford: 1866), p. 74.

486 "Stratford, Conn. One of the Oldest and Best ...," *The New York Times,* July 20, 1866.

487 Catherine C. Lawrence, *Christ Episcopal Church Stratford, CT: Three Hundred Years of History, 1707-2007,* (Stratford, 2008), pp. 60- 61.

that in early February, 1872 she died at age nineteen. Her body was brought home to Connecticut and she was buried in the New Haven Cemetery on February 20th with a small number of grieving family members present. At the time of her death her last name was still Panton, meaning she was not married.[488] Adele was a small girl when she came into the home of grandmother Annie Loomis and her husband Gustavus. The old Colonel and his wife were the only significant parents in her life. Now Gustavus and Annie grieved for their granddaughter who was like a daughter to them, she being the joy of their older years.

The Chapel at Yale University, appearing much as it did at the March 7, 1872 funeral service for brevet Brigadier General Gustavus Loomis.
Source: www.yale.edu/chaplain/ battell_history.

Less than three weeks later, Colonel Gustavus Loomis was dead. There is no record of the cause of death for the old soldier. Perhaps he picked up a tropical illness from his years in the Florida swamps fighting in the Seminole Wars. At his last military assignment at Fort Columbus in New York Harbor the living conditions for many were disease infested. He may have caught pneumonia at the outdoor burial service on that cold February day a few weeks prior at his granddaughter's funeral. Or perhaps he simply died of old age at age eighty-two.

The War department received a telegraph of Loomis' death March 5, 1872. The telegraph message was from Gustavus' wife,

---

488 *Burial Records, Christ Episcopal Church, Stratford, 1872, p. 299.*

M.A.T. Loomis of Stratford, Connecticut, stating the Colonel Gustavus Loomis died at six o'clock that morning.[489] There was no doubt that Gustavus would be buried at the New Haven Cemetery next to the chapel at Yale University. According to the 1870 U.S. Census for New Haven, there were over two hundred people with last name of Loomis living in the area. Not only did Gustavus have family connections in New Haven, but his wife Annie also had family relations in New Haven. About three weeks earlier Annie and Gustavus buried their granddaughter in this cemetery. Now it was time for Annie to bury her devoted husband of twenty-one years. A day after his death, an obituary notice for Gustavus Loomis was printed in New Haven;[490]

DEATH OF COLONEL LOOMIS

Col. G.A. Loomis died at his residence in Stratford, on Tuesday, 5th inst. Col. Loomis was, at the time of his death, the oldest officer in the United States service, and the oldest graduate of West Point. He was in the War of 1812, the Black Hawk, Mexican and Indian wars, and continued active in service up to a very late period. A man of great energy and integrity, his industry was remarkable always. As a citizen, neighbor, and friend, he will be remembered for his excellencies. He died as he had lived, full of faith in his Redeemer. Funeral services from the Chapel on Thursday afternoon at 3 o'clock.

The records of the Christ Episcopal Church in Stratford tell us that Gustavus Loomis was a member of that church when he died and that his pastor, Rev. Daniel Weston, performed the burial service according to the Protestant Episcopal Church rite.

489 Carolyn Thomas Foreman, "Gustavus Loomis: Commandant of Fort Gibson and Fort Towson," *Chronicles of Oklahoma,* (September, 1940), p. 228.
490 *The Evening Register* (New Haven), Wednesday, March 6, 1872, p. 2.

The funeral was at the New Haven Cemetery next to the Chapel at Yale University.[491]

No doubt Gustavus Loomis would have liked his funeral service to be conducted in such a historic building. In this structure, built in 1824, there were numerous revivals and awakenings over the years. The chapel housed a library on the third floor and maintained rooms for divinity students. The inside reflected a typical larger New England meeting house, with its three isles of pews and its grand elevated pulpit. At the time of brevet Brigadier General Loomis' funeral, Christian liberalism had infiltrated Yale and taken away much of the evangelical zeal of the chapel. Nevertheless, independent student groups such as the Student Deacons of the Chapel, the Young Men Christian Association (Y.M.C.A.) and missionary focused Sunday Schools maintained the old biblically focused evangelical message and were active on the Yale campus.[492]

An obituary for Gustavus Loomis appeared a few days after his funeral service in *The New York Times* newspaper. The paragraph began, "One of the oldest and most faithful servants of the country in the United States Army, Col. Gustavus Loomis, died at Stratford, Conn. on Tuesday." The obituary gave a narrative of his military career without mentioning anything about his family. It accurately stated that he was brevetted as a Brigadier General in 1865 and that he served in uniform until 1867. It was a rather impersonal biographical summary of his life, and some of the details were inaccurate.[493]

A more personal and accurate life summary of Gustavus Loomis was provided by the third reunion of West Point gradu-

---

491 Christ Episcopal Church records courtesy of the Stratford Historical Society.
492 "A History of Religion at Yale," www.yale.edu/chaplain/yalehistory. Accessed February 8, 2010. "A History of Battell Chapel," www.yale.edu/chaplain/battell_history. Accessed February 6, 2010.
493 *The New York Times,* March 10, 1872.

ates, held three months after Gustavus Loomis' death. After four detailed paragraphs listing highlights of Loomis' military career, the biographical summary became more personal: "Possessing an eminently ardent and impulsive temperament, with the most inflexible firmness of purpose and a resolute and untiring perseverance, Loomis entered with his whole soul into everything that engaged his special attention." The article called Loomis "no less a valiant soldier of the cross than of his country," and stated, "By his excellent example and Christian counsel he exercised a most salutary influence over both officers and men, and prevented any desecration of the Sabbath within his entire command. He was an exacting disciplinarian; a highly conscientious and excellent soldier; a kind father, husband, and friend; and a good man, who, we think, it is perfectly safe to predict is now reaping the reward of a well-spent forty years of Christian benevolence."[494]

Gustavus Loomis served at Fort Snelling, Minnesota from 1834 to1836 and again from 1849 to 1850. A study of the commandants of Fort Snelling has the following interesting personal and professional synopsis of Loomis' life at that fort.

> LIEUTENANT COLONEL GUSTAVUS Loomis, of Vermont, commander and member of the Sixth Infantry Regiment, was a personality at Fort Snelling, who had a colorful history in his nation's records. Loomis' military career was fairly steady, but it did not rocket him to national fame. He graduated from West Point in 1811. After commanding many garrisons, Loomis found himself commanding at Fort Snelling. He commanded Company C at Fort Snelling as the lieutenant colonel of the Sixth Infantry Regiment, from

494 *Third Annual Reunion of the Association of the Graduates of the U.S. Military Academy at West Point, N.Y. June 14, 1872)*, (New York: Crocker and Company, 1872), pp. 46-47.

June 21, 1849 to February 22, 1850...Loomis will be remembered, in Minnesota, as the most religious of Fort Snelling's commanders. Many exploits record-ed of Loomis bear this distinction out. George Will Feathertonhaugh, in 1835, described Loomis as "bor-ing, with his psalm-singing and exhortations; being a "living-road-in-soak" to tickle-up sluggish Chris-tians. Loomis may have been boring, but he did not let that curtail his zeal. He was said to have initiated a "red-hot revival among the soldiers" for religion in 1835. He, along with Dr. Thomas Smith William-son started the first Christian church in Minnesota, the "First Presbyterian Church of Saint Peter's." He and H.H. Sibley served as elders, for the twenty two members. Loomis earned the friendship and praise of Samuel Pond, and J.H. Stevens, who described him as an "earnest and active Christian."Although a deeply devout Christian, [he] was stern and a first-class sol-dier when need be. He disciplined soldiers humanely, but in such a way as to leave an impression. His fa-vorite punishment was to chain a log of wood on top of a convict's shoulders and compel him to walk in a circle for a given amount of time. He also ordered squatter shacks on the Fort Snelling Military Reser-vation to be destroyed. Finally, not even the Indians could expect this holy man to be lax. Loomis contin-ued the duties of keeping the Indians close to their reservation but far from whiskey sources. He even sent an expedition to force the Winnebagos back to their reservation and out of Wisconsin. On February 27, 1850, as Loomis left to command Fort Leavenworth, he was honored as a "noble old colonel who did much to benefit the northwest and Christianity... the missionaries lost their best friend.[495]

The widow Annie Loomis lost her husband of twenty-one years. But Brigadier General Gustavus Loomis had planned well for his younger wife to outlive him. In his Last Will and Testament, Gustavus left everything to his wife. Further, they had a home in Stratford that Gustavus made sure was in both his name and his wife's name, thus guaranteeing the house would belong to Annie after he died. The old General made some land investments in western areas, investments that Annie could sell for money in her older widowed years. And there was a widow's pension available to her as the wife of a career active duty military officer. By the standards of that day, Gustavus did a remarkable job insuring the economic stability of his wife after he was gone. In early April Annie Loomis approached her U.S. Congressman from Connecticut about receiving her widow's pension. On April 25, 1872 it was granted. In November of that year, Annie Loomis hired an attorney to assist her in managing her husband's estate. There were properties in Leavenworth, Kansas and their home in Stratford, Connecticut that needed to be transferred solely to her name. Her New York City attorney would have the authority to manage her properties and investments for a nominal fee and otherwise administrate her small estate.[496]

Brevet Brigadier General Gustavus Loomis did not write his memoirs, a book, or a journal. He never wrote anything that has survived that was longer than a few paragraphs in length. He was not a man to draw attention to himself. He worked diligently at

495 Joseph S. Micallef, Jr. *The Commandants of Fort Snelling, 1825-1858,* (Minnesota Historical Society, 1986), pp. 15-16.

496 "Mary Ann T. Loomis of Stratford to Rawlins A. Thomas of Staten Island, New York, November 6, 1872." Courtesy of the Stratford Historical Society.

all his tasks and yet deeply desired quiet time alone with God and the Bible. He was robed with humility. His longing at the end of a tiring day was to be home with his wife and family. Some thought it beneath his dignity as an officer in the army to lead psalm singing at prayer meetings, but Loomis never thought so. The West Point educated officer thought nothing of teaching illiterate blacks and Indians the Bible, often to the ridicule of his fellow officers. Some scoffed at his prayer meetings, others showed some support, and some were converted to Christ under Loomis' influence. None ever questioned his military proficiency.

The Thetford, Vermont native was a fascinating individual with an earnest and persevering personality. He exemplified

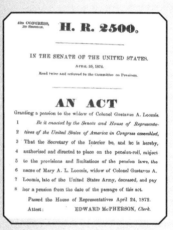

The act of Congress which granted Annie Loomis a widow's military pension.

the best of the puritan attributes he learned through his family heritage and from the pulpit of Rev. Asa Burton at the Congregational Church in Thetford. Gustavus Loomis never outgrew his faith in God. From the time of his conversion as a youth in Thetford, to his death as an almost eighty-three year old man in Stratford, Connecticut, his faith did not waver; in fact his spirituality matured and deepened over the years. Loomis was altogether a splendid army officer. He was driven first by a sense of duty to God, then his family, then his military career. The Lord was always first, the highest priority, the ultimate goal. The *Westminster Shorter Catechism* states, "What is the chief end of man? Man's chief end is to glorify God and to enjoy Him forever." This was the drumbeat to which Loomis marched.

Gustavus Loomis was a warm and humane person who looked for the best in others. He abhorred slavery and violated local laws in teaching blacks and Indians how to read the Bible. One criticism of Loomis is that he was ant-social. It is true that Loomis did not enjoy the pomp and ceremony of formal social occasions he was expected to attend as a military officer. Such pageantry meant nothing to him. Nevertheless, Loomis did attend many social activities related to starting new churches, establishing missionary colleges, creating mission stations for Indians, and the like. It was not that Gustavus Loomis was anti-social, but that he chose meaningful social events in which to participate, events that to him had some enduring or spiritual purpose.

Loomis was self effacing, even to a fault. His brief letters and military dispatches reveal a man who never begrudged the success of others, even when junior officers almost half his age were promoted above him in the Civil War. He never pulled down someone to build up his own reputation. We can look at Loomis' career and ask why he was not promoted earlier to Colonel, or why his promotion to Brigadier General was a brevet promotion. There is no evidence of Loomis ever complaining about his slow but steady rise in the ranks. Instead there is plenty of evidence that Gustavus was full of energy, ability, tactical competence in battle, and possessed an overwhelming sense of benevolence. Loomis was benevolent or charitable to blacks, Indians and to his subordinates in uniform. He was not a despotic or hypocritical or unbalanced leader. To his family he showered love and affection. His wife Julia of thirty-two years, and his second wife Mary Annie of twenty-one years, both adored him. His child and grandchildren loved him, respected him and obeyed him. From all accounts, the Loomis household was happy, his family willingly and even eagerly sharing the faith of Gustavus in his Lord and Savior Jesus Christ.

Gustavus Loomis was articulate but not an intellectual. He was a multifaceted officer known for his administrative abilities, his high professional standards, his competence in the face of enemy forces, his moral integrity, and his tenacity. But most of all he was known as an enthusiastic Christian, dedicated to God and family and his country. He was also popular with junior officers and the regular troops. His conduct was always proper, manly and sincere. Brevet Brigadier General Gustavus Loomis rose through the officer ranks in regular order, serving professionally at every level. Yet he always seemed to have a higher standard, a loftier goal, a more spiritual awareness. As his obituary notice stated, he was "A man of great energy and integrity, his industry was remarkable always. As a citizen, neighbor, and friend, he will be remembered for his excellencies. He died as he had lived, full of faith in his Redeemer."[497]

---

497 *The Evening Register* (New Haven), Wednesday, March 6, 1872, p. 2.

Selected Bibliography

Agnew, Brad. *Fort Gibson: Terminal on the Trail of Tears,* (Norman, OK: University of Oklahoma Press, 1980).

Alstrom, Sydney E. *A Religious History of the American People*, (New Haven: Yale University Press, 1972).

Ambrose, Stephen E. *Duty, Honor, Country: A History of West Point,* (The Johns Hopkins Press, 1999).

The American Almanac and Repository of Useful Knowledge for the Year 1860, (Boston: Crosby, Nichols and Company, 1860).

Babcock, Wiloughby M. "Major Lawrence Taliaferro, Indian Agent," *The Mississippi Valley Historical Review,* Vol.11, No. 3, (December 1924).

Battles and Leaders of the Civil War: The Opening Battles, (1887: reprinted by Castle Books, Edison, NJ in 1956).

Bauer, K. Jack. *Zachary Taylor, Soldier, Planter, Statesman of the Old Southwest,* (Louisiana State University Press, 1993).

Bayard, Frank. "Prince Saunders," *Dictionary of American Negro Biography*, (New York: W.W. Norton & Company, 1983).

Beardsley, Eben E. *History of the Episcopal Church in Connecticut,* (1868: reprinted 2009 by Cornell University Press).

Bemrose, John. *Reminiscences of the Second Seminole War,* (1856[?]: Reprinted by University of Florida Press, 1966).

Berton, Pierre. *The Invasion of Canada, 1812-1813,* (Anchor Canada Books, 2001).

Blake, William P. *A Brief Account of the Life and Patriotic Services of Jonathan Mix of New Haven, being an Autobiographical Memoir,* (New Haven: 1886).

Brackett, Albert G. *History of the United States Cavalry*, (Bibliolife Publishers, 2009).

Bradley, Joshua. *Accounts of Religious Revivals,* (Albany, NY: G.J. Loomis and Co., 1819).

Boettner, Loraine. *The Christian Attitude Toward War,* (Phillipsburg, NJ: Presbyterian and Reformed Publishing, 1985).

"Brighton Heights Reformed Church Demolished," www.preserve.org/stgeorge/bhrc.

"British Post on the Apalachicola," "Attack on the Negro Fort," www.exploresouthernhistory.com/fortgadsden.

Brown, Russell K. *To the Manner Born: The Life of General William H.T. Walker,* (Mercer University Press, 2005).

Buckingham, Samuel G. *The Life of William A. Buckingham, the War Governor of Connecticut*, (Springfield, MA: 1894).

Burton, Asa. *The Life of Asa Burton, Minister in Thetford, Vermont, 1779-1836,* (Thetford Historical Society, 1998).

Byrne, Charles. "The Sixth Regiment of Infantry," www.history.army.mil/books/R&H/R&H-6IN.

Canova, Andrew P. *Life and Adventures in South Florida*, (Palatka, FL: 1885).

"The Capture of Fort George – May 1813," www.war1812.tripod.com/ftgeo.

"Christ Episcopal Church, Stratford," www.christchurchstratford.org/history_5.

"The Coast and Geodetic Survey – The Beginning," www.history.noaa.gov/legacy/coastsurvey.

Coe, Charles H. *Red Patriots: The Story of the Seminoles,* (University of Florida Press, 1974).

Coffman, Edward M. *The Old Army,* (Oxford University Press, 1986).

Collins, Gilbert. *Guidebook to the Historic Sites of the War of 1812*, (Toronto: Dundurn Press, 2006).

Connecticut Military Record 1775-1848: Record of Service of Connecticut Men in the War of the Revolution..., (Hartford, CT: 1889).

"Connecticut – Union Regimental Histories," *The Civil War Archive,* www.civilwararchive.com/Unreghst/unctinfl.

Correspondence from Jerome Brubaker, Old Fort Niagara Museum, October 5, 2009.

Correspondence from Richard Baker, U.S. Army Military History Institute, September 16, 2009.

Covington, James W. *The Billy Bowlegs War,* (Chuluota, FL: Mickler House Publisher, 1981).

Covington, James W. *The Seminoles of Florida*, (University of Florida Press, 1993).

Cowdrey, Albert E. *Land's End: A History of the New Orleans District, U.S. Army Corps of Engineers,* (Office of the District Engineer, 1977).

Cruikshank, Ernest. *The Battle of Fort George,* (Niagara-on-the-Lake Historical Society, 1990).

Cruikshank, Ernest. *The Documentary History of the Campaigns upon the Niagara Frontier in 1812-1814,* (Welland, Ontario: 1908).

Cullum, George W. *Biographical Register of the Officers and Graduates of the United States Military Academy, at West Point, New York,* (New York: 1868).

Denham, James M., Keith L. Hunetcutt, Corrina B. Aldrich, Ellen B. Anderson, *Echoes from a Distant Frontier: The Brown Sister's Correspondence from Antebellum Florida,* (University of South Carolina Press, 2004).

Dodsworth, Robert O. *The Battle of Wisconsin Heights of 1832*, (Wisconsin Department of Natural Resources, 1996).

Dibble, Ernest F. "Giveaway Forts: Territorial Forts and the Settlement of Florida," *Florida Historical Quarterly,* vol. 78, Fall, 1999).

Doubleday, Abner. *My Life in the Old Army*, ([1873?] Edited by Joseph E. Chance. Fort Worth: Texas Christian University Press, 1998).

Draughon, Ralph Jr. *Down by the River: A History of the Baton Rouge Riverfront*, (U.S. Army Corps of Engineers, 1998).

Elderkin, James D. *Biographical Sketches and Antidotes of a Soldier of Three Wars as Written by Himself: The Florida, the Mexican War, and the Great Rebellion Together*, (Detroit: 1899).

Faulk, Odie B. *Crimson Desert: Indian Wars of the American Southwest,* (Oxford University Press, 1974).

Ferris, Robert G. *Soldier and Brave: Historic Places Associated with Indian Affairs and the Indian Wars in the Trans-Mississippi West,* (Washington, DC: National Park Service, 1971).

Foreman, Carolyn T. "Gustavus Loomis: Commandant of Fort Gibson and Fort Towson," *Chronicles of Oklahoma*, vol. 18, no. 3 (September, 1940).

Foreman, Grant. "Fort Gibson – A Brief History," www.freepages.genealogy.rootsweb.ancestry.com.

Foreman, Grant. *The Five Civilized Tribes,* (University of Oklahoma Press, 1982).

"Fort Gadsden in the First Seminole War," www.exploresouthernhistory.com/fortgadsden.

"Fort George History," www.niagaraghosts.com/HFort.

Folwell, William H. *History of Minnesota*, (Minnesota Historical Society Press, 2006).

Gamble, R.D. "Army Chaplains at Frontier Posts," *Historical Magazine of the Protestant Episcopal Church*, (XXVII, December, 1958).

General Orders of the War Department, Embracing the Years 1861, 1862, 1863, (Washington: U.S. War Department, 1864).

Greene, Howard. *The Reverend Richard Fish Cadle,* (Waukesha, Wisconsin: Privately published, 1936).

Gribben, William. *The Churches Militant: The War of 1812 and American Religion,* (New Haven: Yale University Press, 1973).

Guernsey, R.S. *New York City and Vicinity during the War of 1812,* (New York: Charles L. Woodward, 1889).

Guinn, Jeff. *Our Land Before We Die: The Proud Story of the Seminole Negro,* (New York: Tarcher Publications, 2005).

"Gustavus Loomis File," *Probate Court Records, April 8, 1861.* Courtesy of the Stratford Historical Society.

Hansen, Marcus L. *Old Fort Snelling, 1819-1858,* (Cedar Rapids, Iowa: The Torch Press, 1918).

Hatheway, John S. *Frontier Soldier: The Letters of Major John S. Hatheway, 1833-1853,* (Vancouver, WA: Vancouver National Historic Reserve Trust, 1999).

Hattaway, Herman. *General Stephen D. Lee,* (University of Mississippi Press, 1976).

Headley, Joel T. *The Great Riots of New York City,* (Scholarly Publishing Office, University of Michigan Library, 2006).

Hemphill, W. Edwin, Editor. *The Papers of John C. Calhoun, Volume V, 1820-1821,* (University of South Carolina Press, 1971).

Heidler, David S., Editor. "Burbeck, Henry," *Encyclopedia of the War of 1812,* (Naval Institute Press, 2004).

Heidler, David S. and Jeanne T. Heidler, *Old Hickory's War: Andrew Jackson and the Quest for Empire,* (Louisiana State University Press, 2003).

Hinds, J.I.D. "Memorial Sermon for Rev. David Lowry, D.D.," *The Cumberland Presbyterian,* April 12, 1877.

"History of Christ Episcopal Church, Stratford," www.christchcurchstratford.org/history_5.

"Historic Fort Snelling," www.mnhs.org/places/sites/hfs/history.

"History of Fort Towson," www.civilwaralbum.com/indian/towson_history.

"History of New York City," www.inetours.com/New_York/Pages/NYC_History. "New York City and the Developing Republic," www.nyhistory.org/seneca/nyc.

"History of the War of 1812," www.militarysocietyofthewarof1812.com.

"History of Saint Mark's Anglican Church," www.stmarks1792.com/page/historyofsaintmarks.

Historical Sketch of the First Congregational Church, Prairie du Chien, Wisconsin, (Prairie du Chien: 1891).

"History of the First United Methodist Church of Pensacola," www.pensacolafirstchurch.com.

Hitchcock, Ethan A. *Fifty Years in Camp and Field: Diary of General Hitchcock*, W. A. Croffut, editor, (New York: The Knickerbocker Press, 1909).

Howard, Oliver O. *Autobiography of Oliver O. Howard,* (New York: The Baker and Taylor Company, 1908).

Howe, Daniel W. *What Hath God Wrought: The Transformation of America, 1815-1848*, (Oxford University Press, 2007).

Howes, Kelly K. *Mexican American War*, (Farmington Hills, MI: Thomson Gale Publishers, 2003).

Hughes, Nathaniel C. and Timothy D. Johnson, *A Fighter from Way back: The Mexican War Diary of Lieutenant Daniel Harvey Hill, 4th Artillery, USA*, (Kent State University Press, 2002).

Johnson, Lorenzo D. *Chaplains of the General Government,* (New York: 1856).

Jordan, David M. *Winfield Scott Hancock: A Soldier's Life,* (Indiana University Press, 1995).

Journal of the Annual Convention of the Protestant Episcopal Church the Diocese of Connecticut, 1864-1866, (Hartford: 1866).

Journal of the Annual Convention of the Protestant Episcopal Church, Diocese of Maine, (Portland, 1876).

Kimmerer, Gladys, Editor. *A Story of faith: A History of Faith United Methodist Church, Staten Island, New York,* (copyright 1976 by Faith United Methodist Church).

Knapp, Lewis G. *Stratford and the Sea,* (Charleston, SC: Arcadia Publishing, 2002).

Knetch, Joe. *Florida's Seminole Wars, 1817-1858,* (Charleston, SC: Arcadia Press, 2003).

Knoll, Mark A. Editor, *Eerdman's Handbook to Christianity in America,* (Grand Rapids: Eerdman's Publishing, 1983).

"Last Will and Testament of Gustavus Loomis," Stratford, Connecticut Historical Society.

Lawrence, Catherine C. *Christ Episcopal Church Stratford, CT: Three Hundred Years of History, 1707-2007,* (Stratford, 2008).

Lawson, Kenneth E. *Essex Vessels in Times of War: A Study of the Wooden Ships of Essex, Massachusetts in the Revolutionary War, the War of 1812, the Mexican War, the Civil War, the Spanish American War, World War I, and World War II,* (Essex, MA: Essex Historical Society, 2001).

Lawson, Kenneth E. *Religion and the U.S. Army Chaplaincy in the Florida Seminole Wars, 1817-1858,* (Columbia, SC: Eastside Printing, 2006).

Lawson, Kenneth E. *Religion and the U.S. Army in the Utah War, 1857-1858,* (Printed in Puerto Rico, 2009).

Littlefield, Daniel F. *Africans and Seminoles: From Removal to Emancipation*, (University of Mississippi Press, 2001).

Lundrigan, Margaret. *Staten Island*, (Arcadia Publishing, 1999).

Latham, Charles. *A Short History of Thetford, Vermont 1761-1870,* (Lebanon, NH : 1999).

Lewis, James. *The Black Hawk War of 1832,* (Illinois Humanities Council, 2000).

Long, Oscar F. "Changes in the Uniform of the Army, 1774-1895" *US Army Quartermaster Foundation, Fort Lee, Virginia*, www.qmfound.com/changes_in_the_army_uniform_1895.

Loomis, Elias. *The Descendants of Elias Loomis*, (New Haven: 1875).

Loomis, Elias. *The Descendants of Joseph Loomis,* (New Haven, CT: 1875).

The Loomis Family in America, (Hartford, CT: 1905).

Matloff, Maurice. *American Military History,* (Washington, DC: 1973).

Meltzer, Milton. *Hunted Like a Wolf: The Story of the Seminole War*, (New York: Farrar, Straus and Giroux Publishers, 1972).

Mahan, Bruce E. *Old Fort Crawford and the Frontier*, (1926: reprinted by the Prairie du Chien Historical Society, 2000).

Mahon, John K. *History of the Second Seminole War, 1835-1842,* (University of Florida Press, 1985.

Mahon, John K. *The War of 1812*, (Gainesville: University of Florida Press, 1972).

Manning, Thomas G. *U.S. Coastal Survey vs. Hydrographic Office: A Nineteenth Century Rivalry in Science and Politics,* (University of Alabama Press, 1988).

Marshall, Albert B. *History of the First Presbyterian Church of Minneapolis, Minnesota, 1835-1910,* (Minneapolis: Minnesota Printing Company, 1910).

McChristian, Douglas C. *Fort Laramie and the U.S. Army on the High Plains*, (National Park Service Historic Resources Study, 2003).

McDonald, Robert. *Thomas Jefferson's Military Academy,* (University of Virginia Press, 2004).

McPherson, James M. *For Cause and Comrades: Why Men Fought in the Civil War,* (New York: Oxford University Press, 1977).

McReynolds, Edwin C. *The Seminoles*, (University of Oklahoma Press, 1972).

Micallef, Joseph S. Jr. *The Commandants of Fort Snelling, 1825-1858,* (Minnesota Historical Society, 1986).

Millett, Allan R. and Peter Maslowski, *For the Common Defense: A Military History of the United States of America*, (New York: The Free Press, 1994).

"Minnesota Pioneer," *Minnesota Historical Society Holdings*, 4-2-1849 through 1-9-1850.

Missall, John and Mary Lou Missall, *The Seminole Wars: America's Longest Indian Conflict*, (University Press of Florida, 2004).

Mix, Jonathan. *A Brief Account of the Life and Patriotic Services of Jonathan Mix of New Haven,* (New Haven: 1886).

Neill, Edward D. *History of Freeborn County: Including Explorers and Pioneers of Minnesota*, (Minneapolis: Minnesota Historical Society, 1882).

Neill, E.D. *Occurrences in and Around Fort Snelling, from 1819 through 1840,* (Minnesota Historical Society, 1845[?]).

Nevin, David. *The Old West: The Texans,* (New York: Time Life Books, 1975).

Noll, Mark A. Editor, *Eerdman's Handbook to Christianity in America*, (Grand Rapids: Eerdman's Publishers, 1983).

Norton, Herman A. *Struggling for Recognition: The United States Army Chaplaincy, 1791-1865*, (Washington, DC: Office of the Army Chief of Chaplains, 1977).

O'Brien, Sean M. *In Bitterness and in Tears: Andrew Jackson's Destruction of the Creeks and Seminoles,* (Guilford, CT: The Lyons Press, 2005).

Official Army Register of the Volunteer Force of the United States Army for the Years 1861, 1862, 1863, 1864, 1865, New York and New Jersey, (Washington: Adjutant General's Office, 1865).

"The Old Army: History of the Fifth United States Infantry," www.theoldarmy. com/usarmy/5us.

Orcutt, Samuel. *A History of the Old Town of Stratford and the City of Bridgeport, Connecticut,* (Fairfield County Historical Society, 1886).

Palmquist, Peter E. and Thomas R. Kailbourn, *Pioneer Photographers of the Far West,* (Stanford University Press, 2001).

Patterson, John B. editor. *Black Hawk: An Autobiography,* (1833: reprinted in 1955 by the University of Illinois Press).

"Pentagon Barracks," www.nps.gov/history/Nr/travel/louisiana/pen.

Pond, Samuel Jr., *The Story of the Labors of Samuel and Gideon Pond,* (Boston: Congregational Sunday School Publishing, 1893).

Porter, Kenneth W. *The Black Seminoles: History of a Freedom-Seeking People,* (University of Florida Press, 1996).

Prichard, Walter. *History of Baton Rouge and its People,* (States Historical Publication Company, 1932).

Prime, Samuel. *The Power of Prayer: The New York Revival of 1858*, (Carlisle, PA: The Banner of Truth Trust, 1991).

The Records of the Church of Christ, Thetford, Vermont, 1773-1832, (Thetford Historical Society).

"The Regulars – A History of the 6th U.S. Infantry," www.fortatkinsononline.org/6thInfyHistory.

Records of the Governor and Council of the State of Vermont, vol. V, (Montpelier, VT: 1877).

Reports of Maj. Gen. John E. Wool, U.S. Army, Commanding Department of the East, with Orders, & etc. July 13-16, 1863, www. Civil-warhome.com/woolor.

"The Rev. Ezekiel Gilbert Gear, D.D. Chaplain at Fort Snelling, 1838-1858," *Minnesota Historical Society Collections*, 1908, www.anglicanhistory.org/usa/mn/edsall_gear.

"Rev. Robert Addison," www.2ministries-online.org/tbfuller/addison.

"Revival Born in a Prayer Meeting," *Knowing & Doing*, Fall, 2004.

"Rhode Island – Union Regimental Histories," *The Civil War Archive*, www.civilwararchive.com/Unreghst/unriinf.

Rhodes, Elisha Hurt. *All for the Union: The Civil War Diary and Letters of Elijah Hunt Rhodes*, (Vintage Civil War Library Edition, 1992).

Rodenbough, T.F. *The Army of the United States: Historical Sketches of Staff and Line with Portraits of Generals-in-Chief*, (New York: 1896).

Sylvia F. Rodrique, *History of Baton Rouge: An Illustrated History*, (Historical Publications Network, 2006).

"Saint Mark's Began our Diocese, and Continues a Fine Ministry," *Niagara Anglican*, September, 2008.

Sanders, Charles W. *While in the Hands of the Enemy: Military Prisons of the Civil War*, (Louisiana State University Press, 2005).

Scanlan, Peter L. *Prairie du Chien: French, British, American*, (Menasha, Wisconsin: Collegiate Press, 1937).

Schweikart, Larry and Michael Allen, A *Patriot's History of the United States*, (New York: Sentinel Press, 2004).

Scott, Winfield. *Memoirs of Lieutenant General Winfield Scott*, (1864: Reprinted in 1970).

Sibley, Henry H. *Autobiography of Henry Hastings Sibley*, (North Carolina, 1844).

Siebert, Wilber H. *Vermont's Anti-Slavery and Underground Railroad Record*, (Columbus, OH: 1937).

Skelton, William B. *An American Profession of Arms: The Army Officer Corps, 1784-1861,* (University of Kansas Press, 1920).

Smalley, E.V. *The Republican Manual with Biographical Sketches of James Garfield and Chester A. Arthur*, (New York: 1880).

Smith, Edmund B. *Governor's Island: Its History under Three Flags, 1637-1913*, (New York: 1913).

Smith, Sharon B. *Connecticut's Civil War,* (Milford, CT: Featherfield Publishing, 2010).

Speer, Lonnie R. *Portals to Hell: Military Prisons of the Civil War,* (Mechanicsburg, PA: Stackpole Books, 1997).

Sprague, John T. *The Origin, Progress and Conclusion of the Florida War,* (New York: 1847).

Sweeney, Douglas A. and Allen C. Guelzo, *The New England Theology*, (Grand Rapids: Baker Books, 2006).

Tebbel, John and Keith Jennison, *The American Indian Wars,* (London: Phoenix Press, 2001).

"Telegraph from Colonel Gustavus Loomis to General George McClellan, March 9, 1862," *The Abraham Lincoln Papers at the Library of Congress,* letter # 14908.

"The Texas Frontier-Army Movements," *The New York Times,* December 10, 1852.

Thayer, Crawford B. *The Battle of Wisconsin Heights: An Eyewitness Account of the Battle of Wisconsin Heights of 1832*, (published by the author, 1833 [reprinted 1983]).

Third Annual Reunion of the Association of the Graduates of the U.S. Military Academy at West Point, N.Y., June 14, 1872, (New York: Crocker and Company, 1872).

Trask, Kerry A. *Black Hawk: The Battle for the Heart of America,* (New York: Henry Holt & Company, 2006).

"Universalism," *The Quarterly Christian Speculator*, (vol. V, 1833).

Utley, Robert M. *Frontiersmen in Blue: The United States Army and the Indian, 1848-1865,* (University of Nebraska Press, 1967).

Viele, Teresa G. *Following the Drum: A Glimpse of Frontier Life,* (New York: 1858).

"Virtual Vermont Internet Magazine," www.virtualvermont.com/towns/thetford.

Wakefield, John A. *Wakefield's History of the Black Hawk War,* (Jacksonville, Ill: 1834).

Waldman, Carl. *Atlas of the North American Indian*, (New York: Checkmark Books, 2000).

Waselkov, Gregory A. *A Conquering Spirit: Fort Mims and the Redstick War of 1813-1814,* (University of Alabama Press, 2009).

Weems, John E. *To Conquer a Peace: The War between the United States and Mexico,* (New York: Doubleday Books, 1974).

Weins, Janine. "The Church Built on Thetford Hill," www.acornhillfarm-weather.com.

Weisberger, Bernard A. *They Gathered at the River: The Story of the Great Revivalists and their Impact upon Religion in America,* (Boston: Little, Brown & Company, 1958).

West, Anson. *A History of Methodism in Alabama,* (Nashville, TN: 1893).

White, Arthur D. "Prince Saunders: An Instance of Social Mobility among Antebellum New England Blacks," *Journal of Negro History* 55, (1975).

Wilber, LaFayette. *Early History of Vermont*, (Jerico, VT: Roscoe Printers, 1902).

Wright, W. M. "The Second Regiment of Infantry," www.history.army.mil/books/R&H/R&H-2IN.

Yocum, Barbara A. *Fort Jay Historic Structure Report,* (National Park Service, 2005).

INDEX